Presented to

Kingwood Branch Library

By

Kingwood Area

Republican Women's

Club

Harris County
Public Library

your pathway to knowledge

Grassroots Women

M amie
E isenhower
L ibrary
P roject

In Honor of Former First Lady

Mamie D. Eisenhower

This book is presented by

Kingwood Area Republican Women

Club Name

Texas Fed. of Republican Women

State Federation

In Honor/Memory of

Under the sponsorship of the
National Federation of Republican Women
124 N. Alfred Street, Alexandria, VA 22314-3011

A Memoir of the Texas Republican Party

MEG McKAIN GRIER

Grassroots
Women

Wingscape Press, Boerne, Texas

To the thousands of Texas women
who with their commitment and tenacity
made Texas a two-party state
and in the process gave us a model
for grassroots action

Contents

Foreword *by Barbara Bush*

*W*hen George and I were living in Midland during the 1950s, he decided we should become active in local Republican politics. His father was, after all, then a Republican senator from Connecticut and the family had always been active in local and state politics back East. So it seemed only natural that the Texas branch of the Bush family would continue the tradition in Midland.

Except there was one small problem: There was no Republican politics in which to become active. In fact, there were hardly any other Republicans. I can still remember when George and I volunteered to work at the polls during a primary election. Exactly three people voted Republican that day: The two of us and a man who you could say was a little bit inebriated and wasn't sure what he was doing.

Now flash forward more than forty years to the 1998 state-wide elections. It was an amazing night in Texas politics—and not just because George W. Bush became the first Texas governor to be elected to consecutive four-year terms. (I hope you'll forgive a mother who can't help but brag a little.) The more amazing result of that election is that after all the votes were counted, every single statewide office in the state of Texas was held by a Republican for the first time since Reconstruction.

How did that happen?

I can not really answer that question, but I know some people who can—the remarkable women whom you will meet in this book.

Women have always been a very powerful force, whether they were behind or in front of the podium, on the ballot or behind the ballot box. When we first moved here, the women I got to know best were the stay-at-home moms who devoted themselves to their families and their communities. They were the PTA presidents, the hospital volunteers, the scorekeepers at the Little League games, the next-door neighbors who were there for each other in good times and bad.

As the years progressed and women everywhere started playing a more prominent role on the public stage, Texas women were once again among the strongest and the best. They became doctors, astronauts, lawyers, mayors, senators, firefighters, police officers, business owners—and yes, they were still PTA presidents, too.

You will meet all of these women in this book, and they all have one important quality in common: They cared very much for their country, their state, and their communities, and as a result, they became very active in politics. In this particular case, Republican politics.

We first started getting to know many of them way back in 1962 when George ran for chairman of the Republican Party of Harris County. (I was so politically naive then that I thought he had simply been asked; I didn't know he had to "run!") They helped him navigate the very turbulent waters of local politics, and they were there for us again when George ran for the Senate in 1964 (he lost); Congress in 1966 and 1968 (he won); the Senate again in 1970 (he lost); and, well, you know the rest.

Some of these very same, determined women helped our son become governor in 1994 and at this writing, president-elect of the United States of America. One thing is for sure: They never give up on their causes or their candidates.

Their stories are remarkable for their candor, their sense of history, and above all else, their determination to bring two-party politics to the state of Texas. The Bushes are proud to call almost all of them friends. Without them, it's possible George and I would still be volunteer poll workers in Midland, praying that a fellow Republican will walk through those doors.

Barbara Bush

December 15, 2000

Introduction

*H*ave you ever wondered how laws are influenced,
passed, and implemented? I did. During graduate
school in Washington, D. C., I held various internships and jobs,
which afforded me entry into many legislative and executive
branch offices and the opportunity to work with many staffers.
These experiences made me wonder how these dedicated,
hardworking, and qualified people ended up at the fulcrums of
power. I also pondered the source of this power and concluded that
it lay outside of "the Beltway." When I finished school, I moved
to Texas determined to answer the question, "What really makes
things happen in politics?"

    Certain that I would find the answer by following the
money trail, I pursued a career in banking and small business. I
also became involved in the community through a wide variety
of professional and volunteer activities. Still I searched for the
answer to my question.

    Have you ever looked for something and found it right
under your nose? The answer was in my very own family. My
mother-in-law, Mary Lou Grier, and her friends provided it by
their example.

    For years, they had recruited, campaigned for, and advised
governors and presidents, congressmen and senators, state
representatives and state senators in a dogged effort to establish
the Republican Party in Texas. How did they do it? Hard work
and persistence, persistence, persistence. Many became interested
in politics as young women. As they grew to adulthood, they
expressed concern about good government in Texas. Driven by
patriotism, concern for their children and communities, commitment to the Republican philosophy, and interest in conservative
issues, they volunteered as Republican precinct workers and

*rapidly moved up the political ladder. Women broke the stereo-
type of the white-gloved socialites wearing flowered hats and
successfully entered the political arena, making valuable contributions to the fledgling Republican Party of Texas and the
transformation of Texas to a two-party state.*

*Women like my mother-in-law and her friends went
against the norms of the 1950s and 1960s and pursued their
political interests. They made it socially acceptable to be involved
in politics and Republican politics at that! Texas had long been a
one-party state; as in the rest of the South, the Democratic
Party had been entrenched since the Civil War. In fact, all 254
counties did not hold Republican primaries until 1996. Economic and social pressures kept many people Democrats. Most
voters did not want to cause their Democrat grandfathers and
great-grandfathers to roll over in their graves by voting Republican. But these women pursued their desire to make Texas a
two-party state and to clean up the corruption they saw through
competition with the Republican Party of Texas.*

*Mary Lou and her friends volunteered for years, doing
whatever task was needed whether they had experience in that
job or not. Through campaign and Party work, women developed areas of expertise and trained others. They organized precinct,
county, and state party structure, ran campaigns, raised funds,
worked with the press, and ran for office themselves. Through
the years, they won an election here and there. Then the Texas
Republican Party experienced the ultimate victory in 1978—
Republican Bill Clements was elected the governor of Texas.
More victories followed and more Republican women were
elected to office. Through their affiliation with candidates over
the years, women became trusted confidants. They assumed
important advisory rolls both formal and informal and molded
local, state, and national policy. In the process, Texas became a
two-party state with two viable political parties fielding
qualified candidates.*

Grassroots Women *is a collection of memories describing the
kind of hard work, commitment, and persistence needed to*

develop a political party. At every step of the Texas Republican revolution, women worked shoulder to shoulder with men. The women sharing their experiences with us reflect the accomplishments of thousands and thousands of women from all regions of Texas. As these puzzle pieces of recollections and insights are assembled, readers will come to see a complete picture of the development of the Republican Party in Texas. It grew from a disorganized group of people primarily concerned with obtaining patronage from a Republican president to a well-organized political party determined to elect candidates committed to the Republican philosophy to local, state, and national offices.

Grassroots Women *focuses on the 1950s through the early 1980s. Although many important victories were yet to come, Party organization and change in attitudes about Republicans were in place by the early 1980s.*

I interviewed women from all across Texas for this book. They generously shared their time, accomplishments, and wisdom to inspire future generations about the political power they can gain if they work with likeminded people. I made every effort to talk with women who represent the thousands of others who were active at all levels of Republican politics—from the precincts to the Republican National Committee, from county judge to U. S. Senator. Many of those interviewed have been active in the Republican Party since the 1950s, well before precincts were organized and Republican primaries held in Texas. Most remain active today.

Although this book recounts the experiences of women who are Republicans, it is not a history of the Republican Women's Clubs or the Texas Federation of Republican Women. With that said, the important role of the Republican Women's Clubs will be apparent. In fact, all but a handful of those interviewed were active in Republican Women's Clubs, and they consider participation in them a meaningful part of their political careers.

This memoir provides rare insight into the transformation of Texas to a two-party state. Because the human memory rarely cooperates with exact dates and times, I have tried to place these remembrances and insights in context through brief introductory remarks in the chapter openings. In addition, the comments and questions expressed in italics throughout the text are mine, intended to assist the reader's journey through the book. As much as possible, I have allowed the women to speak in their own words and follow their own lines of thought.

The memories of Republican women in Texas form a clear picture of a grassroots model for political action. They reveal that a kernel of interest, combined with vision and follow-through, answers the question, "What really makes things happen in politics?" Despite all the discussion about the role of money in politics today, the experience of thousands of Texas women proves that money alone does not equal election victories.

Grassroots Women

CHAPTER I

Background of the Times

"Everyone has to contribute."
— BETTY STROHACKER

*orld War II and the Depression demanded struggle
and sacrifice from everyone in Texas and the U. S. When
peace and prosperity returned in the 1940s and 1950s, women
wanted to continue to give of themselves in their communities in
addition to raising families. Some women worked but found
career options limited. Community volunteer work became a
way to use their talents while making a valuable contribution
outside their immediate families. Soon women began to expand
their interests and applied concern for their families and community to politics. In doing so, they reevaluated long-held
beliefs and began to look at the Republican philosophy as
better representing their personal philosophy.*

PETER O'DONNELL, DALLAS

In the 1950s, the backbone of our effort was the women. At
that time, the business community by and large was conservative
Democrats and men, but women who might be from a conservative point of view would be active Republicans. The stand-up-and-
be-counted people and the workers were the women. They were
able. They worked hard. They were dependable. We were looking
to get a job done. We had a huge volunteer effort. We knew that
they could perform. Frankly, they had the time. There weren't as
many women in the work force then as there are today. It was successful for us. It worked.

3

BERYL MILBURN, AUSTIN

The reason that I'm active in politics is, first, I am a conservative and, second, I am a Republican. In a one-party state, there's just tremendous corruption. I felt that it would be better for Texas if there were two parties. When I was selected to receive the distinguished alumnus award at the University of Texas, they identified me as a "political activist." Somebody asked me what do they mean when they call you a "political activist?" I said, well a long time ago a group of us got together and decided we wanted to change the government in Texas and we did.

Why were the men willing to give the women the opportunity to participate meaningfully in the political system?

WILLIAM RECTOR, WICHITA FALLS

We love women. Seriously, I think that is as good a reason as any.

Women's Voices in Politics

MARJORIE ARSHT, HOUSTON

Women did not hold office. It was unheard of. In fact, when I attended Rice University, there was only one woman that I knew who studied to be a lawyer. She was a freak. Really! The career open to women was teaching if anything more than working at a store or working as a clerk.

ELLIE SELIG, SEGUIN

My father was involved in politics in New York State. My mother sort of dragged along. It wasn't a time for women to be out cavorting about at meetings. They were supposed to be at home taking care of their children. Women were not in politics and they weren't in politics for a long time. I think they had concern for the needy. Philanthropic organizations sought out the needy and took care of them, and that brought out a lot of people interested in doing civic works.

When did women start making the transition from just being involved
with philanthropic organizations to being active in politics?

When they couldn't get things done, they realized that they
had to get out and get with it.

PAT McCALL, HOUSTON & UVALDE COUNTY

We all knew that women really had to fight to get any recognition at all. It was accepted that we had to work harder than anybody else. Women had done war work. My aunt and my mother
and all of the ladies that we knew worked at the Red Cross regularly. They knitted. They packed boxes. We rolled bandages. I got
to go there after school. Some women drove ambulances. Mother
and Daddy were air raid wardens in Houston. They wouldn't let
just Mother be the air raid warden. It had to be Mother *and* Daddy.

After the war, they didn't want to stay home and do nothing.
So things started happening, like the Methodist Hospital Service
Corps. It gave women the opportunity to use their abilities. We worked
in surgery and in intensive care with the families and kept books.
Women wanted to continue to give of themselves. When we found
out we could volunteer and do something, we found out we could
volunteer for politics too. Politics became a volunteer effort as it
remains to this day. It grew from the war.

WENDY MARSH, AMARILLO

Kay Bailey Hutchison and I were two of the first women at
the University of Texas Law School. I was in her class in 1967. They
kept saying, "Why are you going to law school? You're taking up a
perfectly good space for a man."

GWEN PHARO, DALLAS

I don't think there would be any Republican Party in Texas
without the women who went against the habits of the times and
became very active in Republican politics. We did not mind carrying a sign, calling a page in a phone book, going door-to-door ask-

ing for votes in the least privileged parts of town. That is politics at its finest.

What were the habits of the times?

Being invisible in party politics. The women of Dallas truly made politics socially acceptable.

GLENDA REEDER, SAN ANTONIO

There was nothing, nothing to gain from being a Republican. The reason that women founded the Party was because a businessman felt that he simply could not afford to risk his business. There were two clubs here at that time. One was the Bexar County Republican Women's Club. My husband used to say I spent four days after a meeting talking on the phone to people who attended the meeting. I would say, "Yes, ma'am, I know it was a little cool in there. I will talk to the Bright Shawl about the thermostat. I certainly will. The flowers were little bit high, yes, ma'am. I will see about that." Can you imagine us with flowered hats and gloves having luncheons? Then there was a small businesswomen's group led by Irene Wischer. A good turnout was eight people. I remember visiting the meetings. These were businesswomen as compared with little old ladies in flowered hats. They just got things done.

VIRGINIA EGGERS, WICHITA FALLS & DALLAS

That is the way we women made a contribution in those days. You got self-satisfaction out of helping and finding that, yes, I can run the mental health drive and, yes, I can volunteer and do a good job. I was young and did not know that about myself. I went to junior college, got married, and had babies right away. I was kind of growing up at the same time. The more you did the more you wanted to do. Your eyes are opened to so many things when you get out in the public. Once I became president of the Republican Women's Club and precinct chairman, I learned that I could do these things. It was our work outlet in a way. We were involved in the symphony. We brought the Broadway Theatre League to Wichita Falls. We did all of that and our politics. We were volunteering instead of working in an office.

Patriotism

BILLIE PICKARD, RAYMONDVILLE

We had a number of people move to Raymondville after World War II. Those involved were very dedicated. Part of that was the aftermath of World War II— patriotism, recognition of love of country and of what needed to be done in the country. After being through the war, they saw what could happen in other countries. I think it was also a generation where you had been taught to serve your community and your country. Our families and the schools instilled patriotism. I think television is a factor. We used to get out and visit with people more. With television, we turned inward. We stay inside where it is comfortable now.

Government was becoming more of a factor in people's lives, doing what used to be done by charities. We saw needs and the community as a whole did something about them. That has been diminished by government taking on so much of it. Everything now emanates from Washington or the state. We used to look more to ourselves locally.

Perhaps we were not as self-indulgent. "Things" were not that important. I can look back at the end of World War II. Houses hadn't been built. People coming back from the war were getting married and looking for a place to live. We had an army surplus trailer that we set up and lived in for a while. Friends in town were happy finding a garage that they could make into a room. Our energies were a little bit more down to earth and owning things was not important. There was still a dedication to the community and church.

BETTY STROHACKER, KERRVILLE

I've never discussed this with anybody. We asked our boys to go off and be in the draft and go into World War II. I thought if we are going to ask our boys to go into the service, the least I can do is to do what I can at home for our country. That is the thing that always kept me going. I had to do that. It wasn't very much. Everyone has to contribute.

ANNE BERGMAN, WEATHERFORD

The men who had served our country came back and joined the Rotary club and the Lions club. They worked on every fund drive. They did everything. I think we were an idealistic generation.

ZUBIE WALTERS, YOAKUM

The people united to win the war. We had more women go to work. Education had a big part in that, too, because more women had gone to college. Once they had been to college, they wanted to use their education. A lot of women continued working. When they started working out in the public, they liked it and the additional money that they earned.

Born a Democrat

POLLY SOWELL, McALLEN & AUSTIN

I had been involved in Democratic politics in the 1950s. It is very hard for people to even imagine what it was like to be a Republican in the '50s in Texas. To give a clue, when Dwight Eisenhower was running for president in 1952, the Democrats were so worried that there would be a great Republican sweep that they changed the election code so that everybody could run in both parties. Everybody from the governor on down ran as both a Republican and a Democrat. The Democrats effectively kept the Republican Party from growing during the '50s when Eisenhower was elected. It was all very cleverly done.

RITA PALM, FORT WORTH

My great-great-grandfather was a member of the first Continental Congress. Down through the years members of my family have taken positions of leadership in their hometowns. My grandfather was the state treasurer. When I was a teenager, [*Republican*] Thad Hutcheson ran for the U. S. Senate. He was our neighbor in Houston. He came down and talked to my dad about running. I remember Daddy saying that was the most foolish thing he had ever seen—running as a Republican.

In college, I majored in political science, government, economics, and history. I did my thesis on Andrew Johnson's impeachment trial so I was really knowledgeable from a book standpoint on Reconstruction. President Lincoln had not wanted to punish the South. His policies and Johnson's were alike on that, but after Lincoln died the more radical wing of the Republican Party took over and punished the South. I saw there was a difference in what the parties espoused and what they did when they got to Washington. It was easy to see that if you truly wanted states rights it was not going to be sufficient to be active on the national level as a Republican; you needed to force through to the local level. As for southern Democrats, the conservative wing began to lose out to the liberal wing of the Democratic Party. That was all during the '60s when Kennedy took over. That was when Ed and I married. We just never did see the liberal Democratic point of view, and we just had to switch as far as we were concerned.

When we were in graduate school in Austin, I had a great-aunt there and we lived in a duplex that she owned. Somebody called and asked if we would help pass out literature for Richard Nixon in our neighborhood. We did, on a Thursday night. On Saturday, my great-aunt called and invited us for lunch on Sunday.

We arrived for lunch. Four or five cousins, my uncle, and my aunt were there. We sat around this big table and had such a wonderful time at lunch talking about everything we were doing. At the end of the meal, my great-aunt leaned back in her chair and said, "There is really just one little thing I would like to bring up." She said, "Children, I hope you know that we support Lyndon in anything that he does. In fact, each of us here has given Lyndon quite a bit of money." (Now, it was not polite to discuss money, but my uncle told me that everybody at that table had given him ten grand and that it was an offense to everybody that Ed and I were passing out literature for the opponent.) I was just brazen enough that I said, "It is wonderful if you feel that way but I don't like his politics."

Well, I could have shot a bomb off at that table. It was silence personified. One of my cousins said, "What do you not like about him?" I said, "It's nothing personal, but I don't like how they take our tax money and spend it all on programs that I don't believe in." They could not argue with me. They were so displeased that I had an answer they didn't like that a pall fell over the table. My aunt loves me to death but we never did discuss politics after that. Never! It was a funny experience. In reflection, her father-in-law had been a captured Confederate soldier. When he came home, he was disenfranchised. He could not earn a living. His family had probably grown up in lean years because of it. I can understand where they were coming from but times were different.

BETTE HERVEY, EL PASO

I was interested in current events. Fortunately, my husband was too. The way I got interested in Republicanism is when Lyndon Johnson sold out. He was running against Kennedy and then he accepted the position of vice president. We were very surprised. We were conservative Democrats. Then we got very active in the Republican Party.

JUNE DEASON, SAN ANTONIO

Like most Texans, we were conservative Democrats. You just didn't have a place to go in Texas. I began to see that my philosophy was really not being put to any use. I was in the wrong party. I grew up in a non-affluent family and so did my husband. We had both been used to working hard, saving our money, paying our bills on time, and not running up debt. Every time I looked around, the Democrats had another program. The attitude was you don't really have to take care of yourself because the government's going to do that. The biggest occasion that I remember for my grandparents was the day they burned the mortgage. It was a big thing! Now, what do they care if you get in debt? File bankruptcy.

We Made Time

JOAN GAIDOS, DALLAS

The 1950s and '60s were truly a much more leisurely time. We seemed to have time for our children and for some social events that didn't cost a whole lot of money but were fun. We had a lot of neighborhood parties. There was a lot of talk about politics then. I knew very few women who worked full-time. My neighbors were all stay-at-home people who raised their kids. None of us had much money but we had a good time. The kids were there and we were there. We took them to school and were there when they got home. Nobody seemed to really like Lyndon Johnson particularly because of the Box 13 affair [*in which a ballot box had been tampered with*]. I think that had a lot to do with it. There was a lot of corruption.

MARGARET VICKERY, FORT WORTH

We were busy going to school but took part in things because we didn't sit around and watch TV. You didn't sit and receive. You gave. We were interested in politics. You have to have some interest and education to vote intelligently.

CHAPTER 2

Why Two Parties Were Needed

"We want to give you back your power as a U.S. citizen."
— GAIL WATERFIELD

*A*s women became more politically aware during the 1950s and 1960s, they wanted change. The political system in Texas did not provide enough true choice of candidates, opportunities for participation in an entrenched and complacent system, or an effective way to redress grievances against the government. For generations, "Republican" was a dirty word for the majority of voters because of the resentment Reconstruction generated after the Civil War. For all practical purposes, Texas had only one political party, the Democratic Party. Due to the lack of competition, public officials were in essence elected in the Democratic primary and not on Election Day in November. Lack of competition also affected the way in which women looked at their government. Some saw it as corrupt while others believed it unresponsive to their concerns. A desire to establish balance and give voice to the opposition motivated women to clean up elections, giving fellow citizens a choice of political parties and candidates—a choice many had never had in their lifetimes.

Competition

JOCI STRAUS, SAN ANTONIO

We didn't have competition in politics. Government is the biggest business in this country. It affects more people, more businesses, more individuals, more books that our children read. Texas did not have a competitive two-party system, meaning our largest industry had no competition, which is not healthy. Having one person looking over the other person's shoulder is critical to us all. It breeds a much better climate, a much better legislature, much better decision-making, and a much fairer process. You can't get up in the morning without being involved in politics. I was in the grocery store once pulling all the avocados that were ripe towards me because I had to have a guacamole salad in a hurry. A friend came by and asked what I was doing. I said, "I'm working on a campaign." She said, "I don't know how you can stand politics. It's such a dirty business." I looked at her and said, you know, you get up in the morning and say good morning to your spouse or your mother. You are in politics. You could blow the whole day by the way you get up and say good morning to somebody. It isn't dirty at all. It's interaction with people. It is so wonderful to find someone who doesn't think the way you do and bring them around to what you believe is truth and what is right. It's just fun!

DIANA RYAN, SAN ANGELO

Competition is an issue because when you champion an attitude or a cause, if you're not competitive, you're not willing to see both sides. Competition is the name of the game.

SURRENDEN ANGLY, AUSTIN

In college, one of the first things that I attended was a Young Democrats meeting with Maurice Angly who was later to become my husband. I changed very specifically because of the non-competition within the state. At that point in time, the Democratic Party was very conservative, but there was no competition in the general election. We thought that was wrong.

RAQUEL GONZALEZ, LAREDO

People were little goats, you know, when you ring the bell. There come the Democrats to get money for federal programs. I'm not saying the programs are not good. There was no choice, and that is why I decided to start doing something about it.

Balance

GAIL WATERFIELD, CANADIAN

People admired those of us who went out on a limb and said we think that this is wrong and we want to change it. We want to give you back your power as a U. S. citizen. The more you learn the more dedicated you will become. People did not think that they had a choice or needed one because they did not have much to worry about. You lived in a smaller world then. The world was your county. You did not get CNN. You got fifteen minutes of the evening news. People stayed pretty isolated.

I wanted a choice after the Goldwater election. There is something wrong when it is that much out of balance [*Republican Barry Goldwater lost when Lyndon Johnson was elected president by a landslide in 1964*]. Everything deserves discussion and debate before it is done. I've learned to accept things that I don't agree with by saying, well, it was a balanced group that did it so I guess they've decided.

BILLIE PICKARD, RAYMONDVILLE

Checks and balances are needed. If the Republican Party of Texas had been in charge all of those years without any competition, you would have seen essentially the same thing happen. It is a consequence of power. My father asked me to go to a Democratic precinct convention. It was so cut and dried. Obviously, there was no local input. I didn't care for it. That was another motivation for me.

KATIE HECK, MIDLAND

In those days, the two-party system seemed so important. I had grown up in San Antonio and went to school at a polling place. I can remember buses pulling up to the polling place and my father later explaining about the black vote [*blacks were bused in by Democrats*]. It occurred to me that for the average citizen to ever have a choice in Texas some of the people were going to have to be dyed-in-the-wool Republicans to balance out the dyed-in-the-wool Democrats. So it became kind of a challenge to see if we could balance that. Also, philosophically, the Republicans were more in line with our thinking about how we wanted government to be. The combination was just too good to pass up. It was just too much of a challenge not to try to do something.

HOLLY DECHERD, AUSTIN

I have three children. I saw that our state had a very unbalanced political system, and I wanted them to have a future in our state that was fair and equitable in the workplace. The best way I saw to do that was to get involved in Republican politics and work to make it a two-party state.

One time I was on a talk show with [*Democrat*] Ann Richards chaired by Dave McNeely, a columnist for the *Austin American-Statesman*. I was terrified because I knew Richards to be a hard-nosed, seasoned politician. I met her in the hallway and introduced myself and she said, "Oh, you have been working in state-level Republican politics. Well, you must really be a crackerjack fundraiser." She meant that was the only real reason for influence in politics. Of course, I was in politics for reasons of idealism and making it a better world. She had her priorities very clear.

PATTY BRUCE, EL PASO

We were interested in a two-party system. You need balance in everything. I grew up in a conservative home. Republicans used to be in the conservative wing of the Democratic Party. The Democrats tried to control all of the politics that way. I wasn't interested in being a conservative Democrat. That's why we went to work when Tad Smith became Republican county chairman.

CLAUDETTE LANDESS, AMARILLO

We had a young man who was state representative for Potter County. He was quoted in the paper as saying we don't need the Republican Party. We have two parties within the Democratic

Party—the conservatives and the liberals. A lot of people thought they could make the Democratic Party representative of their viewpoints. They finally realized, no. The Democrats had become very complacent. They had not seen that they really needed to involve citizens. We wanted people elected that we felt would listen and make the difference. We wanted to have someone who would say, we want to do what is best for everyone. If you only convince a few other voters per person, you make a difference.

Corruption

POOLIE PRATT, VICTORIA

We wanted to build a two-party state. Bill and I got involved in the Republican Party as far back as Eisenhower in 1952. My husband was in law school and he worked at the state land office. We knew that things were amiss, but there was no one to tell because there weren't two parties. It seemed to us that Texas should have two political parties so that we could go and tell someone something was amiss.

FLO KAMPMANN CRICHTON, SAN ANTONIO

It was amazing that [*Republican Senator*] John Tower won by 10,000 votes in 1961. We sent the biggest, burliest fellows we knew down to Jim Wells and Duval Counties to sit on the ballot boxes because the election had pretty much been stolen the year before. They sat on the ballot boxes until they got the right count and then he won by 10,000 votes. It was just a question in the election of ballot security.

We learned a hard lesson in the previous fall election [*when Richard Nixon was the Republican presidential candidate*]. There was a law on the Texas books that the governor appointed all of the election judges all over Texas. Well, of course they were going to be from the party of the governor. They had a negative ballot law that said you had to cross out anyone you didn't want and that the judge could throw out any paper ballot that was not correctly marked. The election judge could interpret the intent of the voter. There were Republicans that didn't cross out everyone so their votes got thrown out. We had a lawsuit then because they threw out the ballots in all of the Republican precincts and they didn't go into the Democratic ones at all. We took the position that we didn't see why the Republicans were so much more stupid than the Democrats. We lost Texas by about 46,000 votes. We lost that suit. The Democrats would never allow the ballot boxes to be reopened and recounted. That's when we really knew we had to get a two-party state. We were lost. We were powerless. Cook County in Illinois was another problem. If we could have turned around those two states, Nixon would have won the 1960 presidential election.

A friend of mine, Gabriel Hauge, was chairman of Eisenhower's Council of Economic Advisers. He was sent out to Cook County to handle the recount there. He called me. It was the saddest day. He said, we are within 5,000 votes of turning this election around in Illinois. He said, it's going to be mean. It's going to be horrible. It's going to be violent. There will be all sorts of problems if we turn the election around. There's no point in doing it if we can't turn it around in Texas. I had to tell him we can't.

POLLY SOWELL, McALLEN & AUSTIN
The Democrats in Texas, particularly in the Valley [*the counties of the Lower Rio Grande Valley in South Texas*], bought votes. They made welfare people vote a certain way before they could get their welfare checks. That was one great motivating factor. In order to clean up the corruption in the Democratic Party, we wanted Texas to be a two-party state. That was obviously the only answer. In '60 and '61, I began to meet Republicans in other parts of the state. I was so dazzled by their brains and their character. People like Peter O'Donnell and Flo Kampmann were so smart and so uncorrupt. Issues were another motivating factor. We were in the Cold War. I was violently anti-Communist and thought that the Democrats were too soft on the Communists.

ESTHER BUCKLEY, LAREDO

There was only one party, the Democratic Party. It really was more exclusive than that. Only the people belonging to Laredo's Independent Club could win. Nobody dared run against them because they had no chance. They could get into a lot of trouble. They wouldn't be murdered, but they could lose their jobs. They could lose their homes. They could lose financial assistance. If they wanted a loan, they couldn't get it. They didn't run against members of the Independent Club.

JAYNE HARRIS, SAN ANTONIO

I was born in Alice, Texas, in Jim Wells County. We had a lot of dirty politics. Things were settled by a group of men who gathered around before the primary and, as my grandfather would say, spit and whittled, tossed old so-and-so's name into the ring, and that was it. There was no such thing as a primary in South Texas. My grandfather and grandmother's ranch was in the Box 13 precinct [*where infamous extra ballots were cast in favor of Lyndon Johnson*]. But there were enough old, crusty South Texas people that said, I did not vote that way. Down there you were not even allowed to have poll watchers.

I was really turned off because I had known of the death of a friend of mine. Someone who had gone to the same school as me had been shot walking out his back door [*Buddy Floyd, the son of Jacob Floyd Sr., an outspoken critic of the county's political machine and the probable target, was killed in 1952*]. They never found the murderer. Another murder was that of our radio announcer [*W. H. "Bill" Mason*]. Supporters of the political boss said, if you go on the air one more time and say what you are saying, you are dead. He did and they shot him. That leaves you with a pretty bad taste in your mouth toward anything political. I guess that influenced me to specialize [*as a campaign manager*] in judicial campaigns.

BABS JOHNSON, DALLAS

Once the Republican Party was equal in numbers to the Democratic Party, each party would have to put up the best possible candidate. A system where the parties were so nearly equal that every election would be a toss-up meant that each party's candidate had to be the best possible person we could secure for the office. I thought the day would arrive that you would have to look much more seriously at the Democrat opponents because they were going to put up a person as good as our man or woman if they possibly could find one. I don't think it turned out quite that way.

Why Not Clean Up the Democrats?

BARBARA CULVER CLACK, MIDLAND

I remember going to my first Republican precinct convention. Of course, I had been going to Democrat precinct conventions and they were really knock-down, drag-out fights. I led the rump sessions and everything else. Then I went to this Republican precinct convention and it was a love-in. Everybody was so delighted to see everybody. Anybody who would walk in the door and say they were Republican was welcome. There was much harmony and sweetness and I thought, wow, I like these people. I felt at home with them. They were very interested in the conservative issues that I was interested in— you know, fiscal responsibility, national defense, and all of the things that are on the traditional agenda of the Republicans.

FAY SURRETT GREENWOOD, EL PASO

I had been told all my life that the Democrats were the South, period. I finally woke up and I told my sister-in-law who said that she would never be anything but a Democrat. I said, only a fool never changes his mind. As I look back, now I can think of a lot of people who changed. Democrats were becoming too liberal.

BARBARA HOWELL, FORT WORTH

The Democrats had won so easily here in the state for a century. When you get to be a winner, you start slacking up. When you are running to win and have never won, you are really going to put the muscle to it. That is what took place here. Remember that many of the Republican votes we got were from the Democratic Party. We were getting people who were ready to listen and really hungry to find a place to express their vote.

JANE BUCY, LUBBOCK

I had been brought up a Democrat and I thought that was all there was to it. Then in about 1960 or '61, I began getting more interested in and reading more books on the conservative side. Through the people I met in the John Tower Senate campaign, I knew that was where I wanted to be and work. I had been to one Democratic county convention. The only ones who were recognized were the old-time party hacks and the candidates. I guess they discarded most of the resolutions that were turned in—they did not read them. For delegates to the state convention, they chose all of the officers, the officials, the big donors, and their wives. They did not even have to attend, which I thought was strange. If you cared enough about it, you should be there. I thought, well, that certainly isn't the place for me.

CHAPTER 3

What Sparks Political Interest?

"I thought, this is a real interesting game. This requires
something to play." —BETTY STERQUELL

*W*hy do people get involved then stay active in politics?
*Some call it a "disease" and others a "bug" but no matter
what the impetus the root is idealism. Some might ask, "Where is the
monetary reward?" But these girls, young women, and mothers had
a burning desire to make their world better. Some learned the
importance of the voting privilege when living in a foreign country
while others were horrified by threats to the right of secret ballot.
Parents, friends, and employers influenced and molded these women
along the way. Regardless of the spark, Republican women pioneers
thought for themselves and did not feel compelled to follow the pack.*

Living Outside the U. S.

GLENNA MCCORD, DALLAS

In 1950, we moved to Venezuela. I found out in a period of
about five years what it is like to live under a dictatorship. While
there, we had a very powerful shortwave radio but unfortunately it
was more often than not the Voice of Moscow that we could tune
in and not the Voice of America. I became irate about this. I was
determined that, as soon as I got back to the States, I would become active one way or another.

ANA OCHOA, LAREDO

I had a very strong belief that we desperately needed a two-
party system. I was a Cuban political refugee. I was shocked when

I moved to Laredo and found that we didn't have a totally free political situation. I was expecting and assuming that everywhere in the United States you would have free participation. I thought we had to have the opportunity to elect our officials, not to be intimidated by any political system.

MARY LOU GRIER, SAN ANTONIO & BOERNE

I grew up in the Panama Canal Zone where there were no politics. It was like a military base overseas. There was just no such thing as voting in Panama, although it was always a desire. So you wanted to participate in your government.

Being Interested as Young Women

RUTH SCHIERMEYER, LUBBOCK

As a junior high student living in a rural community, I was very interested in politics. I picked up the paper in the morning after the primary. The headline said, "Allan Shivers Elected Governor." I said, "Daddy, how can this be? I thought this was a primary and the election is not until November?" He said, "Well, kid, you don't understand. In Texas the primary is the election." I said, "But that isn't fair. I thought we were supposed to have another election in November." I decided then that Texas should be a two-party state.

Working in the Democratic Party wasn't going to make it a two-party state. The first campaign that I started working in was Eisenhower's presidential campaign. I had my mother bring me to Lubbock. I got enough brochures to mail out to everyone in our rural telephone directory. I just wanted to be involved. I wanted to do something. I had listened to the national convention on the radio. I made up a grid with all of the states listed in alphabetical order and in columns so that I could keep votes. My daddy let me sit up with him until three o'clock in the morning listening to the convention.

NITA GIBSON, LUBBOCK

My family lived in the Colorado City-Loraine area where the Mahon family lived. George Mahon was the candidate for the Nineteenth Congressional District just after it was carved out. My dad was for him so much that I handed out cards around the square in Lamesa, Texas, and asked people to vote for George Mahon. I can remember going with my mom and dad into town to get the election returns. They posted the returns on a black chalkboard. We sat up late on election night for the results. We were Depression people, very poor but real high in morals and principles that are really so precious to me today. I was taught that America was not an accident. It has to be carried forward from generation to generation. Then I discovered that it takes a little political action and political involvement to do that.

LOUISE FOSTER, AUSTIN

When I was young girl, I listened to the radio. The announcer was Ronald Reagan. I was a sports nut and listened to the games in the afternoon. Ronald Reagan was being criticized because he was going against the owners of the Chicago White Sox and the Cubs. He was doing the play-by-play descriptions for both teams. He criticized them for selling off their better players. Reagan said, "You are never going to win anything if you are selling off your better players. I am in the United States of America and I can say what I believe. This is what being an American is. If you don't like what I say about the owners, there is a dial on your radio. You can switch to another station or turn it off. I am going to keep saying what I'm saying." I went to my mother and told her the wonderful things he said. It stuck with me all my life. We do have the right in America to express our opinions. That stirred my interest in other things that were going on.

NANCY ABDULLAH, DALHART

When my parents took us to Amarillo to visit my aunt and uncle, they talked about ideas and I guess you could say values.

They talked about real things and not just family gossip. My father died when I was about twelve. My mother went to work in the courthouse in Dumas, Moore County, and was later appointed county treasurer. I was in the courthouse a lot. One of my best friends was the sheriff's daughter. Her parents lived on the top floor and her mother cooked for the prisoners. There was a jury room in the courthouse where they used to sequester the jury. We would have slumber parties there. We would go down to the courthouse on election night, which was on Saturday. We sat outside in the car, and when they had the election results they would come out on the courthouse steps and read them.

BETTY STERQUELL, AMARILLO

In the late 1940s, a friend of mine was running for head cheerleader at the University of Texas. We put together the best campaign. We did everything right. Our opponent did nothing. But the morning of the election, we all woke up to see that his fraternity had gone through—with the palms of their hands, their fingers, and ink pads—and plastered bare feet all over everything. Their candidate was Barefoot Sanders. Of course, everyone was so fascinated with the gimmick he was elected. I thought, this is a real interesting game. This requires something to play. This isn't licking stamps and folding envelopes like I had been doing for [*Republican presidential candidate Thomas*] Dewey.

THEO WICKERSHAM, SAN ANTONIO

When I went away for college in 1942, I became very aware that Georgia was a one-party state. I was very conservative because I was brought up on the farm, so I founded the first Republican Party on a college campus in the state of Georgia in 1942. I was also the editor of the newspaper. Colleges always send news back to your hometown newspapers. The next thing I knew the headline of our newspaper was "GOP Activist on College Campus." My dad called me and said, "I think that if I were you, I would kind of keep quiet about this Republican stuff. They're going to be burning crosses on my yard." So that's the way I first became involved.

ANN WALLACE, FORT WORTH & AUSTIN

I don't exactly know why the idea of a two-party state struck me. I went back one time and looked at my high school yearbook. You know how they write things by people's names. One girl wrote, "She's a lot of fun even though she is a Republican." I thought, this is just really funny because this was back in the early '40s. At that point in Texas, everybody was a Democrat.

MARY ANNE COLLINS, DALLAS

I have to say my real beginning was when I was seven years old. At the corner of Beverly and Fairfield here in Dallas another girl and I wrote "Win with Wilke" on notebook paper and tore it in little strips and ran around putting them in people's doors. My father really couldn't stand Franklin Roosevelt. So I guess I heard him talk about Wilke and I decided, well, I should do my part.

CAROLE WOODARD, HOUSTON & GALVESTON

Since I was a child, I followed the Civil Rights Movement. I paid attention to George Bush because at that time he seemed to be the only congressman interested in the Civil Rights Movement and in civil rights legislation before Congress. I read about him when I was in high school before the Kennedy assassination and all of the civil rights legislation. He was the congressman for the Seventh District. I became interested in him and followed him. I became a closet Republican because of George Bush. I didn't care who knew I was a Republican, but I was not actively out working in Republican campaigns. All I did was vote. Then I worked a little when he ran against Ronald Reagan in 1980. When I found out he was going to run for president in 1988, some black Republicans got me involved in the campaign, and I got actively and visibly involved in politics.

DEBORAH BELL, ABILENE

I remember when Barry Goldwater was running for president. I was eleven years old and went to Republican headquarters. They had little gold elephant pins with glasses. I plastered my whole front door with Barry Goldwater signs. You wouldn't think that someone eleven years old would really get involved in politics. But that was my first taste, when Barry Goldwater ran for president. Why the Republican Party? I don't know. I just know that the Republican Party appealed to me. The Republican Party, its theme, its values, even at eleven, I think it can attract children. I am living proof. Maybe I am an odd ball.

Wanting Good Government

JANE ANNE STINNETT, LUBBOCK

I work to get people elected because my only interest is good government. That is what keeps me working in politics.

IRENE COX WISCHER, SAN ANTONIO

I wrote an editorial on morality in government, and it said in part "morality is celestially democratic and it knows no geographical boundaries." It should know no political boundaries.

PENNY BUTLER, HOUSTON

Good government is less government—letting people find their own way and decide for themselves. People need to go back to their most local community, neighborhood, and home-owners associations, and learn what it takes to live with all of their neighbors. Then they should go to the next steps, municipal government then county government and state government and, finally, the federal government. Most people don't even realize that the state government can affect them more than the federal government. Honest people who have good judgment and who have some experience, particularly some experience in business, need to be elected. Business teaches you about ups and downs and how to handle people and problems. Good government also needs to handle our tax money very wisely. All of those things go back to what I consider to be the Republican philosophy of Good Government.

SALLY McKENZIE, DALLAS

There was a man named Frank Barnett who was part of a think tank in New York and a traditional conservative Republican. Peter O'Donnell knew him and would get a group of us together. Barnett would speak as a guest lecturer. We were interested in Good Government. We finally decided that we didn't need Barnett as a catalyst, and those little groups got together as likeminded friends.

BILLIJO PORTER, EL PASO

I got involved in Republican politics because I am a conservative and because every vote that any politician makes affects my life. I thought it was very important to get people who had integrity and whose political philosophy agreed with mine elected.

POLLYANNA STEPHENS, SAN ANGELO

It all starts with a desire to make your town, your community, your country a better place. When you have that desire and you volunteer, then you understand what the governing process is really like. You realize not only that you have a desire to help out but you really have a commitment to help keep the government straight and running right. It's not a selfish feeling at all. You start thinking, if this is affecting my business, what is it doing to somebody down the street who may not be quite as big as I am? It will be harder on them. Then you think about your children growing up. What is the climate going to be like when they grow to be adults? It really does sound corny, but you have to have values in your subconscious or you would not spend all of your time on this.

CAROLYN PALMER, SAN ANTONIO

I finally realized that the people in politics make everything go. If you care about something and don't like the way it is, you need to know who they are and what they stand for. What you read in the paper is not enough. The only way to really find out is to get involved with who is running and learn why they are running and what their background is.

KAY DANKS, GALVESTON & AUSTIN

We moved to Galveston where my husband was doing a radiology residency. One of his former classmates from medical school, Paul Cunningham, lived down the street. His wife, Billie, had always been kind of involved. Billie asked me if I would make some calls for John Tower in 1961. I had two babies and was expecting another baby. When they napped in the afternoon, I sat down on the floor in the hallway and made these calls. What got me really fired up was I called a longshoreman's wife. She told me, "We would really like to vote for him, we really do like him, but you know the union tells us how to vote." I said, "Oh, no, it's a secret ballot and you can vote anyway you want to." She replied, "Oh, honey, they have ways of finding out." It incensed me so much. That is what really sparked my interest.

For the Children

MARY LOU WIGGINS, DALLAS

We were just beginning to have our family and we were very idealistic. We looked at conservatism as a mission. We felt that we were doing this for our children. It was a departure from regular politics because the Democratic Party was totally in control in Texas. We felt like we were pioneers.

JOCI STRAUS, SAN ANTONIO

I don't know whether becoming serious about life was because I had the third child or because I had a new dryer and washing machine and didn't have to hang up diapers anymore. Having a son helped me realize that the world was bigger than I thought. I needed to get with it and start something that really made a difference instead of doing little neighborhood walks for organizations that would call me. It was really critical that we address something that needed nurturing and developing. I often think that if it had been a Republican state I might have been a Democrat.

RUTH POTTER, DALLAS

I actually didn't vote until I had kids. Then you become more aware of what is going on and consider what the future holds. Actually, I voted Democratic two or three times before I realized, I am not really a Democrat. I believe more in the individual instead of the government running everything. At the time I thought, I don't want my kids to grow up in a socialist nation.

The Republican Philosophy

ILLA CLEMENT, KINGSVILLE

It's your belief in which type of government you think is best for the country in addition to which person is best for the country. The Republican Party builds up people's incomes through work possibilities and in other ways rather than just taking care of people. Money makes them independent. It is very important to make people feel that they can do it. Help people that really need help, but you're not going to help people in the long run, giving them the dole. Really, that is the big difference to me in the two parties.

There was such a large Mexican population here. They had always been raised to believe that democracy is Democrat. America is a democracy. You can vote either way and still be a democracy. It is very important to give people the opportunity to learn what the difference is and why you yourself believe in the Republican Party.

ESTHER BUCKLEY, LAREDO

I am an educator. I saw the total lack of knowledge that the voters had in Laredo. I started working in polling places. People couldn't read or write. They didn't know what they were doing. They had instructions on how to vote. It was kind of sad. There was no way for them to improve unless they got educated. I decided that politics was another area that I needed to get into.

Texas Democrats were very, very conservative. If you were a Texas Democrat, you were a conservative Democrat. There wasn't a whole lot of difference between a Republican and a Democrat. It was kind of like voters didn't see a need to move from the Democratic Party because it was in agreement with them. Later, in the '80s, they started saying the party had left them. Republicans have an extremely strong work ethic. You work for what you get. You do not go for charity and you do not ask for welfare. You take care of yourself. It is nobody's business what your problems are at home. You take care of it. That is a Mexican philosophy. In a lot of cases, people here were on the welfare system. They obeyed and they bowed down. They did what they were told in exchange for that job they got. They got us loans when we needed loans. When we were in trouble, they took care of it. The *patrón* system was alive. It was documented on the CBS TV show *60 Minutes* because it was so blatant.

DEANNE CLARK, LUBBOCK & DIMMITT

The Democratic Party changed and left the people of this area. As we were taught so aptly by Royal Masset of the state party, Texans really had a Republican mind-set but they just didn't know it. It has taken all of these years to persuade them that really they were Republican in philosophy. As the Democratic Party got more and more liberal, especially with the inclusion of gay rights and abortion rights, the people in this part of the country said, "No."

DORIS WILLIAMS, LAKE JACKSON

My husband always considered himself a Republican. Quite frankly, I came from a Democrat family. We were conservative Democrats. When I was growing up, there were no Republicans around. So I definitely learned about the actual Republican Party and the philosophy from my husband more than I learned from my parents or my school or anywhere else.

ANNA CLAIRE RICE, HOUSTON

I had always leaned Republican, but I belonged to a union. They would tell us how to vote. We would get a lot of letters and journals. That was one reason I got started. I had voted Republican and the lady that had the South Central Republican Women's Club, Miss Elsie Penk, got my name from that list. She called me and asked if I would come to a meeting. I said I would and really liked it. They talked about the issues.

Union members indicated that they were inclined to vote Republican but they were afraid the leadership would find out. Did you ever feel that way?

No. I was not afraid to tell them that I voted Republican. They didn't like it. I didn't care whether they liked it. People knew that I was working in the Republican Party. There were a lot of union people who would come up to me and say, we agree with the Republicans but we just don't advertise it.

Influential People

Many people influenced the women who built the Republican Party in Texas when they were girls. Local leaders, state leaders, and national leaders all inspired, trained, and advised, but by far family made the greatest impact. Time and again, fathers, mothers, and grandparents persuaded women to be responsible citizens by the example they set.

Family

ROBBIE BORCHERS, NEW BRAUNFELS
Truthfully, I was born a Republican. My mother's family had been Republican for many, many years. My mother has been a Republican. I have always been Republican. Maybe this is a birthright. Some years ago when our children were small, they were looking at Mother's Southwest Texas State yearbook. One of them said, "Grandmother, you didn't tell us that you went to school with Lyndon Johnson." He was president at that time. She indicated

that she really had not had that much respect for him when they were in school together and she sure didn't like him now. It wasn't anything she was proud of.

SYLVIA NUGENT, DALLAS & AMARILLO

My mother was involved with the Republican Party in Maryland and held some sort of office on the district level. I got involved in the Eisenhower campaign hanging door knockers and that sort thing as a youngster. I have had a lot of women who influenced me in lots of ways. My mother always pulled us out of bed at three in the morning to watch the moon shots. I watched every Kennedy-Nixon debate. Election night I stayed up all night. It was such a squeaker. Those things were encouraged in my house. Those were important things.

MARY TEEPLE, AUSTIN

As part of a family that was active in the community, I would have to say that I began my interest in issues important to Texas and issues important to the United States of America and issues important to Midland, Texas when I was a teenager. I was active in college in [*Texas Attorney General*] Waggoner Carr's Senate campaign here in Austin. That was in the '60s. My dad was a member of the Democratic Party in Midland. He even went to the Chicago convention in 1968. His name is Thornton Hardie Jr. His dad had been an active Democrat in El Paso. But Daddy realized that the Democratic Party was not nationally the same as the Democratic Party statewide. When a Democratic caucus was formed in Washington D. C., he was advised that it would be very difficult for a conservative Democrat to have a part to play. After he attended the Chicago convention, he decided that it might be a good idea to switch parties. So he did. That was my influence really.

BECKY CORNELL, SAN ANGELO

I guess I really got involved in politics early on with my father. We discussed politics at the dinner table. It was not a two-party state then. It was important to vote in the Democratic primary to "weed out the riff-raff." That was the 1950s in Dallas. He was always precinct chairman and would have stories about getting thrown out of the state convention because they couldn't get seated. I guess that was what really first started it. I grew up hearing it all of the time.

BUCKY SMITH, NEW BRAUNFELS

My father was a Yankee. He moved here in 1929 when I was four. He along with possibly one or two other people in town were outspoken Republicans. It was hard here in New Braunfels because this was a very Democratic stronghold. I grew up with the philosophy of conservatism and Republicanism all my life. Daddy used to laugh. He'd go vote on Election Day and there'd be maybe ten Republican votes. He'd say, one of these days we are going to change this whole thing. This county is going to go Republican. It did when Eisenhower was elected. They all just got together and laughed and said, we got them.

CAROLE KEETON RYLANDER, AUSTIN

I was blessed to be brought up in a household and a family that thrived on people, problem solving, and being where the action is. My dad was dean of the law school at the University of Texas for twenty-five years. Dad taught the law and Mama was the law. My brother, Richard, and I were the only kids on the block that had bedtime cases instead of bedtime stories before we had our prayers at night. Dad said, "Carole, you are the judge. Here is what happened. What would you do?" Dad never distinguished between myself and my brother. We were both the judges. What I learned from Dad and Mom was that it is not the dollars that you make, it is the difference that you make. I am always quoting Dad on that. The other thing that Dad taught me at a very early age is if you don't have somebody mad at you, you probably haven't done anything. So it paid to have someone mad at you if you are speaking up in the causes of human well-being and human decency. I was taught from a very early age to speak up and speak out.

FRAN CHILES, FORT WORTH

My father's father came from Germany to escape persecution and the overbearing government in Germany. So my father was very much a free enterprise person. Before my husband, Eddie Chiles, [*of "I'm mad too, Eddie" fame*], my father was making anti-socialist government speeches on the East Coast. We had values in our family. It was God, country, and family. My mother was the first Republican committeewoman on Maryland's central committee. We walked precincts with my mother. My mother and father both realized the importance of being involved in the government and trying to preserve the free enterprise system.

GWYN SHEA, IRVING

I grew up in West Texas in Kermit in Winkler County. My mother and father were very involved in politics and were election judges. My dad had actually been on the city council and on commissioners court. He owned the only bakery within a seventy-five-mile radius and then operated a restaurant. Growing up, my brother and I were actually taken to the polls on presidential election nights. We got to have our sandwiches and stay up until two o'clock in the morning because my mother and daddy were counting paper ballots. We thought that was an exquisite thing.

I took as normal that when you sat around the breakfast, lunch, and dinner tables people talked about issues that needed to be resolved or about bringing warring factions together to move things forward. I took the bulk of that experience for granted until I got out into the real world and became an adult. Everybody seemed to vote as a Republican in the presidential elections. But if you wanted to have any stroke in the local community, you voted in the Democratic primary. I came away from my childhood experience understanding my role in the system was very, very important. I should be involved in helping to elect those people that I thought could represent me with their vote.

MARY DENNY, DENTON

I started out in Houston, where I was born and raised. When I was about thirteen or fourteen, I really got involved in the

Goldwater presidential campaign. I had a little bit of exposure to politics before that. Some friends asked me to join them in handing out bumper stickers and literature in a parking lot at a nearby shopping center for a candidate. I thought, well, that sounds like fun. I went home and told my folks what I had done that day. My dad said, that's just great but did you realize that candidate is a Democrat and we are Republicans? I said no. I didn't know the difference and had not paid any attention. But I enjoyed what I did. Right after that, the campaign season of 1964 was upon us. So I got involved in the Goldwater campaign. That is when I really started getting active. My father was somewhat active in that race. I don't remember word for word what was said, but I liked the rationale my father used about why he was a Republican and I understood it. I really didn't question it. But of course as I got older and really got into it, I firmly believed in what the Republican Party stood for.

HARRIET LOWE, DALLAS

My grandfather and my father were both interested in politics. I can still remember my grandfather up on the bandstand giving a speech. I don't know truthfully if he was a Republican or Democrat, but I knew that you were supposed to be involved in politics.

JANELLE McARTHUR, SAN ANTONIO

I was born in McAllen. My grandfather was very much involved in politics. He was on the school board. At dinnertime, whenever he was there, he talked politics. I remember listening to election returns coming in on the radio in McAllen. He just instilled that interest. Later when I was down in McAllen one time—I don't remember what campaign I was doing—he said, "Janelle, nice girls don't belong in politics." I was stunned. Here was a person who lived and breathed politics.

MARGUERITE BINKLEY, HOUSTON

Much of my history includes Warren, for I could not have devoted the bulk of my adult life to the Party without his support.

Many husbands gift their wives with jewels; my husband indulged me the greatest gift a man can accord his wife—my time. In a sense, he was my mentor in that he encouraged my participation when his dental practice precluded his continued involvement.

FRAN ATKINSON, LUFKIN & SAN ANTONIO

My father was always interested. He was the lone Republican in Angelina County. We had the county convention for [*1936 presidential candidate*] Alf Landon in my living room, and there were six people there. This was before there was a Republican Party in Texas. I would always listen to both conventions on the radio and later on TV. I thought that to be effective you had to be involved. You can't do it from the outside. I was raised that way. It was put into me honestly. My daddy did it.

So would you consider him a mentor?

I didn't need one. It was just a charge!

ANNE ARMSTRONG, ARMSTRONG

My aunt and uncle who lived at our ranch, too, were Republican so I think I got indoctrinated, but also part of it was coming to my own conclusions. I could stand on my own feet. I didn't want government telling me what to do, who to hire, or how much tax to pay. So I changed and became a Republican. I was given a big boost in my political career by my Aunt Henrietta Kleberg Larkin Armstrong. She had been Republican committeewoman for our district. She felt she had done enough time there and asked me if I would be willing to take over that job.

Did she act as a mentor to you or did she just suggest this as something you might do?

Yes. She was a mentor. She took me to my first convention. She introduced me around. We would talk about the issues first. The Republican Party in those days was so small that it didn't take a lot before you knew the leadership. I liked it from the beginning.

Others Involved Politically

GWEN PHARO, DALLAS

Actually, I was born into politics. I was born in the little town of Lafayette, Alabama, next door to a United States Senator, Tom Heflin, who never married. In polite society, that means that he never had a family. So I was his little girl. As far back as I can remember, Senator Heflin always took me with him when he campaigned. After college, I went on to become Sam Rayburn's Texas secretary. There weren't any Republicans in Texas at the time.

What duties did you have?

They included being sure that casework was done properly. It wasn't like a standard congressional office since Mr. Sam was the Speaker of the House. If he needed something done in Texas, it was part of my job to see it was done. One of my duties was receiving him when he came home to Bonham—to see that the house was open and that the menus were planned. Several times Harry and Bess Truman came to Bonham. In those days, he didn't have the media or the Secret Service or any of those people. It was just like private citizens coming to be houseguests somewhere. They were just general duties, a person on the ground for the Speaker in his home state.

Rayburn hired you even though you were a Republican?

I always was a Republican. We used to have some colorful arguments. He used quite strong language and he had a sense of humor. I was a good employee. It wouldn't mean the same thing today that it meant then. He thought it funny and just an aberration because there weren't any Republicans. So, it never came up.

We had two big arguments. One of them was when [*World War II General Douglas*] MacArthur was fired. I was livid and did not mind expressing my opinions to the Speaker. The other one was when he called me and told me that he thought it was time I moved to Washington. I said, well, I am not sure I want to move to Washington. He said, you would be moving here to be Lyndon's executive secretary—his personal secretary. I said, well, I am dating a Navy doctor and think I may be getting married. That made him very unhappy. He used quite colorful language to tell me what a fool I was. He said to call him back tomorrow after I had come to my senses. He told me at the time, "Do you not know this man is going to be the president of United States in ten years?" This was 1951. That always stuck in my head. Mr. Sam wanted me to fill that vacancy since he was running the world anyway. So I called him back the next day and said, no, I'm not coming to Washington. Sure enough, in June of that year I did get married and left his job. Mr. Rayburn was very conservative so it was not a chore. In those days, Republicans were not a factor.

LOIS WHITE, SAN ANTONIO

I was a schoolteacher. If you are too narrow you don't have much to offer other people who need encouragement and need to be pushed out and need to distinguish themselves. Politics had been an area that blacks had not been involved in. My father, who was a minister, explained to me as a child how things had gone particularly in the South. You usually were involved in politics at what I call a very low level. People would come ask for your support. The person may not be one of good character. My father had stayed out of that. If you could not be involved in a decent way, if it did not lift you up, well, then leave it alone. If it is going to tear you down, you don't need it.

At last we were at a point where it seemed that blacks were going to be encouraged to be full citizens. I read an article in the newspaper quoting the chairman of the Bexar County Republican Party. He said that a black man here in San Antonio told him blacks on the East Side had all been brainwashed. He said he was the only one on the East Side of San Antonio that voted for Richard Nixon. This was 1963. On an impulse, I called the chairman. He was not in but I talked to his secretary. I told her I had just read the article and not everyone had been brainwashed. I voted for

Richard Nixon. I had friends who voted for him. We thought that Eisenhower sending the troops into Arkansas [*in 1957 to enforce school desegregation*] was a positive move. Since the Civil War, we decided that was the most significant civil rights event that happened. When the Republican county chairman got back to his office, he called me. He said he wanted to talk to me. He also wanted to know if I had any time to get a group together; he would like to come over and talk. I said, no, I didn't have time to get any groups together; that is not what I wanted to do. I just wanted to set the record straight.

JUNE DEASON, SAN ANTONIO

Beryl Milburn is one mentor and Mary Lou Grier another and Anne Armstrong—what a beautiful, rich, talented, intelligent, kind, nice, wonderful, wonderful lady. Janelle McArthur taught me a lot. The first two campaigns I worked in Janelle worked in them. She had done a lot of things I had not. I was just getting started. I watched Janelle in action. If you're smart, you'll watch those people who are successful. Cleo Bohls, who died of cancer in 1976, would have been president of the National Federation of Republican Women if she hadn't been sick. This lady could do anything and never lost her cool. You admire people like that. So, I've had mentors. Great ladies! I learned something from every one of them—something different.

AMELIE COBB, BEAUMONT

Peg Fleming, who I lived with on Sunset Boulevard in Houston, was a contributor early on to the Republican Party. She encouraged a lot of people to get involved in politics. She is probably just one of the many unsung that had very strong Republican beliefs.

KRIS ANNE VOGELPOHL, GALVESTON

There was a wonderful woman, Estelle Tartt. She was the government teacher at the high school. She did everything she could to influence her students. She was the State Republican

Executive Committee member. She also did a lot of the entertaining when the candidates came down. She would attend meetings and hold elections. She came from an old, old Galveston family, and they were quite wealthy. She had been in the school system for so long. She had such a good reputation. She was one of the best teachers. I would say she gave more to the Party in the early days than any other woman. She was also very generous to candidates.

JANE NELSON, FLOWER MOUND

There were some very strong women in my life at the time who encouraged me to get involved in politics from the volunteer perspective. My mother-in-law, Marilyn Nelson, was really one of the pioneers of the Republican Party in Denton County and was certainly one of those who encouraged my involvement. In later years, Fran Chiles played a huge role in encouraging me. There were many, many other women. In Denton County, there were no elected Republicans at the county level. One of the members of that circle, Lee Walker, was big in PTA, very active and involved in the community, and a mother whose daughter was murdered. She took that pain, ran for office, and was the first Republican and first woman to get elected as a county commissioner in Denton County. Lee opened the door for many others. I worked on Lee's campaign. I think in that area, particularly, women ran for office; they didn't just work on campaigns. As a young woman at that time, I didn't really consider running for office. I think that made a big impression on me that women were doing things that were traditionally associated with men only.

It is intriguing that Democrats get the credit for being such strong supporters of women.

No. We were the ones there when the rubber met the road. We elected women to office. It may well have been that the officeholders for the Democrats were males and probably didn't encourage women opponents in the Democratic Party. There were women who were willing to run as Republicans and sure got the support of others, not just other women but other individuals in the area.

CHAPTER 4

What Comes First,
the Candidate or the Party?

"I got involved because we finally had a candidate in our area
running for office . . ."   —DORIS WILLIAMS

*C*an you imagine going to your polling place with your voter's
registration card, checking in, picking up a ballot, and only
having a few races in which to cast your vote? That happened in
each Republican primary across the state for years. How could you
develop a party without candidates to vote for? How could you recruit
candidates without party faithful to check the box or pull the lever?

Several candidates held the key to bringing voters into
Republican primaries statewide. President Dwight Eisenhower
brought respectability with his established reputation and new
patriotic and dedicated followers after World War II. Senator
John Tower provided legitimacy with a statewide win and a
consistent conservative voting record, leading to reelection.
Presidential candidate Barry Goldwater drew to the Republican Party thousands of new volunteers who were eager to vote
for his brand of conservatism and defeat the "Eastern Establishment" candidate within the Republican Party.

Voters in pockets of Texas had local and regional candidates
that they rallied behind and elected. Bruce Alger of Dallas and
Barbara Culver Clack of Midland inspired the Party faithful
and gave voters a face for the Republican philosophy. Thousands
of Republicans "threw their votes away" by voting in the
Republican primary in order to develop a base of voters that
candidates could count on in each subsequent election. At the same
time, many Republicans took the risk and ran for office without
much hope of winning in order to give the voters a choice.

A push-and-pull between the interests of statewide and local candidates continued through the 1960s and 1970s. Some Republicans hoped for strong statewide candidates because "that is all we had," while others resented the state party siphoning off volunteers and dollars, which they thought had a negative impact on their ability to recruit and elect local candidates.

At the bottom line was a tough decision about the allocation of resources to elect the most Republicans to office in Texas. In a state as large and diverse as Texas, a formula did not exist which worked well in each region. Many people devoted time and money to local, regional, state, and national candidates to elect Republicans any way they could.

How did you get the organization growing? Was it different in different parts of the state? Did you push the issues? Did you pursue candidates?

ANNE ARMSTRONG, ARMSTRONG

It really is a chicken and egg situation sometimes. Of course we had our urban strongholds, particularly in Dallas. That was the fountainhead of Republicanism in those days. The rural counties were tough. But luckily our leadership seemed to understand that one size didn't fit all. For instance, in our little county, Kenedy County, that only had about four hundred people, it really got people's backs up if we tried to have election judges looking over the shoulders of our neighbors. In general, our leadership was smart enough to realize that what was necessary in Dallas and Houston might not be in our rural counties.

We had candidates in Dallas early on and some in the Hill Country and up in North Texas. South Texas was quite slow, though I remember we had Chuck Scoggins in the legislature pretty early on. Issues were very important to us. In general, we were against the intrusion of government into our lives exactly the way we are today. One particular issue, right to work, was certainly a big one. We were always very strong on national defense. Strong anti-Communism. So, yes, we pushed issues. We got candidates when we could. But I think we definitely had a philosophy of conservatism in our Party.

AMELIE COBB, BEAUMONT

I don't really want to play down the issues because I do think they are important. But it takes a spokesman for those issues to really get people turned on. There are some issues that are so overwhelming to people that they activate them into politics. But I don't think they will stay hooked for very long on most issues if they don't have a spokesman that they feel can take the message they care about and go do something about it. For me, it was Eisenhower and then it was Goldwater and then it was Bush who sort of embodied the ideals that I had or felt. In general, unless you have a strong commitment to issues, the leaders have brought you into participating in politics.

What Candidates Did for the Republican Party in the Early Years

---

Dwight Eisenhower

Brought Enthusiastic Supporters into the Political Process

MARTHA CROWLEY, DALLAS

Frank and I would get together with other young couples every weekend. We generally ended up talking politics. We were all very opinionated. We all knew exactly how to cure all the problems. All of the people I knew and I respected it turned out were Republicans. The closer primary time came, the more heated the discussions became and most of us, especially the girls, were vehemently in favor of Eisenhower.

My husband, Frank, pointed out to us that we couldn't vote for Eisenhower because Eisenhower wasn't going to win the primary. I said, well, all of us are in favor of him over Taft [*the 1952*

Republican establishment candidate Robert A. Taft]. He said, well, you're not going to be able to vote in the primary because you're not going to be able to find one. When Frank said, you're not going to be able to find a Republican primary, Pat Jordan said, "Well, I'll bet I can find one." Frank told Pat that he'd bet the two of us a hat we wouldn't be able to come up with a Republican primary. He still owes us a hat. He never paid off that debt.

Pat started calling around. I did too and we were informed that there was an Eisenhower campaign office that had just opened. It was downtown in an old, rickety building. Pat was working so I went down the next day and Allie Mae Currie was there. She was the first person I met with any authority at all. Oddly enough, she and her husband were both Republicans, but they split over the candidates. He was for Taft and she was for Eisenhower. I told her where I lived and she looked it up on the list. She said, "Your precinct hasn't been organized at all. It shows a precinct chairman here—have you ever talked to him?" Of course I had not been involved in any kind of politics before, and I wasn't on a list so they hadn't contacted me. But they never had contacted anybody. They were just in name only. She asked if I would organize the precinct. I said, oh sure. I had no more idea what I was getting into. All of us who were getting into it were just stumbling around. We just scratched it out for ourselves.

First of all, Allie Mae said you have to look up these names and the addresses. I looked up all of those phone numbers and started calling them household by household. I asked them whether they were going to support Eisenhower or Taft in the primary. Well, some of them would inform me that I was in the wrong party. Allie Mae got together the leaders in those precincts being organized and gave us instructions. We had to attend the primary. Of course none was scheduled in my precinct so we scheduled one at my house. There weren't many voters. I thought it was going to be a mob scene.

What happened at your precinct convention?

There was a rump convention. We had to bolt our own house

with the Eisenhower people! The man who was the precinct chairman had never been active; his wife, his daughter, and maybe two others were the only Taft people. Allie Mae told us to have a camera and take pictures of the Eisenhower people with signs to indicate that we were for Eisenhower and then somehow get a Taft sign or make one and have them hold the Taft sign. There was a fight between Taft and Eisenhower supporters at the county level and at the state level and all the way to the national convention. We bought our first television set so we could watch the national convention. Texas was one of the contested states. The Eisenhower delegates went armed with all of the pictures and statements by county chairmen and the state chairman. It was certainly a wonderful lesson in civics.

KATIE SEEWALD, AMARILLO

In 1952, a little notice was in the Junior League newsletter, "If you want to help nominate Eisenhower for President, call Emmy O'Brien. If you want to help nominate Taft, call Ruthelle Bacon." So I called Emmy. She was thrilled to death. She said, "You'll have to be chairman in your precinct." So I held a precinct meeting here in this living room. There were only three of us.

I was elected delegate to the county convention. We held that convention in the courthouse. I forget whether we rumped or they rumped but there was a big to-do. Then we went onto the state convention in Mineral Wells. One of us rumped. When we got back from that Mineral Wells convention, Emmy and her husband, Tim, came over here and convinced my husband, Buddy, that I should go to Chicago to the national convention as a witness before the credentials committee. All of the people that were going to testify for Eisenhower from Texas got together. Our coach was William Rogers who later became secretary of state under Nixon. He told me what to wear. He told each of us to go write down in our own handwriting what had happened and why we were doing this. He had it typed up. When I appeared before the credentials committee and then before the national committee, I simply read the following.

"This spring along with hundreds of other Young Texas Republicans, I wanted to make my voice heard against the Democratic administration where it could count in the precinct conventions. National publications and local newspapers had continually emphasized the importance of ordinary citizens participating in these precinct meetings. The opportunity seemed golden and in our enthusiasm and inexperience we never visualized what was about to happen to us.

In my precinct I was unanimously elected delegate to the county convention. Some time later, the Zweifel forces persuaded a man in my precinct to certify that he had held a convention naming another person as delegate. Later, this man became frightened and told the County Clerk that he had not held a convention and that he wished to withdraw the returns filed by him, as illegal. This man's sworn statement is on record with the County Clerk.

The legal county convention was held at Amarillo and it elected 14 Eisenhower delegates to the State Convention, myself included. A few Zweifel supporters stayed on and held a rump convention naming a slate of Zweifel delegates to the State Convention. In our county including all of the illegal rump conventions there were approximately 150 votes cast for the Zweifel machine and over 600 for Eisenhower.

We were hopeful that the judgement of the people in higher authority would be fair and right, but at Mineral Wells we were shocked at what happened. At 4:30 in the morning they gave us 5 minutes to speak and then the axe. The delegate who had been originally selected by an admitted fraudulent precinct convention was seated in my place.

And here is one very important point. If all these young people who are so eager to take an active part in a genuine Texas Republican Party and we really are—if we are denied that right to participate, where are we to turn? We were willing to forfeit the right to have any say in our local or state government. We want to work in and support our chosen party—the Republican Party. We want to help elect a Republican President. Won't you give us that chance?"

That convention and being a witness up there was the most exciting thing. I was just beside myself with terror at having to talk to that many people. Just the excitement of it sort of carried me on.

The influx of new Party members supporting Eisenhower caused distrust among the existing Republicans. In fact, many new people were suspected of being Democrats. As history now records, these were indeed Republicans who made a lifetime commitment to developing a two-party state in Texas. The following quote exemplifies the skepticism about the motivations of new people involved in the Republican precinct conventions.

RUTHELLE BACON, AMARILLO
(As quoted in the September 27, 1952 issue of Collier's*)*

"The Democrats stole it. They invaded our precinct conventions and put over an Eisenhower slate. I've been in Republican politics here 32 years. I know Republicans. These were Democrats. They had no right to dictate our nomination."

JANE JUETT, AMARILLO

Actually, it was the first time that my husband, Bill, and I had ever voted. I think we just assumed that we had to vote Republican to be able to vote for Eisenhower. His parents, my parents, and all our families were very strong Democrats. In fact, my mother and dad were both officeholders on the Democrat ticket. So we were kind of in trouble with both our families when they found out that we had voted Republican.

VERA CARHART, RICHARDSON & HOUSTON

I was in Woman Power for Eisenhower. It was difficult because Johnny was a baby and I had to get a sitter. We were in Alamo Heights in San Antonio. Finding a sitter at that time was not that easy. I had a neighbor who would keep him for me, and I'd go downtown to the headquarters and work. Mostly it was identifying the votes and getting them out—the old basics.

Who taught you "the old basics?"

It was a group of women that were, I think, probably a lot of army wives. I was a newcomer to San Antonio. I just went in totally unknown. They gave me a job. I did it and they asked if I'd come back next week and I said yes.

BETTE JO BUHLER, VICTORIA

The Eisenhower convention helped us tremendously because there was a fight between the Taft and the Eisenhower forces. Most of us were young and inexperienced—it fired us up. If the old guard in 1948 didn't want any new Republicans, there was this new group in 1952 that wanted to open it up. It made a big difference.

Built a Bridge from Democrat to Republican

HELEN ANDERSON, HOUSTON

Eisenhower as a candidate made it sort of easy for someone like myself who had been a Democrat. He formed a bridge for us to cross over. He was someone who would add distinction to the office of president. We felt that he was a man we could be very proud of and therefore we backed him. He was a Republican and, suddenly, *you* were a Republican. In my case, I was aimed that way.

Was it difficult for you to make that switch coming from a long-standing Democrat family and with your father an elected Democrat?

Yes, it was. Therefore, I sort of followed the movement at first. I was certainly no leader, but I was firm in my beliefs and my family supported me. I became involved in a movement that I was proud of, that I could identify with. Suddenly I was very firmly in it and remained so.

The Republicans represented more of what you believed in than your parents' party, and having Eisenhower as the candidate made it more acceptable?

That was the only way because had Taft been the candidate the story might have been different as far as I am concerned.

Eisenhower made it entirely possible to make that switch. I think that represented the way a lot of Democrats felt.

John Tower

Created a Reason for Organizing: The 1960 and 1961 Senate Campaigns

In what areas did you find that candidates helped spark interest and in what areas did you find that an organization helped spark interest?

BETTE JO BUHLER, VICTORIA

To get a good candidate, you need an organization. But you are not going to get an organization until you prove there's a reason for it.

How was Tower's campaign strategy formulated when you started out with so few assets?

That was a miracle. Talk about political novices, we were it. Raising money was a major issue as it still is today. The major problem was raising money to get his name before the public. At that time, newspapers did not cover Republicans. We had to advertise. He was a tireless campaigner. He went to most of the counties even if there was no hope. He made a good impression. If he had half a chance, I think he could sell himself.

BERYL MILBURN, AUSTIN

The big thing was the election of John Tower in the '61 special election. He had been the nominee for U. S. Senate against Lyndon Johnson in '60, and that was funny because at that time we nominated candidates by convention. There was a convention in McAllen, and he wanted to be the candidate for U. S. Senate. We thought, "John Tower has no chance. He's not a very attractive kind of person." We wanted Thad Hutcheson to run again. He wouldn't do it. We begged him. Finally, we gave the nomination to

John Tower and he got defeated. But he just kept right on running for the vacancy caused by Lyndon's election as vice president. When he won, it was really something. It put the Republican Party on the map.

Why was he successful in that run and not earlier?

It was a special election. Everybody runs together, not by party. I think there were some seventy candidates. He got into the runoff and the momentum just carried him in.

How did John Tower become the Party's candidate?

FLO KAMPMANN CRICHTON, SAN ANTONIO
He just plain wanted it. We didn't want to talk him out of it. We just felt like he was gutsy enough to make a run for it. He said, "I'm not going to win this time. As long as I can get forty-three percent of the vote, then I have got something to build on." He took chances. He had a statewide constituency. So in 1961, he was the lead guy. He fought and scrapped. He had been on the state committee and was the chairman of the platform committee. He was a good speaker, a good writer, and very determined.

RUTH MANKIN, HOUSTON
I can remember so well the night of that vote. It was a Saturday night, and the turnout wasn't as good as we had hoped for. We had already identified our voters. We knew from the people working at the polls, our voters had not all turned out. So we gathered together a group. We got in our cars and we went door-to-door to all of the known Republican voters. We got people away from the bridge table. We got people out of the bath. We said you have got to come. This is it. We are the bellwether precinct. We were the largest Republican precinct in the state of Texas in terms of registration or poll taxes in those days. We felt that we were very important to his success.

That means that you knew them well enough to get them out of the bathtub?

Most of our precincts were like this. I am not saying it was just our precinct. This was what was emphasized. You were to know your people. Then you had to get them out by hook or by crook, whatever it took.

VIRGINIA EGGERS, WICHITA FALLS & DALLAS

When John Tower ran in the special election, we had what we called the Tower Belles. We were all dressed up in our little red vests. They were red felt, and we had these little red pillbox hats. We would wear our navy blue skirts and our white blouses. We got on a bus and we just drove down the highway. We would stop in any town. We went in this billiard parlor one time. There were groups in the back playing cards. Not one of them did a thing. They just raised their eyes to us and watched as we paraded around the room. We want you to meet John Tower. He came along in his cowboy hat and boots, and they never moved—their eyes just followed us around the room. We are lucky they didn't shoot at us. I am sure to them it was rather odd to see all of these young girls all dressed up coming to their town.

MARION COLEMAN, PASADENA

I was so energized by Tower's candidacy and the possibility of us really doing it. We kept everything Q. T. We didn't let anyone know what we were doing or how we were doing it. We would find out who the union people were. "Hello, this is the Area 20 Republican Headquarters calling for John Tower." They hung up on us. Then we would write down "UNION" in big red letters. Do not call this house again. We had a lot of those, let me tell you.

MARY LOU WIGGINS, DALLAS

Where I lived, it was not difficult to persuade your friends and neighbors. It was more difficult on the Couples Canvas for Tower because we were covering an area and we would go to towns like Grand Prairie. There wouldn't be enough Republicans in Grand Prairie to go door-to-door. So we would have to take volunteers over there. We would get couples in a precinct signed up and give them a schedule. They would go door-to-door for John Tower. I think that was very impressive. He was elected against all odds.

Why do you think people were impressed?

Because we were responsible young people. They responded to that. It wasn't just the same old thing.

Do you think you contributed to the growth in the Republican Party through your willingness to go outside your neighborhood?

I think so. It helped and encouraged the few Republicans that were in that area. Then you go door-to-door and you meet people. I think they were impressed with the fact that people thought enough of their candidate to go and ring somebody's doorbell and tell them about him.

TAFFY GOLDSMITH, DALLAS

My job was organizing and financing the Tower Trailer, which was a small trailer that had to be hauled from shopping center to shopping center or rally to rally.

Did the Tower Trailer go around the whole state?

No, just Dallas. They considered Dallas County pivotal and important. We already had a Republican congressman [*Bruce Alger*]. I went around the state to rallies on trains and buses. We went wherever we could get anything started. The trips were very well planned. I was pregnant, and it was easy for me to go into any hostile group in a red, white, and blue outfit. It was easy to glad-hand for Tower. I had gotten to know him through Young Republican activities and through the state conventions. I really respected his knowledge of history. People followed him because they knew he had the words and he had the history to back him up. He would always say, "Once more into the breach, my friends." We were always the underdog because we never had the money.

JEAN RAFFETTO, HOUSTON & SEABROOK

I was a newcomer to Houston. I didn't know many people,

but I just wanted to do something to help John Tower. I remember getting together in the evenings after work and going out door-to-door, talking about John Tower and giving out literature. I was living in the southwest part of Houston.

How were you received when you went door-to-door?

I don't recall people being rude. It was kind of a new experience to do that. Ignorance is bliss. People were friendly.

BARBARA HOWELL, FORT WORTH

It basically started with five women in the upstairs of the Republican headquarters for Nixon. The ladies were Pat Kennedy, Mackie Brownfield, Ann Wallace, Betty Andujar, and myself. The five of us really spearheaded the campaign for John Tower here in Fort Worth. By the time we got through, we had many, many enthusiastic and hard-working ladies.

What kinds of things did you do to educate people about John Tower?

Each one of us would go talk our husbands out of plain envelopes from their offices and plain pieces of paper. Then we would proceed to get fliers out or bumper stickers. It was amazing; all of a sudden we were seeing these bumper stickers. One of the women brought up the subject of having a coffee and asking women from every area of the county to this coffee. They asked me if I would have one in our home. We had over two hundred attend. They were women we took off the voters lists in different areas of the city. We sent this little invitation. It was very homemade. We asked each one if they would sign up for a coffee. I remember Betty Andujar spoke at my coffee telling the ladies about Tower. We told them that if they would have a coffee we would have someone there to explain who John Tower was. It just blossomed and went from there.

On Saturday mornings, we had several women who took their station wagons and several restaurants and cafeteria owners who volunteered their equipment. We would plug in our coffee makers at the lamppost in the shopping centers. We also had little micro-phones and would ask people to come over and have coffee. The ladies were very well versed on his qualifications.

LINDA DYSON, HOUSTON

In 1960, state headquarters was here on Montrose. County offices were there also. I went in and worked and just did what-ever. Helen Healey was the executive secretary of the state party. Tad Smith from El Paso was the state chairman. We all worked diligently for Nixon and Tower.

Helen asked me if I would go to work for her in the Tower campaign in the special election. I said, "Well, I really don't know anything, but I will work if you will teach me." I went into the Tower campaign as a paid employee. Maybe it was two hundred dollars. It was big time. I did all the finances. All of the checks would come in and I would deposit them. I would write down the expenditures. That was the bookkeeping of the Tower campaign. But it worked.

How was the Tower campaign set up when he ran against Democrat William Blakely in 1961?

Jimmy Bertron, who was Harris County chairman, took a leave and chaired that special election campaign. They brought in all kinds of field men. We talked to the county chairmen through-out Texas. Everybody was instructed the way they were to report the vote on election night, since the 1960 presidential election was really stolen in Texas. Odessa was a town that we knew we would win, but we couldn't report it as a win. When Odessa officials called election central in Dallas, they were to misreport it. If we had 4,100 votes, they were to report it as 1,400. The Tower campaign did that in a lot of counties throughout the state. We also had federal mar-shals lined up to go into the Valley [*in South Texas where fraud was routine*] and secure the voting boxes. The returns really looked like they were in Blakely's favor. As soon as the boxes were secure, we corrected the election returns. I think it saved us.

KATIE HECK, MIDLAND

I liked Tower a lot, but he was a funny guy to campaign with because he was fairly aloof and shy, believe it or not. He did not want to get out of the car and go shake hands. We would make him get out of the car and go talk to people. We would tease him unmercifully saying things like, "Who is the candidate here? We're not going to the Senate." Of course, we didn't think he was going either. Oh, that was a happy night. At first, it was beginning to look like another step on a long road and he was not going to win. All of a sudden, the announcer comes on and says we made a mistake. The vote from Midland County was reversed. We all burst into tears, grabbed each other and hugged. Our headquarters was chaos. We were yelling and jumping up and down.

MARJORIE ARSIIT, HOUSTON

The results just dribbled in. Everyone went home, but there were a few of us that stayed. During the night, the word got out that Lyndon Johnson had come back to the ranch. We knew that it was all over because all he had to do was go around and do something to the votes. Did you know that no one ever really celebrated that first victory because no one believed it until he was sworn in? [*Republican National Committeeman*] Albert Fay and others went to Washington to the swearing in. There was no big celebration because no one believed it.

JANE ANNE STINNETT, LUBBOCK

Women did the legwork, put rallies together, did the conventions, built precinct organizations, and did the phoning. They did everything. I don't think the women who came before me get the credit that they should get. They are the ones who really worked at it. They did a great job. Women all over Texas were doing that. Of course, John Tower was a great one to rally around and help build the party. Having him elected gave the Republican Party in Texas credibility. Vaude Roper, Terry Tapp, Nita Gibson, and Mrs. Treadaway all worked really hard at bringing people in and recruiting candidates and helping them raise money and putting events together. To put an event together for John Tower in 1960 was a major deal. They would spend a lot of time on the telephone. They had a lot of credibility.

You traveled around the state with John Tower and a lot of women assisted. Why do you think he trusted them so much?

CYNDI TAYLOR KRIER, SAN ANTONIO

When he ran first in 1960 and then in the special election in '61, there were sixty some odd candidates and he got into that run-off. I heard him say a hundred times he was elected because of Republican women in tennis shoes who told their neighbors, held teas, walked with him and for him, and then voted. If we went to Beaumont, Leon Richardson would be there to meet us. When we came to San Antonio, it was Mary Lou Grier, Libba Barnes, Joci Straus, and Janelle McArthur. Everywhere you went there was a Republican woman who was an activist. He continued to be in touch with them.

It Was No Fluke: The 1966 Campaign

FLO KAMPMANN CRICHTON, SAN ANTONIO

Of course, being reelected proves it's not a fluke. It really confirms your legitimacy. Senator Yarborough helped us out [*U. S. Senator from Texas, Democrat Ralph Yarborough*]. I got to know Senator Yarborough pretty well. He didn't get along with John Connally. Of course, he didn't like Attorney General Waggoner Carr either. [*Connally was governor and Carr was running against Tower*] They were just different people. So he seemed willing to help us.

How were you in a position to be talking and negotiating with Senator Yarborough?

I had come to know him through Hemisfair [*San Antonio's 1968 world's fair*]. I was on the executive committee. Senator Yarborough was to introduce the Hemisfair participation bill in the Senate, but he got crosswise with [*Texas Congressman*] Henry B. Gonzalez. He said he was not going to introduce the bill, so that held up the participation of every other country if the U. S. was not going to participate. It was really a serious matter. Bill Sinkin called me and asked me if I would speak to Senator Tower and ask him to speak to Senator Yarborough, which he did. Senator Yarborough still was not going to introduce the bill, but he said he would be very glad to support it if Tower would introduce the bill, which he did.

In the meantime, I had to go to Washington and do some visiting with him about it. He just wasn't going to support Waggoner Carr. So he said he would very quietly support Tower. He sent word to his people that if they couldn't vote for Tower, don't vote at all. That was a very good relationship between Yarborough and Tower. They were so different, but they could sort of respect each other. Senator Yarborough said to me that Senator Tower had never attacked him personally. He said, "Tower has always been very cordial and I have always been able to work with him and our staffs have been able to work with each other." That was good for Texas because most federal appointments went through fairly easily. I was very pleased with that.

In what other activities did you participate in conjunction with the 1966 campaign?

In those involved with John Tower's election, which covered the waterfront. You just do whatever is necessary. I went certain places and made speeches for him. I did just a touch with the finances of the campaign and dealt somewhat with the strategy, but John Tower, more than probably most candidates, liked to run his own campaign. He had good people to run it, but he sort of had an instinct as to what he could do best. So he had a good deal of say-so about the campaign.

NADINE FRANCIS, ODESSA

I received a call that I was to get in contact with a man in Midland with the AFL-CIO. I can't remember his title. I was to very quietly meet him and pick up a list of people and mail it to headquarters in Austin. This was such an important move. It was a big part of helping in the election of John Tower that I'm sure it made a difference. I promptly sent it to the headquarters.

How do you think Tower pulled off the win in 1966?

ANNE ARMSTRONG, ARMSTRONG

We had, particularly in the big cities, some very stalwart backers. We had some persuasive powers at the top of the Party who were able to convince Washington Republicans that we deserved backing from them. We were the future of the South and of the Republican Party. We were also able to convince the national party and the congressional and senatorial campaigns to send money down here. Then you had sophisticated people like Flo [*Kampmann Crichton*]. Flo had a lot of influence nationally. So did some of our other Party leadership. They were respected up there, and the people in Washington knew we would not lead them astray down here by urging them to back certain candidates.

The organization of this state I would venture a guess in those days was the most sophisticated, thorough, and effective of any state party. It had the correct concept and it had fantastic execution. The details were looked after. The enthusiasm that was generated down at the local level got our volunteers to do all of these things that were necessary. It was inspiring. We, down at our county levels, had faith in our leadership that they knew what they were doing. They proved it to us. They had a plan and then they would help teach us how to execute it down at our level. It was a model in those years. It may be now. We were very afraid in those days of being cheated out of what we really won so we had to have the details looked after.

Who formulated the plans?

Mainly the Peter O'Donnell team with the original core from Dallas. They elected the first candidates, and there were a lot of smart people up there. They were fearless because it wasn't easy in those days to go against the Texas establishment. So I give the main credit to that team up there. The rest of the state could have defeated the O'Donnell team after a couple or three years, but we thought it was great. We were glad that they were pointing the way.

People quickly realized that it was a wonderful plan and that we could carry out this plan. We did. We had some terrible disappointments, especially in 1964 [*when Lyndon Johnson defeated Goldwater in the presidential election*], but we rallied. The friendships that were formed helped us along. The band of women that were friends then was something rare in politics. It was unselfish. It was a true bond of friendship—the bonds that you get for believing in the same principles. It was a great time to be in politics. I wouldn't take anything for those days.

It must have been difficult to regroup after the 1964 loss.

FRANCIE FATHEREE CODY, PAMPA

Oh, yes, it was. Right after the election we had some men come over to my house. We talked about what we were going to do to try and make the Party stronger. We were going to raise money. We were going to try and get people to run for office.

It seems like there was a lot of joint effort between the Party and the candidates in the 1960s.

BILLIE PICKARD, RAYMONDVILLE

We were few in number. We didn't have that many people to call on to divide the effort between the Party and the candidates. We needed every warm body that was available to be involved. It is better when you can all be on the same road. It could be that after Tower won that '66 election it strengthened his position. I am guessing that after that the financial support was much greater for him for future campaigns. Possibly in '66, funding was still a bigger factor, and you needed both units working together because of that.

So some people might be willing to give to the Party rather than an individual candidate because they still doubted that candidate had the ability to win?

Yes. It is just a guess.

NITA GIBSON, LUBBOCK

When we would have John Tower here, we would invite people from all around. I'd invite people from every county and all around West Texas. You have them register. You know their names and their addresses. You know that they are interested in John Tower. You keep a good record of these people. When you go into that county, you say, hey, would you like to serve as county chair, or county vice chair, or would you help us with the primary?

RUTH COX MIZELLE, CORPUS CHRISTI

Tower was very popular in Corpus Christi. We decided to have a free tamale dinner. They told me that the music was changing and didn't think that I could get some Guy Lombardo music down there and get the voters out. So we had three different bands and free tamales. They really turned out because it was right on the way from work and it was early in the evening. People went outside and put a Tower sticker on everyone's car. I'm sure that we had a lot of people who came who weren't going to vote for Tower but at least they were going to advertise.

We picked Tower up at the airport. He didn't say anything. We showed him the publicity. When he got up to speak, he really was a statesman and an orator. With all of the clamor, people would just stop and listen to him. He was a great candidate. I think he was writing his speech in his head while driving from the airport.

RUTH McGUCKIN, HOUSTON & WASHINGTON COUNTY

In 1966, I worked for Tower's reelection. One man told me, "I don't know anything about John Tower, but if you are willing to walk in the rain for him, he must be pretty good so I'll vote for him."

How important was it to have someone like John Tower and George Bush elected to Congress to help state and local candidates? Or did you work from the bottom up?

Tower helped some, but a lot of the time we hardly had any other candidates because we couldn't get anyone to run. We wanted one of the precinct chairmen to run for state representative. He said, "I will, but I am really tired of these kamikaze campaigns."

Did you work for John Tower's reelection in 1966?

GLORIA CLAYTON, DALLAS

We did the telephone canvas and the get-out-the-vote. I don't know what the laws are today, but there were some companies that would let us have their phones after they closed. Ebby Holiday was one of the ones that I remember. We would all man a phone on a desk. We had our list of calls to be made, and we would just start in.

RITA PALM, FORT WORTH

The bus tours in '66 were fun. Lou Tower is such a warm, reach-out person. Maybe four or five women from Dallas and four or five from Fort Worth and Weatherford all got on the bus. They would have us booked into maybe ten towns. We would spend maybe one night on the road, and then we would go to ten towns the next day. We would go in and the Republican Women's Clubs generally sponsored a coffee. We would usually pick up the Senator somewhere along the way. I remember him with that gold cigarette case. He would sit there and smoke that cigarette and look just as starched and neat at ten at night as he had at eight that morning. I never knew how he did that.

MARY BODGER, CORPUS CHRISTI

After Tower won, my Democrat father who was living in California called me and said, "I want to congratulate you. Your man won and he is a good man." I said, "Do you mean that, Daddy?" He said, "Yes, you are now working on the right track because it changes every so many years. Republicans are the ones that have it now."

Increased the Party's Visibility

NORMA BENAVIDES, LAREDO

When John Tower made it, it was really wonderful because for a long, long time all of South Texas was considered solidly

Democrat. Of course, it had made a difference because it proved that even in South Texas you could get a Republican elected.

JESS ANN THOMASON, MIDLAND

It was a big boom. It was like we finally accomplished something. It gave us all lifts because we had been voting Republican for so long to no avail. To have John Tower come along, it was like a miracle.

IRIS MANES, HOUSTON

The fact that we could elect someone to that high office showed the conservative Democrats that there was a reason to come over to our Party. We were growing rapidly at that time.

Inspired Loyalty

BILLIJO PORTER, EL PASO

Here was this short guy, and he could open his mouth and talk. He could move a whole crowd into enthusiasm. Also, he voted right. He was a leader in the Senate. He was on the Armed Services Committee, which was important to El Paso. He was a conservative. But when you heard him speak, it was mesmerizing.

LEON RICHARDSON, NEDERLAND

For some reason, he liked me. I have no idea why, but he always boosted me for different leadership roles [*talking about him tearfully*]. He was the most intelligent man I had ever seen. He was also the best speaker and also one of my very best friends. I always picked him up at the airport. I could read his moods. If he was thinking about something or something was on his mind, we would drive to Beaumont and I would drop him at a motel or some function and we might never say a word to each other. Then sometimes he would chat all the way and ask about everybody in the county and ask about the family. A lot of the people thought he was aloof. He wasn't. He was a big kidder. When I had my first grandbaby, he wrote me and said "Dear Granny." I was so upset when he died [*in a commuter plane crash in 1991*].

He was the Party in the '60s. He was our only hope. Of course, he never got beaten because he never wavered from his philosophy. When a vote came up, I knew exactly how John Tower was going to vote. He never disappointed me. He was the head of the Party. It was funny because the only time he ever got angry with me was when John Connally changed over [*former governor John Connally became a Republican in 1973*]. We had a big party in Austin. I said, well, now you are going to have to share the limelight. He just turned around. He was angry with me. He had a big ego.

LIBBA BARNES, SAN ANTONIO

A highlight for me was when we reelected John Tower the last time [*1978*] because that was a hard race. I remember the next day some of the Tower staff ended up in the same restaurant as his Democrat opponent Bob Krueger's staff. Still nobody really knew who had won. We thought we had won. Gary Mauro and other Krueger staff members were all there mumbling and grumbling looking at us with hate. I went to Washington on a San Antonio-to-D.C. trip several months after that. Cathy Obriotti Green and I were standing by the elevator. Congressman Krueger was there. She said, "Congressman Krueger, I'd like you to meet Libba Barnes." I said hello. He said, "I know you, Libba Barnes. You're the one who worked so hard for John Tower. What has he ever done for the state of Texas?" I looked at him and I said, "Well, he beat your ass." Cathy yanked me into that elevator and said, "Are you crazy?" I said as the elevator doors started closing, "How dare he talk about my Senator!" I had had enough. I didn't feel that I had to defend John Tower. Then Krueger ends up marrying my cousin.

Barry Goldwater

Got New People Involved

POLLY SOWELL, McALLEN & AUSTIN

LBJ carried Texas big but the little hearty band of Goldwater followers were so passionate and so committed. That's what came through. Little old ladies with their five and ten dollars came in. The Goldwater partisans were committed. They were passionate about it.

MARTHA PARR, AMARILLO

I was working for the Republicans. We had been offered a building free that had shag carpet and a big heavy chair but no plastic base for the chair. After about a week, it just did terrible things to my back. So I went to the doctor. The doctor said I needed to be in traction. I said, "Doctor, I can not go in the hospital now. I am working in the presidential election. Election Day is only about two weeks away." He said, "Who are you working for?" I said Barry Goldwater. He threw whatever he was holding in his hand up in the air and said, "My God, no, you can't go to the hospital." He gave me muscle relaxants. All of the doctors got behind us.

DIANA STAFFORD, IRVING & AMARILLO

I lived in Irving, Texas. I was teaching school in Arlington, and my husband was in medical school. That was after JFK was killed. Goldwater was coming on the scene. I think that everyone had a lot of respect for Goldwater. I canvassed neighborhoods in Irving.

IRIS MANES, HOUSTON

I just fell in love with Goldwater. I had a two-year-old child. and I would go and pick him up at the nursery and take him home to my mother's. I would go back to work, then come home and feed my family and put him to bed, and I would work on the phone as late as I could. When I went to the Goldwater head-quarters the first day, Noelie Holtz, who is Congressman Bill Archer's cousin, was the executive secretary of the draft Goldwater movement. The first day, she asked me if I would be volunteer chair-man. I called everyone that I could possibly find.

Why do you think so many people were attracted to Barry Goldwater and wanted to be active in his campaign?

He was the first candidate that the conservatives could really rally around. We had lots and lots of volunteers. When I was at the headquarters, I would direct the volunteers looking up phone numbers, doing mailings, that sort of thing. We did everything that could possibly be done. I just couldn't believe that Goldwater wouldn't win. I thought that, if everyone is as dedicated as I am, we have got it won. I didn't know until I was on my way back to headquarters after the polls closed how devastating the loss was. That is a hard way to get your feet wet. I find that I am motivated when I lose. Most of the people that supported Goldwater stayed and helped Reagan.

FLORENCE NEUMEYER, HOUSTON

I really bought into the fact that my opinions about the world were important. If enough of us got together and our voices were heard, we could make a difference. Of course, I was very young and Goldwater inspired so many people just as Reagan did later on. He made it sound like we could make changes if we really wanted to and if we all got out and did the work in the trenches. I was always interested in world events, even as a child. Goldwater inspired me to get involved.

The first thing that I ever did was to go door-to-door. One of my neighbors and myself just said, yes, we will help. We took our assignments and they told us, here is the area you are supposed to cover. We did. It got dark and they were all out looking for us. We didn't know we were to come back. That is how dedicated we were. We were going to do it right.

RUTH McGUCKIN, HOUSTON & WASHINGTON COUNTY

I saw in the paper that the draft Goldwater headquarters was opening and it gave the address. So I went over there. I didn't know anybody, but I had read his book *The Conscience of a Conservative* a few years earlier. That convinced me that he was the kind of man that I wanted. So I went to the headquarters, and Marguerite Binkley was the first person I met. She was working in headquarters. We worked all through the rest of 1963 and 1964.

What about Barry Goldwater and his philosophy attracted you?

We don't need the government doing everything for us. He was a patriot and loved this country and fought for it. He seemed like a true-blue, all-around American.

The election results must have been devastating.

They were. But we went to Goldwater headquarters the next day and answered, "Goldwater in '68." We were all determined to keep working, not for him necessarily but for somebody who could get us back to the values that we thought we should have.

KRIS ANNE VOGELPOHL, GALVESTON
The first election I helped with was for Goldwater. We went on the Elephant Walks that were so popular then. We all met down at a central location every evening and then went out in a team to canvas votes and to get them to turn out and vote Republican. We were completely out of our minds. There weren't many neighborhoods that you could go into in Galveston and talk about Republicans.

RITA CLEMENTS, DALLAS
I had gotten to know a lot of the group that were Goldwater chairmen. They formed a campaign group and they asked me if I would do the door-to-door canvas nationwide. We never had more volunteers! Almost as many volunteers as we got votes. We tried to use the Texas plan and suggest it to other state organizations. When I say the Texas plan, I am just talking about the door-to-door canvas effort that we had had for Senator Tower and during the presidential years prior to '64. A national campaign like that can't make state organizations do the things they don't want to do, but you can provide them with plans and techniques. Most of the state Goldwater chairmen were very receptive to making that part of their campaign.

Peter O'Donnell and Bobbie Biggart and myself and my brother-in-law at that time, Harry Bass, went to New Hampshire in January of 1964 to meet with the New Hampshire organization about organizing for the Goldwater primary up there. A couple of years later Mr. Lyons from Shreveport, a candidate for governor, called Peter O'Donnell and asked if he would bring his team and help organize his campaign. Bobbie Biggart, Peter, and I went over and told them how we had won some of these elections in Texas.

Gave People a Political Education

DOROTHY CROCKETT, ODESSA & MARBLE FALLS

Goldwater educated so many people. He really changed the Republican Party all over the nation. So many people wanted to follow where he led and learn the things that he taught us. For a long time, the Republicans were against everything. We didn't have any positive message. Gradually, from the grassroots, we had some things that we were for. That's what we began to teach and preach. It just grew until finally the Republican message now is a positive message.

PATRICIA LYKOS, HOUSTON

When I was a teenager, I remember reading about Barry Goldwater. I actually saw him. Barry Goldwater probably is the reason why I even considered elective office. The campaign against him was so foul, so demagogic, so reprehensible, and he was a man of principle. He was a man of candor. He was correct about the Vietnam War. He was correct about the Great Society. I think the world would be far different today if he had won. When he lost in 1964, I vowed that I would do anything that I could to avenge that loss simply because of the despicable campaign waged by LBJ and his cohorts.

Taught Us to Deal with Defeat

SALLY McKENZIE, DALLAS

We all worked very hard in the Goldwater effort. Peter O'Donnell was the national chairman of the Draft Goldwater Committee. Rita Bass [*Clements*] went to Washington and ran the national door-to-door campaign. We all worked our souls out. Every bit of that went down the tubes the day that Jack Kennedy was killed in Dallas. I had just finished a door-to-door canvas in

my precinct. I went in that night, not that I was being disrespect-
ful of a deceased president, and just tore up the records. It was
futile after that.

MARGUERITE BINKLEY, HOUSTON

Being completely honest, I don't know why Harris County
Republicans did not get discouraged following the Goldwater loss. It
was probably due to a combination of factors, chief being that social
standing was the dominant force among the establishment whereas
the precinct workers were motivated by conviction.

BARBARA HOWELL, FORT WORTH

In February 1965, Helen and Gordon Fitzgerald called my
husband, John, and me and said we have got to do something
about the Republican and conservative movement in Tarrant
County. They said we want to have Ronald Reagan come and speak.
Our antennas just went up. The four of us ran the show. We had
Ronald Reagan here. It was a sell-out at the Will Rogers Coliseum. We broke all of the fire codes because everyone came and
wanted to hear him. We had him speaking all over Tarrant County
that weekend.

So out of Barry Goldwater's defeat came Ronald Reagan.

Oh, yes. John said after the Goldwater lost there was no hope,
but I'm kind of like an old bulldog. Barry Goldwater was the "sower"
of seeds. So we and the Fitzgeralds decided we would hang in
there with Ronald Reagan.

RUTH COX MIZELLE, CORPUS CHRISTI

I remember one day I was in the swimming pool. I was drown-
ing my sorrows after we lost so big. A man passed by the pool and
said, well, if you want to join the Democratic Party you are welcome because the Republican Party is dead. I said, "Over my dead
body." I remember there were some people who felt like we were,
but I think we started growing our roots then. We knew who the

Republicans were. We had workers and people who grew out of that and went on to do other things.

The Importance of Republican Candidates on the Ballot

What do you think made the Republican Party the dominant party in Harris County?

HELEN ANDERSON, HOUSTON

It was the candidates we put forth. They were fresh. They had never run for office before. It was bringing on a whole new group of actors to the scene.

ANN WALLACE, FORT WORTH & AUSTIN

We met George Bush who came down to one of the state executive committee meetings. Both of the Bushes were so attractive. It was 1963, I guess. I just thought, gosh, if we have candidates like this it is just going to be a wonderful thing.

CATHERINE SMYTH COLGAN, DALLAS

My neighbor in Dallas ran for the state legislature. I started out stuffing envelopes and licking stamps. He was elected to the state legislature. He was Tom James who is now a judge in Dallas. He ran as a Democrat. He decided to change parties in 1964 and sought a judgeship in Dallas and asked me to be his campaign chairman.

It sounds like the candidate might have been more important to you than the Party.

It was before I paid too much attention to the ideology. I did get into it because of the personalities.

GAIL WATERFIELD, CANADIAN

As "down ballot" candidates began to file, like the county judge and sheriff, people started going to the Republican primaries.

DORIS MAYER ROUSSELOT, SONORA

Due to a personal friendship with my father, Edwin Mayer, candidates would come. Because what could a little town like Sonora have to offer a candidate, especially on a statewide level? We would try to have a gathering. John Tower used to come here a lot back when he first started running. We just tried to keep it out in front of the people so they started listening and saw the Republican values.

NANCY LOEFFLER, SAN ANGELO & SAN ANTONIO

In all honesty, Tom's [*Tom Loeffler's*] election to Congress in '78 was the first time there was ever any real strong Republican organization. I think that's due to two or three reasons. Some of it was Tom. He had a lot of friends. He came from an agricultural background, and when you get outside of San Antonio in the Twenty-first Congressional District it's mostly agricultural or oil related. That was very appealing to a lot of people. Tom had made many contacts throughout the Hill Country and West Texas from high school and college football. He began to build a network. A lot of people then decided that they were Republicans. He was the first Republican elected to that seat and a Republican has held it since '78. After that, it got a lot easier to get Republican candidates, to help Republican candidates, and to get people out in West Texas to admit that they were Republicans.

In 1954, Jack Porter, the state chair, didn't take kindly to the idea that women should have more of a say about running the Party.

MARY JESTER, DALLAS

No, he wanted to run the whole thing. It was hard to find people to run. He just knew people, and he let them put their name on the ballot. That was it.

KATIE HECK, MIDLAND

It seemed like there were only twenty-five or thirty of us here. Everybody was involved in everything. If you knew somebody who would make a good candidate, you did what you could to try and get them to run. The best thing that we could do to get them to run was not only demonstrate that we could raise money but demonstrate that the vote was potentially there. That was back to the precinct work. If we could get the votes, we could get the candidates. They were dependent upon each other. We had to have good candidates to get the vote out. Of course, it was easy to campaign for Eisenhower because he was such a popular guy. But locally it was a whole different world.

NITA GIBSON, LUBBOCK

We had to have Republican candidates because it's just tacky to preach the gospel and not have anybody that you can put a check mark by at the ballot box. The county chairman in 1964 really did hit me at the eleventh hour about this. He came to our house. Filing deadline was midnight for candidates. He was looking for candidates really desperately. Well, I was the candidate in 1964 for county judge for whatever that's worth. There wasn't anybody else. George Bush was the candidate for U. S. Senator. There was Barry Goldwater for president, and Nita Gibson for county judge.

What do you think your run for office in 1964 did to help the Republican Party grow?

A man called me in 1964 or '65 from Seagraves, Texas, which is about seventy or eighty miles from here. He said, you know, what you have done has made me declare myself as a Republican. It was a real big thing to declare yourself a Republican. As people began to come forward and as campaigns began to develop and with the election of John Tower, people began to look at the Republican Party. I might have contributed to it in a small way because it might have encouraged people to run who have the intestinal fortitude, the guts. You have got to have people to vote for. Once we got people running for the offices, that forced us to go to the counties and get those counties organized so that they would have a Republican primary.

BILLIE PICKARD, RAYMONDVILLE

I remember when Mary Lou Grier, John Armstrong, and the others running for statewide office came to Raymondville and we had a chance for them to speak locally. I don't know what time of night it was when they got through but they had dedication. I just took my hat off to them for what they were doing. It wasn't easy.

What role did having people willing to run for office in the 1960s and 1970s play?

Tremendous. If it were not for them out there doing it, I do not think that we would have been perceived as a viable party. I don't think that having one senator can do it. You knew they had been here. The local media picked it up. The public perceived it as being a coming Party. They made a tremendous contribution to the state party.

What were the most important steps taken in Waco to build the momentum?

BECKY DIXON, WACO

The emergence of some good solid candidates that would finally bite the bullet and say I am a Republican and I will run as a Republican. We have lost some good candidates, but it has worked out well for them in the long run. Slowly but surely, someone else would step out.

GLENNA McCORD, DALLAS

It was a very frustrating time to try and do all of this because we didn't have anything behind us. Dick West, I recall, right before primary time, would have this article in the *Dallas Morning News* saying Texas does not need a two-party state. We already have one. There are liberal Democrats and conservative Democrats. Trying to get those people who were conservative, who should have been calling themselves Republican, into the Republican primary was a challenge. They wouldn't come because they said we were only running one candidate. At that time, it was Bruce Alger [*for Congress*]. They'd say, we need to go into the Democrat primaries so that we can have the most conservative candidates possible on the ballots in November, but we will vote for your presidential candidate.

How important was it for you to find local people to run for office?

POOLIE PRATT, VICTORIA

It was important, but we didn't have much luck getting people to run for local office. I think we probably made a mistake here. We didn't know it at the time. We ran a slate in the early '60s. We worked and got a candidate for every county commissioners seat. We posed too much of a threat and were wiped out. We didn't elect anybody. It caused a backlash. If we had run one, we might have had better luck. We didn't know that. You know, you learn. We had real good candidates. Then after that, no one would run, for sure.

ANITA DAVIS, HEMPHILL

When we had meetings in Lufkin, there were not a lot of people there. Then when we got over here there was practically nobody. Even people that agreed with us and voted Republican in November always voted Democrat in the primary. You can't build a party without people who will vote for the Republican Party in the primary.

Why wouldn't they vote for the Republican Party in the primary?

Because they wanted to vote for locals, and nobody would run on the Republican ticket for these local offices. They knew that they couldn't be elected. That is still the reason that it is very hard to get credible candidates to run on the tickets because they just don't think that they can get elected in this county [*Sabine County in East Texas*].

CAROLYN KNIGHT, AUSTIN & MARBLE FALLS

I recall the primary in '64 in our home. We thought we were going to have a fairly good turnout. As it turned out, I think there were less than a half a dozen who participated, basically because you couldn't vote for sheriff. I bet they attached more to the sheriff's race than they did to the president at the time.

DORIS WILLIAMS, LAKE JACKSON

I got involved because we finally had a candidate in our area running for office—Ron Paul. He lived in Lake Jackson, and I knew him real well. So one day I decided. I went down to the headquarters and volunteered to work and from then on it was work, work, work. Our house practically became headquarters. I always believed in the Republican philosophy or the conservative idea. Of course, if you were a Texan, the conservative idea came from being a conservative Democrat. Then the party left the Democrats. All of those conservatives I have found through the years have become Republicans because they no longer believed in what the Democratic Party stood for.

Before Ron Paul, my husband would work for people and send money to people who were not in our area but believed in the same things that we believed in. What really triggered my involvement was actually having a Republican candidate from our town.

It really surprised me all of the nice people I met that I had not known before but were involved in his campaign. It seems as if we really had something to work for back then when we just had one candidate. People began to see that we had a candidate that represented their views more than a Democrat candidate did. That is when a lot of people converted in Brazoria County—when we had a candidate to work for. They could listen to him and what he stood for. Then they could compare him to the Democrat candidate.

Early Victories

BARBARA CULVER CLACK, MIDLAND

Being the first woman ever elected on the Republican ticket as a county judge in 1962 sort of broke some ice to make it possible for people to accept the idea of a Republican. We kept saying, well, someday Texas will be a two-party state. You have to start from somewhere. I always thought we had to start at the grassroots. It frustrated me that we would go out and recruit an unknown from somewhere and run him for governor. Nobody knew whether he would be good or not. But if you have some people bubbling up from courthouses or city councils or the school boards or the legislature—people who have a track record that catches your eye, you can grow with them. You can promote them.

FLO KAMPMANN CRICHTON, SAN ANTONIO

We knew that we had to have some local county judges and justices of the peace and that sort of thing. We were very glad when there would be someone who was willing to run. It was 1962 when Barbara Culver ran. She really sort of set the pace for it. Gradually, we collected a lot of Democrats, too. Democrats decided just to move over. Of course, they didn't have money to finance their campaigns, so the state Republican Party tried to help out wherever it could. It was just a very gradual thing. It eventually proved its value.

When you don't have many candidates in the Republican primary, is it hard to persuade people to come and vote?

That's right. They had some candidate on the Democrat ticket that they thought highly of, and they didn't want to lose a vote for that person, particularly the judges. You have lawyers all going into the Democrat primary because they didn't want to lose a vote on who they thought would be a good judge.

MARY ANNE COLLINS, DALLAS

We got Frank Crowley elected county commissioner [*in 1960*]. Then we had a lot of candidates for state legislature win [*in 1962*]. That included Buddy MacAtee, Fred Agnich, and we got a state senator. That really spurred us on because then we could see that we were making headway.

RUTH FOX, HOUSTON & AUSTIN

The people in Harris County were divided in 1980 [*between George Bush and Ronald Reagan in the presidential primary*]. Personally, I was for George Bush. We worked hard. We could not have primaries in some of the precincts on the east side of town, in the Hispanic area, because we could not find people to run the primaries. So we printed that list in the paper where we could not hold primaries between Bush and Reagan. We started getting calls down at county headquarters. People started calling in from the Hispanic areas asking, why can't we have a primary? All of a sudden I thought, "Well, you know what you can do? You can go down and vote at the county courthouse. Write your name at the bottom of the ballot to sign in as precinct chair, and then you won't ever have this happen to you again." As it turned out, we wound up having some contested precinct chairs.

We opened up a whole area over there. We out-voted the Democrats by 20,000 votes in the primary, which had never been done before.

In '74, Jon Lindsay, who had been a Democrat and in '72 had run as a Democrat for the legislature, turned Republican and ran for county judge. Nancy Palm got behind him and all of us women did. He was the first Republican county judge in Harris County. That was another turning point. I think that also helped us in '80, since he had been county judge for six years and had become a very popular person.

GLENDA REEDER, SAN ANTONIO

When Republican Doug Harlan ran in the '70s, Tower said, "I'm telling you right now, Glenda, if you all are running against anybody in that Twenty-first Congressional District out of Bexar County, I'll get right up on that platform and denounce it." I said, "John, you wouldn't do a thing like that, would you?" "Yes, I would." He almost did that to Doug Harlan. The Democratic candidate was the very popular conservative O. C. Fisher in the Hill Country. You left some people alone.

Local or State Candidates

Many expressed frustration that the state party did not do enough to promote local candidates in the 1960s. Looking back, do you think that was a fair criticism?

ANNE ARMSTRONG, ARMSTRONG

It is very tough when you are a Party leader to have to target races and decide where you are going to put the money and the willing hands. Sometimes, when things were really bleak and our funds were low, there had to be some hard decisions made. We were not going to run serious races across the board in Texas. We didn't have the volunteers. We didn't have the other resources, mainly money. So there would be hard feelings. We felt that the number one priority would be maintaining what we had, which was John Tower in the Senate. We worried that sometimes primaries were not always helpful when you are a budding new party. So I think those are some of the reasons, plus normal big-city vying.

How did you develop the Republican Party further if no one would run locally?

POOLIE PRATT, VICTORIA

We focused on Tower. He was the only thing we had. He had a fellow by the name of David Martinez, who was the head of military affairs. John Tower served on the Armed Services Committee, which is a very powerful position. There were lots in the Mexican American community who were in the military and they had a lot of problems. Martinez could solve them in an instant. We made a lot of friends. That was the beginning of our breakthrough. My postman, Adam Hernandez, was very big in either the American Legion or Veterans of Foreign Wars. I finally told him, "Why don't you become the person that all of the people in the armed services can turn to for help? You can call Martinez instead of me." He did. He is a loyal Republican to this day. He helped all of these veterans. He told all of these groups about the help that was available from John Tower. It really was effective. That was our first inroad into the Mexican American voting block.

DEANNE CLARK, LUBBOCK & DIMMITT

Tower came to our county several times. All you would get is newspaper coverage. Still, it was one more way to show the local people that you were a viable organization and that it was okay for them to get on the bandwagon.

RITA CLEMENTS, DALLAS

John Tower certainly was that rallying point. But people who were looking at the future felt that we really would not be considered a true two-party state until we elected a Republican governor. The governor's position is really key. Winning that was the key to making Texas truly a two-party state.

ANNE SHEPARD, VICTORIA & HARLINGEN

We said if you like Bill Clements then you'll like the Republican Party [*Republican Bill Clements first ran for governor in 1978*].

When do you think people realized that they weren't Democrats?

ANN HARRINGTON, PLANO

I don't think it really happened in Texas until the Republicans were working to elect Bill Clements governor. We worked for years, but I don't think people really started to take notice until then. So many people considered Senator Tower's race a fluke.

BECKY FARRAR, HICO

We planned a reception for Clements in 1986 [*when he again ran for governor and won*]. It was one of the first big events in Erath County for Republicans. We turned out about 250 people, which was just unheard of in this area. We played up the idea of a governor coming to our county. This was rare. It was exciting to think that even a former governor was coming to the county. There were people who wanted their children to meet a governor. We had people there with their babies and strollers. People just wanted to be part of the excitement. We even had a heckler there. I invited the sheriff, and he escorted the heckler out. It was a good day and a turning point.

BETTY STERQUELL, AMARILLO

In the late '60s, the state party felt that we were not viable if we did not get governor candidates. There were those of us that said, it's just temporary if you get a governor candidate. You've got to start in the courthouse. Take the courthouse and move up. Then you'll have your machinery, your base.

We set up a committee to select candidates. We figured out about how much it would take for each election and got businesses to volunteer someone to run for office and give them time off and raise the money for them and help them get started. We put quite a few people in the courthouse. That was a real turning point for us.

At that time, I went to the state organization along with Dick Brooks, who was the other county chair, and some others. It was important to say that we couldn't raise our state quota because we were funding our own candidates. So we were able to raise enough money to begin to take the courthouse. Gradually, people were switching from Democrat to Republican. That's when some of the people down south in the Valley, who could raise the money and didn't have candidates, came out and supported us. Polly Sowell and Anne Armstrong and some of those were in there to help support us.

CAROLYN MINTON, SAN ANGELO

Barbara Culver's election as county judge in Midland was the beginning of taking the courthouse. That is the secret of turning the tide for the Republicans. You can work for a presidential candidate but you don't have to have a two-party system. Working on a local, grassroots level converted the community to the Republican Party.

CATHERINE SMYTH COLGAN, DALLAS

Tower asked me when he was chairing the presidential race in Texas, have you got any advice for me? I said, yes. Work from the bottom up. If people will vote for the bottom of the ticket, they will usually support the top. Many people make a mistake by starting at the top of the ticket and working for support there and hoping it will trickle down. I always found the opposite to be true. If you can get somebody to support your county commissioner and work hard at that level, chances are they'll also support the top of the ticket.

You have to work both ends to the middle. You need the top guns to get the publicity and the attention because there are people that don't pay attention except for every four years. If you are meanwhile working at the lower level, they will come together.

CHAPTER 5

What Is the Role of Issues?

When you first started, it was so cause oriented. You almost
had to see it that way for a while to drive all over, go to meetings late,
come home late, and hire a million baby sitters.

—FRANCIE FATHEREE CODY

*I*ssues put the meat on the bones of the Republican philosophy.
Women held strong opinions about many matters affecting
their families, Texas, and the U. S., especially the Cold War,
national defense, taxes, education, social programs, and business
policies. They sought candidates most reflective of their views.
The question of compromise was always at hand—how far do
you compromise your stand on the issues to win an election?

The John Birch Society left an impression upon many
women active in Party politics, for some negative and others
positive. It was the most controversial issue-based group of the
era, bringing new faces to the Republican Party. Many women
felt the group a threat to the viability of the Party. This threat
rejuvenated the women's organizational efforts in many parts of
Texas in order to prohibit the society's takeover of the Party
apparatus.

Issues also provided a mechanism to educate voters and
sway them to the Republican viewpoint. Women educated
themselves and others, resulting in legions of informed, responsible voters. While many idealistically pursued issues important
to them, political reality set in. It was (and is) difficult if not
impossible to elect a bad candidate, even if he or she held positions on the issues with which many agreed.

Party Identification

ANN LEE, HOUSTON

You're drawn both to a party and to candidates that seem to reflect your personal philosophy.

KATIE SEEWALD, AMARILLO

I was sort of an academic liberal going to college. I got out of the university and came to work up here for an airline. Of course, you get to be conservative when you start earning your own living and seeing what they do with taxes. I got real interested and tried to change things. I had not only my husband's blessing but he pushed me.

BARBARA FOREMAN, ODESSA & DALLAS

We moved to Odessa in 1960. That year, Richard Nixon ran against John Kennedy. The oil business was very upset with Kennedy. I started getting involved then. I grew up a Republican, but my husband grew up a Democrat. Ed would go to the chambers of commerce around the area speaking for Nixon. Kennedy was trying to shut down the oil business. That was our bread and butter.

BARBARA BANKER, SAN ANTONIO

I do not have women's issues. I have business issues. I am not talking about getting preferential treatment by the EPA [*Environmental Protection Agency*]. I am talking about a business climate where government does not tax me to death. I'm talking about the state level, too. It got to a point that I thought I was going to close my doors because I could not afford the insurance.

Then I started looking for somebody who wanted to change some laws about the high awards given in lawsuits, and I started wanting conservatives on the court.

GAIL WATERFIELD, CANADIAN

My husband's family was a ranching family in Canadian. He was the third generation. His mother had a very early unfortunate death. Dick and his brother inherited the ranch. Everybody said, "Isn't this just absolutely wonderful?" We did think about it as being security until the government sent us the inheritance tax. Well, we had the ranch, but we didn't have the money. To make a long story short, we went to work very hard. Dick and I and Jim and Sandy, believe it or not, paid it off. When we got through paying the inheritance tax and the attorneys, we could have bought the place. I said to myself, the government doesn't have the right to do that. I'm going to try to change it.

Why do you think the Republican philosophy has been attractive to people in West Texas?

JESS ANN THOMASON, MIDLAND

It is our way of life. West Texans have always been conservative. I think it angers people to think that we are taxed to death in the oil business and our money is thrown away in Washington. All of the give-away programs—I think that is the biggest thing that offends people in our part of the world.

GWEN PHARO, DALLAS

A lot of those who were instrumental in founding a real Republican Party started out as anti-Communists. There was nowhere for us to go politically other than to the Republican Party and try to shape it into a party that understood the Soviets. You have to remember, this was the early '50s. There was [*Communist baiter Senator*] Joe McCarthy and [*convicted State Department spy*] Alger Hiss. I think a lot of prominent people aligned themselves with Republicans simply because they thought that the Democrats were just riddled with subversive people. We weren't necessarily considered pariahs here because we saw the threat of the Soviets.

FRANCIE FATHEREE CODY, PAMPA

When Nixon lost in 1960, my little girl, Susan, was five. I guess I had been brainwashing her too much. I didn't go to bed that night. I was sitting on the couch, and she came out. I told her we lost. She said, crying, oh, we're not going to be free anymore. I said, no, no, no. We're going to be free, but I had to kind of undo what I had done. When you first started, it was so cause oriented. You almost had to see it that way for a while to drive all over, go to meetings late, come home late, and hire a million baby sitters.

Willingness to Compromise

HOLLY DECHERD, AUSTIN

I got active in some associations that were related to my husband's work, which I thought would be in the conservative arena and our values would be much the same. But I found that it was different. Lobbying tends to be bipartisan, even though one would think there arc certain arenas that would demand either conservatism or liberalism. Unfortunately, it is an impure game. People are playing both sides of the fence just to see where they can gain some ground. That was unsatisfactory to me. They would say, we have to support J. J. Pickle because he will be our congressman. They felt like they had to give him financial support for his race. I was unencumbered by those sorts of obligations. I enjoyed pure politics in the sense of trying to elect people who really represented my views. I didn't have to call on those people for favors. I could be a little more pure about it, which I guess is a luxury.

AMELIE COBB, BEAUMONT

I was on the State Republican Executive Committee. The man who was my counterpart [*each state senatorial district was represented by a committeewoman and a committeeman*] was very much more conservative than I was. We were talking and I said to him, "I don't know why we are at odds. You and I believe in all of the same things. The difference is that I am willing to compromise to win an election." He said, "I would rather lose every election that we are in than to compromise on anything. I won't bend on one issue." You can make a case for that. There are a couple of issues that I would never compromise on, but there are some that I would.

If your candidate has got to soften his stand a little in order to get elected so that he can accomplish at least some of the things that you believe in or at least change the momentum a little bit, I don't see great evil in that. But he did. He really believed that if you compromised at all, it wasn't worth it.

So politics isn't black and white?

I don't think so. Lyndon Johnson, for all that I didn't like about him, did say something that I thought was true: "Politics is the art of the possible." It is true. It is what you can get done. If you want your candidate to be totally 100 percent lily-white pure and not be elected, you are not practicing the art of the possible but of the impossible.

There were a lot of women who were accused of just wanting to win elections.

ANNE ARMSTRONG, ARMSTRONG

That is always going to be with us. You can understand it. Some people think that you must not bend your principles, and it is a matter of degree. I happened to be what I would call a more centrist conservative. But I respect people with other viewpoints, and they push as hard as they can. That is fine. That's what primaries are about. That's what precinct battles are about. As you grow, a party is going to have those. I think it is healthy. It can go past the healthy, though, because in my day when I was very active in politics, the John Birch Society was a problem to Republicans. We deserved to be criticized. We were right to say, when people go beyond the pale and accuse good citizens of being intolerant or accuse people of being Communists who are not, we are not proud to call them our Republican brothers and sisters. So at times you have to draw a line in the sand. Anytime someone makes accusations of somebody being a Communist or traitorous in other ways to the country, if you don't have the facts down absolutely without a quibble then you should keep silent. Goldwater himself, as I remember, said he would not support some of the accusations of the John Birch Society.

The John Birch Society

MARJORIE ARSHT, HOUSTON

I wrote an op-ed piece on the John Birch Society. I took it to George Carmack of the *Houston Press*. He gave me the whole editorial page. John Tower saw the letter and asked [*legislative candidate*] Bob Overstreet if he could interview me. So I went to Austin and met him. My thesis was that everyone was exercised about the extremism of the John Birch Society, but no one was asking what caused it to be born. The John Birch Society was born as a result of the feeling of frustration and helplessness in the face of the extreme leftward turn of the Supreme Court just as the Ku Klux Klan was born out of helplessness of Southerners in the face of the abuses of Reconstruction, but because it was outside the law it deteriorated into an organization that had nothing to do with the reasons for its birth. People needed to concentrate on the cause and the reasons for it to be born. Well, Mr. Carmack called me up and said, we have never had this happen. He knew that my essay was controversial, but my theory was something that both sides were praising. So John Tower used that thesis all over Texas. When asked, "What do you think about the John Birch Society?" He would say, "Well, we really need to examine the causes for its birth." Nobody could argue with that. Years later he would say, "That's the best thing you ever wrote."

NANCY CROUCH, HOUSTON

When conservative Democrats came over to the Republican Party, a lot of them were members of the John Birch Society. It was never really clear who was and who wasn't a member. There were a lot of "fellow travelers." They were very conservative and didn't seem to have what was in the best interest of the Republican Party as their goal. They packed the conventions and elected their people. A lot of people don't understand the importance of precinct conventions, and as a result they took over the county [*Harris County*].

What was the influence of the John Birch Society?

NANCY PALM, HOUSTON

It seems to me that it wasn't an influence. I was not a member. I maybe knew two or three members. What everybody has to understand is that you're not going to agree with another segment of your party 100 percent. If you come up 85 to 90 percent, everybody has to be willing to give a little bit to make a party grow. I don't like the phrase Big Tent, but you have to be willing to welcome people into the Party and try to find a way for them to be used. I put people in spots where they were exceptionally good doing the work.

Was the John Birch Society very active in Houston and Harris County?

IRIS MANES, HOUSTON

Yes. I know a bunch of precinct chairmen that are still active today who were members of the John Birch Society. Yes, I would say they were very active.

What effect do you think the John Birch Society had on the Republican Party in Harris County?

Directly, I don't think they had any, but I think some of the people who were members were certainly above average in their political knowledge. They were more of the leadership type. You never heard the John Birch Society being mentioned. There was one man who used to give their literature out. He would never mention their name. A lot of people didn't approve of it. It didn't bother me because I found that I agreed philosophically with those people I knew had been members almost right down the line and still do today. I do know they still have good memories of being members. My husband, Archie, and I almost joined. We were invited to our closest friend's home for a meeting when it was first formed. We were very interested. We even wrote a letter to [*FBI director, J. Edgar*] Hoover and asked him what its background was and if there was any reason that we shouldn't become involved. He wrote a letter back saying that they were just what they appeared to be. That he had investigated them and they were organized primarily to fight Communism. But we still didn't join. That was before all of the persecution of the [*Communist and alleged Communist*] people in Hollywood and all of that. We felt that it was possible that it could hurt Archie's business.

Concerns of a John Bircher

WILDA LINDSTROM, HOUSTON

The John Birch Society was just a conservative organization. It was maligned and criticized so much. Guess who was the leader in the district? Me. I was very active in the John Birch Society. I lived in Channelview [*near Houston*]. It was known to be one of the most liberal areas in America. We had our little John Birch meetings. I learned more and more about the conservative movement and why we should get involved. It was just an educational thing. Mass ignorance is one thing that is wrong with this country.

My husband is a very quiet man. You have to work hard to get a word out of him, but he listens. He was active in the John Birch Society but not as much as I was. He worked for Exxon. When he started, they wanted him to take money out of his check for the United Way. He said, I'm not going to do that. They said, Mr. Lindstrom, you have to do that. He said, who said I have to? Then they wanted to take money out of his paycheck to support the liberal candidates. He said those are not my candidates. You can not take money out of my check to support those people. They're not the people that I vote for. He got labeled real quick. When John F. Kennedy was killed, his workers rushed up to him and literally held him. They said, I guess you are happy now your bunch has killed our president.

I was in real danger, too. I happened to know some photographers. They were conservative. I went to their studio to have my children's picture made. While I was in there, I was talking about the liberals and some other people were in there. I still haven't learned how to guard my word. I still think I am in a free country. I was spouting off about the liberals. The day that Kennedy was killed some people came in and asked the manager, "Do you remember the lady that was in here that day? Do you have her name?" The photographers said, "What lady?" The people said, "You know, that lady talking." I don't remember if I mentioned the John Birch Society, but I may have because I've always been pretty big mouthed. My friends caught on and knew pretty quickly they were dangerous. The photographers said, "I don't know who you are talking about." They said, "We want that lady. We want to know who she is. How can we find her? She killed Kennedy. She is responsible for his death." This was no fun.

How do you think the John Birch Society influenced the Republican Party?

It was a tremendous boost and help to the Republican Party. The Republican Party does not have any training program per se to teach its people anything. We needed an educational wing for members. There were scores of people in Houston and Harris County who got informed through the John Birch Society and then came to work for the conservatives in the Republican Party. They were very influential and very effective.

What impact do you think Kennedy's death had on the John Birch Society?

When Johnson was running for president and we were for Goldwater, a man that my husband worked with said, "Well, I'm going to vote for Johnson simply because your John Birch Society killed my man. I'm going to support Johnson out of sympathy for Kennedy." They did that all over the country. Very few people realized that the Communists were right here in Houston working for Johnson. I have a lot of documentation. After that, the best I can piece together, there were a lot of people who were in the John Birch Society who became frightened that the enemy achieved exactly what they wanted. A lot of people kind of dropped out. A lot of people were so frightened—the average person. Many people were not bodily attacked like my husband was and accused of killing the president. The world is not full of strong people. And that is the effect it had. After that, the conservative movement suffered, but then Reagan came along and through the help of the Goldwater people it never let up. The conservative movement is alive.

Rescuing the Republican Party

MAYETTA PARR, AMARILLO

We had a group of Birch people that came into headquarters every evening just before closing time, and they would put out their literature. How they got it done with us watching I don't know. We had gotten an ultimatum from Barry Goldwater—this is my campaign and it will be run like this. Every morning we had to dig through and get their stuff out and put out what Goldwater said we could distribute. Then at night it happened all over again. I got so I hated to go to headquarters in the morning because we were throwing stuff away. Money was going into the trash. We must have had 5,000 copies of *A Texan Looks at Lyndon* [*a book by ultraconservative historian and political activist J. Evetts Haley*] go into the trash because Goldwater said he did not want that in his headquarters. You just couldn't talk to the Birch people. They just wouldn't listen. I thought I was a radical Republican, but . . .

How did you get the Party back?

BETTY STERQUELL, AMARILLO

J. Evetts Haley got up at the 1964 county convention, took a broken pool cue, and cracked it down on the table and wouldn't let people speak. He had made out the delegate list and wouldn't allow any differences. It was just a real railroad. Several people came to me and said, "Betty, you organized this in the beginning, won't you help us?" I said, "Yes, we've got two years to do it."

I said, now here is what we do. We will get a group together at my house, and we will talk about strategy. First, we need to have our statistics. We know how many votes it takes to control a precinct. Our projected figures can tell us how many people are straight ticket voters, how many people are voting split tickets, and how many it's going to take to control the precinct.

Now, we needed to have some very non-threatening precinct people who would be precinct chairmen. People the John Birch Society hardly knew were whose names should be on the ballot. It should not be presented until about an hour before the deadline. So we did that in every precinct. The opposition thought, we don't know these people. They're no threat. They won't be elected. Then we went out on a vote hunt. We said we need you to vote in the Republican primary and vote for this person and come to the precinct convention so you can be a delegate to the county convention. Then you are off the hook. You don't need to do anything else, but we need to do it to recapture the Party. Nobody knew we were calling.

The night of the election I didn't go down to election central until right at the end. A couple of us just dropped in. I think I was an election judge, and I just didn't put my box in until late. But members of our opposition were saying, I don't understand how he could be elected. Who is he? Of course, we had the control. Then, the first thing that we did at the convention was promote openness. We explained to everyone that they were welcome and that nobody would be turned away. The idea was to have openness and Party growth.

Putting It in Perspective

PAT McCALL, HOUSTON

The John Birch Society started off as I recall doing the right conservative thing, and then they got radical. Any group that becomes radical is wrong. I don't care if you are right or left or whatever, if you become radical you shoot yourself in the foot. That is what the John Birch Society did.

POLLY SOWELL, McALLEN & AUSTIN

We had the John Birch problem in 1964. The John Birch Society was a bunch of radical ultraright people that claimed Eisenhower was a Communist. Somehow or other they infiltrated the Republican Party. After the election we didn't know what to do with them. We had our first, to my knowledge, infighting. It was hard for us because we had been such a wonderful team—all so dedicated to the same things and all going in the same direction. We loved each other and got along just great, and then we had this big intraparty dispute about the John Birchers and what to do about them. I can remember going to a State Republican Executive Committee meeting, and there was a resolution that we were supposed to vote on disdaining the John Birchers or something like that. Oh, we just had this knock-down drag-out fight over that resolution.

I remember walking out of that meeting, and I was crying. I was walking out between Peter O'Donnell and George Bush. They said to me, Polly, this is nothing. Don't let it upset you. Wait until we win something, and then you'll see how bad the fights get. They were right, of course. It kind of worked itself out. For a true believer, it was hard to go through the first Party fight.

RITA CLEMENTS, DALLAS

I have a lot of friends who were members of the John Birch Society. I never had any interest in being a member. Yes, it was strong and certainly probably in many ways the predecessor of what I call the right-wing political groups that still exist. It was not into abortion or any of those subjects; it was into the basics of conservative vs. liberal politics.

When you mention Texas Republicans to people who were observing things at that time from outside Texas, they respond, "Those crazy ultra right-wing people." In talking with the people who were running the Party then, they were not.

No, they weren't. In fact, as the Texas Republican Party grew, it was very mainstream. Maybe more conservative than back in the Eisenhower years when Texas Republicans were maybe a little more liberal.

Political Education
Being a Responsible Voter

DEBBIE FRANCIS, DALLAS

I was raised in our family to be responsible. To me it's just— I know it sounds so goody two-shoes—part of every American's responsibility to vote and to be aware. Hillary Clinton talks about, and a lot of people disagree with, "it takes the village to raise a child." We all are part of a larger thing. We do have a responsibility. If you want the system to work, you have got to work with it. For me, it's worth fighting for.

On the forty-fifth anniversary of D-Day, my husband, Jim, and I were at the Normandy beaches. I wish that every American could go see them. That to me is part of what it is all about. We are so lucky. We take so much for granted—so much that most people today can't imagine or fathom. We are spoiled. What people were willing to do!

People say, I don't even know when Election Day is, much less, I would give my life for our country if it needed it. That kind of thing has a powerful impact on your life even though it was fairly recent. I just wish every American, I don't care what your political persuasion is, could go and stand on those beaches and think about how many people literally gave their lives. So maybe I can just pay attention and hold my local, state, and national leaders responsible. And when I know that they really are not, am I willing to stand up and say so and support somebody else who will represent the people more dutifully?

RUTH POTTER, DALLAS

Not everyone should vote if they're not informed. They can't cast an intelligent vote if they don't know what the election is about. That's why elections turn out so crazy.

Educating Yourself

BARBARA BANKER, SAN ANTONIO

I was standing in line to vote, and there was a group of people around me saying, do you know any of these people who are running for judges? The offices that are not highly visible because they are not high profile don't get a lot of media play. I thought about it, and I said, "Well, do I know enough about them to make rational decisions myself?" I determined, no, so are you just going to vote the Republican one-lever vote in the general election and hope? That was one of my first encounters with not spending enough time getting to know the candidates.

KATHRYN McDANIEL, BORGER

We had a group, which we called Republican Women's Study Group. We didn't have bylaws, officers, year books, any of that kind of stuff. We just met regularly to study the issues and government. Mainly, we studied things like what the government—state, local, or national—should be doing or should not be doing, trying to keep ourselves informed. Back then, in this area particularly, there was considerable concern about importing foreign oil. Independent oil producers kept saying there's no security to our nation in foreign oil. So we studied issues like that. We didn't want the federal government dictating education so one of the policies was no federal aid to education. We studied the whys and wherefores. That spreads as you talk to your family and talk to your friends.

Educating Others

THEO WICKERSHAM, SAN ANTONIO

I respected Barbara Campbell [*Texas Federation of Republican Women president, 1983-1986*] for conveying to me that political education is very important and we need to set an example. I didn't go anyplace that I didn't wear a button. If I was on an airplane, I had some kind of button and people would always ask, what is that or what does that mean? Not necessarily a campaign button but something like "Republicans Want You." When I send my mail, I send these little Republican stickers.

People are not politically educated. Somebody would say, vote for so-and-so. Well, that's what the Democrats were doing and that's what they're still doing—vote for me. Republicans must be politically educated. You can always find out how your representatives vote and why they are voting a certain way. I think political education is one of the main things in getting people involved and getting them to stay involved. Give them something to do.

CHRIS HOOVER, CORPUS CHRISTI

When I was vice chair of the Nueces County Republican Party, I was concerned with women's participation. So often the wives voted the way the husbands told them to. I wanted to educate and to inform and to give women the feeling that they had an input into their government. There are just so many things that government officials do that affect families. Women needed to be informed. They needed to know both sides of the issues. I believe that everyone has the right and freedom to vote their choice, but on the other hand I believe that everybody has an obligation to know both sides and make a choice and make it intelligently. You can't do that unless you are informed.

Issues Are Important but
You Can't Elect a Bad Candidate

From your observation, what has been more important, candidates or issues?

RITA CLEMENTS, DALLAS

They each have their importance, but it is very difficult to elect a bad candidate. As the years have gone by and as the quality of our candidates has improved, the better off you are as far as electing them. The quality of the candidates is really the key.

How would you define a good quality candidate?

In this day and time, someone who is good on television, expresses herself or himself well, is good with recruiting people and getting people to help, and knows the issues. One of the key things that George W. did both times he ran for governor was to pick out three or four major issues and concentrate on those. He hammered at them and hammered at them. The press will drive you crazy with that because they are looking for a new story every day. Those traveling with you on the campaign trail will egg you on and try to get you off on some other things. George W., in the first campaign in particular, was just amazing at hanging in there and sticking with education, criminal justice, and the issues he said were important.

CHAPTER 6

State Party Organization

"... as time went on we realized that we had to build from the ground up rather than the top down." —FLO KAMPMANN CRICHTON

ourishing the seeds of Republican interest that were beginning to crop up in the state and helping them grow provided the focus for state visionaries. Leaders fanned the embers of activity, concentrating on developing county organizations wherever interested Republicans lived. Gradually, the Republican Party changed from a party of Presidential patronage to a philosophically based party united to elect candidates. Leaders built from the bottom up and from the top down—whatever method had a chance in divergent parts of Texas.

Interdependence among candidates, issues, and party structure characterized the growth of Republican politics. Voters needed issues to motivate them, candidates to rally behind, and an organization to provide a way to express themselves on Election Day. During the 1950s and 1960s, Party leaders focused their efforts on party structure and organization by recruiting county chairs. The goal for years was to have a chair, vice chair, and primary in each of Texas's 254 counties. The Republican Party achieved this goal in 1996, nearly fifty years after the effort began.

The statewide Republican volunteer organization consisted of a state chair and vice chair, and a committeeman and committeewoman from each state senatorial district. The committeewomen worked with the committeemen to raise money, recruit candidates and county chairs, organize primaries, and, especially in the 1950s and 1960s, help campaigns. In the mid-1960s, the positions of deputy state chair and deputy vice chair were created. They served regions of the state, improving communication between the state chair and the rest of the Texas organization. Leaders struggled constantly to organize counties. Names of possible county chairs and vice chairs were as good as gold. While trying to build the organization, leaders also battled redistricting plans that nullified their progress.

SHIRLEY GREEN, AUSTIN & SAN ANTONIO

The most effective way to build the Party was through the commitment of individuals in individual locations—people who really had vision and would persuade and convince. Building a party is not a one shot affair—"here's the magic bullet." It was a long, long, long time of commitment, making many tiny baby steps until the steps finally got big enough that they started making a difference.

One of the things that I think was the most significant in deterring the growth of the Party was the incessant, long-running, constantly evolving intraparty fight. Before I got involved, the two factions had been Taft and Eisenhower. Then in the '60s there were the factions of one versus the other in state leadership. Then as we got into the '70s, there were the Ford and the Reagan factions. Then as we got into the '80s there were the Reagan, Bush, and Connally factions. Basically, it broke down ideologically into one slightly more moderate or conservative than the other. To me, there shouldn't be this much worry about the Party fights.

Vision

BETTE JO BUHLER, VICTORIA

When I started in the Republican Party, I moved here from Seattle in the '50s. I went to the district committeeman to volunteer, and he didn't want any help. Billy Murphy and Connie Anderson and myself were determined to get something started in the state because we had so few Republican votes. A two-party state was always our goal.

KATIE HECK, MIDLAND

In those days, we did everything by convention. We didn't have primaries, we went to precinct conventions the night of the primary and elected delegates to the succeeding convention. It was a small enough convention that at a couple of parties you could literally meet everybody. Albert Fay was the national committeeman. Flo Kampmann was national committeewoman. They were just as accessible as they possibly could be. They encouraged any activity out here.

How was Flo Kampmann (Crichton) able to help support you?

Primarily by example and encouragement. She'd come out now and then. She arranged for Nixon and Lodge [*presidential candidate Richard Nixon's running mate, Henry Cabot Lodge Jr.*] to come. Flo arranged that kind of thing. It had never happened in Midland before. She arranged for the national chairman to come out here. That was big. In fact, I can remember going down to the newspaper to tell them he was coming and ask if they would like to cover it—"Oh, yes, ma'am, we certainly would." The national chairman had never been to Midland. It was all such a new thing. Flo could help because she had lots of contacts at levels we couldn't reach. The Party was changing from the old patronage guys. There was still a bunch of the old diehards who didn't want the Party to grow, and here were all of us young types. We were the young turks of the day, upsetting their little applecarts because as long as there was a Republican president then they might control the patronage. Well, we weren't interested in that. We were interested in local Republicans and statewide Republicans. Some of those people were horrified. It wasn't all smooth. There were some hurt feelings.

FLO KAMPMANN CRICHTON, SAN ANTONIO

We really were interested in recruiting good candidates. In 1960 we began to do that. In the beginning, it was just people who wanted to run, and after that we had a candidate recruiting committee. Then as time went on we realized that we had to build from the ground up rather than the top down, and we began to elect county judges and county commissioners and justices of the peace. It really was a good decision.

PETER O'DONNELL, DALLAS

We had a couple ideas when I was state chairman. One was that you needed to select your targets carefully and recruit good candidates, and the other was our basic door-to-door effort to identify the voters and ultimately turn them out. We developed a pattern that we tried to get other candidates to follow. It finally evolved into understanding that there were big counties, like Dallas, Houston [*Harris County*], and so on, and then medium-size counties and then rural areas, and we developed campaign materials for each of them. For Tower's campaign in 1966, we broke it down: State Organization Chairman—Rita Bass [*Clements*]; Operation Early Bird—Sally McKenzie; State Undecided Voter Chairman—Nola Smith; State Absentee Voter Chairman—Liz French; Get Out the Vote—Ginny Pearson. They worked at it for years.

> *Why were so many women involved in heading up these committees?*

Rita, Sally, Nola, and the others knew all of the programs. They knew them inside-out so they could tell people. They were better able to recruit because of it.

> *What made you want to keep working despite the near certainty of defeat?*

FRANCIE FATHEREE CODY, PAMPA

You got started and you would think, well, maybe we can do this. I served on the state committee because I thought we could do better and maybe we could elect a few Republicans. My goal was trying to get a primary in every county, and there were twenty counties in the thirty-first senatorial district. The state party organization was talking mostly about urban areas. They wanted us to go door-to-door. That worked in Pampa, but I had rural counties like Roberts County. They could vote in Miami and someone out on somebody's ranch could hold an election. But door-to-door? These were huge ranches. There might not be anybody that lived within ten miles of each other. The rural areas, you just had to work the best you could. Like taking the one town in that county and trying to get someone working there. I was in Lefors in Gray County trying to find someone who was a Republican. I called, introduced myself, and said I was looking for a Republican who would hold a primary for us. This man said, "Well, you know, there was a Republican down here but he died."

What were the goals of the state party during the 1960s?

BILLIE PICKARD, RAYMONDVILLE

To have county chairmen in all the counties, increase the voters, get out the vote, have fundraisers, call people and get them to attend rallies, and get that enthusiasm going. Personal contact. My effort was to get county chairmen in some of the outlying counties so that we could have an election. Women very often were the ones that would tell some man who had a good presence locally, if you will do it I'll help you. Mrs. Wells in Alice was wonderful about that. She would say, "Well, why don't you call the president of the bank or some highly respected local figure and tell him that I will help him?"

We were very few in numbers so we still needed assistance from the state to keep our spirits up. During the '60s, we were really united and focused on the same things. We didn't have the splintering that has taken place, I guess beginning in the '80s. We couldn't afford the luxury of being divisive. It was really grassroots organization and unity that carried us even when there began to be splinter groups.

FRAN ATKINSON, LUFKIN & SAN ANTONIO

Peter O'Donnell used to quote very often the old expression, "You can't make an omelet without breaking eggs." When it comes to personal feelings in politics, sometimes that's not our primary consideration.

Leadership of Women

There is an image of smoke-filled rooms that would not neces-
sarily include a whole lot of women back in the '6os. But many
women were involved in setting strategy. How did that happen?

RITA CLEMENTS, DALLAS

Peter O'Donnell. He had confidence in women. He had a
good sense of picking good women to take leadership positions.

ANNE ARMSTRONG, ARMSTRONG

We had strong leaders in those days. I would say that about
Senator John Tower as our top officeholder and Peter O'Donnell
as our state chairman and then national committeeman. Party
officials Tad Smith and Bill Steger then came in. When you go
back to the late '5os and '6os, it was not unusual to have men who
thought they could do it all and didn't need the women. Our Party
had in its leadership in the beginning males who were not typical
of that era—not one of them was a chauvinist. We had strong
women who were willing to give the time and effort, and in many
cases their own money, and in all cases their own brains and elbow
grease. It was an ideal situation. I never felt put down by our Texas
leadership. When I got up to Washington, I had a few harder
knocks, but not down here.

When you have the whole world open to you and could go in any
direction, how did you decide to set political strategy?

We felt the Democratic Party was stuck in the mud. We had
no competition and in a great state like ours it was holding us
back, economically as well as politically and morally. So we could
go in any direction and basically I would say it was a conservative
direction and it was full of young people.

Women did have the whole world open to them in Republican Texas politics. Since there weren't many Republicans around
and since our male leadership was extremely open-minded, they
were delighted to have the women in the forefront with them. I

have always thought that a candidate's ultimate proof of faith in women was if he had a woman campaign chairman. That's what John Tower did. Also, he had a woman chief of staff. Peter O'Donnell and [*National Committeeman*] Albert Fay and others of the top male leadership were extremely open. Particularly O'Donnell. He really reached out to women who he thought could be effective and helpful. So it was a glory day for women. We made strides that women in other states still haven't made.

LEON RICHARDSON, NEDERLAND
Women were in on the decision-making and the planning and the recruiting. People like Anne Armstrong and Beryl Milburn were in on the planning and strategy meetings. I have been in a lot of smoke-filled rooms where decisions were made and candidates and money were discussed.

State Vice Chairs

Your mother, Emmy O'Brien, was state vice chair in the early 1950s.

WENDY MARSH, AMARILLO
Yes. Her job was to find somebody who would chair every county. Amarillo was forty or fifty thousand people. I can't imagine how small some of these counties must have been. Do you know that women were not allowed to sit on a jury until 1954 in Texas? They could vote, but they couldn't sit on a jury.

When you were vice chair, do you think you were able to make contributions in all areas of Party operation—organization, political strategy, and fundraising?

FLO KAMPMANN CRICHTON, SAN ANTONIO
When I was vice chair, I dealt with the state committeewomen. There were thirty-one. I had to keep in touch with them. They were then in touch with the county vice chairs. I didn't do any

fundraising. It was all local. I did get involved in some strategy. Thad Hutcheson was chairman then and a good friend, so he included me in everything. [*National Committeeman*] Jack Porter was a great friend so we worked very well together. I never gave it a second thought.

KATHRYN McDANIEL, BORGER

We wanted a Republican organization in all 254 counties—a chairman and a vice chairman. At that time, the chairman most of the time was a man and the vice chairman was a woman. Then we had a chairman for every precinct and a vice chairman for every precinct. If we had that kind of an organization in all the counties, then we could take it from there when it came election time.

One time, when we were having a state committee meeting, the press was excluded from it. There were other people in the room who were not members of the press but were also not members of the state committee. They were spouses. There was an objection raised about this. So the state chairman ruled that these jobs were community property [*laughing*]; therefore, if the spouse wanted to be present he could. These were not paying jobs. In fact, it was expensive. You paid your own expenses to go to meetings and for your hotel.

This is the text of an October 1960 memo written to state committeewomen after Kathryn McDaniel's election as state vice chair.

"Name a woman to serve as vice chairman in each of your counties. Every woman should know and be able to discuss intelligently issues in this campaign—Study both platforms. Have political coffees in each precinct—Discuss the issues with friends and neighbors. Invite undecided voters. Make a habit of passing onto others worthwhile newspaper and magazine articles. Assist in completing the telephone surveys in your county. Arrange listening parties for political broadcasts. Set up *now* telephone committees by precinct, provide them with names and instructions so that they will be ready to call when there is to be a rally, a fundraising affair, a workers meeting, and finally to get out the vote on Election Day—the conservative vote that is. Help staff county headquarters. Work with Young Republicans, Youth for Nixon, etc. Work with women's clubs who are interested in having political programs. Keep in mind that undecided voters are often influenced by appearance of active, enthusiastic participation of many people. So let public know what you're doing. We have a great cause. Leave us not to be too modest. Also you will please pass on to me any suggestions you have to strengthen and improve the work of the women's division. I am new at this job and will surely need all of the help that I can get. We have less than 30 days left."

What did you do as vice chair?

BERYL MILBURN, AUSTIN

Recruited county chairmen, urged the Texas Federation of Republican Women to keep growing, raised money, and wrote programs for campaigning.

Deputy State Vice Chairs

FRAN ATKINSON, LUFKIN & SAN ANTONIO

I went on as committeewoman in '65. Then after that I was asked to serve as deputy state chairman for one-fifth of the state—the eastern part of the state. I went from Brazoria County nearly up to Dallas. Peter O'Donnell was the state chairman at the time, and he was just inundated by telephone calls and nitty-gritty. He wanted some help. He wanted to divide the state up and let one person take charge of that area of the state and report to him. So just a division of labor was all that it amounted to.

Do you remember the other women in that position for other parts of Texas?

Bobbie Biggart, Polly Sowell, Mary Lou Grier, and Dorothy

Langford were a few. Polly was made the big cheese over her district without a "vice." Eventually, I was in mine and Mary Lou was in hers.

Did you have any awareness at that point that you were making a difference?

Yes, I did. That's what we were working for. I was gol' dern stubborn. I wasn't going to stop until we got a governor elected. And I didn't. It was an avocation, but it was eight or nine hours a day. My telephone bill was astronomical because I had fifty counties that I had to deal with. I traveled it all. I was in every county at least three times a year. That was at my expense. The Party didn't pay for that.

Was your husband, Basil, supportive of your activities?

Oh, yes! I got him a little button that said, "Pity me. My wife belongs to the GOP."

Did he get much pity?

No. I was just a loud-mouth broad who didn't mind getting knocked down a few times and getting back up. It just was constant. Some of the Democrats' party people who wanted to keep the Republicans excluded used ridicule as their technique. Then others just kind of chuckled behind my back. Not to my face.

You must have developed a thick skin.

Oh, you never get thick enough. Occasionally a barb gets through, by somebody you don't expect it from.

POOLIE PRATT, VICTORIA

The regional program was probably the most efficient thing that we accomplished in the '60s. We were small enough. Say our state committee meeting was to be Saturday morning. We would have a regional committee meeting on Friday afternoon. Our region had the same problems, but our problems were different than Amarillo or Houston. We would compare notes on what worked.

We met late in the afternoon, and we all went to dinner together. We got to be great friends.

FRANCIE FATHEREE CODY, PAMPA

Our deputy state vice chairman was Virginia Eggers. It is always a neat thing to bring in an expert from out of town. We used to have regular meetings of the county chairmen in our senatorial district. It lent credibility. The Party is bigger than just our county.

VIRGINIA EGGERS, WICHITA FALLS & DALLAS

I was appointed deputy vice chair for Region 5 in 1965. There was so much work to do. Instead of having all the county chairmen out doing their own thing with the state program, you went by and made a visit to make sure that they were doing it like they were supposed to. A lot of people in any organization always think they know how to do it better. But it was important to follow the state program so everybody was doing the same thing and wasn't getting in trouble with the local Democrats and making enemies.

What elements of the program were you concerned about implementing correctly?

It was the door-to-door campaigns and the telephone campaigns. You had to make sure that, if they decided they would telephone precincts, they were using phrases that weren't offensive. You couldn't just call up somebody and say, how do you plan to vote? You always needed to identify yourself and why you were calling. Often, we did surveys over the phone or door-to-door trying to find out whether people considered themselves Republicans, Democrats, or Independents. A lot of people had never thought of that. As time went on, more people moved from not knowing what they were to being Independents because they had voted Democratic and then later realized they were Republicans.

We could appoint county chairmen in all of these smaller counties, but we needed to give them a little something to do because they would get disinterested, especially if the candidate was not from their county. We talked some older, longtime citizens into being county chairmen. I would call them up and ask them if they were doing the state program. Had they delivered their campaign literature? I will never forget one older man said, "Mrs. Streeter [*now Eggers*], I am doing what I need to do." I said, "Well, thank you, I will report that." We had no idea what he was doing, but he knew that in his county if you put out one piece of Republican literature they would just throw it back in the front yard. He was doing it kind of by word of mouth.

State Committeewomen

When you served on the State Republican Executive Committee (SREC) as a state committeewoman, what goals did you have for your senatorial district?

NADINE FRANCIS, ODESSA

Goals upper most in my mind from the beginning were to get good candidates and work to get them elected.

What did West Texas volunteer (the late) Maxine Browne do to help get people to vote Republican?

JOHN TEDFORD, SONORA

She didn't mind asking people to do things. She was a real go-getter. She was a very convincing, charming, and talented person. She had a way of recruiting people. She then began to be asked to visit other towns and give talks and help get them organized. Later on she became state committeewoman. She did a great deal of travel. An oilman in San Angelo who was a staunch Republican and may have been a state committeeman at some time, John I. Moore, encouraged Maxine to go after it. He said he'd help her offset some of the cost of it. I know that he was influential in encouraging her.

Why do you think John I. Moore wanted to support Maxine Browne's efforts?

She had a great deal of energy. She was the perfect person to get in the trenches and do the legwork.

BILLIJO PORTER, EL PASO

When I was county chairman and working statewide with the Texas Federation of Republican Women [*TFRW*], Patty Bruce was my committeewoman and Ward Koehler was committeeman. They were a lot of help to me. I would go with them to the SREC meetings. Patty would come with me to the TFRW meetings. We were so cohesive. It wasn't just work, it was fun.

How did you come to serve on the SREC?

POOLIE PRATT, VICTORIA

About 1965, Bette Jo Buhler was going to resign, and I wanted to take her place. She took me to every county and introduced me to everyone so I would be certain to be elected. Someone else wanted the post. I went on a county-by-county campaign and met every county chairman.

ANN WALLACE, FORT WORTH & AUSTIN

The woman who had been on the SREC had been just sitting waiting to retire. She said she wasn't going to until she found somebody. She found me. Then by '63 or '64, we had sort of maintained the Republican presence and headquarters in Tarrant County. I felt very strongly that anybody who said they were Republican should have a forum. I had a lot of people who did not feel that way. They said, you mean if [*presidential contender Nelson A.*] Rockefeller comes down here you would have something? I said that you should present all sides. I'm not for him, but he is a known Republican. Well, that drew a line in the sand and people decided that I was just a wild-eyed liberal. I was very strong for Goldwater. There was a woman who was in that group who knocked my elementary-school-age daughter down in the hall one day. A teacher saw the whole thing. My husband said, well, you're out of politics. So I got out of politics. Tower would call me after that for a reference on somebody being considered for a nomination.

BARBARA FOREMAN, ODESSA & DALLAS

I did a stint on the state committee from 1979 to 1982, from Dallas. Jo Kanowsky was the committeewoman before me. I was appointed. That's where you can run into men who don't want to share the credit with women.

Why were you interested in serving on the SREC?

I knew Jo, and her health was failing. She convinced me that I should serve. Every once in a while I like to hit myself with a new challenge.

What kind of leader was Jo Kanowsky?

She was one of the ones that if something was going to happen, everyone went to her. She was a feisty thing. She could hold her own with all of the men. Jo really hated to give it up. She talked to me for about a year about being her replacement. I think it was what kept her going. After I talked to her a couple of times, I knew that I could never do the same kind of job that she did. But I decided to go ahead and take the job, try to do my homework, and see if I could contribute anything.

ROBBIE BORCHERS, NEW BRAUNFELS

In 1981, during the time of redistricting, I had the idea that it was time for us to get a new state representative because we felt that ours was not going to run again. I invited the leadership from Kendall County and Guadalupe County to my home in Comal County one evening for dinner to talk the matter over and try to secure a commitment from them to this project—to discuss possibilities for candidates and what might be looming in their counties. I felt that Comal County had had the state representative for ten years. After that event, we came up with Edmund Kuempel. We have had him as our state representative for sometime. Then the next year, someone in Guadalupe County, I can't remember whether it was Barbara Schoolcraft or Marjorie Donegan, called to see if I might be interested in running for the State Republican Executive Committee, which I agreed to do.

I served two terms and spent many, many hours and days traveling South Texas with Pulse Martinez trying to get some of those counties organized. Many of them did have a nice nucleus of people. So we were able to organize a few of those. In some cases, we at least got people organized to the extent that they would do some serious campaigning and some mail-outs for statewide candidates, even though they maybe didn't have any candidates themselves.

What was the most successful way to get the nucleus to open up to involve more people?

I never found that to be a problem. Generally, it was a matter of them not knowing exactly what to do and how to go about it. We would explain the basics. It was more a matter of laying out for them what has to happen in the way of structure. They just needed the basic executive committee and some precinct chairmen and some willingness to do whatever it was the candidates needed. Basically, they had to have a commitment of their own before they would even talk to us. It was again a matter of pointing out the great advantage of a two-party system in their area. That person we were talking to needed to step out and get it started.

Was it easy for people to take that risk?

Sometimes. Sometimes not. Frequently we found that we would be dealing with someone who was pretty well insulated and didn't have to worry about the slings and arrows that would come their way.

Voter Registration

LEON RICHARDSON, NEDERLAND

Peter O'Donnell appointed me at the suggestion of Senator Tower to be state chairman for voter registration in 1969. I traveled all over the state at my own expense. Our goal was to get all of the Republicans that we could registered. Beryl Milburn was with me most of the time. When we came up to East Texas, Fran

Atkinson joined us. We had material for the workers to go out and register people. Ann Steger joined us at one point. We went to the big towns, the large cities, the small towns, and four or five counties for regional meetings.

You would register anyone who wanted to register?

You register people in your best precincts. We didn't register anyone in Newton County because we would probably register Democrats. We were targeting the best Republican counties in the state of Texas.

Rules

MARGUERITE BINKLEY, HOUSTON

State Chair George Strake was not power hungry and was responsive to allowing the Party rules to become more "delegate friendly" during that time. "Delegate friendly" is my description of convention rules that provide for delegates to have a real voice in the business of the convention. Of necessity, much of the business to come before the body is prepared by staff and filtered through pre-convention committees. Usually, all main motions are brought before the delegates in the form of committee reports. An example of a "delegate friendly" rule is one that permits debate and amendments from the floor. You can easily understand why the serious delegate would prefer "delegate friendly" rules, although there are some organizations whose constituent representatives actually prefer that virtually all business be predetermined, left only to be rubber-stamped. Not so, Texas Republicans!

While there are those who decry the democratization of procedure, and I myself sometimes became impatient with the lack of discipline, I nevertheless defended open convention as essential to the Party's growth in Texas. This lack of discipline refers not to a rule itself but rather to persons who seek to pervert a rule or amend it in a way that the opposition is denied opportunity. Some newcomers to the Party do not appreciate that they are accorded current privileges because those who came before them strove to level the playing field. I fear that I am being credited and/or blamed for some recent rules changes that occurred after my time.

How have Republican Party rules developed through the years, and how has that contributed to the development of the Party?

JAYNE BRAINARD, AMARILLO

Some of them are very good, and some of them do not exactly follow Robert's Rules of Order. Any organization may have the right to make their rules. They would supersede Robert's Rules of Order. Some of the rules of the Republican Party are a little too stringent on what the member can do, but it seems to work. I think some are slanted maybe more to the right than to the center, where parliamentary law is right down the middle, black or white.

Have you seen situations where people abused rules to have their way because the rest of the people were not knowledgeable?

Oh, yes. I have sat in conventions both for political and other organizations where people have a very poor knowledge. Usually, there will be one or two who do have some knowledge but not enough. People are so intimidated that either they don't vote or they vote with them. I have seen it used that way in the Republican Party in the last ten years. Parliamentary law was never written to take over a precinct meeting. It was written to be fair. The majority will prevail, but the minority shall be heard.

County Chairman Association

JACQUE ALLEN, WICHITA FALLS

When I was county chairman, they had field men who taught you what to do. My goal on the SREC was to see what we could do to change that. [*State Chair*] Ray Hutchison let the chairmen organize. County chairmen have a lot in common. We had forums going on constantly trying to teach us how to hold a primary, how to recruit precinct chairmen, how to raise money, and all of the things you need to do. It's different from going to conventions. Nobody is running for anything for one thing. You all have something in common. Most of them are hungry to learn so that they won't make a fool of themselves. They talk with each other about what the county clerks are doing and what they are doing about it. They encourage each other.

NANCY CANION DAVIS, GALVESTON COUNTY

I was secretary for the state county chair organization. We had that going very actively at the time. We took the responsibility of ballot security in the Bill Clements gubernatorial election. We had the best ballot security program anybody ever had in the state of Texas.

We sent people out and taught Texas law. We had a lot of people at the polls. We had recounts. I don't even want to think about the recounts we went through in those unair-conditioned warehouses. It was certainly very highly organized. I take more pride in that than anything I did on the state committee because on the state committee you have the agenda set and policy is practically made for you.

Were you able to help the Party develop in the more fledgling counties?

I made trips to Matagorda and Aransas and the smaller counties. We exchanged lists because I might have a national donor list that had some donors they weren't aware of. We shared them for local candidates. It worked because they elected a bunch. Actually they did a lot better than Galveston did, locally.

Has the County Chairman Association been effective in both urban and rural counties?

ANN PEDEN, HONDO

It has been extremely effective in rural counties because a lot of the urban counties already have some type of organization. In the last fourteen years, many times we started out in a county when the only person recognized as a Republican was the county chair.

There was no organization, and they were not holding primaries. It was almost just a title. In 1996, I was the primary administrator for the state party and wanted to have a primary in every single county. It had never been done before. I was determined—and I mean determined to the point of almost being a fanatic—that we were going to have it. I did it by calling and calling and calling and by recruiting people to hold a primary. You cannot hold a primary if you do not have a county chairman. We went through five county chairmen in one week in one county. We had people who said, "I'm not going to hold a primary. I don't have time." And I said, "It is terribly unfair of us to ask that of you. If you'll send us your letter of resignation, we will find someone who will do it." We had a primary in every single county in the state of Texas in 1996, and we repeated that in 1998.

State Party Employees

SHIRLEY GREEN, AUSTIN & SAN ANTONIO
My experience working at state headquarters was a wonderful one. I learned as much about management as I have ever learned in my life. My degree from the University of Texas was in business. I learned more about management from Marvin Collins [*then state Republican executive director*] than I did from anybody. The state headquarters was well organized and well run. There was an executive director. There was an organization director who was in charge of the county party operations. We had at that time ten field reps that worked the counties in their regions. There was the PR director, John Knaggs, who did all the newsletters and was press spokesman. We had an excellent research director, Lance Torrance. The Texas Federation of Republican Women and the Young Republican Federation were at headquarters. It was a fairly simple structure, but when you get right down to it, that is what all campaigns have. You have to have a director, a field operations director, somebody who schedules the candidate, someone who does the PR, somebody who raises the money, and somebody who

does the research. The basics, whether it's a presidential or a state rep race, are pretty much the same. It wasn't brain surgery. It was a matter of paying attention to details.

Media

Editorial

POOLIE PRATT, VICTORIA

We always took candidates to the newspaper. We courted the press. The newspaper publisher was my godfather. That helped a lot. He was a very good friend of mine, and he liked George Bush and John Tower. If we had a candidate, that was always the first place we went because we didn't have a TV station then. We would have the radio station come to the rally. We worked on the press a lot. We worked on it in all the counties. We had mail-outs from the state, and they taught us how important it was to work with the press. It paid off with good publicity for candidates.

JACQUE ALLEN, WICHITA FALLS

An older man, Mr. Howard, owned the newspaper. When George Bush ran for Senate in 1970, I was working with George W. We'd drag into the paper whether they were nice to us or not. We had to walk down this hallway through Democratic candidate Lloyd Bentsen's posters. We were walking along, and Mr. Howard's son-in-law came up behind us and said, "The old man wants to see you." Well, it was scary enough. By the time we got down to the end of the hallway, George and I were holding hands. The man behind us said, "He doesn't eat women and young boys. Don't be scared." We went in and he said, "Young man, you know I'm Bensten's chairman here, but I wanted to meet somebody that was working as hard as you are for your dad. He's a nice man and if he wins I will be happy." Then he said to me, "And don't you ever come in here without saying hello to me." I was so surprised.

John Tower had always been told, "The paper doesn't like you." So after that they said, get a picture of John for the old man. The whole back of his desk was covered with Lyndon Johnson pictures and all of the big Democrats. My husband, Dave, said, "Get a picture of John and take it down there." So I got a picture, and it stayed in the back of my car until it was almost faded. I called and said I'm coming. The old man had me greeted. There was a picture in the paper of me giving Tower's pictures to him.

When Tower came in the next time, I said, "You know, I think you ought to go call on Mr. Howard." He said, "I'm not going. He doesn't like me." We drove around a while, and I said fine, then don't go. But I will never go for you again. So John said, "Well, will you pick me up in the morning?" When we got there, I said, "You want me to go in with you?" He said, no. Well I laughed until I hurt. I was sitting out there reading, and here comes John. He jumps up and kicks his heels together right in front of my car. He said, "You know what? My picture is right by Lyndon. I should have sent a better picture."

LOUISE FOSTER, AUSTIN

I remember one of the editors of the *Austin American-Statesman* came and spoke to Austin Republican Women in the early '80s. The question was asked of him, why don't you ever have anything in your paper about Republicans? He said it wasn't local interest. That was the answer we were given. I believe it is getting to be of more local interest now because you do see more coverage.

How did you make the transition from being a member of the press to working in the Party?

DOTTIE DE LA GARZA, DALLAS

It is easy when you think about it. Karen Parfitt Hughes [*presidential candidate George W. Bush advisor*] has done a perfect job of it. Most of your good political media people came out of media jobs because they know the media. You know what the media process is, their deadlines, what they think is huckstering, and what they think is informational. You know their mind-set because you have been in the newsroom with them. I knew the ones that didn't think a whole lot of the Republicans, and I knew those that had a secret admiration for them. Dick Morehead, for instance, the bureau chief of the *Dallas Morning News* was a closet Republican. You know how they operate and how best to get your message in their hands in a usable form that will project the best image for the Party. I always took the approach not to massage the media. I was not one of those spin-doctor people. That came along a little bit later.

My job was assistant PR director for the Party in the Littlefield Building in Austin in '68. You felt like you were in a kind of subversive mentality. I was a kid. You did feel like you were in kind of a revolution, which is ironic since we were supposedly conservative. But we were part of a revolution in Texas. To think that conservative Republicans were part of an upheaval that upset the status quo rather than conserve it. Do you see the irony in that?

Ads

KAY DANKS, GALVESTON & AUSTIN

We aired a thirty-minute Reagan broadcast in Austin. Also, Maurice Angly did what we called "the voice of God" on drive-time radio. We went down to the station, and he made the voice-overs and aired those tapes in drive time and we paid for it. One of the funny things was that I went down to [*the Johnson-owned station*] KLBJ to buy time. They have to sell you time. The guy who sold time walked out and was gone for two hours. But I outwaited him. He had to sell me the time.

This was in 1976? LBJ was dead by then wasn't he?

Yes, but you know Lady Bird still owned the station at the time. That's sort of what went on in those days as far as the Republicans were concerned in Austin.

As a Tool for Party Expansion

BILLIJO PORTER, EL PASO

I was the first woman county chairman in El Paso. Then the Democrats elected a woman as county chairman, Mary Haynes. The press loved it. They followed us around all of the time. I found out that it was very important to cultivate the press. They will do more for you because they like you than because of what your position is.

If we had a press conference at Republican headquarters, we always had food and drinks for them. We always made them feel at home and talked to them. I always got a fair shake, I felt. I was one that told it how it was. They kind of liked that, too. They really were quite generous with coverage. I kept saying, don't you want to talk to my candidates? They just wanted to see Mary and me get into it. We disagreed a lot on how government should work, but on the integrity of the governmental process we did not disagree. That is why we could get along.

ZUBIE WALTERS, YOAKUM

We had articles in the newspaper. It was not too cooperative a lot of times when we had an out-of-town speaker. We would ask them to come and take a picture, and usually they would say, oh, we can not come that night. It was the same story every time. That is frustrating, especially when you have someone running for state office. We would submit a piece to the paper about the candidates being there. Sometimes they would publish that. Sometimes we would buy an ad.

NANCY PALM, HOUSTON

I was such a novelty. Let's face it. We had had almost no women elected to anything. I never was afraid of them. They saw that I did not call them or discuss things with them unless I thought it had news value. I had worked with the media my four years at Vanderbilt and the seven years I was with the Harris County Medical Society. So I felt like I was one of them. I wrote all of my own press releases.

How did you get the nickname "Napalm"?

I was very active in support of the war. Nixon, I thought, deserved all of our support after he was in there. My name is so totally given to that expression. People thought I was very, very firm. Let's just put it that way. It never occurred to me to be afraid of a politician or a person in public office, period. I just figured that I knew as much or more about it than they did.

In 1974, we carried the county judge's position, which had never been held by a Republican. I recruited Jon Lindsay. It amused me that night on television, the county judge, Bill Elliott from Pasadena, said, "It's all because of 'that woman' that I've lost the election." He said it over and over again. It was all over television. I attacked the commissioners court very heavily. That must have been where "Napalm" came from.

RUTH MANKIN, HOUSTON

We had to find forums and platforms to make our policies known. We did that through a good little publication called the *Republican Banner.* I was editor of it for some time. We sent it out to all of the registered Republicans. For me, it was a bully platform to bring together, first, as much Party harmony as we could. It was very divisive in those years, and we worked to pull everyone together. Second, and probably more important, we were concerned with local races and local issues. I often wrote editorials critical of positions that were taken by the Democrats—city council, mayor, and commissioners court. There was an outbreak of encephalitis in Harris County. That was back in the '60s when we had open bayous, and mosquitoes used to breed and infect people. A bunch of us went door-to-door getting a petition signed to create a Mosquito Control District. When all of the petitions were turned in and approved, we had people backing it but the Harris County Commissioners Court refused to accept the responsibility to do it. So we used the *Banner* and said, this is not just for Republicans, this is for all of the community. They eventually saw the light.

Redistricting

NANCY JUDY, DALLAS

In 1970, I was the Republican chosen by Dallas County to be responsible for redrawing legislative districts. I did it following all the proper legislative requirements, and it turned out beautifully. We had eighteen districts, and we had nine Democrat districts and nine Republican districts, just by following the proper guidelines. Of course, the state legislature was primarily Democrat, so it didn't turn out that way. Republicans embraced it, but then it was sent to the state redistricting committee. They weren't responsive to the logic of it. They weren't interested in logic. They were interested in power. It was wildly gerrymandered.

CHAPTER 7

Precinct Organization

"A good precinct chairman does it all, helping the candidates
in every way possible and staying in touch with the voters
in the precinct."   —BARBARA NOWLIN

*P*recincts are the building blocks of grassroots political
efforts. County chairs and vice chairs directed their effort to
build a county organization by recruiting precinct chairs as the
foundation. Many men agreed to be precinct chairs in the 1950s
and 1960s, when their wives promised to "help out." Soon
women wanted to serve as precinct chairs because they were
already the de facto chairs and wanted the title and recognition.

When people begin anything new, the question arises,
"Where do we learn how to get the job done?" Some of the new
Republican activists had been involved in Democratic politics.
Many called upon Democrat friends and precinct chairmen to
give them tips. One unlikely source of information, the AFL-CIO
organization manual, provided many women insight into building
a framework to elect Republicans.

Precinct chairs approached their duties professionally. They
developed an organization by recruiting others to be block
captains and in some cases organizing precinct women's clubs to
provide workers. They knew their voters and effectively got
them to the polls on Election Day. Battles about candidates and
issues sometimes erupted during the primary, but most women
found common ground on which to stand and work together to
elect Republicans in the November general election.

Precinct Chairs

Recruiting

How did you end up as a precinct chair?

PETER O'DONNELL, DALLAS

In our precinct, there was a vacancy in 1956, and they asked me to be precinct chairman. My wife said, if you do it, I will help you [*laughing*]. I said, okay, I will do it.

ANNE BERGMAN, WEATHERFORD

At first, I used to say to my husband, "Bob, you be the precinct chairman, and I will do the work." Now, wasn't that ridiculous? The Tower chairman, the Bush chairman, whatever chairman—the men would be the chairmen and we would do the work. Well, we learned pretty soon that wasn't a good idea. By 1958, I was precinct chairman.

WILDA LINDSTROM, HOUSTON

When I get on the phone, I get timid and I am always afraid that I am infringing on someone's life. But in the back of my mind, I'd know that, no matter what they say, they couldn't hurt me. One lady said to me, "Lady, what do you want?" I said, "I want to talk to someone about being precinct chairman." She said, "Why don't you say what you want?" I said, "What would you have me say?" She said, "Say, hello, my name is Wilda Lindstrom. You don't know me, but I am trying to find someone in your precinct that would talk to me about being precinct chairman. Would you talk to me?" I said, "Well, that sure sounds good. Would you mind if I hang up and call back and practice on you?" So I called her up and I said, "Hello. My name is Wilda Lindstrom. You don't know me, but I am trying to find someone who would talk to me about getting involved in politics. Would you talk to me or maybe your husband?" She said, "I couldn't do it, but I'll let you talk to my husband." I talked to him, and he became a precinct chairman. So it worked. I have recruited hundreds and hundreds and hundreds of precinct chairmen.

ANN LEE, HOUSTON

We moved here in 1968; 1970 was the year that George Bush was running for the Senate. I called Republican headquarters to find out who was the precinct chairman. Low and behold, there was not one. They asked me to run the primary and to run by write-in vote for precinct chairman. I think I had four votes. All it took was just one. I was precinct chairman for twenty-two years. We have organized the precinct pretty well. The thing that we have always done is to put out a letter that goes door-to-door to everyone. People will call if they don't get the letter soon enough. We put signs in our yards so people know who to vote for on the whole ballot.

BEVERLY KAUFMAN, HOUSTON

I married the right man. We have shared conservative views. We are both patriots and love our country. I learned that he had been active in the Republican Party. At that point, I was twenty-two years old, and I never had a chance to vote. Soon after we married there was a special election in 1968 for state representative in Harris County, and he got called to work at the phone banks. He didn't have time and wanted to know if I would go. I said, sure, it sounded like an adventure to me. That was my first experience as a campaign volunteer. I really enjoyed it. I quickly found a home in the Republican Party.

We worked with our precinct chairman, and then two years later, as the area grew, the precinct was split up and there was an opening in the new precinct for another chairman. The precinct chairman came over and said he was going to recommend my husband. I said, wait a minute, guys. I'm one that's been doing all the volunteer work, throwing parties at the house and recruiting all these people. I would like to be the precinct chairman. Impertinent little me. I was like twenty-four years old.

How were you elected precinct chair?

LEON RICHARDSON, NEDERLAND

We moderates decided that we were going to take over from the extreme right wing.

How would you define moderate? You supported Barry Goldwater.

I was a conservative but not a John Bircher. These people were in the John Birch Society. Howell Cobb ran for county chairman against Dr. Walker, who was extremely conservative. We organized, and we got somebody to run in all of the precincts. We worked. We got out and beat the bushes. In my precinct, six people had voted two years before then. When I ran [*for precinct chair*] against Harold Jackson, 168 voted. Dr. Walker counted the votes, and I lost by one. Of course, when you've lost by a certain percentage you are entitled to a recount. Cobb and I posted the fifty dollars it cost, and we had a recount. I won by two.

Duties

HARRIET LOWE, DALLAS

I learned an awful lot from my Democrat precinct chairman. I had a funny thing happen. I had a Bruce Alger [*for Congress*] sign on my car that I drove around with. A big sign. I parked outside the distance markers at the polling place at Southern Methodist University [*no campaign signs are allowed inside the distance markers, or within 100 feet*]. I went out for lunch, and my Bruce Alger sign was gone. There was a rose in my front seat. I never used to lock my car. I know that Jack Harkey did it. He was the Democrat precinct chairman.

What did you learn from him?

How to work a precinct. There were all kinds of things to learn.

Why do you suppose he was so forthcoming? You were a political rival.

Oh, no. I wasn't that type of a politician. His wife and I are still friends. I remember when I was a Cub Scout leader. We were taking a group of kids somewhere, and one of the other women had a Kennedy sign on her car. The kids said, don't ride in that car. I said, if you don't you can't go on the field trip. I'm not that kind of a politician. Yes, I can disagree with you, but there is no use being disagreeable about it.

LINDA CUSTARD, DALLAS

In 1960, the man who had been precinct chairman in our precinct in the Park Cities was unable to meet his responsibilities. As a bride of a few weeks at the age of twenty-one, I was asked by Peter O'Donnell to assume the responsibilities of precinct chairman. I became the youngest precinct chairman in Dallas County. That was pre-computers. Everything was done on three-by-five cards and by telephoning. We did door-to-door canvassing. Couples would come in the evenings, and I would organize and feed them dinner and have everything ready for them to go out and do the canvassing in their area. Then they came back and reported. Then I would report to the county structure. I held that position for five years until I had a newborn baby, a second child. One night, my husband came down at two in the morning, and I was nursing with my left hand and going through three-by-five cards for the precinct with my right hand. He said, I think enough is enough. It's time to let someone else take over. So that's when I retired from being a precinct chairman.

My husband and I and son, Allen, lived next door to Robert Stovall, the Democrat precinct chairman. So there were very lively discussions and disagreements. They did an article on the two of us for the *Dallas Morning News*. We were on the cover of the weekend magazine with a picture of Allen Custard with a big pin that said, "If I were 21, I would vote for Barry." They said, don't you all disagree and argue? Are you still friends? I said, we are because it is the American way to have a mutual respect for differences of opinion, which is what we did have. Of course, this was pre-assassination and all the dreadful things that happened in the city in 1963.

The interesting thing is that there was never a problem finding volunteers. I was able to gather people because so many believed in the Republican cause and wanted to see a choice in Texas. The Democrats were so smug and so arrogant and self-satisfied. There just needed to be a change. A lot of people felt that way. We were willing to provide it. We had the highest percentage Republican vote in the county. We also turned out the vote.

The challenge for me personally was simply to take care of little children and still do all of the work that was involved and do it well. Of course, the precinct chairman has to be at the polls. So you are up at four in the morning and at the polls at six for each and every election. It's easy to discount the importance of a precinct chairman, and yet it all begins there at the grassroots. I am grateful to have had the experience because it's really just the bedrock of our political system.

BARBARA NOWLIN, HOUSTON & FRIENDSWOOD

In 1962, we moved to Sharpstown in the southwest part of Houston. It was a brand new area. We needed to get that area organized for the Party. So my husband and I did that and held the first primary in the area. I walked door-to-door and started a women's club and got people to come to my house. About twenty-five or thirty women showed up. A district director spoke to us and told us what we needed to get started.

Why did you want to start a women's club at that point?

I just had the idea that we could do more if we had a group of women. I knew that women get things done. I just thought that if we had a women's club we could organize our area and ourselves better. It is not always easy to find a good precinct chairman. A lot of people sign on with the idea that they would like to be an election judge and run the elections. That's just all that they do. A good precinct chairman does it all, helping the candidates in every way possible and staying in touch with the voters in the precinct. It is a good idea for a precinct chairman to hold meetings on a regular basis for a while at least. Precinct chairmen need to do a lot more than just run a primary election.

RUTH MANKIN, HOUSTON

When we first moved to Houston in 1957, my husband was a precinct chairman. I said, "Good grief, what is that?" And he said, "A lot of work for us." The first thing I did was get the AFL-CIO handbook *How to Win* and study it. It was strictly a door-to-door precinct organization with block captains and district chairman. I rewrote the book into a handbook for Republican precincts called *Politics Is Not a Spectator Sport*. The book was adopted by the county headquarters and given to every precinct chairman. I felt that was one of the best contributions I ever made. In those days we literally went door-to-door, greeted everyone that was new to the precinct, made friends with everyone, identified them on our card file—nothing electronic, just shoe boxes.

When it came time to vote, we knew who our people were and turned them out. One time a man called in about 1957 or '58. He said, "Why haven't your people ever called on me?" I looked him up in the card file and said, "We have your son's bar mitzvah on such-and-such date, you moved into your house on such-and-such day, you voted in the primary." "How do you know that?" he asked. "We had our block chairman call on you." That shows what it was all about when you're on that kind of personal level. Our insistence on turning out the vote really paid off. It lay the foundation of what was to come.

ANNE ARMSTRONG, ARMSTRONG

It was down in the precincts where I think the women made the biggest difference. That's where we had such a tremendous advantage over the Democrats. There weren't a whole lot of enthusiastic females working for Democrats down in the precincts in the old days. We brought a spirit. We were like missionaries. I rose quickly, but there were women who chose to stay in the trenches or had to because they were working or couldn't leave. I was lucky. I had help at home. I had a husband who supported me. He let me go statewide and let me go to Washington. Ninety-eight percent of women were not in that position or wouldn't have wanted it if they were in that position. They were the ones that gave us an enormous leg up on the Democrats. Those are the unsung heroines. Overwhelmingly, they did the work in the towns and the cities.

Canvassing

Phone

GLENNA McCORD, DALLAS

In 1955, I joined the Valley View Republican Women's Club in Dallas. Mary Ann Lesch was the precinct chairman, and she was the founder of that club. There weren't too many of us. One of the other people in that club was Margot Perot. Margot was a very hard worker. One thing led to another. It wasn't too long before I got a call. Could I go down to Republican headquarters and do some telephoning? They had put together these precinct lists of telephone numbers. Harry Bass had done most of this work himself. As many women as they could get down there during the day were there. We were calling people domicile by domicile—I think that was Harry's favorite word—trying to identify people. We never asked them if they were Democrat or Republican. I think that's one mistake the Party made. We asked them if they were conservative or liberal. The funny thing about it was eight of every ten people that we called had no idea of the definition of either word. So we would have to stop and explain to them what conservative and liberal really meant. If they were conservative, then we would put them down as a possible Republican. Whenever you got 10,000 bad, bad words thrown at you or were hung up on, you knew you were in the wrong precinct.

How did you define conservative and liberal to those people that didn't know?

It was a simple definition: do you believe in less government in your lives; do you believe in freedom and a few words on what freedom meant to us. In the '60s, the liberals dominated the government in Washington and interfered in our private lives. That is probably oversimplifying. Maybe it is not simple enough.

WINNIE MOORE, LUBBOCK

We were organizing the precincts. Our precinct chairman called and asked me to do some telephoning to get out the vote. I said, sure. When he brought this stack of cards, it was everybody in the precinct. I thought there would just be a few names that I would need to call. I called them all, not knowing any better.

What did people say when you called them on the phone?

Nobody was ugly when I called them. I'm sure some of them appreciated me calling.

Bus Canvas

MARY ANNE COLLINS, DALLAS

Women organized bus canvas groups. We would meet in Preston Center [*a shopping mall*]. We would have buses, and we would go to places like Lancaster and Oak Cliff. We went door-to-door. That was in the days when you could still do things like that at night. Everybody you knew was doing it. There was a huge level of commitment.

Door-to-Door

DOUTHEA AND BILL SHANER, MIDLAND

Douthea: We organized our precinct. We knocked on every door. Found out who lived there and if they were of voting age and canvassed them as to what Party they considered themselves belonging to. We entered the information into punch cards and put it into the computer. We started with automation in '62. I'm not sure why. I guess it just seemed a neat way to do it rather than transfer all of this information page to page.

Bill: Douthea's background is as a geophysics programmer. Then she became a computer programmer. She had a really good bunch of people that she was working with. This was a project that they just took on. So then in '64, she was ready.

What were you ready for?

Douthea: Ready to know that we were going to carry the precinct by ten votes.

Bill: We had a chairman who said, well, it is a forgone conclusion that east of Big Spring Street Republicans had to write off winning. Well, we happened to live east of Big Spring Street. We said, no way.

Douthea: That was probably the inspiration for all of the hard work—saying that we couldn't do it. We only carried by four votes. We did have an impact. You can't contact all of these people and have nothing happen. At the worse, somebody is going to say, "I had a Republican come to my door last night." His neighbor says, "Well, so did I."

BETTE HERVEY, EL PASO

Door-to-door was our way of contacting people without spending a lot of money. We didn't have money. We would arrange a walk on Saturday morning. I remember the night before packing the packets for the block walkers to hand out. I guess I enjoyed meeting people. I wanted to spread the word whether we won or not. At least I let them know we were here.

PATTY BRUCE, EL PASO

Tad Smith started a house-to-house survey in the '50s to locate our conservative vote. It took years and years. We went door-to-door. I had a kid on my hip and one by the hand.

MARY DONELSON, AMARILLO

In 1956 and 1957, we were out knocking on doors identifying who was Democrat and who was Republican. We went door-to-door. We were assigned a whole block to do. We went to everybody. We tried to identify whether they were Yellow Dog Democrats [*party loyalists who would "vote for a yellow dog if it was a Demo-*

crat"], which we put up in the corner "YDD" on the cards that we filled out. We also asked for contributions. The state chairmen said, if they will give you a little money they will be more inclined to vote with you, and so we always asked for support. The watchword was "Texas needs a two-party system."

What was your strategy to grow the Party at the local level?

MARGARET BAIRD, HOUSTON

It was grassroots activism. Knocking on doors. Generating enthusiasm and patriotism. I would do the same things that I would ask anyone else to do. We generated a lot of enthusiasm. I know that big money counts, but interacting with people is the most important part of politics. It was how we won most of the things in the Clear Lake area and the Houston area. I made badges for everything. People began to feel that they wanted to vote. They would say things like, "I really didn't care about politics before, but now I really have gotten interested." It had an impact. Enthusiasm is contagious.

RUTH FOX, HOUSTON & AUSTIN

In the early '70s, we did go door-to-door. We made a practice of not asking people if they were Republican or Democrat. I can remember years afterwards people came up to me and said, "I remember you coming to my door and registering me. I said, 'Well, I'm a Democrat,' and you said, 'Well, I don't really care, I just want to register you to vote.'" That changed their minds. Several people said that to me.

Knowing Your People

BETTY STERQUELL, AMARILLO

I used in Potter County the technique that I had learned from Duval County. The five letters of Duval stood for the degrees of loyalty to your Party. The first two "DU" were Democrat. "V" was the independent. "AL" were either ones who did not vote or could not be counted on to vote for you. What I used in Potter County was T-E-X-A-S, and when I typed the mailing labels I just underlined T, E, X, A, or S. "X's" were the independents we sent letters to. To this day, that precinct still is one of the strongest precincts and that was in 1952. When you really organize one well, it holds.

When I moved to Randall County, I worked with a man named E. W. Glenn. He was considerably older than I was. He used to call me "girl." He said, "Girl, let's just go out and get this county organized. We just need to find out where these Republicans are, then get them done." We went out to the farthermost rural precincts first. We would drive up, and he'd go out and talk to the farmer and I'd go in and talk to his wife. We had some funny things happen. I asked one lady, "Do you vote?" She looked around and said her husband was watching. Then, when he was outside, she said, "Yes, honey, and I don't always vote the way he tells me to." Another one I went to told me that she voted. I said, "Do you consider yourself a liberal or a conservative?" She said, "Honey, I am a conservative." She took her fist and pounded the kitchen table and said, "I hope to die if this county ever goes wet." So we still had to educate. People didn't know what conservatives were.

THEO WICKERSHAM, SAN ANTONIO

Mary Morton Jackson used to tell me, "know your people." I knew everybody who was a voter in my precinct at the time. She taught me that. She would walk into a room or a convention and she would say, "Hi, Bonnie. Hi, Olla." That meant a lot to people. She didn't drive, so she would have people take her out to the poorest neighborhoods in Bexar County on the south side, and she would sit there on an old wooden box with a lemon pie covered with flies. She'd do it, and those people would follow her. They would vote because they knew Mary Morton Jackson. Barbara Schoolcraft was a real worker, and I got my get-up-and-go from her. I'd say, we couldn't possibly do that, Barbara. We can't drive down to Laredo. She'd say, yes, we are doing that and we are going to Zapata from

there. She thought nothing about it. She didn't care that it was in-
fested with Democrats. I did a lot of country politics out in these rural
communities. Country politics means you sit down with them and eat
lemon pie with flies on it. I don't guess they're that much different, but
they do expect you to take up a little more time with them.

VIC KING, FORT WORTH & BOERNE

About 1962, Betty Andujar lived just around the corner from
us, and she was very active in politics at that time. She got me
interested in politics. As a result, I became precinct chairman in
her precinct when she gave up that position. When we went to the
first county convention after I took over, we had maybe twenty-
three delegates. When the first real vote came up for permanent
chairman of the county convention, they asked us to poll our delegation. I didn't say anything to encourage the vote one way or
another. When we took the vote it came out twenty-one to two. I
think my wife, Fran, and I were the only ones who voted for a
certain candidate and everyone else voted the other way. I had to
give all the votes to the candidate that I did not want. After the
meeting, some of the women in the delegation came up to me and
said that I seemed sort of surprised or disappointed about the vote.
They said that Betty had called them up last night and told them
how to vote. Right after that, Betty came up to me and slapped me
on the back and said, "Well, you learned something about politics
today, didn't you?" I learned I needed to know what the delegates
think before I step into the convention.

Precinct Battles

MARY LOU WIGGINS, DALLAS

We had battles here in Dallas in the presidential primaries of
1968. I was a precinct chairman. You do learn that, when you can
control the county delegates, the state delegates, and the national
delegates, then you can influence your future. You are not helpless.

We had precinct battles of course. That was even true in the Eisenhower-Taft race. Later, it was between Reagan and Nixon. That was a big battle, and that was tough on me. I am not a confrontational kind of person. We had to call everybody in the precinct and get them to the meeting. We had really good friends that were for Reagan, and we were for Nixon. It was very difficult for me because I don't like to be a part of controversy.

When you have big battles, there can be some hurt feelings. How do you get those repaired so people can work together again?

You try to mend fences. We realized that we were ultimately on the same side.

CHAPTER 8

County Organization

"You can't stay at home and get to know the precinct chairmen
and get a working organization going."   —WANDA EIDSON

*C*ounty chairs had a challenge ahead. Management responsibilities
fell on their shoulders, including running elections, recruiting volunteers and candidates, opening headquarters, organizing the county to get out the vote on Election Day, and raising
money. Women initially were vice chairs of the county organization, but by the end of the 1960s women had taken on the
position of county chair in large and small counties alike.

In the 1950s and 1960s, most women raised their children
and found their work outlet in volunteer endeavors. Women had
time to give during the day, and as county vice chairs they could
keep the county headquarters open, increasing Republican
visibility. Women maintained the consistent organizational
efforts needed to develop an effective structure ready for action
in campaigns and on Election Day. They did the tedious jobs,
such as looking up phone numbers and creating a voter card file,
as well as those jobs with high recognition, like escorting visiting
candidates and raising money. In the 1970s, primary participation began to grow and so did the Republican Party, finally
giving voters the choices that women active in the 1950s wanted
to offer.

Rural counties provided different challenges than urban
counties. State leaders worked to coax men and women out of the
shadows and publicly admit to being Republicans. In many
small counties, that was a nearly impossible feat. Instead of

organizing a county party, leaders set up women's clubs to carry the Republican banner. Small counties identified voters any way possible, often not by following the prescribed formula. These tried-and-true methods for county organization continue to be in use today.

County Chairs

Qualities

What do you think desirable qualities are for a good county chair?

WANDA EIDSON, WEATHERFORD

Be a good politician. Understand both sides. Get publicity for things. Involve everybody that you can. Push people into taking things that maybe they don't have time to do. It takes time to keep in touch with all of the organizations. You can't stay at home and get to know the precinct chairmen and get a working organization going.

Recruiting

In the early days, how did you find people to be county chairs?

BETTE JO BUHLER, VICTORIA

Knocking on doors, talking to service station attendants.

RUTH SCHIERMEYER, LUBBOCK

We thought we needed a man as a chairman. The women were the workers, but we needed a man as chairman for the name. Terry Tapp was one of the few women chairman of the county party during that time. She and her husband, Raymond, were a team. If you got Raymond, you got Terry. If you got Terry, you got Raymond. Had it not been for that, I don't know if they would have put a woman in as chairman then.

MARTHA CROWLEY, DALLAS

Frank and I were in Washington working for Congressman Bruce Alger, and the people at home had a lot of faith in Frank's opinion of people and things. Anything serious, they would call Frank and want to know what he thought. Harry Bass had been sitting in, I think, as county chairman. He could not do it any longer. So they called our house one evening and said, "What do you think about Peter O'Donnell?" Frank turned from the phone and said, "Do you know who Peter O'Donnell is?" I said, "Yes, he is the fellow I sat with all day at Mineral Wells when we bolted the convention with Mrs. Black [*Mrs. John R. Black (Thelma), the national committeewoman*]." He and Mrs. Black and I were sitting together in the lobby all afternoon. He said, "What do you think?" And I said, "He's a nice guy and smart, he'd be fine." I knew that he was from an affluent family and could afford it. But it was another Peter from another family. I had never laid eyes on Peter O'Donnell before, and Frank didn't know him either. Now, if we had and didn't like him, they may have paid no attention to us whatsoever. It was Peter Stewart. I told Peter Stewart about it recently and he laughed.

Duties

JANE JUETT, AMARILLO

We did have a female county chairman in 1965. She tried her best to raise money to keep headquarters open. We have had a headquarters since the '60s open all year-round in Potter County, which is unusual for a place no larger than this. I used to get so tickled at Betty Hervey [*not to be confused with Bette Hervey from El Paso*]. She would be totally out of money, and there was a man named Ed Roberts who was pretty wealthy. She would go to him and say, "Uncle Ed, I just don't have the rent money. Do you think you could help me out, please?" He would give her check. She was always trying to get people to be precinct chairs and to work the primaries.

How did a woman end up as county chair?

Men just didn't want to be bothered a lot of times. They're busy. Men are good, and they certainly have their place. When it comes to details, they just can't be bothered. Whereas a woman will get in there and do what needs to be done. Men either assume it's going to be done, or they would like to find somebody else to do the detail work. If you are going to do a good job, there has got to be attention paid to details to come out successfully.

Why do you think Nancy Palm was able to make changes as county chair?

PATRICIA LYKOS, HOUSTON

She was the only Republican presence that we had of prominence. She would go down and confront commissioners court. Let me tell you something, that was a tough court in those days. They would get into fistfights. They were very rude to her, and she stood up to them. She was not a country-club Republican. She was very innovative. She took the initiative. Nancy Palm made the Republican Party possible for both men and women. She blazed a path for women to follow. No path is easy.

NANCY PALM, HOUSTON

A vice chair is supposed to be, of course, supportive of the chairman. The chairman, Dudley Sharp, had not quite yet learned that women in politics were here to stay. He got just terribly upset at a meeting where the rules that had been previously adopted were submitted for renewal. He walked out on me in a very contentious meeting of the Republican Party at the county courthouse and resigned in the middle of the meeting. I turned to his parliamentarian, Marguerite Binkley, and said, "What do I do now?" She said "Carry on." And I carried on. Then I was actually elected to the chairmanship by the executive committee.

What was so controversial about the rules?

With Marguerite Binkley's help and Nora Elich's help from

a parliamentary standpoint and with my knowledge of election law, we divided the Harris County structure so it would be controlled by state senatorial districts. This was the main thing that Dudley Sharp resigned over. It actually lessened the authority of the county chairman he thought. When I took over, there were four senatorial districts and now there are parts of seven or eight. One person, from an organizational standpoint, cannot cover a county the size of Harris County because it is bigger than eighteen states. The people in different parts of the county were so very different from the so-called old guard that we had been depending on to carry elections. I had opposition the first three times I ran. By then, the other side had become accustomed to me.

What did you do to organize the county?

I worked the senatorial districts, and we started immediately calling everybody that had voted in a primary. We didn't have primaries of any stature until 1968. Back in those days, the Republican Party, not the state, had to pay for the primary. We started calling every voter in the precincts. We started building up the number of precinct chairmen. The precinct chairmen were the main engines of the Republican Party or any political party. With this large county, you simply had to divide it and get it down to the level of the actual voting public. I am extremely, extremely fortunate in the type of people who supported me. They were unusually dedicated and knowledgeable and very, very practical. We had to bring in Democrats as well as stimulate Republicans to come and vote.

Marguerite Binkley assisted you with the rules?

She was a licensed parliamentarian, and she certainly was a genius at organization. Lee Stevens became the treasurer. None of these people were paid, and when I think of the time and intelligence and hard work that we all put into it . . .

How long did it take you to put the system into place?

I went in July as the county chairman, and we had an election in November. It was a very full-time job. We would not have been successful if it had not been for all of the wonderful people who worked as hard as they did. We were building an organization that was the envy of the country. Then, after the election, we had a relatively cool period to continue to make contacts. So I worked with the media. You had to depend on free media back then. We didn't have any money. In the early '70s, the media was coming to us rather than to the Democrats for the news of the day, particularly where elections were concerned. I could call a news conference and get a room full of reporters because I knew how to speak and what I was talking about. I educated them and they helped me. Then it was so much more the print media than the video media. I would never have been able to do this without their help. We had two major newspapers and a large number of radio stations.

Why were you interested in politics?

When I came to Texas, I thought the way that elections were held in the state was so grossly unfair. When I started studying the election laws of the state, I became even more certain that the only way that things in Texas could be changed would be by changing the election laws. I did help change election law in this state.

I fought constantly for at least the first four years of my office to secure Republican election judges, which is necessary to prevent fraud. Later on, I was appointed by George Strake [*of the state party*] to be the one Republican on the committee appointed by the secretary of state to re-codify the election code. They had assigned me the chapters on voting machines, and I became known all over the country as the authority on voting machines. They can be manipulated so tremendously. It has taken a very long time to change the fact that the Democrats had total control of the elections.

Here in Harris County, everybody told me I did not have the authority. I took the county clerk to task for the way he had set up the voting machines, which was absolutely narrow-minded, illegal, and unfair. As the chairman of the Harris County Republican Party, I took him before the Texas attorney general for an opinion. He was forced to back down in the middle of the election and redo the voting machines. This strengthened my conviction that you have to start at the bottom, meaning the county level, rather than what previous Republican county chairman had done by starting at the top, carrying the county for the president. I am for that, but the bedrock of a political party is centered in the county courthouses of the 254 counties around the state. The county commissioners court is the one that appoints the election judges, decides the voting dates largely, and decides what kinds of voting machines there are. The reason the Party is so successful thirty years later is because we got control of the county courthouses.

JACQUE ALLEN, WICHITA FALLS

It was rough when I started in 1976. We would go get our supply cans [*at the courthouse*] and fill them up [*with election supplies*] at our headquarters. Then we would take them out to the polling places, bring them back, count the ballots, and take them back to the courthouse. I did that once. I knew the Democrat county chairman. He had been the county chairman for years. The next time he and the county clerk were having their meeting, I just went in and said, "I heard you were having a meeting." I said, "I've just been appointed the Republican county chairman and I don't know anything about it. You are going to have to teach me. You fix up the Democrat cans down here at the courthouse, and I need that help." They were nice about it after that. We just never had asked. We sort of knew they didn't like us, so we stayed away.

When you are the county chairman, you are not the same as a campaign worker. Particularly since 1972, when the secretary of state tells you what to do [*the funding of primaries changed in 1972, when the state began assessing filing fees instead of the political parties*]. You are doing the same thing that the Democrat county chairman is doing. After I got acquainted with the county clerks through the years, if we got new Democrat county chairmen, the county clerk and I would take them to lunch. We would say very bluntly, we both do the same thing so there is no point in us having any fusses. We will work together. It worked.

Conflicts

MARGUERITE BINKLEY, HOUSTON

The John Tower Senate victory followed by Goldwater's presidential defeat paradoxically combined to usher in a wave of volunteerism that fueled a fundamental change in political organization in the county. Unlike other areas of the state, Goldwater's defeat did not extinguish the local conservative zeal, despite an unbelievably arrogant call by the Old Guard extorting the newcomers to retrench and meekly vest control of the newly energized party to those who wouldn't or couldn't acknowledge that politics in Texas had undergone a revolution.

The conservative activists were not to be denied. The genie was out of the bottle. There was not an anointed leader among us early on, but we were dependent upon James C. Fourmy, a level-headed precinct chairman who helped us keep our focus through his consistent, practical direction. The several district headquarters and phone banks from the Tower and Goldwater campaigns had spawned district leaders who were even more valuable to our goal than a single leader.

Following a contentious county chairman's election in '65, those of us who had been volunteering at county headquarters were replaced by a staff person, and only she and the county vice chair were permitted to answer the phone. Additionally, not only were the primary voter lists verboten but also the list of precinct chairmen was kept under lock and key, available only to selected persons. The proverbial straw that broke our backs occurred when the new county chairman announced his committee appointments; out of fifty-six appointees, fifty-three were persons who had been his active supporters, leaving three inconsequential committee slots for his opposition. I should interject that the rules in effect at that time, such as they were, permitted near dictatorial power on the part of the county chairman, leaving us no option except to change the bylaws governing the county executive committee, a task much easier said than done.

It required months of meetings around the county in groups large and small. We began by using our existing district organization that had developed during the Tower and Goldwater campaigns. The most critical rules changes related to committees. We allotted district committee members based on the number of precinct chairmen in the district. They were elected by the precinct chairmen within the district. Further, each committee chairman was elected by the committee membership. The county chairman was allotted three at-large appointees. Thus, the committee structure broke open the Party for development.

The most influential committee was the one assigned to fill vacancies in the positions of precinct chairmen that occur between primary elections. In an urban county with many precincts, 200 then and over 1,000 now, it is an ongoing task to fill these vacancies. The procedure for so doing can significantly impact the political divide. Texas election statutes allow the county executive committee to make the legal replacement for a precinct chairman who has died, moved, or resigned; however, the law requires that a majority of the executive committee's membership must "participate" according to the statute in filling vacancies. Those selected must receive a majority vote of those participating. The faction that holds the balance of power on the executive committee tightens its grip through control of the vacancy committee.

After the '66 primary, the Goldwaterites held a clear majority on the executive committee. When compromise candidate Dudley Sharp resigned as county chairman over a rules dispute, Nancy Palm as vice chairman ascended to the chairmanship and the coup de grace was complete.

Those rules, which dissipated the virtual total control exercised by the county chairmen of that era, contributed immeasurably to the Party's growth. The administration of Nancy Palm, a strong chairman by any definition, proved without a doubt that power doesn't have to be absolute in order to be respected. These rules were developed with input from our district leaders and were largely based on the experience of their workers. They were endorsed by a large majority of the county executive committee who appreciated the fair treatment assured by their concept—a far cry from the dictatorial tone of earlier bylaws. Nancy Palm's years as a county chairman, '68 through '77, and my tenure as Party secretary and unofficial organization director coincided. It was a complementary relationship. Our emphases differed but never conflicted. Nancy was issue oriented and a master of public relations, leaving me to quietly keep the organizational machinery in working order. Suffice it to say that all of our work was volunteer—no monetary compensation.

How did you get involved in running the headquarters in 1962?

FRAN ATKINSON, LUFKIN & SAN ANTONIO
Well, there wasn't anybody else doing it. So somebody had to. It turned out to be me. The county chair at that time was an old fellow. The women volunteers just didn't respond to him as well as they did to me.

He was smart to get you involved.

He didn't get me involved. I got myself involved. There were times he'd have liked to throw me out. I wouldn't do everything he said lockstep, Indian file. That didn't exactly appeal to him. I believed in a much more public operation than he did. But we were lucky to have somebody as county chairman.

County Vice Chairs

MARY LOU GRIER, SAN ANTONIO & BOERNE
In 1961, I became Bexar County vice chairman. The common practice was that a man was always county chairman, and he named a woman to be county vice chairman.

Was that an informal arrangement or was that mandated by the state Republican Party?

It was mainly a structural arrangement to enable more work to get done. As county vice chair, I could be at Party headquarters every day. I served with four county chairmen, and they couldn't be there on a daily basis. To get things done, you needed a woman with the time to spend on it.

Did Glenna McCord and Bobbie Biggart have different approaches and goals when they were Dallas County vice chairs?

BABS JOHNSON, DALLAS

They were both single-minded in goals. In methods, Bobbie Biggart was a staunch ally of the county chairman, and they were a good team. Glenna followed and worked with the same county chairman and was more aggressive than Bobbie in making suggestions and implementing them. Bobbie was truly a remarkable woman. She was a graduate of Sophie Newcomb and had a little softer approach. She persuaded people but underneath was an iron backbone about what had to be done. Glenna didn't have that soft of an approach but certainly was equally effective in getting things done and more innovative.

DOROTHY REED, AMARILLO

What were your responsibilities as the vice chair of the county party?

They were to work in the headquarters, get volunteers for headquarters, set up card files, and get lists of our voters. Then, of course, we started running the primaries. I didn't have to do any fundraising. When candidates would come to town, we tried to support them and get people out to meet them. It was just Party building and laying the groundwork for what's happening now.

GLORIA CLAYTON, DALLAS

Bob Porter asked me to be his vice chairman in 1972. I was a very low-key vice chairman. I knew a lot of people in Dallas County from all of the campaigns that I had worked on. Bob seemed to think that was what was needed to get volunteers back into headquarters. A feeling of "come help, you are welcome." Apparently, headquarters had gotten away from that a little bit.

Was it a challenge to recruit volunteers during Watergate?

No. We all needed to pull together. It made us stronger because it seemed like much ado about nothing at the outset. We would address envelopes, lick stamps, and watch TV. I was satisfied with achieving that. I felt like we had lots of volunteers to come by and stay on a regular basis. We wanted the door to headquarters open again.

How were you received as a woman participant in political meetings?

NADINE FRANCIS, ODESSA

I was welcomed because I was doing the work. I was always glad to have a good strong chairman because he could take over when there was a public meeting. I was interested in doing the background work. When I first got into working with the Republican Party there were two things that were evident to me. First, men assumed that I wanted to have an affair. I was a mother of four, a housewife, and supposedly bored. Well, when they saw that wasn't the case, they decided that I wanted to run for public office. That was equally as far from my mind. In the first place, I knew I couldn't win and I wasn't about to run.

The men were all very respectful, very helpful. I could go into any office in Odessa. If I called for an appointment, I could get in. They would sit back in their chairs, and I would listen to them tell me for fifteen or twenty minutes, sometimes longer, what they thought about what was going on and what we needed to do. Then they would say, "I have talked long enough. What did you come for?" They would be surprised that I came in just to talk to them and to hear their ideas.

MARY ANNE COLLINS, DALLAS

When I was the county vice chairman in 1963, the chair raised the money and I tended to the organization. It was a match made in heaven because he didn't tell me what to do and I didn't tell him what to do, and it just worked out great.

County Area Chairs

DOROTHY DOEHNE, SAN ANTONIO

I became an area chairman. Their responsibilities were to contact precinct chairmen within that area and keep in touch with them and try to get them to do the work that they were supposed to do.

VERA CARHART, RICHARDSON & HOUSTON

I was an area chairman in Richardson. I kept in touch with people and gave them gentle prodding—has he done this, you've got a deadline, can you do this for us, do you need some help?

County Headquarters

JOAN WOOD, WACO

We would find an old house somewhere, and people would contribute desks, chairs, and file cabinets. I don't even remember if Dorothy Wood was paid. It gave us visibility. People came in off the street and volunteered because they knew we were here.

BETTY KING BOYD, WACO

Dorothy Wood would open headquarters about 9:00 a.m. and close about 4:30 or 5:00. They kept excellent records. Everyone who could vote in McLennan County was on a 3-by-5 card. They had the telephone number and the address and how they voted, if we knew. We would check periodically on the county's voter registration list.

What was a typical day like at Republican headquarters?

BECKY HUSBANDS, WACO

We contacted people and reminded them what was going on. People called us, and there were other headquarters in other towns that would contact us. Then national would send us materials that we had to distribute. When John Tower ran for Senate, we went door-to-door and saw people. It worked. The main thing was there was always somebody there.

KAY DANKS, GALVESTON & AUSTIN

In 1967, I worked down at the county headquarters with Ruth Price who was running the headquarters. I went in the mornings and worked. Then I came home and picked up my daughter from kindergarten and took her down there. She played in the back room and we worked. We looked up phone numbers. We gave out literature. We had all the meetings down there. We set up for those, arranged for food, or did whatever needed to be done.

MARY DONELSON, AMARILLO

In 1982, I volunteered as a typist at headquarters. I have been at it ever since. We used to try and send out mailings. People still want us to send out a monthly newsletter. We can't do that. We have such a mailing list. Around '89 or '90, we sent out a first-class mailing. We came up with some figures then that have held true. There were 14 percent moved or lost people in nearly every precinct over the two-year period. We just couldn't afford that. Not even bulk mail.

JUNE DEASON, SAN ANTONIO

You'd have to get out a 20,000-piece mail-out. The days of direct mail were not operational then, and the money wasn't there, so it was women, women, women. They would pour into those headquarters and bring their lunch, or Ruth Baker would cook for twenty or thirty people every day. If you ever let them get out for lunch, you don't get them back. It doesn't take you long to realize that it's the women. If the Democrat women ever got a clue in their head as to why the Republicans are effective, one of the big reasons is we've got the women power. For years and years, we did it without money because we didn't have any money. Who's going to give to Republicans in Texas? So it was the women, and they've done everything from raising the money to being the drivers to doing the scheduling to running the campaigns.

They've done it all. Regardless of what the job is, they don't care. Yes, I'll do it. I don't know how, but I can learn. Sure.

Paid County Staff

DIXIE CLEM, PLANO

In 1968, the committeeman and the county chairman, who were Connor Harrington and Jack Carter, came to me. It looked like we were going to carry for Richard Nixon and also elect a constable. When we won, we thought we would open a county headquarters. So they called around and gathered up $350 and opened an office—a cubby-hole room just about the size of a bathroom. We had a filing cabinet and a desk and a table. There was only one other county comparable to Collin County that had a headquarters and that was in Waco. Dorothy Wood ran the office. I went down to visit her and patterned our records after the records in Waco. I stayed all day looking over everything and came back and tried the same things.

It was my job to set up a program for the county and find Republicans. So I chose every Monday as my visitation day in the county. I started out going to McKinney and then to Melissa. I visited John McVeigh, the justice of the peace. John would go with me and we would visit the people out in his area. We would go to Weston and Westminster. We had coffee in homes with people. That's how we found Republicans. I have a little book with all of my Monday visitations and things that I would say about the people after I visited with them.

On commissioners court day, I would visit. I was the only Republican going in. When I walked into the courthouse, they knew it from one floor to another. Since I was going to work with the tax assessor during the elections, I made sure we were friends. I could go into the office and be kind, and they would do anything for me. I knew they talked about me as soon as I left, but they were very nice. I always took the county clerk for coffee so that I'd find out anything I could find out. Targeting races made the biggest impact for the Republicans in the county. I looked at the vulnerable seats. That's why I visited all of the different offices. Even though I didn't know all there was to know about county government, you can learn pretty fast. You can see who is weak and who is strong. Then I would pick the vulnerable spots.

Jack Carter was our county chairman. He and I would go and visit people. Of course, we tried to talk two or three people into running for county judge back in those days, and they didn't want to do that. They just couldn't let their name be out there on the Republican ticket. Finally, we had two people who wanted to run for justice of the peace. We won those races. We ran George Smith for sheriff. We won that race. That gave us a constable, two J. P.'s, and a sheriff. That was our start.

Holding an Election

Finding a Location

BETTY STROHACKER, KERRVILLE

We got more people to participate in the Republican Party, and actually it was hard to find a place to have a primary election. The only type of building in the whole area of seventy-six square miles was a little one-room schoolhouse. It was after World War II, probably 1952.

We started having the primary in our living room. An election inspector came out one time. I went out and met him and his wife out on the road. I talked to him about what we were doing and the election. He came in, and he approved us and went on his way.

RUTH SCHIERMEYER, LUBBOCK

Early on, the Democrat primary voters entered the front of the schools and the Republicans were somewhere around the back of the building if you could find them. We had our sign on the door. I thought this was ridiculous. The first year I was in charge of the elections, I went to the school system and talked to the man in charge of all of the facilities. I asked, "How do you determine who gets the front of the school and who gets the other entrance?" He said, "It's first come, first served." I said, "Well, good, then I need to reserve the front of the schools for the primaries." He said, "Well, it's about time you got here. So it's the Democratic Party in the front entrance of the schools." I said, "No, sir, that's the Republican Party." He said, "Oh, I don't know if we can do that; we have always done it this way." I said that you just said it was first come, first served. I said that I was a really nice person and I would agree for both parties to use the front entrance of the school, then one could go one direction and the other go the other direction. Otherwise, I wanted the front entrance. He said, "I'm going to have to call the Democratic Party chair." I said, "You call him and tell him that I either want the front entrance or I am willing to have both parties go in the same entrance." It really was a milestone. People now can not believe that we used to have to go through the back door of the schools. That was the beginning of the recognition of the Republican Party as an equal.

SITTY WILKES, AUSTIN

I was involved in establishing a precinct in my area. They discriminated against us. I had to have the precinct meeting here in my living room. I remember serving beer. Maybe eight or ten people came. Then years later, Marvin Collins was the state director and they wanted to have a Republican primary in Bastrop County. They wouldn't allow it. We have a forty-three-year-old business in Bastrop. So Marvin went out there and met with my husband, Bob, who had a big payroll. It was one of the few industries in the town at that time. They went to the county courthouse and said, "We are going to have a Republican primary."

Running the Election

CAROLE RAGLAND, LEAGUE CITY

Before an election, I used to have all my workers over and work out a system step by step. I have a reputation for running smooth elections. The process is broken into components with each voter processed at one place. We divide the alphabet up according to what the demand will be with a team of two people at each station. The first takes voters' identification and looks them up in the book, and the other takes the I. D. and then the voter signs the ballot sheet. The voters don't get their I. D. back until they sign. We have about 6,500 voters and 800 early voters.

WINNIE MOORE, LUBBOCK

When people came to vote we would be sure that they were registered. We told them about the precinct convention, which we held right after the polls closed. As they were coming through the line I asked people if they would like to be a delegate to the county convention. I'd take their names down, so that when we had the precinct convention we would have something to go on. That took a lot of doing as they registered and went through the line.

Back then you had to have everybody you could think of working because you needed three people at every table counting votes. Two tallied and one called. There could have been three tallying and one calling at each table, so that if two of them were alike and the other one missed the count we had the correct total. We didn't have machines. As for the general election, when Republicans and Democrats were all on the same ballot, it might be ten or eleven o'clock at night before we got through because there were so many voting. The Democrats always had the presiding judge.

At first, they had the presiding judge and the alternate judge. The county commissioners are the ones that appoint them. Jane Bucy and I went down to the county commissioners and told them we thought we should have a Republican as an alternate judge. The Republicans never had any position back then. So they appointed Republicans as alternate judges.

ESTHER BUCKLEY, LAREDO

I was an election clerk. I learned how the Democrats ran the elections and when the Republicans started organizing their elections, I went over to work for them. There used to be one polling place in the whole city. By the time I finished my tenure as county chair, we had ten to fifteen polling places. We identified that we were going to be here and have primaries.

In organizing the elections, you had to establish a big structure. You must understand that this is a poor city. So a lot of the control that the Democrats had was through saying, I am going to hire you today for three dollars an hour or whatever. That was a lot of money. So when we said to them we are going to hire you as a judge, and you can bring all of your family in on that day, and I will pay for all of your family to come and work for me, this was different. We were able to start breaking that hold because we had jobs for them. When we hired the poll watchers, the Clements people understood what we were doing and the Tower people understood what we were doing when we told them we needed to hire an absentee poll watcher and we wanted them to be there and we wanted to pay them. Can you imagine what it means to a small family to have $400 or $500 come into their home?

We were damaging the Democrat structure. It was aggravating to the Democrats to have to say, yes, we have two parties. You can have that little tiny room over there in the back to count your ballots. It aggravated them that we were getting money from the state.

I was lucky because the county clerk I started with was a very nice old gentleman. Then the new county clerks that succeeded him were always extremely courteous and polite to me and respected me as an individual. I went to a lot of ballot security workshops. I studied the election code. They recognized that I spoke out of knowledge. They allowed me to criticize. I was even a presenter for the Democratic Party's election schools. Just imagine having a Republican telling the election judges what the law was.

County Conventions

NORA RAY, FORT WORTH

We had differences of opinions at county conventions even back then. Betty Andujar knew how to get her point across, bring in the vote, and get the right delegates. She did it in such a nice way. You didn't have the same bad taste with her after it was over and you lost. She could always make you feel like everything was okay and get the troops back together. I bet I've heard that speech a million times. She usually convinced all of us that it was the thing to do.

HARDY CHILDRESS, SAN ANTONIO

My wife, Beulah, enjoyed meeting people and working the crowd. What I would call the background politics. When we went to a convention and there was a person or an item on the agenda, she talked to people and persuaded them to believe like she did. Bob West, the head of Tesoro Petroleum, would go to senatorial district conventions. He would always tell Beulah, "Save me a seat. I want to sit by you. I don't know how to vote, so I want you to save me a seat. You tell me how to vote."

Rural County Organization

Recruiting Rural County Chairs

How did you recruit people to be county chairs in rural areas?

KATIE HECK, MIDLAND

Face to face. Just literally go to the city and talk to the people who were Republicans. That was a big problem in a place like Kermit or Pecos. You might get some people who sympathized with you and would secretly vote for you, but to get them to come out and be county chairman with the responsibility that involved was difficult. Being a county chairman has always been a chore. There are things that have to be filed and have to be done. They might not get done because the judges and all the people in the courthouse were Democrats. That's another reason that I admire Tad Smith so much. He was a lawyer in El Paso and took on the job. I hear it hurt him financially to a certain measure.

BERYL MILBURN, AUSTIN

We weren't really that successful in those rural small counties. It was really tough. But you just get on the phone and you talk to one person and then that person sends you to somebody else. You get a group together and you say, somebody has to be chairman because you have all these legal requirements, and eventually somebody will volunteer. Way back, many of those county chairmen were really regarded as the village idiot. They weren't very strong, and they didn't have any influence.

What was the participation in the Republican Party in the Marble Falls area in 1970?

CAROLYN KNIGHT, AUSTIN & MARBLE FALLS

Well, believe it or not they had a primary that year. They had had a very strong county chair, Mary Jane Allen from Burnet. She carried the banner for the Republican Party for any number of years in that county. Her husband was a doctor so she felt free to do that.

DEANNE CLARK, LUBBOCK & DIMMITT

When I lived in Lubbock in 1964, my boss's wife invited me to some things. She decided that I would be a good worker. When Goldwater was running, I got involved in phoning and meeting and so on. You could say I was hooked. I served in Lubbock first as a worker, then as a committee person telephoning, and so on. Leadership was sparse, especially out here and at that time because this area was primarily Democrat. You just had to have a little courage and conviction to work as a Republican. I ended up being the president of the Republican Women [*the Republican Women's Clubs became known as simply Republican Women*] here and then I went as a delegate to the National Federation of Republican Women convention. Those two things, with the tutelage of Vaude Roper, really got me started.

When I went to Castro County as a new bride, I didn't want to be involved in anything for a while. So after I had been there for about four years, I attended the county convention. There may have been ten of us. My friend wrote my name in as candidate for chairman. No one knew me there. So the committee went through the list of nominees and asked each one if he or she would serve. Each one turned them down until they came to me. I said yes. That was in 1976. Of course, I had a lot to learn. Fortunately for me, two of the ladies who had done the work in the past there, one as the vice chair of the Party and the other as the chair, helped me. I served until I moved in 1998. People are just grateful if you will do the work and take the responsibility. So I never considered not running or not serving during that period of time even though it certainly was hard. There were times when people would ridicule you or they wouldn't work with us at the courthouse. I believed in the party philosophy and in the candidates, and there was a nucleus of workers. Through working together and socializing together, you became friends and close, and I just stayed.

One of the things that helped us greatly was when the state of Texas started funding the elections. We would send in a budget of proposed election expenses. How much the ballots were going to cost. How much it cost to rent the place to hold the election. How much the workers would make. Then they would approve it and send us 75 percent and the final part at the end. Well, that turned everything around for the local party, having a chance to hold a primary and raise some funds for candidates.

In recent years, the secretary of state would send the chairman of both parties to Austin. Pay their expenses to attend the county chairmen seminar. It was excellent. That helped us not feel so disjointed. It gave us some training and encouraged us. At the state level, they were beginning to notice that there were going to be two parties.

MARY ANNE COLLINS, DALLAS

For the first time ever in 1996, we were able to have a primary in all 254 counties. My job with the Republican Party of Texas was to be sure that we had county chairman in every county. I love working with the county chairmen. You cannot have a good organization if you don't have good county chairs. The rural areas really inspire me because these people are working so hard. Some of them now have their first local candidates. I can just see the growth of their county parties. I went down to Goliad, and they hadn't had a primary. Their party got going and now they have local candidates. They carried for George Bush. So you see a lot of progress.

Rural Obstacles

KATIE SEEWALD, AMARILLO

Jack Porter was the Eisenhower head man in Texas. I told him when we were at the 1952 Chicago Republican convention, "I want to go back to Texas and work for Ike's election, but I can't do much without a telephone. I really need a telephone." He was the big honcho in the telephone company at that point. I got a phone in a very few months. None of us out here had phones. I put those two little children in the back seat of my two-door coupe, and we went all over this huge rural precinct, which was a big waste of time. So few people involved. But that was what I thought I was supposed to do.

What was the main obstacle to Republican Party development in your area?

LEON RICHARDSON, NEDERLAND

Labor. The oil industry was the main industry and still is, and there are a lot more workers than there are other voters. They were afraid. Back then the labor bosses told them how to vote. In fact, when I ran for the legislature, one of the sons of a family that lived across the street worked as a pipe fitter. He came over and said, "Mrs. Richardson, I would sure like to vote for you, I just can't do it because our chairman out at the pipe fitters' union says I have to vote for the Democrats." I told him you have to do what your conscience tells you to do. I'm sure he voted against me.

It's supposed to be a secret ballot.

I know. They had people thinking that they would know.

ANITA DAVIS, HEMPHILL

I'm about to tell you something that embarrasses me a lot. In '68, we really got angry at the fact that it seemed like there wasn't a lot of difference between parties. The Republican Party was not as conservative as we wanted it to be. We went with George Wallace. It had nothing to do with race. He believed in states rights, small government, and, we felt, truly conservative values. On election night that year, I had a sick headache because I was so afraid that [*Democratic presidential candidate Hubert*] Humphrey was going to win, and I promised that I would never do that again because if Nixon had lost it would have been due to George Wallace's campaign. I promised. I really was sorry that we did that.

DEANNE CLARK, LUBBOCK & DIMMITT

The first year that I served as county chair we took our election boxes to the courthouse and that particular county clerk said, "Oh, we don't take those." I said, "Who does?" and she said, "I don't know." I said, "Well, I think you do." "No," she said, "we don't. I only take the Democrat boxes." I said, "No, you take both sets of boxes." So we really had to train her. Someone turned in a complaint, and she immediately accused us of doing it. I said we didn't turn in any complaints. She named the person, and I said he has never even given a dime to us and never comes to anything. He is not a Republican.

The newspaper owner was a dyed-in-the-wool Democrat and had no patience with us. When his son came to run the paper, he tried to be fair and truly is one of my friends. He has confessed to me that in Arizona he was a Republican. He just had to be who he was as long as his father was living. Another thing that helped us in the long run was voting early. That meant people who wanted to change their vote could go in privately. Even though the county clerk knew who they were, and they had to ask for a certain kind of ballot, they didn't have to go to the polls on Election Day and show everybody that they had changed. Democrats had a grip on people by saying, this is what you have always been. They even had promoted through the years the theory that if you voted in the primary you had to vote for those candidates in the fall. We told them, no one is to know how you vote in the fall. You can vote anyway you want to. It took us a long, long time to even promote that idea. We were breaking a stronghold. Most of us lived around the corner, and we were neighbors. We weren't two-headed monsters. You know, it might be okay to be a Republican. I was Citizen of the Year one year. When I gave my little speech, I said, "I guess it is all right to be a Republican now." People thought it was funny.

Breaking into Closed Communities

BILLIJO PORTER, EL PASO

When Clements ran and Tower ran at the same time, it really helped the situation in West Texas—in Pecos and all of these little counties—because people liked them. They didn't like the liberal Democrats. Even though they might have been old-line Democrats, they were conservative. They were the John Connally Democrats. When he switched over, it was a shock to them, but then they came over. Even if we didn't have an organization in the rural areas, they would still vote with us in November. What has helped El Paso is the influx of people from other states.

How successful were you in growing the Party by starting Republican Women's Clubs in little towns in West Texas?

We got one started in Fort Stockton and one in Alpine. That was about it. I went to Dell City and Fort Hancock and other places. It was all they could do to have a county chair in some of these towns. Why not make the effort and let them know that you care about them as a Party? The Democrats never organized like we did. A lot of people in rural towns were afraid to become involved with the Republicans because they said, "My business [*would suffer*]." It was very difficult in the beginning to even get a chairman or somebody that would admit to being a Republican.

*When you were chair of the State Rural County Task Force,
what did you do to get the counties organized?*

ELLIE SELIG, SEGUIN

First of all, I would try and put people in categories. You are
not supposed to do it, but I did because it was the only way I could
figure out how to accomplish something. I had a list of people who
were farmers. I had a list of people in the dry goods business. I
would call the farmers at 6:30 in the morning because that was
when people would be in. It is awfully hard for people to say yes
when you have awakened them. So I stayed away from that. I
had a list of people who went to PTA meetings. It worked pretty
well.

DORIS MAYER ROUSSELOT, SONORA

The biggest challenge was getting the mind-set changed from
having to vote Democrat because my daddy was a Democrat and
my granddaddy was a Democrat. Back thirty or forty years ago
that's what people really thought. The only way my dad and Maxine
Browne did it was to just thrust it out in front of the people all of
the time and have a headquarters here even if nobody came in.
That's where people got the idea of what this was all about—maybe
we ought to look into it. Eventually, they just started winning people
over. Maybe people would think, "I don't have to vote for this guy
if I don't like him just because he is a Democrat." A lot of it had to
do with good Republican candidates. Good honest people who
were running—that worked to make this a two-party state.

FRANCIE FATHEREE CODY, PAMPA

Betty Brown and I were looking for someone to run a primary
in McLean. We were down there scouting it out. Somehow we got
in touch with this man. He invited us out to his house. They wanted
to know if we wanted some rhubarb pie. I said, "Oh, yes, that would
be lovely." Betty didn't like it but ate it. After the meeting, she said,
"I hate rhubarb pie." I said we had to get him to work with us.

DOROTHY CROCKETT, ODESSA & MARBLE FALLS

I was Llano County chairman and that was by default. We had a county chairman who was just sort of all by himself. He asked me to be his co-chairman. Then he said, "Take over," which I did. I started having regular monthly meetings of all the county's precinct chairmen. That is a common practice now, but then it had not been done. It was hard to get precinct chairmen to come to meetings. We had to meet at night.

In the mid-1970s, the first time I went up to the county courthouse to see about the ballot boxes and take the absentee ballots, I walked in the office. This old county clerk said, "Lady, we don't handle Republican absentee ballots, and we don't deliver your boxes." So I had to go around the back door and force him to take those ballots. He told me flat out he was not going to take them. The other people in the office stared at me like I was some kind of freak.

LISA COMPTON, CLYDE

The first time I lived in Callahan County and voted Republican was in 1994. We had sixty-eight people vote Republican. It took one person who rented a motel room and we voted there. Our first precinct meetings consisted of about five or six of us. Our county convention was at my kitchen table. There were about four of us. We had a congressional candidate, a state senate candidate, and a judge candidate running. They said, "We're going to put up a big tent." Luckily, I knew people in the community. I went to the church and got some women to make homemade ice cream. We sent a postcard to everyone who voted Republican saying we are going to have an old-fashioned ice cream social—come out and meet these candidates. They said, "How many people do you think will be here?" And I said, "I'll be happy if we have twenty-five people." We had over 100 people show up. We stayed and talked until we had to turn the headlights on because it was dark. They were hungry for somebody to come and talk to them. It didn't matter that the candidates were Republicans, they were just hungry for someone to talk to them.

RUTH McGUCKIN, HOUSTON & WASHINGTON COUNTY

We moved to Washington County. I became precinct chairman for about six years. It was interesting because when we moved up there in 1982 Washington County was like Harris County had been years before. It was all Democrats. There were no Republican precinct chairmen. If a person wanted to be a Republican, they had to go to the one place in downtown Brenham to vote.

State laws had changed and said that if the election judge was a Democrat counties had to have at least one Republican clerk. I called and said that I am a Republican and I would like to be a clerk at the election. He said we have never had any Republicans before. I said I would like to be the first one. He said we have never had any ladies work before. I said that would be great to be the first one to work. He said we can't pay very much. I said I worked for nothing for the first twenty years when I was election judge. He said you have to be here at 6:30 in the morning and you cannot leave until 7:30 at night. I said I used to work until midnight so that sounds fine. Finally, he said there won't be anything but men here. I thought, I like men. So I went and worked. They were very cool to me for the first few hours. After three or four hours the other two guys came over and said, "We really are glad that you are here because you make everyone show their voter registration certificates. They will never show them to us. They just say, oh, Bob, you know who I am." After that, he called and asked me to work the next election.

CHAPTER 9

National Politics

"The real purpose when you are in a Party position as far as I am concerned is to help get Republicans elected."   —PENNY BUTLER

*T*he Texas Republican Party made itself known on a national level, in part through efforts of the national committeewomen. Elected every four years by the delegates at the Republican state convention, the national committeewoman represented the state party on the Republican National Committee along with the state chair and the national committeeman. In addition, she raised money, recruited candidates, opened the doors of opinion leaders and financial donors to candidates, encouraged people to participate in the Party, and influenced national-level appointments. National committeewomen gave their all to elect Republicans at both the state and national levels. On occasion, their independent thinking produced surprises.

Every four years, the Party gave a pat on the back to loyal workers at the national conventions. Although there may have been some delegates or alternates appointed as repayment for financial support, women campaigned hard for the honor of representing Texas at national conventions. By their example, delegates often inspired others to get involved in Party work. "Spontaneous demonstrations" and nomination speeches interrupted long hours of Party business on the convention floor. In 1972, the whirlwind of history caught up with those attending the convention in Miami and gave them a glimpse of the underbelly of American society and a new reason to fight for the ideals they believed in.

Watergate hit Texas Republicans hard. Dissatisfaction and disappointment affected Republicans in every corner of the state.

They worked to keep one another's spirits up, most of the time
unsuccessfully. Only the integrity of local, state, and national Texas
leaders had the power to see the state party through this difficult
time. Not until 1978 did the Party have a strong unifying force in
the person of Governor Bill Clements to pull it out of the doldrums.

National Committeewomen

What makes a good national committeewoman?

BERYL MILBURN, AUSTIN

The ability to raise money, to travel, and to know people of
influence.

Did you know Thelma Black—Mrs. John R. Black—the na-
tional committeewoman?

MARY JESTER, DALLAS

Mrs. Black was great. She was national committeewoman for
quite a while. She was always helpful. One of the things that I
remember about her is she held receptions at her house and she
had a cattle counter in her hand. She shook hands and counted
how many people came. She knew what was going on. She was
generous and she raised money.

FLO KAMPMANN CRICHTON, SAN ANTONIO

Mrs. Black was national committeewoman. She sort of said
that she wouldn't continue on. So I put myself up for it. Then she
decided she would run, so I had to run against her. It was a little
bit dicey because they thought I was too young to be national committeewoman. I didn't think I was, but they had never had one that
young. Thad Hutcheson, John Tower, and others convinced enough
delegates that I wasn't too young to be national committeewoman,
and they got it through by acclamation. I went on the Republican
National Committee, and I was the youngest member there.

As the state vice chairman, I really did all the national
committeewoman's work from 1958 to 1960. Mainly, when you are

on the national committee you okay the appointments. Mrs. Black didn't have any particular interest in that, so I had to okay them. If somebody wanted to be the postmaster, they would write to me and I would write to the general counsel and to Jack Porter [*the national committeeman*] and it took a lot of time.

What did you do as national committeewoman?

BARBARA MAN, WICHITA FALLS & DALLAS

We were just trying to build the Party. I was going places to make speeches and just doing what I could to get people to turn around and become Republicans. I traveled to Brownsville, Amarillo, Wilbarger County, El Paso, Victoria, and Weatherford. I also campaigned for candidates.

RITA CLEMENTS, DALLAS

It was just a wonderful group to work with here in Texas, and the experience of getting to know Republican leadership around the country was great. I just served for a couple of years, the reason being that, when I married Bill, he was the deputy secretary of defense and had to be nonpartisan. He had to work with Democrat chairmen in the House and in the Senate. This whole discussion even went to the level of President Ford about whether it would be appropriate for me to stay on as national committeewoman. We all decided that it really wasn't. I resigned when I moved to Washington.

At that time, it was a big responsibility of the national committee people to help raise funds for the Republican Party of Texas. We really worked as leaders in Texas trying to help build the Party.

FRAN CHILES, FORT WORTH

National committeewoman is a wonderful job—influencing the platform and influencing the distribution of money. The national party actually controlled many things that we did. They didn't control Texas, but we tried to be good partners.

I set up an office and worked full time. There's no job description. I was committed to what we could do to make a difference. I always felt we could make Texas a really strong state. Our officers at the state level were in the position that, when the president made appointments, we could encourage certain people to be appointed. Sometimes we had some influence but not always. We did background material on appointments. But, basically, it was trying to get the vote out and get the candidates elected.

PENNY BUTLER, HOUSTON

The main reason I ran for national committeewoman was that George Bush was running for president. I knew that we needed to elect him. My opponent in that race was not for George Bush. I felt very sincerely that he needed every bit of support from the state of Texas that he could get. Fran Chiles, who was then the national committeewoman for Texas, was retiring so that is the only reason.

Once you were elected, what did you do to get Bush elected?

I became his state co-chairman for the campaign. I worked to get support for him and talked to various groups and urged them on. I would go to Republican Women's Clubs, Rotary clubs, and different business groups as well as to civic and neighborhood groups that wanted information and history or government classes in schools.

I served two terms, which is eight years. The state party decided to impose term limits on its elected officials. My partner was [*committeeman*] Ernie Angelo, who had been on the national committee for at least twenty years. I had no intention of being on the national committee for any more than twelve years. Maybe three terms. The national committee is made up of two elected people from each state, a man and a woman, and the chairman of the state party for each state. You really only see each other maybe twice a year, so it takes a while to gain seniority and to be on more committees or head a committee.

The real purpose when you are in a Party position as far as I am concerned is to help get Republicans elected. Mainly, you want people who can be elected and do a good job representing voters—and not based on two or three very narrow issues. We don't want to become a Party that is all so much the same and so narrow-minded that we think outside the square. We don't gain anything from that, and we don't draw other people in. We need new blood all of the time. We need young people and people who have wisdom to get involved.

When you are on the national committee, you can make it whatever you want it to be. You can sit back and go to meetings or you can raise money and talk to prospective candidates. You can remain neutral but you can still remain active with candidates who need advice and direction and need to find out how to raise money and need other mentors. All of these candidates need people along the way to say, "I will be glad to set the meeting for you with so-and-so who might be your finance chairman." I served in that capacity a lot.

What impact do you think being Republican National Committee co-chair and holding cabinet-level appointments had on the Texas Republican Party and its development?

ANNE ARMSTRONG, ARMSTRONG

I think they were proud that one of ours, and one who had been there from the early days, was chosen to be co-chairman of the Republican National Committee and later ambassador to Great Britain. I hope that it gave an impetus for people to think Texans are appreciated and our leadership is respected enough that they can hold national and international positions.

National Conventions

IDALOU SMITH, WACO

I went to San Francisco as a delegate for Eisenhower's second term. That was a great experience. To go someplace and hear them paging senators and governors and think they were Republicans made quite an impression on us and was very thrilling. The convention itself was pretty dull since it was all cut-and-dried, except I did discover that the spontaneous demonstrations are anything but.

MARY ANNE COLLINS, DALLAS

I was for Goldwater in 1960. [*Dallas County Republican leader*] Walter Fleming had sort of gotten me into the Goldwater thing. I had read [*Goldwater's book*] *The Conscience of a Conservative*. There was a Goldwater demonstration, and I got up there. I had my Goldwater placard. The sergeant at arms wasn't going to let me back out on the floor. That was in the days of high heels. I kicked that guy and I was back on the floor. That was the only way there was to get back on the floor.

BERYL MILBURN, AUSTIN

I was a delegate in '64 when Barry Goldwater was nominated. I was a Goldwater delegate. That was an exciting time. We thought we had finally defeated the liberal establishment in the east. That was really a watershed in the national Republican Party because Goldwater's nomination was a defeat of the Dewey-Rockefeller branch of the Party, the liberal Republicans. I remember at that '64 convention, I was so excited and thrilled. I would come out and talk to my husband, Malcolm, who was in the back. He wasn't a delegate and was watching all the TV people. He said, "They are just killing you on TV." I couldn't believe it. I thought it was just wonderful, just wonderful. Well, he was right. They had killed us.

How did you get to make a nomination speech in 1968?

FLO KAMPMANN CRICHTON, SAN ANTONIO

I thought a great deal of Richard Nixon at the time. He really had a side to him that was very thoughtful. We were friends. We were on a Flo and Dick basis. I was not happy with some of the people around him and some of the things that were being done. It was purely instinct. At the convention, I was an alternate. [*Texas activist*] Jack Porter called me and said, "Governor Reagan would like someone from Texas to second his nomination [*for president*]. Would you be interested in doing it?" I said, "Well, no, I'm really not. It's a nice invitation, but no thanks." He said, "Well, do me a favor. Would you go over and talk with him about it?" I said, "Well, that is embarrassing, Jack, if I'm not going to do it." He said, "Please, do it for me."

He was a friend who had done me a lot of favors. So I said all right. Helen Healey who used to be executive secretary of the Texas Republican Party was working for Reagan then. It was kind of easy to go over and see her, and then I went in and met with him.

It was a day or so before the nominations. I had a very pleasant visit with him. We never discussed it at all. We chatted away for about thirty minutes. I thought he was absolutely charming. I said goodbye and that was it. I happened to see a friend in the Rockefeller camp. I told him about this and said if I had my choice I would rather second Governor Rockefeller's nomination. He said, "Oh, I think he would be very happy to have you." So he went and talked to him. Then Len Hall, an old friend who was running the Rockefeller campaign, called me and asked me to do it. I said I couldn't do it until I told my delegation. So I called John Tower and I think I got Lou. John wasn't there. I said, "Go ahead and inform the delegation." Then I called George Bush and he said, "I'll go down and put a note in the box of every delegate."

How was it received by the Texas delegation and other delegations?

John Tower said they were just like a good little man [*laughing*]. They stood up when you came to the podium to second his nomination. I could count the delegates [*and know that there were not enough votes at the convention to nominate Rockefeller for president*]. I just decided that I would do what I wanted to do. The Governor had been very strong on national security and other things I was interested in, so I did it. I ran into Charlie McWhorter who was a big Nixon worker. He was so mad at me. He had been with Nixon a long time. It was like a sign of betrayal. But it really wasn't. I very much felt that Rockefeller would be a good president and a good administrator. The secret of the presidency is staffing anyway.

Well, it turned out all right. John Tower was shaking his head, but he came down to see me shortly after that. He explained that it really had helped some because there had been criticism of Texas voters that they were terribly right wing, and that was not going to sell nationally. So they were able to explain that there was one in the group who supported Nelson Rockefeller. We weren't all ultra right-wing.

JANELLE McARTHUR, SAN ANTONIO

Putting both the state and the national conventions together was a great experience. I was involved with three nationals. There have been some dangerous times, too. Miami was one of them [*in 1972, due to violent protesting*]. I remember walking with Senator Tower to the convention center and being told to lock arms and walk in the middle of the street. You didn't want to be out off the street. There were police everywhere. Of course, they had gas. You could see the smoke bombs. It was a dangerous period of history and you just hoped you'd get back safely. It was almost as if we were in a compound there at the Doral Hotel because no one could come in.

RITA PALM, FORT WORTH

My husband, Ed, was a delegate to the 1972 convention in Miami. I wanted to go, but I didn't want to go as just a guest. Matt Williams was the head of the *Fort Worth Press*, and he wanted me to be a press delegate. I sat in the press section. I loved it. The Texas delegation was staying seventeen miles from the convention center. You had to go by bus. You couldn't get through if you didn't have proper credentials. If you missed your bus, you just didn't go that day. They lined up city buses that had been burned out for something like four miles from the convention center. There were no cars. The bus that you were on went right between those buses to the convention center. It was a scary time.

Ed got a letter from the Republican National Committee that told him delegates could not bring children to the convention. Based on some of the intelligence work being done that indicated terrorists were going to put LSD in the water supply, it would be extremely risky to bring your wife or family. We had a big discussion on whether I would go. My dad decided that he would go. So Dad, Ed's assistant chairman who was a delegate, Ed, and I drove to Miami because we were even afraid to fly.

When we got to the convention center the first day, I sat next to Bishop Kinsolving who was a very liberal Episcopalian writer and the editor and publisher of a Greenville, South Carolina paper. When they brought the colors out, not one single press person

stood up. They were just up there talking. They played the national anthem. I was just so horrified. I couldn't believe that press
people weren't professional. So I stood up. They all looked at me
like, where is she from? That was a really memorable time because
of my stance. By the last day of the convention, everybody on our
side of the press stood up. I must have had two hundred of them
standing up. So it just takes one person to do something.

There was a guy over in Tyler who owned a bunch of television and radio stations. He said, "If you really wanted to write a
story, you'd go down to Flamingo Park." I said, "Okay." He said we
couldn't tell anybody because they wouldn't let us go. They didn't
want press down there. He said, "We're going to take a cab down
there and we're going to walk blocks. I have an NBC television
camera going with us, and I have got a *Time* magazine writer with
us, so there'll be four of us. There will be three men, so you will be
okay." It was one of the most memorable times of my life.

First of all, I had seen the protesting on television, but to be
in a beautiful city park and watch women without clothes on, the
effect of drugs, and Vietnam veterans sitting right there making
hash in their little tents . . . There were also a lot of splinter groups
like the Charles Manson-type people who were really way out.
They had Communist Party people down there. They had the Red
Chinese down there and there was a huge red Chinese flag. We
walked and took pictures for about two hours. Somebody jumped
the cameraman, and he got nervous and left. The *Time* reporter
and I saw pretty much everything.

It was the most decadent existence. I remember thinking, I
wonder if this is what America is going to come to? When we
want to make a change, we go to violence? We go to the ugly side
of life. I'm sure the 1968 Chicago Democratic convention was like
that. This was the inside of the country bleeding.

I wrote several articles for the *Press*. I would call in the story
and send it over the wire and then call in any particulars. Basically,
they wanted to know the social details. What were the ladies wearing? What were they eating? Life was still la-la land my children
say to this day. What came out in the press was little of what was

really going on. We had just been to the moon. We were going up, up, and away. Miami was the nasty side.

BARBARA NOWLIN, HOUSTON & FRIENDSWOOD

National conventions are very motivating. They are kind of like pep rallies. They get the troops motivated and moving. Some of the best motivators were Ronald Reagan and Jack Kemp. I did leave with the feeling that I had to go home and get busy. I doubt that a delegate leaves the convention and doesn't feel that way.

BIRDIE MORGAN, ABILENE

In 1984 when Kathy Webster and I were delegates, our husbands put us in. They said this is the time for the wives to be delegates. We enjoyed it. Of course our husbands were telling us what to do the whole time [*laughing*].

It sounds like you supported your husband's efforts through the years. Why did you think that was important?

I guess I'm a good wife. I believed as he did.

ALICIA CANTU, LAREDO

I guess the high point of my career was being a delegate to the national convention for Reagan. It's been hard work, and you realize that you have accomplished something and that people respect you and elected you to represent them.

CAROLE RAGLAND, LEAGUE CITY

You have to put in thirty years of hard labor to go to the national convention. It should be a reward for years of hard work. Giving some money to a few campaigns is not enough.

GLORIA CLAYTON, DALLAS

Going to the national convention as a delegate was so exciting. A reporter from the *Dallas Times Herald* called me and said it was a cinch that Nixon was going to be nominated. What was the thrill about going? I thought, where is he coming from? This is history being made, and I am part of it. It was an honor. I was very pleased to go. They didn't change any of my philosophy on politics, my thinking, or the way I look at candidates. It was just a real honor.

Many people think you have to give the Party a lot of money to be a delegate.

That wasn't the case with me! In those days we were known as the country-club party. That isn't totally true. There are money people in the Republican Party, but they are also in the Democratic Party. I don't know where we ever got that label. My gang was not big-money people. We were just dedicated.

DOTTIE SANDERS, HOUSTON

Do you know how to run for national delegate? You are not appointed. You get out and go to all of the clubs and speak to all of the different precincts. To get votes, you send out literature. You go to precincts and to the precinct chairmen. They are the ones that elect you. You work hard to get elected.

JEAN RAFFETTO, HOUSTON & SEABROOK

The biggest thrill for me was being able to be an alternate to the national convention in 1992. I never dreamed that would ever come about. As far as I was concerned, it was really an honorary thing. I don't think that you really influence anything at that level. It is pretty much all cut-and-dried by the time it all rolls around. It is fun to be on the floor with all of the speeches, but as far as having an influence at that point, I think it is done.

It gives delegates a charge to go back and work for the candidate?

Yes, I think so. I remember seeing Anna Claire Rice's picture on the front page of the *Houston Chronicle*. The fact that she was a union worker and a Republican made such an impression on me.

ANNA CLAIRE RICE, HOUSTON

I was at the national convention in Dallas in 1984. I was a delegate appointed by Senator John Tower. I was a union member.

It was so unusual for union members to be Republicans that the news media wanted to interview me. They asked all kinds of questions—how I got into it, why I became a Republican. I said that is what I believed. I have always felt like I was more conservative than the union people. Mostly, the union was Democrat. The *Houston Chronicle* man came and said, "I want to take your picture. We are going to put this in the paper." I didn't believe him. He put it on the front page of the paper. The news media just drove me crazy.

Hang In There—Watergate Years

Let Down

DOROTHY DOEHNE, SAN ANTONIO

In the early '70s, we had Watergate, and that was a bad time for the Party. We tried to raise enough money to keep the doors open and to help candidates and to recruit candidates. Of course, at that time, you couldn't get too many.

JANE BUCY, LUBBOCK

Nixon and Watergate. I worked my heart out for him and to have that happen, it just hurt. That same year [*1972*] someone broke into Republican headquarters in Lubbock and bugged the telephone. It was front-page news. All of the information was sent to the state election commission. They were all Democrats, and they didn't act. How ironic!

LEON RICHARDSON, NEDERLAND

Nixon. That was devastating. We all had worked so hard. I think it was devastating. I don't think it affected Texas as much as it did other states.

Drifting

How did you try and keep things together after Watergate?

PATTY BRUCE, EL PASO

It is really amazing. Vincent Kamendo was our county chairman. If he found an article on anything that was the least bit sympathetic towards Nixon, he would bring it into the office and Billijo Porter would run it off on the mimeograph and mail it out to everyone on our mailing list, just trying to keep our chins up. Then there would be people who would sit all day, watch the Watergate trials on television, and then come in and moan and groan. That was very hard to take, especially when they were members of the Party.

BARBARA PATTON, HOUSTON

I was elected president of Post Oak Republican Women during Watergate time. I felt it was incumbent upon me to rally support for our president and continue to boost everybody's morale. It was a dreadful time. People were terribly upset. "Republican" became a dirty word in a sense. Being identified with Nixon was no fun. I would type these letters and try to hold the club together. Of course, Nixon resigned. On a local level, as far as the Republican Women went, we had a meeting about a slate of candidates to run our club, and I was asked to stay on as president of the club. People wanted to just lay low. I thought that was not a good idea. So I passed the torch to someone who was sort of going to keep the name only. It really just dissolved. There was no more Post Oak Republican Women's Club. Years later, a number of the women who had been involved did end up belonging to Magic Circle Republican Women's Club, one of the most dynamic clubs in the country now.

BILLIJO PORTER, EL PASO

In 1973, I was hired to run the local Republican headquarters here. We got a lot of threats. I moved my office to the back because I didn't know what was going to come through that window. I got very ugly phone calls.

Why did you want to keep going to headquarters day after day after receiving threats?

Because Nixon and what he did was not the Republican Party! We still had a Republican Party and elected people with a lot of integrity out there. We needed to keep going. Some of the worst conversations I had were with people who were Republicans. They were the most angry and disappointed. I don't blame them. I was disappointed, too. But we kept on going. In 1974, we had 1,500 people who voted in the Republican primary in this county. That was nothing. We were really in bad shape, but the hard core hung in there and kept our headquarters and functioned as a Party. That was a really bleak year for us.

In '74 we had some statewide candidates. We kept calling people that had been with us for years and tried to keep them involved. We subscribed to a commercial recorder that listed everybody who bought a house in El Paso. We sent them a "Welcome to El Paso" letter, including precinct chairmen's names and where to register to vote. We didn't know if they were Republicans or Democrats, but we hoped that we were the first contact so maybe they would like us. I used to send out about fifty of those every month. We did get some response. It was just like building from the ground up. It was very difficult because there were a lot of people who didn't want to be identified as a Republican in those years. John Tower stuck with us. He would come into town and raise money for the local party.

Pressure in Harris County

NANCY PALM, HOUSTON

We had a terrible blow to the Party in 1972 when the Watergate situation developed. It was very obvious that it was going to be very big even from the time of the convention. I never felt like I was mistreated because I was a woman, but I think they thought I was a sitting duck. I have discussed this with very, very few people. During the '72 election, which was a very difficult one, I had five FBI men in the Harris County Republican office for approximately three to four weeks investigating the finances of the Party. They thought that money was being laundered through my finance committee. That is where Lee Stevens became such a real stalwart. I said, "Give them every piece of material that they want." I felt that way from the beginning about the local party. One of the members of my finance committee had given a very large check. The FBI thought that particular check was what financed the Watergate burglary. They thought that I would crumble, but I didn't have anything to begin with. It was all there in black and white. I became very interested in following the financial laws as they developed after that. I was meticulous about records.

Personal Disappointment

ANNE ARMSTRONG, ARMSTRONG

I was in the Nixon White House [*as counselor to the President with cabinet status*]. Luckily, I think I came out of Watergate with most people feeling I had no part in the shoddy part of that. I would have hated to reflect discredit on Texas. I don't think that I did. I was truly innocent. I even went to Nixon. I haven't told that story very often—about when I was in the White House and started hearing things about Nixon and Watergate that really troubled me. I was out traveling to other countries standing up for Nixon, our Party, and our issues. I went to Al Haig, who was then chief of staff in the White House. I said, "Al, I have got to talk to the President about these things and have him tell me that they are not true." Nixon was at Bethesda [*in the hospital*]. He had had pneumonia, but he was well enough at that point. Haig and I went out to Bethesda and I was alone with President Nixon and sat beside his bed and asked him these questions. He told me that none of this was true. He looked me in the eye. So I proceeded to defend him some more until midsummer of 1974 when we heard the awful tapes and I knew that was the end. There were several of us in the White House that went to Haig and said we were resigning. He said, "Hold it. This is going to be set right within a week or two or three." So we did not resign. Sure enough, with the help of certain senators Nixon voluntarily resigned, which is exactly what he should have done.

It was shocking to me. I guess I was still pretty naive when I went up there but, you know, as many people have said many, many times—if only he had told the truth. He had to have been disappointed in his people. If he had told the truth, it would have been gone. But it was very disillusioning to me.

I had admired Nixon. Certainly, there were stands that I didn't agree with. We had a big fight on wage and price controls. I didn't believe in them. Connally and Nixon did. But you are either going to get on board or you are going to resign if it is something you can't stand. Well, that one I decided to stay on—wage and price controls. On Watergate, I was ready to resign. I guess it was disillusioning to an extent but not ultimately because if he had done the right thing, which you and I have been taught since we were kids to tell the truth, he would've been okay. So politics is not unfair. Even in Watergate. If you hew to the eternal, you will be all right even in the toughest arena of the presidency.

How did the Republican Party manage to survive and later flourish?

With good people like George Bush. George Bush was chairman of the Republican Party during Watergate. His integrity was such that it was extremely reassuring to our people. I think that is what saved us, that and not despairing that good people agreed that Nixon had done a disservice to his country. Look at Gerald Ford—the soul of integrity. I think his character and that of others reassured people like me and other Texans at the local level. Overwhelmingly, people who represented our Party were wonderful people, good people, fine citizens. So the president had done wrong. He suffered the rest of his life. We lost his brilliance and his many qualifications, and he brought shame on the Party. But I think people we could be proud of were banners to hold up to reassure ourselves that there basically wasn't anything wrong with our Party. It was the president who had done wrong things.

CHAPTER 10

Cadre of Volunteers

"There were a lot of people who felt the same way I did.
They just needed to be gotten out of bed and out of the house
and down to work." —KATIE SEEWALD

*T*he Republican Party could not have developed in Texas without
volunteers. Volunteers organized, recruited candidates and
workers, raised money, ran campaigns and elections, developed
strategy, and worked with the media to name just a few of the
many jobs they did. When the time came to implement the
organization and campaign strategies and follow them through
to completion, the army of Republican volunteers was the
essential ingredient for success. As the Republican Party grew
and raised more money, paid managers and staff came on board.

Nothing impeded volunteer recruitment like the lack of
Republican social acceptability. Members of the economic, political,
and social establishment were Democrats. This establishment
threatened businessmen with economic repercussions if they participated. Women, however, were not subjected to the same constraints.
Many husbands gave tacit support to their wives as a substitute for
their own open participation. Prominent women across Texas
became involved in Republican politics, bringing with them their
friends and neighbors. Additionally, ranks grew with the influx of
new Texans drawn to the state by military transfers, growth in
business and industry, and the arrival of the space agency, NASA.

Once recruited, volunteers started at the bottom and
earned their way up by working hard and learning the ropes.
Volunteer management is a tricky business. Since volunteers can
come and go as they please, keeping them interested and motivated was a constant challenge. County chairs and headquarters

*and campaign managers discovered, though, that in many cases it
only required a simple "thank you."*

Acceptability

The In-Crowd

How were you able to get people to participate?

PATTY BRUCE, EL PASO

They were mostly young women. I found a lot of them were
embarrassed. There was still a lot of the attitude that this is a man's
business and I'll do what my husband tells me to do. This is a
terrible thing, isn't it? But it was very true.

When did the Republican Women's Club start up in El Paso?

It started up fairly soon because when he was county chairman Tad Smith's mother and his wife and his sister Dorothy Purse
all headed up these clubs. They had been well-known Democrats.
When Tad said, this is nonsense, we are not conservative Democrats we are Republicans, he brought his brother and mother along
with him. They were very influential among the women. The early
club was like a huge social event, too. That was the way they brought
all of these women out. This was something new, something great.

*It was important to gain social acceptability before you started
talking about the Party.*

Yes, exactly.

*What would you say you have been able to contribute during
your political career?*

Making it socially acceptable for a woman to be active and to
have strong opinions on politics. I was talking to the bridge club
I've belonged to for twenty-five years the other day. I said, "Do
you realize that I never, ever told any of you how to vote?" They all
said, "You knew we were going to vote with you." I said, "No, not

from some of the things that I heard about the husbands." There was a lot of laughing and talking about how they had been able to convince their husbands from things they had learned. It is perfectly all right for women to be politically active.

PATTILOU DAWKINS, AMARILLO

Emmy O'Brien was one that made politics not popular, exactly, but prudent. It didn't ruin your reputation if you went down and helped somebody run for office. She took it out of the smoke-filled rooms and made it respectable for women to work on a campaign.

SITTY WILKES, AUSTIN

You're ostracized socially. You're hurt economically. You have to be a strong person. My friend had put me up for one of the clubs here. They said that I was too controversial because of my Republican leanings.

Beryl Milburn was always socially in. She was a Buckley. She was already established—a member of the Junior League and everything. It didn't hurt her socially. We would meet at her house and go door-to-door. Malcolm [*Milburn's husband*] was always behind her. They were highly regarded. Her friends were the bankers downtown who were Democrats. She made a profound impact.

She invited Bill Buckley [*conservative author and commentator William F. Buckley Jr.*] to come down and speak. We had so many people buy tickets that we had to keep moving where he was going to speak from one place to another. Over one thousand people came. Even she was shocked. He was just going to come and address us as a conservative. It was before he was "in."

ELLIE SELIG, SEGUIN

I damn near lost all of my friends when they found out that we were Republicans. People took us off the guest list. It wasn't that easy to be Republican.

What motivated you to withstand the pressure not to be a Republican?

I couldn't stand what was going on. I figured that some of my ideas were just as good as the ones that weren't working now. I just don't believe that people should have one voice. It is always good to have another opinion, another voice.

Why did you need a thick skin?

ANA OCHOA, LAREDO

Because of the animosity we experienced with local people. We encountered a lot of it. I remember being warned by people: don't get involved because you are going to be ostracized. Whether we were, I really don't know.

I'm a person of principles, sometimes to my own detriment. I felt very sincerely that this was desperately needed. It was almost a mission to be able to bring bipartisan politics to this town. I felt very strongly. Whenever I tackle something and set a goal for myself, I usually succeed. I never cared much what people think.

GWEN PHARO, DALLAS

Republicanism was becoming socially acceptable in Dallas. Many of the Junior League members were involved in Republican politics. I would say most of them, because of the frustration of thinking that our whole government was being influenced by foreign elements. We also subscribed to *Human Events*, and we read books. Working in the Republican Party became the thing to do. It was the late '50s and early '60s.

DEE COATS, HOUSTON

George and Barbara Bush were popular people. On our side of town, they were just "in" people, and all of the people that you knew wanted to work. It was just a fun place to be.

Economic Pressure

LOIS WHITE, SAN ANTONIO

There were just three of us over here. They told us we should be precinct chairs. So we volunteered. We got materials, and they invited us to events. We started trying to find people who would work with us. We really didn't. I found somehow six people in my precinct. The other ladies found about that many. Many people liked what we were doing but didn't want to be identified with the Party. People had been involved here politically, and it has been said that there was a machine here among the blacks. The boss had all of the black people's poll taxes in his safe, and when someone was running the candidate gave him some money and the boss would vote for them. We three women had all come here from other parts of Texas. We thought we found an attitude here we didn't find among blacks in other towns. People were very wary of getting involved in politics because someone might harm you economically because of the way you had voted.

FRANKIE LEE HARLOW, DEL RIO

I would go and talk to the president of the bank. I would say, "Why are you still voting for the Democrats?" He said, "I couldn't afford to get mixed up in politics." A lot of businesspeople told me that. They said, "We will go vote right, but we can't take a stand." It wasn't safe. Americans put the dollar first always.

POLLY SOWELL, McALLEN & AUSTIN

My husband was a merchant, and he used to say that he lost business because of my activities in politics. He probably did, but then he probably gained some. It was an excuse that people used if they didn't want to do politics. It's a legitimate excuse. You can't argue with people when they say that to you. It was particularly hard for lawyers. They had to practice in front of Democrat judges. Always take off your hat to a lawyer who has been the first in his area to change parties.

CAROLE WOODARD, HOUSTON & GALVESTON

When I first started being very active in Republican politics in the 1980s, there was quite a bit of opposition in Houston among blacks. I was penalized tremendously for being a black Republican. I lost a contract with the city of Houston. I worked for AT&T.

I lost a contract for AT&T because I was a black Republican, and we came in the lowest bidder.

It was devastating. You can't believe people would lack that much character and integrity. You can't believe that politics could let those kinds of things happen, but I learned very early on that it did. They thought I would lose my job, but I didn't. The black Democratic structure was such that they went out of their way to try and penalize black people for being Republican, especially if your business was something that they would have direct influence on. We were ostracized from anything that basically had black Democrats in positions of authority or in positions of power in city government or local government. They made sure that you were penalized. It was very mean spirited. I would think that any intelligent black person would see that having a two-party system is very healthy for any race of people and in our government. Why would all black people want to be Democrats?

How have women helped the Republican Party gain a foothold in El Paso?

BETTE HERVEY, EL PASO

I think the women made a difference because they weren't locked in like men were. We were freer to think about it without regard to our jobs. Women could be more outspoken and have less to risk. So many of us women were not working. We had time to get together and talk about it.

Recruiting Methods

CAROLINE PIERCE, HOUSTON

My main pitch is just to be involved. Our greatest problem in the country today is apathy. If nothing else, even if you can't come to the meetings, just looking at any club's newsletter will keep you a better informed citizen. I suppose that is my main pitch—try and become a better informed citizen. I have never had a problem getting people to volunteer.

WANDA EIDSON, WEATHERFORD

We had an advantage here. We knew the people. The town was about half the size then. Later on we did some telephoning, too, and located some help and found out who was supporting us. You had to find out who lived where. Of course, then some thought that it was too much or too hard, and it wasn't. They just didn't know what they were supposed to do. That was about all there was to it. You just had to talk to them.

MARY LOU WIGGINS, DALLAS

I called ten people and asked them to be a captain. Then they could get ten people. That was really it. You would do it on a precinct level. Of course, you do it a lot with precinct chairmen. You have a hierarchy.

Personal Influence

KATIE SEEWALD, AMARILLO

The only way that I ever got people to work was to say, follow me. I got out in front and worked my ass off and tried to get them to do the same thing. There were a lot of people who felt the same way I did. They just needed to be gotten out of bed and out of the house and down to work.

JAYNE HARRIS, SAN ANTONIO

In the early '60s, I had become deeply involved in the schools. Through the Northeast school system, I met one of the most unique, wonderful women I have ever known in politics in my life—Cleo Bohls. We became very good friends. In the migration from school to politics, she took some of us with her and I was one of them. Cleo convinced me that there was something to be said for this.

CAROLE RAGLAND, LEAGUE CITY

Whenever people express an interest to me, I ask, "Why don't you join the Republican Women's Club or help out at a phone bank?" My husband gets angry with me. I always ask whether they are a Republican or a Democrat. People just need to be asked. Sometimes it surprises me because I'm not aggressively trying to recruit. It's not like I am trying to sell Amway.

LAVERNE EVANS, EL PASO

It has been really on a one-to-one basis, just talking to people and inviting them. The surprising thing is you can know people for years thinking that you don't discuss politics, and then all of sudden you find out that they are Republicans and all the time you thought they were Democrats. I taught for a long time, and we could not discuss politics at work. Then you find all of a sudden, very cautiously, that someone has the same beliefs that you do. Then you can approach them about joining.

DONA BRUNS, NEW BRAUNFELS

When we moved into town, Robbie Borchers saw me at the library. She knew that we were Republicans. I was walking into the library where the Republican Women met. She saw me and came out and said, "I want you to be at the club meeting today." Somebody said, "Who is going to volunteer to have the membership luncheon at her house?" Robbie turned around and said, "Dona, you have enough room. Would you like to have it?" I reminded her of it recently and she said, "Did I really do that to you?"

What did you find effective to influence people?

MARY GARRETT, DANBURY

Person to person if you don't push, and I don't. But I always talked about the candidates I liked and who I was for.

In what ways did it help to have people like you who were well known in the community say that they were Republicans?

It means so much if they are respected. It does mean everything. I knew the Democrats would vote Republican once they knew me. Just the fact that you're not disliked.

THEO WICKERSHAM, SAN ANTONIO

Barbara Schoolcraft got me involved. We played bridge together. She got everybody involved. She'd say, "Come with me, Theo, you'll enjoy it. I guarantee that you'll enjoy it or I'll give you your money back." That was her slogan. I thought, well, she sets a fine example because people would see what a workaholic she was and how much she believed in her candidates. I think people respected her, and I looked up to her. I still think that one of the best ways to get people involved is to set a good example.

Volunteers Who "Volunteered"

GLENNA McCORD, DALLAS

After the 1962 election, I was down at Republican headquarters one day when these three lovely ladies came in. One was a retired schoolteacher, one was the widow of a very prominent doctor, and the third was also a retired schoolteacher. They were black ladies. They wanted to know if I would help them organize a Republican Women's Club. That was one of the most delightful experiences that I had. Mrs. McKinley was one of the retired schoolteachers. She told me how she had attended a teachers' meeting before school started one fall. Dr. White was the school superintendent in Dallas. In the course of his talk to the teachers, he turned to those teachers of color and said, "From now on, I don't want to hear any of you ever teach about Abraham Lincoln, that he freed the slaves, and that he was a Republican. Don't you ever, ever teach that in your classroom." It was at this point that Mrs. McKinley stood up and resigned.

I went to a luncheon at the home of one of these ladies, and she had invited all of these folks in. They said that they knew what had been going on in their neighborhoods on Election Day and they wanted to try and do something to stop it.

HOLLY DECHERD, AUSTIN

I actually found a meeting and just showed up. I quickly learned how much you appreciate anybody that did that. I soon began to fall on people's shoulders with a hug if they would just show up at meetings and say that they were interested in Republican politics.

New Texans and Population Shifts

MARY LOU GRIER, SAN ANTONIO & BOERNE

The poll list had the state of birth and year of birth of each voter. We found that if we would go down those poll lists and look for people who came from traditionally Republican states like Ohio, Indiana, Nebraska, and Kansas we could almost call them cold turkey. At least we'd feel safe that they wouldn't hang up in our ear. We got some volunteers that way.

CAROLYN KNIGHT, AUSTIN & MARBLE FALLS

My husband had been very active in Republican politics in South Dakota. I got involved shortly after I retired from the U. S. Air Force in 1963. You couldn't actively support political parties in the military because of the Hatch Act.

MARGARET COSBY, BOERNE

It wasn't that we wanted to change things as newcomers, it's just that you brought other things with you from wherever you were before and introduced them. Maybe they were good and maybe they weren't. Maybe they'd work and maybe they didn't. A lot of the old-timers didn't want to hear it. They didn't like change. I don't think the newcomers really wanted to change things, they just wanted to bring what they had with them. That's the way the country evolved in the first place. People coming over from England brought what they had with them and did what they could with what they had. I just lucked out with a whole bunch of nice ladies. You have to respect each other, and I think the Republican ladies are pretty terrific. They accepted new ideas or tried them anyway. If they didn't work, well, then you can abandon them. Sometimes it's worth a try. They tried everything.

MARY DENNY, DENTON

The county party was really only organized in the city of Denton. Johnia Everett and Phyllis Babcock ran things through the '70s, probably starting in the late '60s. We tried to branch out, but we had not really seen the growth in the south part of Denton County, which is heavily Republican now. That's where all of the Republicans have come from as they moved north, mostly from Dallas County.

BETTY AND KEN RUMINER, SEABROOK

Ken: There was a big melting pot of people coming from all over the country for either industry or for NASA [*just southeast of Houston*]. It was unusual to meet a native Texan like Betty. Industry made us a cross section of the country, professional and higher-level people, I would say. Most of those have a tendency not to think "socialism" and to think "free enterprise and less government."

Betty: A few of the early girls lived in Seabrook and some lived in El Lago, but few people I knew in the early years were ever from Texas. They moved from elsewhere.

PATTI ROSE TRIPPET, WACO

There was a big influx of people in Waco after the war. They made all the difference. They were a help to get us started in the Republican Party. One girl had lived in Oklahoma before she married. One was from California. There were people here with new industry. There were people who were stationed here during the war at our two air force bases who came back and settled here. They were so helpful in maintaining headquarters primarily and putting the name "Republican" before the public. Up until then, everybody in the county was a Democrat. It was so helpful to have new people move here with new industry in the '50s and '60s. We got a lot of northerners but they were Republicans.

Party Switchers

RUTH COX MIZELLE, CORPUS CHRISTI

We tried to be friendly to the Democrats because our life was made up mostly with friends who were Democrats. I always told them, "You are a Republican and just don't know it." We would talk with them and introduce them to the candidates we had, and they turned.

JOAN BIGGERSTAFF, PLANO

My husband and I are both from Plano, and we have deep roots here. We were in [*Democrat and Speaker of the House*] Sam Rayburn's congressional district. Our grandfathers contributed to the train ticket to send him to Washington the first time. They worked his district, and we were raised from that perspective. We became business owners, and so we have a business perspective. We were very interested in the overall view of the community. The Democratic Party had become very complacent and really bogged down. There were longtime officeholders who were probably never qualified. It became very apparent that there was a lot of stagnation.

How did you decide to associate with the Republicans and break from family tradition?

It was a rational process. We were in business. There was a need for conservatism. It certainly did not mean that you could not be concerned about issues. One day the county chairman, Roland Dickey, and I went out driving around on the far edge of Plano. He said, "Joan, you look at those new houses out there. Three out of five of them will be Republicans." He was wrong. It was five out of five. They brought with them a more moderate conservatism that made it more comfortable for me. There were things that I could identify with that I wanted to work for, and at the same time we did have a duty to look after our place and the people in it.

BARBARA NOWLIN, HOUSTON & FRIENDSWOOD

We met once a month at precinct meetings and had speakers. When Hank Grover [*Democrat state representative later Republican candidate for governor*] switched parties and became a Republican, he met with us very early on. We tried to pick his brain about how Democrats do things. He was not as helpful as we had hoped he would be. He wasn't trying not to be helpful, it was just that he had come unprepared to answer those questions. We were saying, we want to know about what you plan to do and what you want to run for, but tell us about how the Democrats do this.

IRIS MANES, HOUSTON

I didn't call on the Democrats unless they first indicated they were interested. There were a lot of them that came in. People who belonged to organizations like Pro America would volunteer every day.

Do you think that former Texas governor John Connally switching parties brought in more people?

RITA CLEMENTS, DALLAS

Certainly. John Connally switching had a major impact. I was Republican National Committeewoman when he did it [*1973*]. I remember well the public announcement that we had in Washington. We felt like it was very helpful.

Why did people switch to the Republican Party?

JOAN GAIDOS, DALLAS

The line that you hear nowadays is the Democratic Party left the more conservative Democrats behind. They were looking for an alternative. The Dallas County group was very hard working and industrious. People just kind of figured out that the Republican Party was a little more to their way of thinking at the time. It was just a philosophical thing.

Nobody really liked [*Lyndon*] Johnson, and nobody liked [*Senator Ralph*] Yarborough as far as the people I knew. I don't remember knowing a Democrat in those days that did. They might call themselves Democrats, but they were really more along the Republican line. They didn't like Sam Rayburn, Ralph Yarborough, or Lyndon Johnson. In fact, we really didn't much like John Connally [*laughing*].

RUTH POTTER, DALLAS

When the Republicans finally got a foothold, we became a viable party. People began to switch to the Republican Party. It happened in degrees. Most of the Democrats were conservative. The national party left the Texas Democrats when it became so socialistic.

CAROLE KEETON RYLANDER, AUSTIN

I, like everybody else in Texas, was born a Democrat. When I had to choose [*a party to run for office*], I chose to become a Republican. When I ran for my third term as mayor [*of Austin*], every single Democrat organization endorsed my opponent, but I won the election. I have always been a fiscal conservative. I switched parties back in 1985. It really is true that I did not leave the party, the party left me. There used to be a place for someone of conservative thought in the Democrat Party. That is not the case anymore. In 1985, everyone looked at me like, why in the world are you doing this? I knew that my party of the past was not the party of the future.

I don't really talk Republican or Democrat. I talk Texan. I think Texans, mainstream Texans, are very conservative. I want reform and results. I want to shake the rafters of bureaucracy from top to bottom. I found that was the Republican agenda. So I proudly became a Republican. When I went to the University of Texas, one of my professors said, "This is a one-party state, and it will always be a one-party state." I found a paper I wrote my senior year at the university that said if the Democrats were not careful they were going to create a two-party state. Democrats were running those of conservative thought out of the party. That is precisely what happened.

NANCY CANION DAVIS, GALVESTON COUNTY

You can not run without issues in a traditionally Democratic area. You have got to have a wedge issue that strikes at the heart of some large group in your area. If you don't, you can forget it. I don't care how much money you dump in there, you are not going to change them. I am just absolutely convinced of that.

> *Once you're able to get them to vote for a Republican, were you able to hold on to them?*

A lot of the people were on the edge anyway. It gave them the nerve to switch.

> *How important was it to try and get Democrats to change parties?*

FLORENCE NEUMEYER, HOUSTON

That was something that I guess all of us worked on more in our neighborhoods than anything else. My particular precinct was a Democrat precinct. The way I handled it in my precinct was I just took literature around. I put it on doors with a note. That is the way that many of us did it. By sticking with it and continuing to let them see that we thought it was really important. It gradually made a difference to your neighbors. It didn't happen overnight. We had Bill Archer, who was a Democrat [*and state representative*]. That was a big deal when he switched. His philosophy was so Republican, so conservative. Many people related to it, and the very fact that he came out and said "the Democrats left me" made it easier for other people to realize that and own up to it.

> *How did you keep Democrats who jumped on the bandwagon from dropping out?*

It was always a battle. We tried to know what was really going on at the local level and what motivated people. Issues can be presented in such away that you don't endear yourself to the people who are on the opposite side, or who would come in and not feel like they were really one of you yet. It is a constant battle. You have got to be genuine. If your approach is consistent, it may take years, but that is how you win.

Latin American Women

POOLIE PRATT, VICTORIA

We worked so hard to get Latin Americans in the Party in the 1960s. We could see that we were never going to carry Texas without them. There was a lady named Lupe Ortiz that Bette Jo [*Buhler*] and I both worked with. She was a devout Republican. We got her to go to Washington as a member of the Texas delegation to the National Federation of Republican Women's Clubs convention. She was wonderful. She did a lot of work for us. The only problem was that Mexican Americans kind of resented a woman having so much authority and power. I don't know whether it helped us with them or not, but she was certainly wonderful.

Young Republican Organizations

ANN QUIRK, AUSTIN

I got started in Young Republicans the last part of my junior year in high school. At that time the Teenage Republicans, the College Republicans, and the Young Adult Republicans were all in one group with one convention and one set of fights and factions. When you graduated from high school, you were already locked into a group or faction of friends. When you went to college, you continued the same battles. In 1974, I believe, the Teenage Republicans, the College Republicans, and the Young Adult Republicans separated.

I ended up being the state co-chairman of the Young Republicans and doing the national Republican deal. I had continual

Young Republican activity from about '67 through '81. Obviously, we didn't have the officeholders or candidates that exist now. It was Senator Tower and one or two congressmen and Jim Nowlin [*state representative*] from San Antonio. The pool of people to move into campaign volunteer activity or to work on campaigns was quite a bit smaller. The impact of a bus of Teenage and College Republicans on a special election in the Valley or in Dallas for a weekend of block walking was a real shot in the arm to a candidate, particularly in a special election.

It was different from the Republican Women's Clubs that worked in their own communities?

There were a lot of differences. There was also a period of time that I was real involved in TFRW [*Texas Federation of Republican Women*]. The differences were obvious. The women who were such driving forces with the TFRW had families and had social lives, whereas the Young Republicans was a group who could take the whole weekend and go to the Valley. When you are that age, you can pick up and do things on weekends. Instead of going to football games, we went to our quarterly board meetings. The women had a leadership track. You pretty well knew if you were third vice president that you would be president in three cycles. I don't think I ever recall a really divisive TFRW convention. The Young Republicans were always very competitive, with lots of money spent on these conventions. I put Watts lines in our house in order to make phone calls in the state for free. It was a really sophisticated and wonderful training ground for convention politics.

Why did you decide you wanted to sponsor a Teenage Republicans club?

BILLIE WHITEFIELD, HOUSTON

I had two interested teenagers. We had a young man running for the statehouse. At that time my daughter, Patricia, who was the president of the group, was the only one who could drive. They were so thrilled because she could take a whole carload over to the headquarters. They would come home and say, "Mama, he has got a refrigerator full of all kinds of cold drinks and lunchmeat and cookies." It was an opportunity for them to do something on their own. It kept them busy.

GAYNOR GALECK, AMARILLO

We would take our children with us to go door-to-door and put flyers in the doors. So we raised our children as Republicans. They were the legs.

Why did you decide to work with teenagers instead of building a precinct organization?

ANA OCHOA, LAREDO

They were the future. Whatever happened here was going to take a long time. I got the idea at a state convention. I came home all fired up. I called the few kids I knew that babysat for me. They said, yes, that sounds great. Then I remember calling a young man to work with us. His mother answered the phone and said, "You know, Ana, we vote that way, but we don't want our son to become involved because we are afraid of the repercussions that the involvement would have for us on a business and a social basis." I said, "That's all right. I don't want to cause problems for you." From then on, every young person that I would think of, I would call their parents to get their authorization. The kids were involved in everything at school. They were the top students and the most popular, so it was a fun, fun group. They helped us with the campaigns. They were so enthusiastic. It was fun working with these kids and getting them fired up. It caused quite a bit of talk in the town because this had never happened before.

TAFFY GOLDSMITH, DALLAS

I could see that we were not drawing young people in and that we needed them to come into the Party. The best hope for us seemed to be Young Republicans. As we began to grow, we got a lot more help. It was so hard to get young people involved. We had to educate high school and college kids about the Republican philosophy.

LINDA UNDERWOOD, HOUSTON

I would say one of the Young Republicans' best efforts was "Registration Day" to register Republicans and especially young people. That was where we felt we could do the most. We went to shopping centers and grocery stores. We set up a card table in front of a grocery store. We usually wore red, white, and blue straw hats and were real friendly and tried to get people registered to vote. We organized this all over the state. We had certain times of the year that we would have drives.

POOLIE PRATT, VICTORIA

In the '60s, I was worried that the Young Republicans might embarrass us. The state chairman was worried there might be some sort of scandal at one of their meetings that would embarrass the Party. He thought they should be chaperoned. Of course, the Young Republicans took a very dim view of this. They had never been chaperoned. Chet Upham from Mineral Wells and myself were appointed the liaisons from the state committee to the YRs.

They were about to impeach their president. It was around the 1968 national election. We did not want them to impeach their president. You had two factions in the YRs. They fought all of the time. The weather was so bad that Chet could not fly in. I got there, and I was going to talk with everyone in both groups. They bugged my room. They were so sure that we were going to interfere. Chet drove down and when he got there, he smelled a rat. He opened the door to the room next door, and you had never seen such a sophisticated system. The YR faction operating the system was on the far right. Chet and I had to call Peter [*state chair Peter O'Donnell*] and tell him that, in spite of us, they impeached their president. Fortunately, it didn't make much news.

MAYETTA PARR, AMARILLO

We had a real good Young Republicans group. In fact we elected Kenneth Kohler a state representative. The Young Republicans did a big part of that with the help of the county chairman, who was Brice Beard, and Jean Wedding, the vice chairman. I felt so sorry for her because we would go in and say, Jean, we'd like to do thus. She'd say we couldn't do that. Oh. Well, we did that already. We helped get [*Congressman*] Bob Price and Senator Tower elected.

LOIS WHITE, SAN ANTONIO

I was a teacher, so there were a lot of things I could get kids to help me do. I had a party in my yard, and we would make signs. I was able to start a Teen Republicans club. I would ask the children to help, and I would ask their parents. Many parents would not get involved, but they wanted good experiences for the kids. We had a good time.

SYLVIA NUGENT, DALLAS & AMARILLO

I moved to Dallas and got involved with the Dallas County Young Adult Republicans. This was a group that was very active in Dallas. I was on their executive committee. The Young Adult Republicans were twenty-two to forty years old, basically. It was designed in such a way to attract young people. There was a big social component, with a happy-hour type meeting every month, ski trips, and that sort of thing. Then we did a lot of things to help "down ballot" candidates. It was a very grassroots kind of an operation.

It was key in helping develop my philosophy because it was the height of the Vietnam War. There were war protests going on everywhere by young people in our age group. We were kind of in favor of the war. We were supporting our troops. We felt that it was shameful for the most powerful country in the world to be at war with a country half the size of Texas and not winning. It was a big mistake, and our group learned from that. My ideas were forming and being set in stone. The exposure had a big impact on my beliefs.

Team Effort

BETTY AND KEN RUMINER, SEABROOK

Ken: I am retired now, but when I was working I just really didn't have time to go do the things and make the contacts—so it was all through osmosis that I did whatever I did.

Betty: He allowed me to be gone sometimes twelve hours a day to do the telephone banks.

TEDDY PETERSON, SAN ANTONIO

One of the greatest things about Lou Tower was when I was working in Senator Tower's phone bank and she visited. She asked everyone to come and bring his or her spouse. When she came to shake hands with my husband, she would always say, "Tom, I want to thank you so much for letting your wife do all of this work for my husband." Not very many candidates' wives thought of doing that sort of thing. They don't stop to think that he was giving something for me to do that. A lot of times, I wouldn't feel like fixing dinner when I got home because I was tired. That was just super for her to do that.

JOAN GAIDOS, DALLAS

I had a traveling husband, and there were times I wanted to go do something. Friends watched my kids after school so that I could volunteer. If you had two- and three-year-old kids, you could hardly go off and leave them.

So it was a neighborhood effort?

Yes. That was the kind of thing that my neighbors did for me.

Volunteer Management

What kinds of qualities did you look for when you were recruit-ing people to help you?

DEE COATS, HOUSTON

The main thing was that they were reliable. After they have been with you a little bit, you start to give them more responsibil-ity and trust as they earn it. Of course, you like enthusiasm. As far as volunteers, you are kind of stuck with who walks in the door.

I worked with Sarah Gee when Bush ran for Congress in 1966. She ran the volunteer operation from the beginning for the

Bush campaign. I started out one day a week. Pretty soon, I proved that I could take on responsibility and was trustworthy. She started giving me more interesting jobs. She would say, "When you come on Wednesday, I want you to do the letters. I can trust you to read this." She ran a tight ship. I learned a lot from her.

CAROLINE PIERCE, HOUSTON

One year, when I was the state coordinator, I went to my Republican Women's Club. The speaker that month talked about "how to say no." I nearly died. If there was one time we didn't need a speaker saying how to say no . . .

The most important thing of all is, when a volunteer comes in to a phone bank or to do a mail-out, thank them for coming. Make sure someone in charge speaks to them and makes them feel welcome so they want to come back. Nothing upsets me more than seeing a volunteer that has spent three hours on the phone start to leave and no one says a word to him or her as they leave. In the next campaign, how many people want to volunteer again? That is an easy thing to forget, because a certain candidate may not be running again for two more years. But if volunteers have not been treated well, the chances they will volunteer for another campaign are very low.

It is so important that the chiefs of staff for any given candidate realize there are certain perks that you can do for volunteers to reward them, which they are really thrilled over. Like the best volunteers getting to go to a special dinner, maybe a very expensive fundraiser that otherwise they couldn't attend, and help with it.

MARY DENNY, DENTON

There is always work to be done. As long as you don't raise people's expectations and don't ever ask anybody to do something that you are not willing to do yourself. We are all humans. We know what tasks are required to do anything. Somebody's got to clean the bathrooms from time to time. If you spread it around so everybody's got the crummy job every once in a while, it is okay as long as everyone is doing it and sharing in it. People don't mind doing that especially if there is fun and some socializing along the way. Candidates for the longest time have always made sure that voluntcers would get free tickets to a fundraising event or something whether they could afford the ticket or not, just as a thank you for their hard work, and people appreciate that.

JOAN GAIDOS, DALLAS

Make them feel like what they do is worthwhile. Make them feel wanted. Make them feel loved. Dorothy Herbert made me feel like sweeping the floor of the Nixon headquarters was one of the most important things I could be doing for the movement. Everybody said thank you. Everybody was glad to sec you whether they were or not. We moved to Kansas in August of '68. The first thing I did was seek out a Republican Women's Club. I volunteered at the local headquarters. They didn't say, "Gee whiz, we are glad to have you. What were you doing in Texas?" But they had been Republicans so long. They truly were complacent. It's not that they didn't work hard, it's just that they didn't have to.

CATHERINE SMYTH COLGAN, DALLAS

You have got to make any volunteer activity fun. People have only the same number of hours in every day. The few hours they have to volunteer will be very carefully selected. If they are not enjoying it, they are not going to do it. Politics is like any other volunteer activity. Unless there are some good laughs, your organization does not succeed.

You have to have a sense of humor to laugh at your own mistakes. I have my "ABC's of Leadership." "A" is attitudes. Attitudes are contagious, and you have to be positive. If you are not a positive, forward-looking leader, then your troops aren't either. "B" is budget. That is not so much about money because if you run out of money you can go borrow some or you can raise a little more. I am talking about budgeting of time. You have to organize your time and not waste your time or waste the time of your colleagues. You have to have agendas and plan ahead. "C" is communication. Communicate not only to the press and to the outside world but communicate within your own ranks so that everybody is moving in the same direction.

FLORENCE NEUMEYER, HOUSTON

As the volunteer chairman, I organized a phone tree. When you needed to get a message out, volunteers had certain people that they called. As we got more volunteers, we had to get more people to serve on the phone bank committee. Marilyn Allen was the chairman for that because she could work from her house. She had children at home and wanted to do something meaningful. She did a beautiful job. She rarely got to come to an event. We talked on the phone sometimes two or three times a week, but we never met. We laughed about that because we were best of friends over the phone for years. That is just the way people were then. She didn't care that anybody saw her. She was doing it because she felt very strongly that it was important to build the Republican Party.

NANCY ABDULLAH, DALHART

At a Lou Tower tea at Mrs. Jimmie Pigman's home, I was sitting on the hearth with two of my friends. Tissie Silberberg and Dorothy Chaloupka. They were coming around to meet everyone, and they said, "The girls are right here altogether." They had seen our names in a part of the world where there were not that many unusual names, and we were all sitting there together. Everyone wanted to come over and see us because they wondered who in the world these women were.

NANCY CROUCH, HOUSTON

My career in politics kind of parallels George Bush. I gave a seminar on how to be a national delegate. They asked me, "Nancy, how did you have so much fun?" I said, "You hitch your wagon to a star—a young politician. You are there for him every time he needs you, then you get to do all of these fun things in the end." I got into politics basically because I thought I could make a difference. I never wanted to run for office. You find a candidate that you really like and you can really support. If he is good enough, you get as far as I did. If he is not, you have not wasted your time because you have ultimately improved government and politics with the right kind of candidate. There's only one president at a time, but there are congressmen. I just happened to find a really good star, but there are young men out there now I feel the same way about as I did George. If I had to tell somebody where to go, I would say go there because they are honest people.

Risks of Volunteering

BARBARA PATTON, HOUSTON

I have been at risk. If you agree to have responsibilities in a campaign and in the Party or as a delegate, you are setting yourself up for consequences that you don't expect. People might think twice about doing that. It is the women, I think, who feel it more than the men do. Men are tough guys; they can handle anything. Women are more emotional about their commitments, and you can get hurt. The emotional toll can be tremendous.

Why have you been willing in the past to risk that?

It is the right thing to do. You do have choices.

MARION COLEMAN, PASADENA

Most of the harassment was directed towards headquarters and towards me because I was putting the organization in Pasadena together. I was so intent on doing what I believed in that I didn't realize how scary it really was. I would not allow myself to consider the danger. I just didn't realize that the unions were as bad as they were until I got beaten up.

Pasadena was going to have a Rodeo Show. We were gaining members. I was handing out Nixon and Lodge literature [*during the 1960 presidential campaign*]. They came and surrounded me and beat me. In those days, sack suits were popular. The jacket was kind of short, and I got cut on my back. It was the kind of thing where they hit you and you can really see it. The next thing people in our booth saw was me on the ground. I just collapsed. They rushed out, and the police came. They got an ambulance and took me to the hospital. They said that I would be badly bruised. I went right back out there because I didn't want them to think that they could do that and be able to get away with it. I knew that I had to do it. They sort of left me alone after that. I gained their respect because I didn't retaliate verbally. I'd always say, "Hello, Mr. So-and-So," and they would either nod or just kind of look at me. I was always bubbly and pretended like nothing happened.

Was it hard to find people to volunteer when you were threatened physically?

That was a very hard thing for me to decide, whether to let them know what was going on to protect them. I didn't want to scare everybody. I thought I'd just let it go for a couple weeks and see if it was just me. Then when the headquarters was vandalized everybody got concerned. I truly thought that I would lose some volunteers, but I didn't. They just got mad. They had to start all over again. Then we just took the files home. We never kept anything again at the headquarters—just furniture. We even took the maps down off the wall.

Volunteer Sacrifice

BARBARA NOWLIN, HOUSTON & FRIENDSWOOD

We basically take the primary list from the last election and work from that to find campaign volunteers. I use club members and neighbors and anybody and everybody that I can think of. The primary list is an invaluable resource. The problem, though, is that it's like beating a dead horse. You keep calling the same people all of the time—ones that have proven to be a wonderful help. They can suffer burnout too. There are so many women working. Those numbers have increased so much. Now that my husband's retired, I wonder how much money I would have made if I hadn't been a professional volunteer all my life. But I can't imagine that it would have been as rewarding—frustrating, and tiring, and all the rest but rewarding at the same time. I have some regrets about it now, thinking, well, it would be nice to have a pension and retire from somewhere and have that income, but there are a lot of things I would not have gotten to do. It's a trade-off, and I made the right decision. You always hope that you are contributing something to make this world better. It sounds like you're trying to be noble, but that is basically it—to make the country and the state better.

CHAPTER 11

Texas Federation
of Republican Women

"Many times there would be a Republican Women's Club
before there was a county chairman or a county organization."

—KAY BAILEY HUTCHISON

*R*epublican Women's Clubs made an immeasurable impact
upon the development of the Party in Texas. Beginning in
Dallas with the election of Bruce Alger to Congress in 1954 through
today, candidates could always depend upon Republican Women, as
the clubs came to be called, to step to the line and staff their campaigns. Clubs developed at a rapid pace beginning in the 1950s.
Women found enthusiasm, camaraderie, and safety in numbers.
Club popularity can be attributed to the same factors that drew
individuals to the Party. Reasons for joining included belief in the
Republican philosophy, a desire to make Texas a two-party state,
and the enjoyment of working with friends and neighbors. Another
reason that can not be overlooked is the increase in social acceptability of belonging to and working with a group. Many women who
were not interested in volunteering directly for the Party or candidates would do the same work as part of a Republican Women's Club.

Clubs popped up all over Texas. Some were formed in conjunction with precinct and county organizations, but many times
the early clubs were the local Party organization. When precinct or
county chairs could not be found, Republican state leaders attempted
to form women's clubs to start local activity. Republican Women
generated enthusiasm in many counties during non-election years.
Then when the campaigns swung into action a group of volunteers
existed from which to recruit campaign, headquarters, and phone
bank chairs. Many an up-and-coming candidate made his or her
first speech at a Republican Women's Club.

As Republican Women's Clubs' campaign and organizational expertise began to grow, they shared it with other members of the Party. They held campaign schools, which today continue to teach candidates organization from A to Z. Although many candidates hire campaign managers, the schools are a place they can get an overview of the campaign process and an idea of what to expect. At one time, Republican Women even conducted polling for state and local candidates. The results assisted many campaigns in implementing their plans.

Republican Women have consistently contributed financially to campaigns. In the early days, they raised money by selling anything with an elephant on it, holding bake sales, and publishing fundraising cookbooks. Between their monetary contributions and time donated, Republican Women have contributed millions and millions of dollars to the Party and candidates through the years.

KAY BAILEY HUTCHISON, HOUSTON & DALLAS

If you are going to talk about building the Party in Texas, you have *got* to talk about the Republican Women's Clubs. Because I was such a pioneer going around the state, I know what it was like out there. Many times there would be a Republican Women's Club before there was a county chairman or a county organization. They would form because they wanted an alternative to the Democrats, who had been running the state or the county for years and years. They would form, and then they would recruit a candidate to run against an incumbent county commissioner or sheriff or justice of the peace who wasn't doing a good job or who was doing something that people felt was wrong. They were the only entity that would support this lone candidate. From that, you would start the formation of a party. You would have a county chairman who would come probably from that club, or the club would say we have got to have a county chairman now. From that, the state party would hold a primary. There would be maybe one primary location in the whole county.

The first time I voted in a Republican primary was when I was on the ballot running for state representative. Why? Because Galveston County, where I grew up, didn't have a Republican primary! I had no choice but to vote in the Democrat primary. That was the case all over. It was only in Houston, Dallas, Austin, and San Antonio that you would start having a Republican primary. It wasn't maybe until the 1970s that you started seeing primaries in twenty counties. It wasn't until the '80s that it was fifty. It wasn't until 1996 that we had 254. They started so often with the Republican Women's Clubs that had ten members. It grew truly from the grassroots. Without the Republican Women's Clubs we would *never* be where we are today.

Starting Clubs

BABS JOHNSON, DALLAS

In the fall of 1953, Jan Kelly, who was the wife of the Republican precinct chairman, invited her neighbors to join her at a morning coffee. She told us that she thought it would be so nice if the neighborhood became a little more cohesive and would we like to form a garden club or would we be interested in a political club? I don't know what she would have done if we had all opted to be a garden club. It seemed that the time was right for women to become much more interested and active in politics.

Probably it arose from the fact that there was a program to raise money for Eisenhower. Women went door-to-door in their neighborhoods and raised money. I'm sure that was one of the contributing factors—there was enough interest evidenced in this door-to-door campaign that the powers that be were convinced that women were truly interested enough to be more active.

Preston West was the first club that organized in Dallas County aside from the old Republican County Club, which organized for a visit by President McKinley. Those people who were interested became its charter members on, if not that day, within a week at a follow-up meeting. Jan thought of more people to include who were not in the immediate neighborhood. We had had a Republican congressional candidate in this precinct. Bill Burrow was his name.

Burrow lived just a few blocks away and was applauded on arriving at places because people thought it was such a courageous thing to run for office on the Republican ticket. Bill was a good friend of Jan and her Republican precinct chairman husband. He also might have been some behind-the-scenes encouragement for Jan.

Preston West's first speaker was [*congressional candidate*] Bruce Alger. I knew that he was going to be a real winner because he looked absolutely entranced with my reading of the bylaws. I was the charter secretary so it was my great honor to read these bylaws. Bruce sat there looking enraptured. He just looked as if he had never heard anything more fascinating in his entire life. This was, if I recall, his first appearance before a women's group.

Why did you get behind him as candidate?

Just the fact that he was there. He was willing, and he was obviously a knowledgeable man about women's responses or he never would have endured looking that happy hearing minutes and bylaws. He proceeded to give that first talk, which convinced women that surely enough we had done a wonderful thing in forming this club and deciding to be active in his campaign.

Had you decided to be active in his campaign?

We had on the spot! Have you seen his picture? He was tall. He was athletically graceful. He was dark. He was a very handsome man with a very nice voice.

Surely that's not the reason a lot of you decided to get him elected?

No. But after all, we were women who had given this small evidence of interest. This was in the days when any Democrat who was running was a winner. It didn't make any difference what they stood for. The brass collar, you know—any dog can win. To speak to someone that you instinctively felt was going to give some Democrat some trouble . . . Those of us who heard Mr. Alger that first time were convinced that, hey, here is somebody who really has a chance. The women all signed up to be hostesses for coffees for Mr. Alger. We hosted meetings of whatever kind he liked so that we could have our husbands meet our candidate. Republican Women's Clubs sprang up.

So more of them started right away?

Yes. In fact Prestonwood was the name of the club that never did quite agree that we were all that far ahead of them. As far as I know, they started quite soon thereafter. We wound up with a number of Republican Women's Clubs. We went door-to-door in our precincts to count houses and blocks, because this was all rather new territory and wasn't by any means solidly built, block after block. We did it in our cars. I would have at least one small child along. Jan Kelly gave me the assignment of which blocks to cover and did the same with all of the members.

We went up and down blocks to houses as they were built. We wrote down the house number, the streets. We covered our entire precinct that way so that the precinct chairman had a card file. When the person moved into that new house, we were assigned to call upon the residents, find out their political persuasion, and ask for telephone numbers because they weren't in the telephone books yet. Then, of course, our whole plan was to be able to persuade them to vote when the time came. That is how precinct chairmen originally had any records for their precincts.

But it took many women in Dallas County to achieve what has finally been achieved. It was a long hard road. We worked at the polls. We were all volunteers. The state did not pay Republican primary officials. We raised money. You name a way that inexperienced women could get together to raise money for our candidate and we tried it. I'm sure we didn't raise by any means the significant amount of money that was needed, but we certainly put our little hearts into it. We made all kinds of crafts, as I recall, probably just dreadful things. We made aprons with elephants of all description. I'm sure that everybody made any kind of elephant that you can dream up to take to political affairs. The clubs joined hands and had summer fairs, which were really watermelon parties that gave us an opportunity to show our wares.

You all must have been thrilled when Alger won.

Oh, you can imagine [*laughing*]. It was an incredible victory! It really produced cohesiveness in Dallas County, which was a great foundation for what came after. We worked together, and that opportunity to have a winner might never have arrived had it not been an all-county effort. It was an invaluable experience.

ELLIE SELIG, SEGUIN

I had friends, and I couldn't stand to be away from politics. Years ago one did not have babysitting services. You had to be wealthy enough to have somebody that came in to take care of your children. In lieu of that, this other woman and myself decided we needed to have a place to meet and bring the children. So that is how we had the first Republican Women's meetings. Then I got Marvin interested.

BERYL MILBURN, AUSTIN

The TFRW organizing convention was in San Antonio in 1955. The clubs that could send delegates had to have at least ten members. When we organized our club, we scratched around and finally found ten members. Men didn't want their wives identified as Republican even though they both were Republicans. They were scared for their businesses. When we moved here, people told my husband, Malcolm, that if he called himself a Republican, he was just not going to be able to be a success at his business. Socially it was not acceptable. We were just left out of a lot of things here in Austin because we were Republicans and made no bones about it. It took a long time before that changed.

I really think that the Republican Women's Clubs were the real levers that got people going because the women were freer economically to join and be Republicans than their husbands were. They were very devoted and dedicated. Republicans were ideologically committed.

KATIE HECK, MIDLAND

We didn't have a Republican Women's Club for the first four or five years that I was active because the precinct work was the main thrust. After a while, the club got started and it did very, very well. The precinct work came first in the late '50s and early '60s. We got it started, and good women took it and ran with it. There were about ten of us that thought it was a good idea having a Women's Club, but we didn't want to belong to it. We had a meeting and got all of the wives of the precinct chairmen and friends and so forth. We said here are the bylaws that we can use, and we elected some officers that would do it and didn't want to do precinct work. I think that our first president was a woman named Gloria Stewart. She liked organizing things and did a beautiful job of it. Joan Paxton was another one. We did a sustaining membership. If we paid twice as much dues, we wouldn't have to go to anything. They did keep the women together in the off years, which was a useful thing. Then the club would be the pool from which the precinct and telephone bank workers came.

The state party encouraged you and others active in Midland to form a club?

Yes. It was really more of a request from the state level. They would tell us, we need this and we need that and we need this amount of money. We would try and do what we could. But in a lot of places there was more club than Party. It was getting the job done that we were doing as a Party. But since we had gotten started the other way, I didn't want to dilute that. I was not enthusiastic about it, but then when we had plenty of people who could do both club and Party work, we just thought, why not?

KATIE SEEWALD, AMARILLO

It was in '61, shortly after the election. Martha Parr and I got in the car and drove over to Borger to see Kathryn McDaniel and ask her what we could do to build for the future here. She was adamant that we needed a Republican Women's Club. I respected her judgment. So we got back over here, and we talked Martha Ann

Duke into being the president. She was from a highly respected, wealthy family in Amarillo and married to a highly respected doctor. She was in the Junior League and was a good face and name to put in front of the people. Dr. Reed's wife, Dorothy, was the vice president. We worked out the slate, the bylaws, and the whole thing. We decided to have our meeting at noon so that professional women could come too. We had a vote on which day of the week and which week of the month would be best for them so that we could get the best turnout. We got it off to a good start. It has been very healthy ever since.

Was there any reluctance that you observed to get involved politically?

Well, only to this extent—I never had particularly wanted to have a Republican Women's Club. I couldn't see any point in it. Why not just go to work in the Party? But there were women who didn't want to do that, and they would work in a women's club. So it worked out fine. I became district committeewoman for the Texas Federation of Republican Women soon after we organized that club in 1961. I would go to the state meetings, come back, and bring ideas and so forth. I tried to organize clubs in some of the little towns around here.

How did you formulate the strategy and identify the best areas to form women's clubs?

LIZ GHRIST, HOUSTON

Where people voted in our primary, we knew we had people who were very interested in the Republican Party. They were our nucleus. We would go down the record, see where they lived, get them involved, and organize them into a Republican Women's group. We didn't care what their faction as long as they were Republicans. It was strictly getting this Republican group together. We knew Houston had a lot of people transferring here from other parts of the country at that time. They knew about being Republican. We were talking conservative Democrats into joining the Republican Party because of what was going on in the Democratic

Party. We were working off of the liberalization of the Democratic Party nationally in order to build our Republican Party locally. Democrats, particularly from the southern states, felt that the issue of states' rights was very, very important. They couldn't make a difference in the Democratic Party, but they could in the Republican Party. Houston began to boom at that time from the oil industry, from the medical industry, from the airports, and from the use of air conditioning. The space center gave us visibility throughout the country. As the city grew and the county grew, we grew.

BARBARA NOWLIN, HOUSTON & FRIENDSWOOD

We were in a newly developed neighborhood in southwest Houston. I had two small children. I held them by the hand, and we went door-to-door. I told the women in the neighborhood that I would like to start a Republican Women's Club. I invited them to come to my house on a particular night. The first meeting we had in the neighborhood thirty people attended. Soon it was fifty people, sixty people, and it just kept growing. It was one precinct in Harris County. It was really a great group of people. It was a very young neighborhood. Young mothers had a hard time doing these things because of their babies and young children, yet we had a wonderful group. They were so willing.

Why did you decide to organize a Republican Women's Club?

LOUISE NIXON, FREDERICKSBURG

Men were not speaking up about Republicans. There was pressure on businessmen to be noncommittal. We took a stand for Republicanism. We wanted a voice in our town. Gillespie County was Republican, but no one would speak up.

ALICIA CANTU, LAREDO

After I ran for the school board in 1973, I realized that we had to organize the Republican Party. We didn't have a group of women. It was just a few men that got together and tried to make some changes, but they didn't have enough support.

When I ran for the school board, I ran all by myself. I didn't have anyone to help me except my family. I remember that the day of the election I felt so lonely. I said that if I had had a group, a support group, I might have won. I had 33 percent of the vote without any help. If I had a support group, I might have more. That's when I said. "Let's organize." I called all of the ladies that showed some interest, and we started the Republican Women's Club. They really are the workers. We started going to the city council meetings because that was the only way we figured we would get noticed. They would frown when we would go, but they paid attention to us because we were dignified and presented our case. We were not there to do anything but to fight for our cause.

ANNE BERGMAN, WEATHERFORD

We took a chamber of commerce political action course. We got a discussion group together of eight or ten women and built around it to organize the Republican Women's Club. We met maybe five or six sessions. We learned how to organize a precinct. It was just a good theory of grassroots politics. One thing that was explained was how you could win an election even if you had just about a quarter of the vote. You turn out the vote big in your strong precincts. We organized in 1963 or 1964. We recruited from the phone bank that we had going in '63 at the time of the assassination of Kennedy. We were on the telephone that day at 11:30 in the morning. We were calling and saying, "Do you plan to support Kennedy this year?" Our response was very good. They were saying no. I got home at noon, and my mother called me and she said, "Well, are you satisfied now?" She was so upset. It was sort of rash to get into political activity like that at the time.

NITA GIBSON, LUBBOCK

I saw a need for there to be a lot of Republican Women's Clubs because the women were the volunteers and I thought this is the way you do it. If you don't like what's going on, don't just complain about it, do something about it. I would suggest to these women, look, if you don't like something, get together with a group and make a resolution and send it to your congressman or send it to your senator or just go down to courthouse square and raise hell about it. If you feel something, well, do something about it. Don't just sit back.

Forming a State Organization

Why did you decide that TFRW was an organization the state needed?

BETTE JO BUHLER, VICTORIA
We needed volunteers.

BERYL MILBURN, AUSTIN
I was chairman of the convention that organized the TFRW. I was active from then on. It was 1955. There was a big fight at that convention because the national committeewoman, who was Thelma Black, quite an older woman, wanted also to be president of TFRW. A lot of us felt that that should not happen because we were too small and we wanted to spread the jobs and the positions and get more people involved. Most of us supported Aileen O'Callaghan. To defeat the national committeewoman is really something. So Aileen became the first president.

DOROTHY CROCKETT, ODESSA & MARBLE FALLS
I was a delegate for the Republican Party of Texas convention in San Antonio. The women were organizing their state organization. I heard that they were going to have the meeting, and I decided to go over there. I sort of hate to even say this. I walked in the room, and there were about fifteen or twenty women in front of the room by the podium. I walked in and everyone looked at me in sort of a strange way. They didn't know who I was or what I was doing there. I felt like they thought I was a spy of some kind. I sat down and listened for a little while. No one ever welcomed me or made me feel like I belonged there, and so I left.

JANE BUCY, LUBBOCK

The women's club held a large luncheon at the country club in 1964. Irene Cox Wischer came, and she was our guest speaker. She was just wonderful. The newspaper did a big write-up and had a picture of Irene. She had wonderful, new ideas. She would tell us what other clubs were doing and what progress they were making. She made us feel like we were part of a larger organization. We weren't here all by ourselves.

What are the responsibilities of TFRW district directors?

DOTTIE SANDERS, HOUSTON

You oversee all of the clubs and help organize new clubs.

BILLIJO PORTER, EL PASO

Vera Carhart and I traveled around to little counties. We went to Alpine and towns like that to try to organize Republican Women's organizations because these counties had no organizations. A Republican Women's Club could be an impetus to a county party.

What were your responsibilities as deputy president of TFRW?

JOANNE POWELL, SAN ANGELO

Clubs were divided into areas and regions. I attended the board meetings and got the information out to them. They were to keep us posted. The main thing that we were working on then was to try and get more involvement and more people for TFRW. The way that you do it is you get more clubs out there and get more people in the clubs. It just takes ten people who are interested in good government to get it started. I guess depending on the people you get involved, it either grows or dies on the vine.

FLO KAMPMANN CRICHTON, SAN ANTONIO

Every state committee meeting had a report from the president of TFRW. It just seemed natural because they were doing an awful lot of work. We just assumed that she would be there. Women were always available to work at the headquarters and in the national campaign. They were great. Men worked so they couldn't staff headquarters.

You were looking at the TFRW for volunteers?

Yes. They were the regulars. When campaigns came along, they would attract other women who weren't necessarily members of a club to work. It worked pretty well.

Leaders

FLO KAMPMANN CRICHTON, SAN ANTONIO
You always knew that Aileen O'Callaghan [*founding president of TFRW*] was there. The first one to do anything in a new organization always has a harder job.

The early presidents are no longer with us. Do any of them stand out in your mind?

MARY JESTER, DALLAS
The one I knew best was Maxine Elam. She was great. She was well organized. She knew what she was looking for, and she could get people to work. She was instrumental.

BABS JOHNSON, DALLAS
I attended the Fort Worth convention when Barbara Man was elected president. She was nominated from the floor to oppose the slated presidential nominee. That was an exciting time. I was rooming with Dorothy Cameron, the parliamentarian. She got back from the last meeting of the evening, and I lay in bed and shivered because I was so excited. She just went right to sleep. Barbara Man was elected president. Barbara then paid all of her own expenses to cover the state. It was never reimbursed. After that, the TFRW decided that there must be some financial arrangements for the president.

Who was the slated candidate?

Allie Mae Currie. She was older, and she was the national committeewoman Mrs. Black's good friend. It was so exciting that

I couldn't go to sleep. I had never been in on that sort of battle. It also gave me a glimpse of women playing hardball. It was not all wearing gloves and going to tea. We really were into hard politics.

I voted for Barbara Man. I felt Barbara was going to be more innovative. She was younger. She was more in touch. Mrs. Currie was more inclined to talk about things that we had been hearing for a long time. Barbara had some refreshing new ideas for the organization—how we could grow and how we could reach out—and I felt that was important. It was time to reach out and not be the country-club set. She certainly did a good job as president. I think Mrs. Currie was severely hurt and disappointed. I think that's one reason I couldn't go to sleep that night. It was traumatic.

It wasn't that important to the average club member who the county chairman was. It just didn't seem to matter as long as we did our part. Our club did well and did what we wanted it to achieve. We didn't really care who was at the top and calling signals. It was all a bit removed. Our leader was the county vice chair. She was in charge of women's activities. Of course, her view of leadership was important to us. It wasn't policy that I am speaking of, it was the personal factions. We thought that it was sort of small, really, to be worried about the rivalries of this small group or that small group at the top.

IRENE COX WISCHER, SAN ANTONIO

I was founder of the federation's quota system and Pink Elephant project, which resulted in raising more than $40,000 during my presidency from 1963 to 1964. We also got a national award for having gained the largest increase in members in the whole nation during my regime. We had school activities. Our women were so dedicated, and they were determined to make the Republican Party grow. The Republican Women in the state and the TFRW in its early years had a lot to do with helping this become a two-party state. We were very active and had a number of social events as well as meetings.

The Republican Women had social events for fundraising?

Yes, we were all business. We also held other meetings to seek members. That was our big goal: to get more members. It was also during my time that we had the first state office. That was done because they [*the state party*] recognized how much money we raised. They gave us a space in Austin. The women organizing all of these clubs in the various cities gave the Party a boost because we became visible. I didn't realize at the time we were doing that much good, but we did.

Our publicity helped the Republican Party a great deal. We had good news coverage in those days, especially on the women's pages. We grew to a large number in a hurry. People were getting sick of the Democrats about that time, too. That helped.

BERYL MILBURN, AUSTIN

I remember in '68, John Tower called me and said, "We need you to be the candidate for the president of the TFRW." I said, "Well, I retired from politics." He said, "We really need you to do it." I said, "Well, I'll do it if you will let me be a delegate to the convention in '68." By golly, he kept his word. I was one of the at-large delegates.

The Party must have thought that TFRW was important for Senator Tower to call you.

Well, it was. The women in those clubs are the backbone. They do all the dirty work and they raise money—not a lot of money but some. They man the headquarters and the phone banks. I don't think that the Republicans would have done any good at all if it hadn't been for the Republican Women's Clubs.

What kind of programs did you institute in 1968 when you were president?

We urged the clubs to take on some kind of community service because the Republicans had a reputation of being rich and not caring and not compassionate about people in need. We redid the *Party Line,* the little newspaper. We developed the logo and the color. We got political consultants, John Knaggs and Marvin

Collins, to look at the TFRW and come up with recommendations about what we could do. We pretty much followed their recommendations.

We were financed by the Party and shared space in the headquarters. It made an enormous difference. They don't do that anymore. It's too bad because what can happen and has happened in some other states is the Republican Party and the women's groups have been at loggerheads and going in different directions. I thought it was important to have that financial support coming from the Party, to work with them and not be in opposition. Peter O'Donnell agreed with that.

LAVERNE CUDABAC, CANYON LAKE

I worked with Cleo Bohls who was president from 1969 to 1970. She was outgoing. She was a person who could get things done. You know some people can't. She was one of those who could. She was a smart lady, and she could organize well. That is another attribute of getting people to work for you—if you are a good organizer.

CATHERINE SMYTH COLGAN, DALLAS

I was able to build the membership from a little over 6,000 to about 9,600. I figured it out at one time that within the first six months of my office I traveled over 30,000 miles. People used to laugh and say, "Where do you live?" And I would grin and say, "On Southwest Airlines." I took the membership vice president, Beulah Childress. She and I drove West Texas. We drove all of the way out in the Panhandle organizing clubs along the way. We organized a number of clubs.

I happened to be in an enviable position because I was vice chairman in Dallas County. Bill McKenzie, the chair, had a lot of problems with his back and had to have surgery. He didn't do a lot of traveling out of town so I was the representative for Dallas County in the County Chairman Association and knew the county chairmen throughout the state. I would simply contact the county chairmen and then work through them. They would help set it up or tell me whom to contact. Beulah worked very hard on logistics, and we pulled together. We would go in and have either a morning or an evening meeting. The secret to organizing these groups or any group of volunteers is to remember that there is a job for everybody. It is a matter of fitting the person to the responsibilities and finding what they like to do. Beulah would share a grin with me on this.

We were out in West Texas. I don't remember where we were. After we got volunteers to take offices, a cute little lady who must have been eighty years old came up and said, "How I wish I were young enough to be an officer, but, alas, I am no longer able to do that." Somebody had told me earlier that she made cookies. I said, "There is a job for you." She said, "What is that?" I said, "I understand that you are a fantastic cookie baker, so you are going to be the cookie chairman." Well, she just beamed. Some months later, at the state convention, one of those members came up to me and said, "Boy, are you in our doghouse. We have all gained five pounds." The lady brought three and four kinds of delicious cookies to every single meeting. That to me proves there is a job for everybody. When you're working with big volunteer organizations in politics, the secret to success is to find the right job for the right person. What appeals to them? You start cramming people into positions and it doesn't work.

SURRENDEN ANGLY, AUSTIN

I felt I brought expertise and aimed at being a morale builder, and that's what I did visiting clubs. I was coming from the hotbed of Lyndon Johnson—his fortress. If it worked here, where wouldn't it work? I traveled with Beryl Milburn, Anne Armstrong, and Rita Clements. We would go up to Washington together, and I felt unbelievably honored to be in this group.

What was your biggest accomplishment as TFRW president?

That youth could get involved. You did not have to be a fifty- or sixty-year-old woman to get involved in the political process. When I made my acceptance speech in San Antonio, my husband, Maurice, brought the children down to hear me. The two children were older, but my toddler, little Surrenden, was about two. I hadn't seen her in four days. Maurice is standing in the back of the hall with her in his arms. She sees Mommy starting to deliver an address, and she just says, "I want my Mommy." I stopped my speech, and I said, "Darling, you come right on up here." I gave the remainder of my address with my child in my arms. It was a whole new concept for people to realize that you could be a lot younger.

What were your most outstanding accomplishments during your term as TFRW president from 1983 to 1987?

BARBARA CAMPBELL, DALLAS

We were able to give women more recognition. When I first took office, we had just a file cabinet in the Republican headquarters. They [*the state party*] gave us a little bit of help but not a lot. I went to Austin my first day on the job. The then executive director, when I asked a question or asked for some help, he said, "When are you women going to pull your own weight around here? When are you going to stop being a leech on the Party? When are you going to do something for yourself? When are you going to do something worthwhile?" I was a redhead at the time, and let me tell you steam started to come out. I then went to the files and pulled information of what we had done over the years and what we were doing and what our goals were to continue to be. There were some people that definitely did not feel that an auxiliary had any right to speak, even to the executive committee. If we wanted to talk, then we could do it through someone who was already on the committee. When the women found out, it didn't go over too well.

We didn't have a vote on the executive committee, and we weren't asking for a vote, but we didn't want our voice taken away from us and they tried to do that. We came up with the "Mother May I Amendment." To make a long story short, that was defeated and I got the nickname "Tough Red" because my women were not going to be treated in a way that they didn't deserve. Even back then, showing the amount of money that we contributed and our hours worked, it would be well over $1 million. It took a long time for the women volunteers to get recognition. I can tell you that that executive director was not around a whole lot longer. Now, I won't say that we had anything to do with it, but the party didn't need somebody like that.

ZUBIE WALTERS, YOAKUM

A good club president is active, takes an interest in the politics, and is always trying to get new members. It takes somebody who does not drag out the meetings. We've had some where we would spend time at the meetings, and we didn't accomplish much.

Source of Volunteers

GAIL WATERFIELD, CANADIAN

I think that it can be said without any doubt it was the Republican women who built the Panhandle. Number one by starting the Republican Women's Clubs, which grew and educated their members. After the political education was done for a year or two, they got out and worked. Nobody was going to waste their time going to those meetings if they were not going to go out and work. Then we moved into going door-to-door, and the telephone calls came later. It took a long time for Republicans to come out of the closet. We knew who thought Republican and who voted Republican, but they weren't going to come out and vote in the primary because they wanted a voice in that courthouse, which was controlled by the Democrats. They weren't going to get it until they got qualified people on the Republican ticket.

Why did you found the Young Republican Women's Club?

LIBBA BARNES, SAN ANTONIO

We didn't have a young group. I belonged to Bexar County Republican Women's Club. It really was to the advantage of the Bexar County group to sponsor another group. They said, all you need are ten people and you can start your own club. There were twenty-six of us who started the first club. It dissolved after about ten years. We all got older and were ready to join the big ladies.

Since you are not a member, what do you think Republican Women's Clubs have done to benefit Republican candidates and the growth of the Party within Dallas County?

MARY LOU WIGGINS, DALLAS

They recruited workers. If speakers can go to a Republican Women's Club meeting and get them enthusiastic, you've got people on your side automatically. It is part of the political strategy, getting your own workers enthusiastic. Clubs are a good nucleus for workers. People feel more willing to work for a cause when they think others are doing it, too. You don't feel isolated. It's good to have that group around you and working with you on a campaign. It reassures you. I don't know why I didn't join except I'm just not a women's club kind of a person.

GLORIA CLAYTON, DALLAS

I had a Republican Women's Club meeting here at my house. That morning, half an hour before meeting time, the doorbell rang and there was a lady on my doorstep. She said she saw in the paper that I was having a meeting of the Republican Women's Club and asked, "May I join you? I am Jennie Foster." I said, "Well, of course, come in. You are welcome." She joined the club, and she went on and became a state committeewoman.

CINDY BROCKWELL, BOERNE

When I moved to Boerne, I saw an ad in the Boerne paper about an inch and half long that said the Kendall County Republican Women was going to have a meeting. So I just thought I would go and see what a Republican club was like. The very first meeting you attend they act like you are their long lost sister. They are so happy to see new members. I met Mona Wetzel, Mary Jane Griffin, Willie Lawley, and Margaret Cosby. They immediately put me on the board. I said that I like to write. Instantly, I was hooked because I was their new newsletter chairman. Once they get you, they don't let you go.

Publicity and Raising Visibility

BABS JOHNSON, DALLAS

A newspaper reporter from the *Dallas Morning News* called our president to ask if they could send a photographer out to take a picture of the newly elected officers of the Preston West Republican Women's Club, almost in disbelief that there was such an organization. She said, "Yes, that's our name." He said, well, yes, we would like to have that picture. So the photographer arrived, looked at the five of us, and said "You know, four really make a better picture." I said, "Wonderful, leave me out." My grandmother felt very strongly that women's names should be in the paper at birth, at marriage, and at death, period. It just wasn't ladylike to be in the paper otherwise. But, secondly, as a Republican woman—a Republican woman? Politics was bad enough, but to be a Republican was unheard of.

What kind of community relations projects did you do?

LAVERNE CUDABAC, CANYON LAKE

First of all, we raised money for our volunteer fire department. We raised money for our Canyon Lake Action Center and for the St. Jude's Children's Home. TFRW as well as NFRW encouraged us to do community affairs so that we would be known in the community. We have parades up here—at Fourth of July and then one at Christmas. We always have floats in those. We always win either first or second place. It keeps our name in front of the public. We have pictures in the paper for making contributions to these different things.

That is the reason we have a big membership up here. People see us, and they know that we are active. They know that we contribute to things in the community and work in the community, and that makes someone want to join.

MARY BODGER, CORPUS CHRISTI

After Chuck Scoggins was elected [*to the state legislature*] in a special election in 1963, I was president of the Republican Women's

Club. There was a film called *Inside the Legislature* by [*Representative*] Hank Grover. It didn't say too much about either political party. I talked all of the high schools into letting me come and show it in 1965 and 1966. I invited a representative of the Democrat women's club. They didn't show up, so Chuck and I would go to the schools and show the film and answer their questions. It was surprising to me how smart kids were. They asked good questions. We took it to civic clubs, too.

LAVERNE EVANS, EL PASO

We have helped battered women, and our literacy program is helping also. With members getting out and working for people, eventually they will know that Republicans are not all rich, as they are categorized. Republicans are just regular people. The first thing, though, is to have good candidates.

Why did you want to promote literacy?

ANNETTE HOPKINS, SAN ANGELO

If a person can't read, how can they vote intelligently? It's amazing how many people can not read. It's very important that our people are educated and able to read about the candidate and know what he stands for. You can't take anything for granted. I also work with our literacy council here. It is so important to me.

ALICIA CANTU, LAREDO

In 1976, during the Bicentennial celebration, I was appointed to the local committee. I got the Republican Women's Club involved in organizing the serenades to give the Republican Party and the Republican Women's Club more publicity. It really brought in a lot of people to the downtown area every Sunday. We had the place packed.

Campaign Schools

Why did you decide to serve on the board of the National Federation of Republican Women?

RITA CLEMENTS, DALLAS

It was mainly because they asked me to be campaign activities chairman. I felt that was the purpose of Republican Women's Clubs, and that is what they needed to concentrate on. It was my opportunity not only to learn from other states but also to tell them all we had done in Texas. Texas was really the pioneer on door-to-door canvassing. We ran campaign schools, and they sent out monthly correspondence to all of the clubs. I would write columns for that.

CATHERINE SMYTH COLGAN, DALLAS

I was asked by Connie Armitage to be the vice chairman of the national campaign committee for the national federation. I worked on the campaign manual with a lady from North Carolina. In 1978, we started the national federation campaign management schools. I still have the first books from that. We started the pilot class in Dallas. We had people like Julian Reed, who had been John Connally's PR man; Mitch Daniels, who became one of the political gurus during the Reagan administration; Bob Odell, who was a nationally known fundraiser from Baltimore; and Mary Ellen Miller, who invented phone banks.

What types of subjects do they discuss in the campaign schools?

BETSY LAKE, HOUSTON

Everything from how to dress to how to write a speech to talking points is covered. How you can raise money. How you can target and what groups to target, particularly in a county like Harris County that is so large. How to get volunteers.

BARBARA JORDAN, KINGWOOD

I was vice president of campaign activities for four years. I don't remember how many schools we put on. We had at least fifty people at each one of those. A lot of them were candidates, and a lot of them were working in campaigns. We held them in Corpus, Amarillo, Plano, in East Texas, and here in Houston. We had them all over the state.

What do you think candidates get out of them?

They see the whole campaign. Some of them have no idea what a whole campaign is like. The campaign schools are a day to a day and a half. They really go into detail on each subject candidates need to know to organize and finance a campaign. They get an overall picture that they wouldn't see any other way. On a day-to-day basis, candidates are not always there at the office. Coming to the schools, they do see how it is put together and how it works.

Polling Schools

DOROTHY REED, AMARILLO

I attended a Republican Women polling school in 1980 in Indianapolis. There were about twenty of us from all over the country. There were five of us from Texas. Vern Kennedy was the instructor. They taught us how to do a scientific poll. We were to come back to our states and conduct polls. I did quite a few. At one time, I was on the TFRW board as the first polling chairman. I did a couple for [*Congressman*] Bob Price. I did one for Dennis Wallace, when he was a state house candidate. I did one for a group of Randall County candidates. I did one for Gene Stores, who was running for Congress. Then for some reason they terminated the project. I don't know why. We did all the sheets for the questions on the script, and then when we got them all marked we would send them to Vern Kennedy and they would be analyzed. Then they would send us the data analyzed. It was very helpful to the candidates concerning their level of support and what the issues were.

RUTH FOX, HOUSTON & AUSTIN

We learned how to poll in Indianapolis. The state and county parties started using Republican Women to poll, and I would teach them in our local area how to do it. Our results were a lot of the time less than three percentage points [*statistical margin of error*] whereas most of the other polls which are being taken now may be five or six points. It took a lot of volunteer training to teach them how to do it. We would get teenagers to come in at night. The preparation would take one or two nights. We polled over a period of two or three nights. There were specific dates, times, and conversations that we were supposed to use when we polled.

Why did TFRW want to conduct polls?

You know where to really put in your efforts to get out the vote and to get volunteers. We'd tell the candidates where they needed to go door-to-door, because that was the most effective way of campaigning. Having done so much of it ourselves, we knew the proof of the pudding.

Fundraisers

SHIRLEY GREEN, AUSTIN & SAN ANTONIO

In the 1960s and '70s, a lot of the Republican Women's Clubs would adopt a candidate. When they had a barbecue or a fundraiser, it wasn't a matter of those dollars being apportioned between twenty-five candidates. They did that fundraiser for a whole campaign. My club adopted me in 1964. It was like $2,000 or $3,000 dollars, which in 1964 for a no-name, know-nothing young woman who had agreed to do this foolishness jousting at windmills was very helpful. There were ways that those pennies and bake sales could be bundled up to make it of benefit.

BETTY RUMINER, SEABROOK

Our first president was Mia Giles. We began doing garage sales. We registered voters in Nassau Bay and at a grocery store. We made about fifty cents a person that we registered.

Who paid you to register voters?

I am not sure. It may have been Harris County. We had bake sales. We had style shows. We had all kinds of things. We had luncheons to make money. We grew in numbers, but we had a terrible time making money.

JANE BUCY, LUBBOCK

I really worked hard on the cookbook. Vaude Roper did most of the letter writing to senators to get their favorite recipes. I didn't start with it until the recipes were collected, and then I started typing it up and doing illustrations.

Do you have any idea how much money you made?

Between $2,000 and $3,000. Vaude didn't charter it for the Republican Women's Club. She had it done for the cookbook committee. We figured that the money would come to us and not the Republican Women's Club. There was a huge controversy. We sold a lot of copies, and we saved nearly $3,000 for a reprint. We still had a lot of copies at our headquarters, then we had a tornado and they were all gone. Some of the members of the club decided that the money belonged to them. They were going to form a new rule that all money made by the Republican members under the Republican name had to belong to the club and not to the committee. Vaude and I went down that afternoon before the meeting and went through all of the money and gave it to Jim Granberry to help him pay his debts after he was defeated for governor. So then there was no money. Vaude didn't want to use it for anything but candidates.

What are "tasting teas" and how did you raise money with them?

WINNIE MOORE, LUBBOCK

We would have tea and tidbits. Everyone would bring their favorite recipes, like what you have at party. We sold tickets. They were a dollar or five dollars. We raised quite of bit of money like that. We did it every year for a while. At the time, that was really something new. We made money from tasting tea recipe books. Whatever they brought, they were supposed to bring the recipe for it. We made them into a book they could buy.

ESTELLE TEAGUE, HURST

I started the TFRW Patrons Program. We needed funds other than our membership. You can't get it by selling notepaper, you need big donations. The Patrons Program started at $250 a year. In

January, we send out notices inviting everyone to join. Then, by the end of March, the membership had just about all come in. Then I started the direct mail. I started the Friends, where the donations were $25, $50, $75, and $100. I designed little pins with the year on them. That program gives funds for the TFRW overhead, the director, and the secretary.

Barbara Campbell, who was TFRW president for four years, was the one who said, "We have got to have a fundraiser. We can't do it on potholders and notepaper." Other states had Friends, but they didn't have a Patron Program. I patterned it after the NFRW Regent Program, which is $1,000. If you have a program like that you have to give them perks. The first year I got the governor to make them all Honorary Yellow Roses. The next year, I got George Bush to make them admirals in the Texas Navy.

BUCKY SMITH, NEW BRAUNFELS

Once the group got going, we had to find some way to make money. We first started off with little things. We did some garage sales. We called them White Elephant Sales. We held some bridge teas. We made good little bits.

We had these little things and realized we weren't going very far, very fast and weren't getting very much money for this. At the same time, Wurstfest began [*New Braunfels' annual fall German festival*]. We were in on the ground floor. It was Robbie Borchers, Margie Waldrip, and myself. It was around 1966. We did so well. We had what we called a "Matschig Berger." It was chopped beef on a bun. We had a hard time finding something to sell that no one else had. We did very well and added something the second year.

We realized by this time that they put a sausage on a stick so you can hold it with a beer. As soon as the concept of food on a stick went over, we had a meeting with our group. We decided to do shrimp. Nobody had shrimp.

A member had been to a party the night before, and they had had sausage cheese balls. We said, "Well, let's try it. We will make them bigger and put them on a stick and it will be nice to have with a beer." Over the years, we have made millions of cheese balls.

We are now, luckily, able to go down to the bakery to mix the stuff in huge vats. We used to make up to 20,000 of them or more to sell during the week. We brought $5,000 in on a Saturday night. We would take this money in paper bags, put them in the car, go home, then throw it out on the table and just start counting the money. Over ten days, we would take in probably $25,000. All the money went to candidates. Mostly state candidates because we didn't have that many running here.

So we have all of this money to dole out. They are courting us. We didn't need to worry at all about money problems. Then there got to be a problem with the PAC [*Political Action Committee*] fund. We needed to find ways to raise money because we couldn't use our PAC fund money for our regular club operating expenses. So here we are again doing garage sales and all the stupid little things to raise money. What we do now is our Christmas home tour. It has just gone over fabulously. Last year we took in about $3,000. So all of the money that we make at Wurstfest goes to the candidates.

JAN KENNADY, NEW BRAUNFELS

TFRW doesn't give money directly to the state party except for the $1,000 to be a Key Republican. We have made some contributions to support a particular candidate or program. Generally, our PAC fund gives strictly to Republican candidates. Our committee recommends who to the board, and the board decides. The TFRW as a board gave about $30,000 to candidates in 1998. But I know of a single club in Houston that gave just about that much. That club has about 500 some members. So if you look at each of the clubs and how much money they have given together to candidates it would be a lot.

Focal Point

PATTILOU DAWKINS, AMARILLO

If you look at the women in TFRW, so many of them are the leaders in their communities. They have made being a Republican and involvement in the Republican organization not only respectable but something that needs to be done. When I have to do something, the first list I pull out is my Republican Women's list.

BILL SHANER, MIDLAND

Midland does not have a Republican men's organization because the women have such good meetings and such good programs. They have allowed us to be non-voting, associate members. We don't have to have a women's club bringing in one of the statewide candidates and then a men's club bringing in a statewide candidate and taking up two days of a month. So we all go to the Republican Women's meeting. That's the way Midland is.

ROBBIE BORCHERS, NEW BRAUNFELS

The club has served as a focal point for the business that goes on. They are good about having candidates in and fundraising. They are a great deal more active than the county executive committee. The county committee seems to tend more toward getting the primary together, and maybe the county committee works harder at candidate recruitment. There's kind of an unspoken division of labor. Republican Women always fund and run the headquarters, and they deal with all of the volunteers and phone banks and so forth. The county committee just kind of takes care of the primary and candidate recruitment.

Area Councils

BABS JOHNSON, DALLAS

Melzia MacIver was the county vice chairman. Melzia discovered that all her brand new Republican Women's Clubs were overlapping or else really competing with one another in area efforts, such as studies that they were doing. So she had a meeting. I suppose it was with the club presidents, I don't know. She said that it was imperative that we have some central organization. So the Republican Women's council was formed. It outlined programs dividing the county in various ways when we all wanted to work together on one particular project. We did a study on the Dallas county courts. There was a central effort to divide the various aspects of the study so the clubs didn't all go calling on the same poor judge at the same time and duplicate our efforts. Mary Jester was the first president of the council.

MARY JESTER, DALLAS

The area council was formed to encourage other clubs to be strong and to get everybody together so they would know what the others were doing—so no one would have secrets. If they dreamed something up, then we wanted to know about it.

Why did you decide to form a council?

BARBARA NOWLIN, HOUSTON & FRIENDSWOOD

I guess because we really thought that with a team effort we would get more done. We really were all new at it then. We needed to learn from each other. I don't think that there was anyone in that club that had ever done anything political. We were all friends and wanted to organize our precincts. It was really the first time out for all of us.

How did the area council help develop the Party structure in Harris County?

It provided workers for the elections. We did the door-to-door canvases regularly and registered voters and had ongoing recruitment of volunteers. We made sure we knew our people and their party affiliations.

In the '60s, we adopted a state representative or state senate candidate, and we became that candidate's chief source of volunteers. It was small back then, very few clubs; now it is huge. Back then, there might have been twenty or thirty clubs.

Was having an area council an efficient way of using time?

FLORENCE NEUMEYER, HOUSTON

It was, because all of the club presidents could know the same information within a few hours of meeting. We used to call people out if the president or a senator was coming into the city.

Hard Work

There was a passage in From Token to Triumph *by Roger M.*
Olien quoting the San Antonio Express News: *"Jack Porter*
[who was national committeeman] also had problems with the
new activists, women volunteers." The author went on to talk
about how Republican Women played a role in getting Bruce
Alger elected to Congress in the 1950s, but Mr. Porter's reaction
regarding that was that women might have rung a few door-
bells but they didn't raise any money. Is that fair?

RITA CLEMENTS, DALLAS

The Texas Republican Party had been dominated by a few
people, mainly men, who did raise enough funds to kind of keep it
going. Republican Women getting out and ringing doorbells broad-
ened the base, and I don't think that women's clubs have ever been
known for big money raising. They had money-raising activities,
but that time is long past. Many women are active fundraisers for
big money now. A few people ran the Republican Party for many
years in Texas. They liked it that way, so there was bound to be
some stepping on toes when more new people started getting involved.

GWEN PHARO, DALLAS

In 1965, I was president of the Park Cities Republican Women.
I had a member named Esther Vermooten. She thought that everybody that lived in the Park Cities should be a member of the
Republican Women's Club. She took it upon herself to walk up
and down the streets of Highland Park and maybe University Park
and knock on doors and sign them up. The dues were $2. People
would give Esther $2 to get her off their doorstep. We had never
had more than 92 members. Ever. By the time Esther got through,
we were the second largest club in the country. There was one in
California that was a little bit larger. We had 892 members. As a
gift to Esther we couldn't think of anything important enough to
give her. We bronzed her shoes. It was like a tiger out of control.

We used to meet in homes, and then we couldn't meet anywhere—there wasn't anywhere big enough to hold us. It wasn't more than two years before it fell back to 92. At least it was manageable again.

MARION COLEMAN, PASADENA

The Republican Women's Club would have teas and coffees for John Tower. We would have two teams. Four to six women would go in and set up the coffee or tea at whoever's house. They would stay around. They knew all of the issues. They taught themselves, and we trained them to go around with the people that were there in case they had any questions about Tower that he didn't have a chance to answer. Those four or six would go on with Tower to the next tea. Another group would come in and clean up so that the hostess wouldn't have to worry about it.

Did the Republican Women's Clubs assist in your husband's campaign?

POLLYANNA STEPHENS, SAN ANGELO

Oh, yes. People like Annette Hopkins and Janie Brock—those are the two, even back in 1984, who set up the room, called the people, licked the envelopes, passed out the posters, and did all that was needed. You can not do something without them.

JACQUE ALLEN, WICHITA FALLS

Mildred Staley was always the district director in the Republican Women's Club. I guess this whole neighborhood was involved in some way. Dorothy Langford was the deputy state vice chairman. They traveled together. After I became county chairman, I went with them. Naturally, through them, I met people who preceded me into politics. They were a gracious group of nice ladies. They are the ones that started that women's club. All of us were members.

When you were involved with TFRW, did you find yourself able to help develop political strategy for the Texas Republican Party?

VERA CARHART, RICHARDSON & HOUSTON

When Ray Hutchison was chairman, yes. At that point, I knew more about what was going on in the state than practically anyone else because I traveled all about Texas. Many times I stayed in homes with people where you talked until three o'clock in the morning. So you know what was going on. Whereas the state chairman, he was home earning a living and had to rely on whomever he hired to be his administrative assistants.

Why do you think the Party was so willing to rely upon TFRW to go in and develop some of the areas that needed to be developed?

We had the time and the resources to do it. We had people that were willing to say I have a cousin that lives in such-and-such county and there is not a chairman there. A lot of the county chairmen did not want women's organizations. We made them insecure. Walker County is a good example. The man that was chairman there would not talk to you. He would just slam the phone down. This went on for years. Finally, I called him and I said, "You listen to me. I've got names of people over there that are interested. They'll work with you, and they want to form a club." He said, "Well, I guess I have been awfully rough on the ladies."

TEDDY PETERSON, SAN ANTONIO

Congressman Jim Collins was down from Dallas when Tom Loeffler was running for Congress in 1978. He was making a speech to a Republican Women's group. He said, "The Republican Women are the best street walkers in the world." I don't think it came out quite like he meant for it to.

CHAPTER 12

Candidate Recruitment

"We had to really twist people's arms and talk them into running
for these statewide offices because, of course, they had no shot at
winning most of the time."   —POLLY SOWELL

*Many attribute the growth of the Republican Party in
Texas to the high quality of its candidates. Party
officials looked for stand-out citizens in their communities who
would be willing to put their names on the ballot as Republicans. It took guts to step out and run for office in the early days,
likely to suffer ridicule and rejection. As time went on, recruiters
looked for those hungry enough to make the sacrifices demanded
by a run for office. Were they willing to raise money and look for
voters outside the Party faithful? Could they inspire workers
and find the right set of issues to attract votes? Many candidates
learned that the success of their campaigns depended on some
very simple phrases: "I want your vote" and "thank you."*

*Personal and committee interviews revealed whether or not
potential recruits had the combination of qualities that volunteers
could rally behind and voters could cast their ballots for on Election
Day. The Party had no control over those filing for a place on the
ballot, and occasionally a Party leader would face the challenging
job of discouraging someone from running. Recruiters sought
qualified women as candidates for important seats, and like men,
they overcame their reluctance. Due to the Party's limited resources,
leaders often had to make difficult choices as to which races were the
most important to support. The decisions were sometimes controversial but nevertheless required.*

Recruiting Committees, State & Local

HARRIET LOWE, DALLAS

I was on a committee to recruit legislators in the '50s. We must have interviewed fifty or sixty people and got down to what we thought was the cream of the crop. Then we had our meeting before the convention, and Walter Fleming, a good friend of mine, came in with tousled hair. "You won't believe what happened. All the people you got to run for the legislature voted in the Democratic primary. Go out and tell everybody we don't have any legislators to run." I believed him. Then, after I had done my job thoroughly of talking to everyone, I met one of these fellows and I said, "Why did you vote in the Democrat primary?" He said, "I didn't, and neither did any of the rest of us." It was a little deal. The Democrats would let us run Bruce Alger [*for Congress*] if we wouldn't mess up anything else. I fell right in that hole. They probably made the deal with Walter Fleming. I don't know.

FRANCIE FATHEREE CODY, PAMPA

Malouf Abraham ran for state rep. I remember trying to talk him into it. I said we need some representation in Austin. It can't all just be Democrats. This is a fairly conservative area, and you are well known and very electable. You can afford to go to Austin and stay for a few months. It would be a good experience in your life. I remember talking to him in the Killarney Cafe in Canadian.

MARTHA CROWLEY, DALLAS

Republicans were running for the first time. It wasn't easy to get candidates. It was before the [*Kennedy*] assassination, so it must have been in '62. We were at Republican headquarters on filing deadline night. Peter O'Donnell was county chairman. Mary Anne Collins was there, and I don't remember who else, but there were eight to ten of us. We tried to think of who we could get to run for the legislature. They were all running at-large at the time. Ike Harris had just graduated from Southern Methodist University law school. His sister-in-law was down there, and she said, "I wonder if Ike would do it." Well, Ike hadn't even decided what party he was in when we called him that night. She talked him into coming down and running. There were six of them that we talked into running. They all came down and filed. They all won. Everybody on our ticket won.

How did that happen? How did you pull that off?

They knew and liked Congressman Bruce Alger. Somebody made the remark afterwards that we could have won with Mickey Mouse. My husband, Frank, wasn't up for reelection as county commissioner. We just got out and campaigned for everybody. There was one special election—Hughes Brown was our candidate. Hughes won that right before the assassination. Everything that came up, we could win.

With Frank Crowley's county commissioner win in 1960, did others want to run for office in Dallas?

GLENNA McCORD, DALLAS

Not until 1962. It was a while. I had been on the candidate recruitment committee a couple of terms. We begged people to run for office who would be not only good officeholders but good candidates as well. People do not realize the sacrifices the candidate makes. With that primary being so early, if they are in business for themselves, they had better have a good partner because otherwise their business is just going to be put aside. If they get elected, then what?

What did you say to them when trying to recruit them?

Usually, it was someone that somebody on the committee knew. You would sit down and talk to them and ask them if they would please come before the committee and let us talk to them about it. Rob Hannay was a delightful lady. She was straight Republican all the way through. No monkey business. She sat there, and she would not ask many questions until we got towards the end of the interview. Then she would say, "I must ask this question." Everybody in the room on the committee knew what it was going to be. "Do you have any skeletons in your closet? If you do run on the Republican ticket, that skeleton will be pulled out of your closet." In 1962, the John Birch Society had raised its ugly head. We were so dumb we didn't know who these people were or what it was all about. These people were coming in to us. They wanted to run for the state legislature. We would ask, "Why do you want to run?" More times than not the reply would come back, "We want to fight Communism." I'd think, "In Austin, Texas?"

POLLY SOWELL, McALLEN & AUSTIN

One of the things we worked hardest at and I felt strongly about was recruiting good candidates. In those early days, you couldn't just sit back and wait for people to say, "I think I'll run for railroad commission." We had to really go out and beat the bushes. We had to really twist people's arms and talk them into running for these statewide offices because, of course, they had no shot at winning most of the time. We tried to convince them that they did. We looked at the election returns and said, "Senator Tower carried the district. You can too." Sometimes it worked, and sometimes it didn't. Candidate recruitment was one of the things we had to constantly work at. I recruited so many candidates and I've had so many lose, but invariably they'd tell me that it was the most fascinating experience of their lives, even when they'd lose.

LOU BROWN, MIDLAND

The Party here had a candidate recruitment committee. We would sit down and try and look for those people who would be good standard bearers for the Republican Party and want to serve in public office.

In a town our size, which was under 100,000 at the time, you know who your leaders are. Leaders came through the different organizations. You have PTA leaders. You have church leaders. You have different people that were doing different things. The committee was made up of people from different walks of life. You just get together and bounce ideas off of one another. It's like a nominating committee—you try and seal in blood everything that is said around the table. If something came up that somebody knew would not make a person a good candidate, you would not work to recruit him or her. After a few years, we had many people coming out of the woodwork that wanted to run for political office.

JUANDELLE LACY, MIDLAND

In '76, I was state chairman of the committee to recruit men and women to run for U. S. Congress. Jim Collins from Dallas, a U. S. Congressman, was national chairman. I worked with a young man out of the national office in Washington. He came to Texas. We were trying at that stage to fill every congressional race in the state of Texas with really good Republican candidates. That was when we began to make some inroads for the Party as far as our U. S. Congressmen. We had lots of names. We would meet in Dallas with Collins and Barbara Lewis, the president of TFRW at that time.

Was this a TFRW function?

No. When Jim Collins called Barbara Lewis and asked if she could help in this endeavor, she said only if she could appoint a chairman. We traveled the state. We interviewed men and women. What we were trying to do was find men and women who were not only capable. Their integrity and honesty were important to us before we would even approach them to run for the office.

When you found people who seemed good, how did you convince them to run?

Most of them wanted to be assured of financial support. The Party has never really given unless we had races that were targeted where national funds came in. In most cases, we rarely had money to fund candidates. But in 1976, we filled every single congressional race. A lot of the candidates were in heavily Democrat areas.

NANCY CANION DAVIS, GALVESTON COUNTY

I organized the district eleven Senatorial District Candidate Recruitment Committee. It was composed of the county chairmen and the two state committee people. We decided what we wanted to target and what we thought was winnable based on past election statistics. Then we went and recruited. I have to say we did pretty darn well with Buster Brown and Tom Delay.

> *What makes an attractive candidate when you are recruiting for a Party that doesn't have many victories?*

People that want the job, number one. Number two, people that have some kind of base in the local community and have a natural constituency they can appeal to, whether it is the business community or the farming community. Bringing some stranger in doesn't work, especially in the more rural areas. We looked at philosophy. Did we think they would do what we thought they would do once they got in office? The other very controversial thing we did was we agreed as a district candidate recruitment committee that, even as county chairmen who were supposed to be neutral, we would endorse in the primary if there was any opposition. We wanted to recruit really good candidates. We felt, as Party leaders, if we went to these people and had them put their necks on the line in traditional Democratic areas the least we could do as a Party would be to stand up for them in the primary. We caught a lot of flack for it, but it worked.

AMELIE COBB, BEAUMONT

We had dreams of someday controlling the Texas Legislature and getting people elected statewide. There was a real push for statewide candidates. By then, Bush had been elected [*to Congress*] in Houston, and there were other Republicans elected. When Ray Hutchison was state chairman, he had a Republican campaign committee for the state. I was one of the members. We looked at the demographics. We looked at congressional races. We looked at state legislative races. We did get down to some of the county levels, but there were not many people running then. There was a debate about where the best place was to start. We needed to start in both places.

We didn't have big bucks initially, but we had some money. If they knew, number one, that they had to put together a campaign plan, and that they had to have a professional manager, it made those candidates get themselves on a much higher plane and not just wander around their district not knowing what to do. They had to put their plans together. They had to raise a certain amount of money. They had to have it all put together before they came to the committee. We met in regions, and all the candidates in that area would come see us. We had a field rep from the Republican National Committee who sat in with us. They may not have gotten a lot of money from us, maybe $500 or $1,000, but then they could say to the people back home, "The Republican campaign committee has enough faith that I have put together a good campaign that they are willing to fund me. Will you give money to my campaign?" It did work. We interviewed first-time-out people like Tom Delay. Tom Loeffler came to our committee. They were fresh.

Interviewing Candidates

ANN WALLACE, FORT WORTH & AUSTIN

We would have our county Republican meetings, trying to recruit good people. You can't tell somebody they can't run. You can try to discourage them or try to find somebody else who is so outstanding that maybe they won't.

How could you convince good people to run when there wasn't much chance of winning?

They had to have some sort of fire in their belly and something that they wanted to do. You couldn't guarantee them any money. You could tell them that you would get out and help raise money. But it was not easy. In those days, women volunteered if you found a good candidate. Really, they were so loyal. They would do anything. They would reach in their pockets and buy stamps if you ran out of stamps. They knew somebody that would do some printing for you. It was the "borrow and scrounge days." You could do things on very little money as long as you had people out really gung ho for it. That's what you needed.

NADINE FRANCIS, ODESSA

In recruiting candidates and talking to candidates, I tried very hard to get them to listen to people. If people were coming to meet a candidate, chances were pretty good that they had something to say to him. They didn't want those candidates to stand up there and tell them what they believed. They were interested, but they had something they wanted to say. Asking for their vote was the hardest thing for candidates. I never understood it. If you ask somebody and tell somebody you need their vote, you want their vote, you appreciate and thank them. It's important to tell people thank you. Thank you for coming. Thank you for taking time away from your business to help us.

FLO KAMPMANN CRICHTON, SAN ANTONIO

Of course, the trouble was, and always is, you can't decide who is going to run in your primary. Anybody who has got the money for the filing fee can go into the primary and they are yours. We tried to control it through candidate recruitment committees and then through persuasion. So often somebody decided to run for office without a clue as to how much money it would cost. Not having any source of money, they just wanted to have their name on the ballot. You have to talk to them and let them reason this out.

Who was picked to go to those meetings?

There were a lot of those meetings. It depended on who was the official in the particular part of the country. I used to be the one to go talk to some of them. It just was my job to do. I remember several people, nice guys who had not a clue what it was all about or what it involved or what you had to put together to run a campaign with no backing. They just felt that they would be a good officeholder and signed up.

How can you let somebody down gently?

You just suggest to them that they look at their own situation. Just say, "Look at your money, supporters, and organization.

Do you really think that it will work?" Generally, when they took a good hard look at it, it wouldn't work. Then they would run for something else. They would think about it. A lot of them have gotten some money and supporters together and run for another office next time.

BARBARA CULVER CLACK, MIDLAND

I met Phil Gramm way back there. He was a professor at A&M [*Texas A&M University*}, and he was thinking about running for Congress. He was wandering around the state meeting people and trying to decide whether he was going to run as a Democrat or a Republican. I got invited to a little committee meeting, and we met this strange professor from A&M. He talked and talked. And we talked and talked, and finally I said, "You know, you make up your mind what you want to be, and then if you want to be a Republican we'll help you. But we can't make this decision for you." No telling what he heard in other places, but he ran as a Democrat. Then the Democrats treated him shabbily, and he resigned as a Democrat and went back, had a special election, ran as a Republican, and won.

Do you have a way of identifying whether or not a candidate has what it takes to win?

BETSY LAKE, HOUSTON

After I have talked to them for thirty minutes, I can probably tell you if that candidate is even going to be able to come close. I've talked a lot of people out of running. Many walked in and didn't have a clue. It takes a year and a half of your life. Young men in particular may not want to run for judge or for Congress. I would say, "Why don't you wait a few years? You have a baby and a two year old. Your wife might need you more right now." They don't think about that. A lot of them come in thinking that the Party is going to pay for it, even in the primary. Of course, you don't do that in a primary. Every candidate is on his own. Sometimes people would come, and I would say, "I don't think that you should run. There are other ways you can be a public servant without running for state rep. Maybe you would like to run for water district or school board." I like to see people pay their dues.

PAT JACOBSON, FORT WORTH

Not only do they have to be talented and have some charisma, the main thing is that they are willing to work. Dick Armey came to me asking for help. I liked his looks. I liked what he stood for. He was a teacher at North Texas [*State University, now the University of North Texas*] in economics. He was very bright. I had been impressed a couple of times with other people, and they didn't work. They wanted me to do all the work for them. Dick had heard of me and knew that I was a fundraiser and could get the money and people involved. I told Dick that I would help him and I would call these people, but he would have to go see them to get the money. I wanted to see if he was willing to work. Not only did he go and get all of that money, I had people tell me he did not stand one chance. My friends who gave $1,000, their limit, laughed at me because they said he could not make it against Tom Vandergriff. They didn't know this guy. He was one gutsy guy. He walked this whole area. He got the contacts. Dick, as we all know now, is the majority leader in the House and is terrific. I'm very proud of him. He started at my kitchen table.

JOCI STRAUS, SAN ANTONIO

John Tower was at our house for dinner. He called and asked for a meeting. He wanted a meeting of four or five of us. He wanted to talk about his future. He wanted to talk about whether he should run again because his drinking tarnished his reputation. We had to rebuild his image. We told him, "You're going to have to leave it to us to do it. It's going to be tough." First thing I did was have an event for him at our house. I started with the hard people first. I invited the conservative Democrats—the Louis Stumbergs and the Woodward Altgelts—the people that wouldn't just come to Tower because he's the father of the Republican Party of Texas. "We're going to have to make it tough on you," we told him, "and you're going to have to sit there and answer all these questions." He did.

We had twelve or eighteen conservative Democrat leaders in our living room. I left the room and I let the men—it was all men there, good old boys—sit and talk about how he envisioned his upcoming campaign. This was 1978, when Clements was running for governor and John was trying to decide whether he should run.

Have a lot of people come to you seeking advice about running for office?

SHAROLYN WOOD, HOUSTON

Some do and some don't. It's not as common anymore because the political consultants have discovered judicial elections. The climate is very different than it was twenty years ago. As other people wanted to run, I was very glad to pass on to them my experiences [*as a judge*]. But in the last seven or eight years, consultants have come in wanting to earn a living. When they hear someone wants to run, they go solicit them and get them to come to them for advice. It has changed, and I am sad to see the change. Judges are different than other people. Our elections are different. One of the reasons that the political consultants have had to come to the judicial races is that is the only place there are contested races anymore. The legislators have all had their districts drawn so that they are all safe.

MARY JESTER, DALLAS

Bobbie Biggart and I would recruit candidates. She called it "the bovine look" because sometimes you would go and talk to them and they would just kind of look at you, like, what are you suggesting? What is all of this?

Being Recruited

CYNDI TAYLOR KRIER, SAN ANTONIO

My first race for the state senate resulted directly from John Tower approaching Norman Newton and the Associated Republicans of Texas. He asked them to do some analysis of election returns to find races where Republican Hispanics had done well in the past so that he might nominate Hispanic Republicans to run in races that had never been won by Republicans before. They did that analysis in Bexar County and found two races—one was the twenty-sixth senatorial district. We tried and thought we had recruited a Hispanic Republican, Ernesto Ancira, to run a senate race, and then at the last minute we found out that, while his business was in the heart of the district, his residence was two blocks outside of it. They literally came to me a week before that race and said, "You have been such an effective advocate for why this race should be run and how it could be run that we would like you to run, Cyndi." So it sort of shifted from Hispanics to women. Initially they said, "File for office and see what you think, and then if you change your mind you can pull out." At that time, if you pulled out, somebody else could be nominated. They suckered me. Once they got your name on the line, there really wasn't a graceful way to say "I changed my mind" without looking really silly. When I counsel people who are thinking of running and when I am trying to recruit candidates now, I always tell them you need to run for office because of what you want to do in office not because you want to be the state senator or the county judge.

SHAROLYN WOOD, HOUSTON

I was interested in being a judge. I had been practicing for about eight years. I got a call one day from a lawyer, John Cavin, that I practiced law with for a long time who was an active Republican. Several of the lawyers that I practiced with were active Republicans. He said Commissioner Echols just called and they need people to run for office. They would love a woman to run. You have always wanted to be a judge. Why don't you just move your timetable up? My first response was, "John, I am too young." So it got me thinking. You have to pick whether to be a Republican or Democrat.

Was that difficult for you to do?

At that point, every judge in Harris County was a Democrat. Except for justices of the peace, there weren't any Republicans. There were no Republicans on the Texas Supreme Court or any appellate judges. My husband and I carpool together. I remember deciding to drive around the block one more time. I decided I could not run for office as a Democrat. This was 1980. I looked at where they were and what you had to say in order to run as a Democrat. I didn't know anyone in the Republican Party, I just decided as a person I could not run as a Democrat.

MARY DENNY, DENTON

Running for the legislature, I got encouragement from Jim Horn and Ben Campbell who were both serving in the legislature during the last redistricting in the 1990s. They said, "Mary look at this district. We drew it for you. You have that rural area, and you know all those people out there." Of course, it takes in two other counties besides Denton where I knew no one. But I really got to thinking about what they said. You know, I thought, maybe I could do this. I was county chairman at the time, and part of the job was to recruit candidates to run for this new district. I couldn't find anybody that I thought was suitable. So I thought, you know, maybe they really were serious. Maybe I could do this. We're so full of self-doubt. We always think that there has got to be more to a job than there really is or that we're not qualified or that we don't have proper training. I had all those questions and all those doubts. Gosh, I bet I wasn't in the legislature two weeks, and I looked around me. Honestly, I don't mean to sound like I am bragging because I'm just an average human being who also has some political experience, but I knew a lot more about a whole lot of stuff than those folks did—less than some, but certainly more than a lot. I thought, I'm every bit as qualified to be here as anybody is. We citizens shortchange ourselves when it comes to thinking about running for political office. Most people who have had some life experience and have reasonable intelligence and care about the world in which we live would be just great running for public office. That is what we need more of. It's not as hard as you think.

NANCY JUDY, DALLAS

My congressman, Alan Steelman, ran for the United States Senate against Lloyd Bentsen. I was in contact with him because of legislative issues pertaining to children throughout my years on the school board. I also continued on in my precinct chairman position. He was an absolutely dazzling personality. A star. When he wanted to run for the U. S. Senate, his staff did an analysis of the community. They felt that I would be the strongest candidate to run as the Republican candidate in the fifth district, so they asked me to run and I did. I don't think I had any opposition in the Republican primary. This was in 1976. I resigned my job on the school board with great reluctance. I ran against Jim Mattox who was a state legislator and with whom I conferred as well as other members of the Dallas delegation on a regular basis. I lost. I received almost 46 percent of the vote. This was after Watergate. That was the year Jimmy Carter won, and the Republicans lost many seats in the House and Senate. I was the strongest contender for an open seat in the state but lost. I will also note that Jim Mattox had more out-of-state labor contributions than any other candidate for Congress in 1976.

Qualities

What kinds of qualities did you look for in possible candidates?

ANNE ARMSTRONG, ARMSTRONG

We had certain basic qualifications that we insisted on. Integrity was the first one, then capability, intelligence, and family. Then you would look into the things that were more practical, like whether they could get the backing of the local people. We used the state committee often for such things, but I well remember specific candidate committees that were charged by this state committee to do spade work on analyzing each race and making the often agonizing decisions as to which ones we could go all out for, which ones we could go medium out for, and occasionally which ones we didn't even want a candidate because there was such a strong Democrat that could command money and efforts against some of our other candidates. If we ran against him, then it would be counter productive. Oftentimes, local people couldn't understand what we leaders up there in Austin were trying to do to them. But we did it scientifically. That makes it sound neater than it was. But it was intelligently approached. It began working.

POLLY SOWELL, McALLEN & AUSTIN

Of course, you'd look for people qualified for the office. You wanted them to be able to raise money. That was the most difficult thing. You wanted them to be hardworking. You wanted them to be right on the issues, too. You'd take advantage of people's ego. You'd plant a little seed saying, "John, you know you'd be a great state rep." Then you'd wait. John looks at himself in the mirror in the morning and says, "You know, I might be a good state rep." Then you'd call again in two or three weeks. You'd get some friends to call and, as one of my friends in politics said, "Three calls and you think it's a landslide." We always tried to recruit women because they always do better. Nowadays they say five percentage points is the advantage that a woman has over a man.

Let's say there are several people who want to run for governor or congressman. All of these people want your financial support. How do you discern which one of them has the character that you want?

JUDY JONES MATTHEWS, ABILENE

Out here, it is not all that hard because everyone knows everyone. If you don't know someone who is running, say, from Amarillo, you can call up there and find out. You know in the case of judges because they have records. You ought to be able to tell what you are getting. A man who is running for the first time might be a little different, but if he has been in law practice or he has been in business, he has some background.

How do you attract the best candidates?

SURRENDEN ANGLY, AUSTIN

They almost need to come forward. They have got to have it

in their blood. It's like taking a horse to water. If I have to pull someone into running, it is going to be a fiasco from beginning to end. I wouldn't go out and beg someone to run. If they want to run, they will run. They develop their own organization and style.

MARTHA WEISEND, DALLAS

Their motive has to be right. They have to understand the cost, not in dollars but in their time and energy. They have to be realistic about winning. I like to know that they have the intelligence and comprehension to do the task at hand, whether it is for sheriff or for congressman or for governor. I like to know that they will represent the people well and that the taxpayers will get their dollar's worth. They need a philosophy of hard work, respect for the Constitution and our government. In a state election, for example, do they care about our state? If they are looking for a job, I'm not interested. If they are looking for public service and have an appreciation of taxpayers' dollars, I'm interested.

Governor Clements has an old saying, "Once burned twice leery." When you sit with a candidate, you can know if he or she is in the real world about what they think they can do. You can certainly figure out how much of their time and energy and money they are going to put into the race and if it is short-term or long-term, or if this is a stepping stone to something bigger. You can pretty well tell the ones that are going to be there to get a job done rather than to build a bio. It is not hard for me. A short forty-five-minute interview and you can pretty well know how serious and how technical they are.

BEVERLY KAUFMAN, HOUSTON

After twenty years of experience, I really was qualified to do the job [*of county clerk*]. I had focused on the area of elections. I was an election judge and a Party worker for years. I was appointed county clerk in March of '94. I had to be nominated by the Party to have my name on the ballot because my predecessor, who passed away while in office, had already filed for reelection before her death. I was challenged by a gentleman who had been on the SREC.

I had a tough fight on my hands. I worked harder than I've ever worked in my life. I am grateful for the women in particular. Because I had worked in the Party for many years, I had a reputation for being fair and dedicated. They respected that. By the time we got to the meeting, I had secured enough votes to get the nomination.

They Had Guts

SITTY WILKES, AUSTIN

Beryl Milburn really was the backbone here. She went door-to-door when she ran for the legislature in the '50s, knowing she wasn't going to win. It took guts to do all that. She knew it when she started out. She just wanted to show that a Republican could run, and it shocked people. I don't think that they had ever had a Republican candidate before. Women had not come into their liberation. What a coup for her to be on the board of regents at UT [*University of Texas*]. None of those people ever thought that any of us would ever get a plum like that. They had it all to themselves.

DOROTHY CROCKETT, ODESSA & MARBLE FALLS

Most of them were token candidates, but they believed in what they were doing. We were so dumb. We thought that maybe we did have a chance. We really believed so strongly in what we were doing. We thought that everyone ought to see the value of having a Republican. We were pretty naive. Some of those candidates, of course, we knew didn't have a chance. But there were some of them that we really thought did.

What do you think your biggest challenge was running for office in the 1960s and 1970s?

MARY LOU GRIER, SAN ANTONIO & BOERNE

Just trying to accomplish some kind of a showing that would help the Party on down the road. The idea that there would be candidates on the ballot to give people a choice and to show that there was more than just a presidential election.

REBA BOYD SMITH, ODESSA & ABILENE

When I ran for office [*county treasurer*] back in '62, I had to make up my mind that I could win or I could lose. It wasn't until I lost that I found out it takes a bigger person to win than it does to lose. People are nice to you when you've lost. They say to you, I am so sorry, you would have been the greatest whatever. When you get elected, then they get to be demanding. I think there is a difference. I didn't know that. Now, when I talk to anybody about running, I tell him or her to make sure that you can lose or you can win.

SHIRLEY GREEN, AUSTIN & SAN ANTONIO

Coming up to '64, the state party theory was, with Goldwater planning to run, run as full a slate as possible so that all of the Democrats would have to be tied down protecting their own seats, as opposed to everybody being able to reelect then President Johnson. There were four state reps for Travis County, and they all were at-large. For some reason or another, they wanted at least one of those candidates for state rep to be a woman and asked me if I would do it. I was young and foolish enough that, after discussing it with my husband and children, I said yes. We were all handily defeated. The good thing about losing a race like that is you knew you weren't going to win so your heart wasn't going to be broken. You were just willing to do it to rack up a few more points for the home team.

SYLVIA NUGENT, DALLAS & AMARILLO

I'll be in a shop buying something, writing a check, and the girl behind the counter will say, "I voted for you." Then I think it's painful to lose office. In politics, winning is everything. Second place doesn't matter much. To know that there were that many people who made an effort to go vote for me is so special. In some ways, it blazes the trail for other women. I'm very proud of taking the risk. I know a lot of men who will not take the risk to put themselves out there. Running for office is hardball. In lots of ways, it gave me credibility that I did not have before. I was not a dilet-tante doctor's wife. I could get out there and fight in the arena of ideas and play hardball.

CHAPTER 13

Women as Candidates

"A close friend in Dallas once said the Republican Party
in Texas is never going to achieve its place in history
until the caliber of the men equals that of the women."
—CATHERINE SMYTH COLGAN

*B*eginning in the 1950s, women willingly put their names
on the ballot as Republicans and exposed themselves to failure
in order to contribute to the growth of the Party. Often they learned
as they campaigned, and in the early years they even ran their own
campaigns. Raising money was a challenge then for women
candidates, as it is today. Money usually follows the victors, and
until Republicans began to win, the quest for campaign funds was
often uphill. They worked hard for endorsements from local papers
and occasionally got the nod from the influential media.

As time went on and the Republican Party became more
sophisticated, so did women running for office. Managers refined
campaign plans. Women who had been early candidates used
their experiences to assist others in developing more effective
campaign plans. Women ran hard against the odds and began to
win. They were not treated with kid gloves because of gender,
and they proved they had the stomach for the vigor of the
campaign trail. They asked for votes and they got them.

Just like men, women Democratic elected officials began to
switch parties. Republican women started learning how to run
for judge and educated volunteers on the special nature of
judicial campaigns. Press relationships began to develop and
were used effectively to raise their visibility. Women staffers
decided to run for their bosses' open seats and learned to successfully represent themselves and parlay their experience into
positions as elected officials.

Putting a Campaign Together

BERYL MILBURN, AUSTIN

I ran for the state legislature. That was in '58, I think. Well, it was just terrible. I didn't know how to run a campaign. There was no money, no support, really. I was active in the Party and I wanted somebody to start running, so I thought, well, I'll do it. Double whammy. A woman and a Republican. My opponent was O. B. Jones, and he only had one leg. Most of the time he had a false leg that he could walk around on, but when elections came around, he'd take his leg off and go on his crutches to generate sympathy.

How were you recruited to run for office at that time?

I just made up my own mind. I remember walking around the offices downtown and handing out a card. People were so amused. They just couldn't visualize a woman running for office, and they couldn't visualize a Republican woman.

BARBARA CULVER CLACK, MIDLAND

I ran in '62. They [*the Party*] said, "We're going to run a slate of candidates." They came around to see if I would run for county judge. Of course, no one expected any of us to win. My husband and I talked about it a long time. I thought, well, it couldn't hurt to run. It could even help get your name bandied about, and it may help the law practice. We were still practicing together. I had been active in quite a few women's organizations, and some of my strange friends ran me as a write-in candidate for mayor. That got my name bandied around but not all favorably.

Women rallied around. We just campaigned vigorously. I was running against an incumbent Democrat who was a very nice person, a retired FBI man, and a pillar in the First Baptist Church. His wife was a charming high school teacher. They had three respectable children. Everybody thought you couldn't beat him. The women and the Republicans and my friends were having coffees and teas all over town. We were going door-to-door. We were standing on street corners handing out literature. In late October this gentleman realized that he had an opponent! If he had started earlier, he would've won. I won by less than 51 percent. He didn't do much of anything, and we had worked our heads off.

Did you have a campaign manager and a campaign plan?

Oh, we had everything and everybody. Anybody who was kind to me was on my campaign committee. We had a large committee instead of one campaign manager. I did have a campaign manager, but everyone talked strategy and tried to raise a few dollars for newspaper ads and radio. It was just a lot of fun. Nobody thought that we could win. We were just out having fun and working.

We didn't raise that much money, but I had a good friend, one of these early day admitted Republicans, named Payton Anderson who had been on the State Republican Executive Committee and who was well placed within the community. He buttonholed some of these Republicans and got some money out of them.

Did you have a problem with the idea of a woman being county judge?

Yes. The beautiful thing was that being a Republican was so much worse. They got off of being a female pretty quickly.

We ran an issue-oriented campaign. We had to go on the offensive. His dockets were a bit behind. We made a lot of points on what could be done with juveniles. We talked about the county budget and how to spend it—all of the issues pertaining to the office. A candidate should be focused on the issues.

How did you get recruited to run for state legislature in 1962?

MARJORIE ARSHT, HOUSTON
They called me up before the vacancy committee. I enjoyed it a great deal because I was a curiosity. Here was a Jewish woman from Yoakum, Texas. I was such an enigma. They had such limited perspective, with yes-or-no answers. They would ask questions like, "Are you for or against capital punishment?" I would say, "Well, until our system is geared so that really serious criminals can be kept behind bars for life without parole, we have no choice." The

answer wasn't on their paper. One of them who was a friend of mine called me one day and said, "I think it is hysterical they don't know what to do with you." Because I was such a curiosity, I really attracted a crowd. Mostly they wanted to ask how I could be Jewish and not a Communist. My husband, Raymond, would say, "I'd love to come along, but I'm sick of the Jewish question." Then I started asking them how many Jewish people did they think were in Houston, and I got answers like a million. Houston's population was about 400,000 people. I said there are 25,000 men, women, and children, which means there might be 5,000 to 7,000 votes in metropolitan Houston. From the back of the room a man called out and said, "Marjorie, are you sure? They must all live around me." That's one of millions of things that happened.

I had $8,000. I had no district—that was part of my problem—because there were nineteen legislators running around Harris County. So I went to the newspapers, and I knew I would have no problem with George Carmack of the *Houston Press* and the Negro newspaper. I went to the *Houston Chronicle*. I interviewed with the political editor, and he said to me. "Who is your opponent?" I said, "Don't you know who Wally Miller is? You endorsed him last time." With that, I went all the way up to John Jones, the newspaper owner. I said, "Your political editor doesn't even know whom you're endorsing just because he is a Democrat, and that is not worthy of this paper. If you want decent people to run for office, then you ought to know them." He knew my family, who was well known in Houston. They waited until the last day, and they endorsed me. So I had every endorsement.

I beat the gubernatorial candidate, who was Jack Cox, on the west side of Houston. But I had to stay on the west side to convince the Republicans that were there that I was not Communist. I went day and night. If I had only had enough time to spend in the black community. Later, I had a lot of blacks say to me, "We had no idea. Why didn't you come?" I just didn't have time. I appeared before the labor unions, which no Republican had ever done. Of course, Wally Miller didn't go. He was a conservative Democrat. Somebody in the audience said to me, "How could someone of your nationality support somebody like Goldwater?" I said, "Wait a minute. I am an American." Well, the Mexicans just rose to their feet and cheered. Somebody said to me, "Are you a Goldwater Republican?" I said, "No, a Marjorie Arsht Republican." They all just clapped. When I got through, the labor union man said, "You got a lot of votes in this hall tonight." It really was an exciting thing.

LOIS WHITE, SAN ANTONIO

In 1966, they [*the Bexar County Republican Party*] said, "We want you to run for state representative." It was Brotherhood Week, which was February 7 through 12. Black History Month has kind of taken over now. A young man at Republican headquarters asked me to come to his youth group on a Sunday afternoon and talk about the race problem. It went off very well. I think that was probably to see if I could handle myself and make a speech. My husband and I talked about it. I said, "I will still teach, whether I go to Austin or not." That just turned out to be a shot heard around the county. A black woman running for state legislature on the Republican ticket?

I had people that were supporting me, but they weren't going to cross the line and be called Republicans. We never had more than ten blacks that would admit to being Republicans. I had the best teachers in the world. They took me step-by-step. The Republican Party had a fantastic esprit de corps and a fantastic structure. Joci Straus and Mary Lou Grier were our committeewomen. I learned very early that volunteers did much of what was done here. I found out what I was supposed to do. I got people to help me. I got friends who volunteered to do this for free.

What we ran into was the East Side was galvanized during district-wide political campaigns. Lots of people were dangling money in front of these people to get workers for this candidate or that candidate. These people would do a little work for a nice bit of money coming in to their households for grocery money. I got these friends, some of them were teachers, and they would work for free. We didn't have money to pay people. At the end, I had six people that volunteered, and we paid three. My campaign manager was Mary Johns. She contacted the churches and saw how many would let me come and speak. I found that they were very reluctant. What I did was, I said to people, "I don't want to offend you, but it is time that you woke up, and if you don't have any attachment to anybody come hear what I have to say." I seemed like a threat to some of them. There were a number that did support me. I got some contributions. What I wanted to do was give blacks a chance to have something besides one party to vote for. I had a fundraiser. The East Side had never had something like that. The attendance was quite good. Kids volunteered to help me at headquarters. I opened my little headquarters, and one night the boys helped me and one night the girls helped me because I didn't want to be suborning romance. Kids made their parents come out and help. Mrs. Johns kept the place open for me during the day.

I walked the East Side area. In a barbershop, an elderly white gentleman getting his haircut said, "We've got to help her." A younger man in a pawnshop said, "You've got that much nerve, I just might vote for you."

When people asked me to come, I would go to speak at night. There were picnics and things with Republicans all over the county. My principal asked me, "Well, how is it going?" The night before I had been out at a very good meeting. I said to myself quickly, "What does he really want to hear?" I said, "I don't think I'm going to make it." The man looked so relieved. The expression on his face was such that I almost died laughing. I turned and ran into one of my friend's classroom and started laughing. He said, "What is going on?" and I told him. Of course, if I had told the principal things were really going well, he would've found something for me to do. I was free for another week.

SITTY WILKES, AUSTIN

Charlotte Ferris, Beryl Milburn, and Yvonne Gardner talked me into running for the school board. They kept saying, "It is a nonpartisan race. You can win." Somehow or another they talked me into it. I cannot imagine, looking back, why I did it because I knew I didn't have a prayer even though it was a nonpartisan race. There was a guy here, Mark Yancey. He was with the highway department. He was brilliant, and he would brief me on the issues and on how to make speeches. So I went down and registered as a candidate and ran. It was in a field of about five, and you had to have a majority vote to win. I campaigned and won, if you can believe. But I went to one of my husband's furniture manufacturing business clients, Louis Shanks, who was an LBJ man, and asked him if he would get his friends to support me. He said, "Why are you running? What is in it for you? Are you going to sell furniture to the school district?" That motivation had never occurred to me. I said, "Oh, no, we make upholstered furniture. We would never be able to sell to the schools." I got a few people like that to help me. Then there was a woman named Mitchell, she was one of the past presidents of the Republican Women's Clubs. It was her idea to get up call sheets to call the voters. I had never seen that done before. She got call sheets for everybody and gave them a list of thirty people to call that day to see if they had gone and voted. I ran in '67 and was elected in '68.

MARY LOU GRIER, SAN ANTONIO & BOERNE

In '74, we had a full ticket statewide. It was something we had wanted to do for a long time. I ran for Texas Land Commissioner and traveled all over the state. We had a motor home. I'd say, 90 percent of the time all the candidates were on board. We'd stop at night at motels. The next morning we'd head out again. Sometimes we'd get out and walk down Main Street, go to a luncheon, or talk to a Republican Women's Club or some other group. There'd usually be a barbecue or something in the evening. We'd stop here and there in different cities. We got good press. The media were always there. We had some of the major city press traveling with us. TV and radio showed up. Everybody likes to be asked for their vote, even though they don't plan to vote for you. So we were pretty well received. We covered a lot of the state. Everybody got along real well. We had camaraderie. Even though most of the men thought they were going to win.

You didn't think you were going to win?

No. I didn't think I would win. But I thought I had a better chance than I did in '62 when I ran for Bexar County District Clerk.

Why didn't you win in 1974?

Well, I think it was too early [*laughing*].

Too early for a Republican or too early for a woman?

Nobody seemed to say you couldn't win because you're a woman. But it was still too early. You know, we just had the problem with Nixon and Watergate.

How do you think that your run for office in 1962 helped your future run for office?

I made a great number of speeches, and I was pretty articulate. I think that was a great deal of the reason behind the Party recruiting me, because they figured I could get up and talk on my feet, which I could do. I think that's why I was recruited. They didn't think I'd be an embarrassment. I could hold my own.

I had been involved in campaigns, so it wasn't as though I didn't know how they were run or what you did in a campaign. I guess I had been involved in almost every aspect of it, other than being a candidate, so there weren't any surprises.

When she ran for land commissioner in 1974, was Mary Lou Grier the first woman to run for statewide office since former governor Ma Ferguson?

CATHERINE SMYTH COLGAN, DALLAS
That's right.

How did people react to having a modern woman candidate?

I never saw a bit of problem. Of course she was such a capable, excellent person, excellent speaker. She was a stronger spokesman than some of the men. I did not see in that particular tour any discrimination because of her wearing a skirt. She could truly communicate with her audience. They were fascinated because of her demeanor and her presence. Had she been another type of female, perhaps it would have been different. She was a strong candidate that just happened to be a woman. That to me is important. Through the years, from what I have seen, the Texas Republican Party really was an open arena for women candidates. I never saw any discrimination. A close friend in Dallas once said the Republican Party in Texas is never going to achieve its place in history until the caliber of the men equals that of the women. You know what, that was correct. As the Party grew in strength, it became socially and professionally acceptable for a man to jump in the ranks.

Did your run for Congress in 1982 and also your run for state treasurer in 1990 affect how you put your campaign together when you ran for the Senate in 1993?

KAY BAILEY HUTCHISON, HOUSTON & DALLAS

I ran for the legislature in 1972 and was elected and served from 1973 to 1976. The legislative campaign was very grassroots oriented. The congressional campaign certainly was, too. I learned a lot from that because it was my only loss, and you learn as much or more from losses as you do from wins. Then in the state treasurer's race, everyone said you couldn't run a statewide race grassroots. It takes too much time. It takes money. It takes effort away from what you have to do to win, and don't do it. I said, "No, that is my strength, and it is the only way I know to run. It's the only way that we can elect a candidate at the down ballot level, because I will never have enough money to be on TV so that people will know who I am. If I don't have a grassroots organization, I don't see how I win against a Democrat in a Democrat state." So I did. I learned grassroots and I stuck to grassroots and it was all very much a stair-step effort. But I never forgot my base and that grassroots effort.

Why would advisors think that it is more expensive than running a standard media-based campaign?

Because they thought to have a volunteer organization, you had to feed it, and you had to have a staff person to make contact and keep generating enthusiasm. People would expect you, if you had a grassroots organization, to communicate with it, and therefore the thought was, you don't have enough effort to do it. But my grassroots effort was mostly volunteers. My whole campaign for state treasurer had only three paid staffers in the beginning and four in the end. I had a campaign manager, a finance director, and a scheduler, who were paid. I had a volunteer press secretary and a volunteer volunteer coordinator, and that was all. I didn't even have a travel aide. I traveled by myself. Later, I traveled with my volunteer press secretary. Then, right at the end, I gave her a nominal salary, nothing like what she was worth. That was it. I won with grassroots. In 1990, the governor of our Party was not elected. Nobody else was either except for myself and Rick Perry [*as agriculture commissioner*]. I believe that the only reason I was in the leading role to be Senator is because I was the highest ranking statewide elected official in Texas. I was a natural, with the grassroots-based organization, to be the nominee for the Senate because we didn't have anyone else.

ANITA HILL, GARLAND

It was a summer election for an open seat in the legislature. People don't think about elections during the summer. My husband insisted that I do it. I had never planned to run. Finally, I agreed. In 1972, my husband had been asked to run for the legislature. He said, "I can't think of a better thing to do to ruin your reputation." Then five years later, I ran. Now, I wouldn't take anything for it.

You ran as a Democrat?

Right. It really didn't come down to party affiliation but being known in the community. It was a three-person race, and we had a runoff. It was real tight. My husband and I had been very active in Democratic Party politics. After I was elected in 1977, one of the questions the Dallas County media asked was, "Are you going to support the candidate of your party in the presidential election?" At that time, it was either going to be Ted Kennedy or Jimmy Carter. I knew I wasn't going to vote for the Democrat. I always voted for the Republican in November. Democrats in Dallas County were having a fight between the established faction and the George Wallace faction. My husband usually was the chairman of the district convention. We saw a little of everything and a lot of hatred. When I decided to change parties, my husband was the secretary of the Dallas County Democratic Party. He resigned the day I made the announcement. They found somebody to run against me. A lot of people thought I should resign my seat. I didn't see it that way because I had been representing my district.

What was the reaction of the Democrats when you switched?

Some anger, but there weren't that many Democrats in Garland. Most of them were very nice about it. I still get along with them. John Bryant, a Congressman who was sort of the Democratic leader for Dallas County, made a statement that if you don't like Democratic Party politics then just get out. Now I am an avid Republican.

What was the reaction of the Republicans when you switched parties?

Enthusiasm! Soon after that, the Republican men's club started. The Garland Republican Women already existed.

When you switched and ran in your first election as a Republican, was there a difference between how you campaigned as a Republican and as a Democrat?

No, not really, but it was harder. My son took a leave from law school for one semester and came home and ran my campaign. The Republican Women from Dallas came up two or three nights to do telephone polls. It showed then that I would win with 65 percent. I actually won with 62 percent. When I ran the first time, I had never made a public speech. My mouth would get very dry. I would always have to go first. Finally, I would say, "I don't want to take advantage of my gender. Let Mike go first." Then I would say, "You have heard the sublime; here is the ridiculous." There are not many people who are very good speakers, so you get a lot more sympathy if you do that.

When I ran as a Republican, my opponent's family was very active in the Democratic Party. It was rough. I do not blame the woman who ran against me. One time they stole my yard signs. A man called and said, "Are you the Anita Hill that has all of these signs out on the lake shore?" Supporters who had my bumper stickers were forced off the road.

LEON RICHARDSON, NEDERLAND

In '76, we were able to get redistricted and thought we might be able to elect a state representative. No one would run. After we fought to get the redistricting, somebody had to do it. So I put a lot into it. Of course, I lost, but I got more votes than anybody ever had before. If I had had a real bad opponent I probably could have won, but he was real popular and I liked him myself. It's terrible to like your opponent.

Who managed your campaign?

One of the extreme right wing [*laughing*]. I have a letter, and she said, "Leon, it's getting hard to dislike you." One of the presidents of the bank was my finance manager. [*Senator*] John Tower came down for my announcement, and he went door-to-door in Nederland with me. He volunteered. Our relationship was platonic. We were buddies. He was here for the whole weekend. We went door-to-door one day, and we went to a high school football game. We had a luncheon and coffees.

How did people react when they opened the door and saw you and the Senator?

Their mouths dropped open. We stopped after a dog chased us.

MARJORIE VICKERY, COPPER CANYON

In the early '70s, I complained to my husband about our children's school. He said, "If you feel that strongly why don't you run for the board?" I never thought of that. I ran and won that election, and I became the first woman ever elected to the Lewisville school board. That was great preparation for me to serve on the state board of education.

After I went off the Lewisville school board, I decided I wanted to run for the state board of education. So I filed. Lots of people in the school system and, in fact, the whole community got behind me. The boundaries for the state board of education at that time were the same as the congressional boundaries. I grew up in Dallas, so I was familiar with a lot of people in North Dallas, and they were very, very supportive of me. In the primary, I had two opponents, both of whom were men. One of them was the former school superintendent in Irving. The other one had been a president of a school board in a parochial school system. When the election came, I almost won. We had to have a runoff. I started immediately getting on the telephone and calling the people who had helped me. I started early and told them that this was going to be the only runoff for the whole Republican Party in the Third Congressional District, so it was really vital that, if they would like for me to be their representative, they should take the time to put it on their calendars and vote one more time. They said that they would. The next time I won with like 70 percent. I had opponents in the general election, and I won.

How were you able to build your core of supporters?

First of all, my husband's company had a gentleman who had run many, many political campaigns. He offered to help me in my campaign. He gave invaluable advice and information on how to run a campaign and promote name recognition. He said it starts with your brochure. It has to be concise and, of course, all truthful. It was. It also had to describe my qualifications for the job. We mailed them out at bulk rate. To do that all over the district was very expensive but very worthwhile.

Because I had grown up in the Park Cities and graduated from high school there and graduated from SMU [*Southern Methodist University in Dallas*], I knew a lot of people in North Dallas and Park Cities that helped me to become known. I didn't have to start from scratch, so to speak. I relied on the Republican Women's Clubs. After I filed, they immediately started extending invitations to me to speak at their meetings.

SHAROLYN WOOD, HOUSTON

I had to make it clear very early on, because a lot of people want you to take political stands. Every time I got questionnaires from people, I sent them back a letter trying to be courteous, telling them, you go elect the legislators and congressmen who will enact the laws that you think are important. As a judge, I will keep my oath to uphold those laws. Of course, that means I uphold laws that I may not personally agree with.

My husband's office manager, Joyce Streeter, had run Jack Kemp's first two congressional campaigns. She had run Republican gubernatorial campaigns. She grew up politically in California with Lynn Nofzinger and all of the Reagan crew. I had Joyce as a secret weapon. She told me the first thing you do is you get a card that says you are a candidate. Next thing, you get some Monarch stationery and you put your name on it and the fact that you're a candidate. Then write a letter to every elected Republican and tell them that you're running. She said to get a list of the Republican clubs and start calling the presidents. They were so appreciative of candidates that wanted to run. The Republican Women's Clubs very quickly understood what judges were about and knew that judges couldn't get involved in the politics. They just wanted people. That's why I encouraged so many people to run as Republicans when they came to me about running for judge. I said, "The Republican Women are wonderful. They are just looking for good, honest, hardworking people. They just want a commitment from you that you're going to be a good judge." That's what they did for me.

When I spent $40,000, I thought that was a fortune. By 1984, I had had a contested primary, a contested runoff, and a contested general [election] in '80; a contested primary in '82; a contested general in '82; and a contested general in '84—six elections in two and a half years. You had better believe that for my husband and me and our two older boys—my sons were four and one—those were very tough years. From 1980 to 1984 was basically one continuous election, one continuous race. It was very difficult to be a judge and a Republican in those days. You had to really work for it. It was much easier to just be a Democrat. You were assured a big block of votes just from the lever—the straight-ticket voters. Republicans were so proud of picking who they knew and only voting for people they knew well. That's because for many years they could only vote for Democrats and had to be very careful about which Democrat they voted for. If the Republicans did not support all the candidates, we couldn't win. By 1984, we got that message across, and we elected our entire slate. It helped to have the president. Running with Ronald Reagan was wonderful. That was the turning point. We knew it was safe to be a Republican.

BARBARA CULVER CLACK, MIDLAND

Governor Clements called me and said, "Barbara, I want to appoint you to the Texas Supreme Court to fill a vacated seat." I said okay. That was a great experience. It was a year like the supreme court has never had and never will have again. Remember that justice had been for sale in Texas. We had had a very liberal court. Tom Phillips was getting situated as chief justice, and I came on.

Then, after a year, there were the normal people that were running. There were six vacancies on the supreme court in 1988, all of us out groveling for money and all of us with opponents. It was just the most unnatural year. I'd work Sunday night until whenever. Go Monday, Tuesday, Wednesday, leave Wednesday afternoon and hit the campaign trail. You must do fundraising to run for statewide office. I raised over $550,000.

Jack Hightower was my opponent. Of course, I had known him for years. He was a former state senator, a former congressman, a lobbyist in Austin, and he was an original good old boy. He campaigned pretty hard. All of the lobbyists really helped him. They felt so virtuous because they backed Phillips and they backed the others and then they backed Hightower. That did not make them look like they were just backing Republicans because they were backing a Democrat. He trounced me.

What did you learn about campaigning for statewide office?

It's hard work, and it is a lot of fun. You meet a lot of wonderful people, but the whole point of your going out is usually to raise funds. How in the world can anybody meet many voters when you catch yourself going back to Dallas or San Antonio, and you see the same twenty people every time you go there? Loyal Republicans come out, but you know that you are not reaching the man on street, the voters, and the people. You have to raise millions of dollars to do enough TV to really reach people. You can't run an ad in Dallas at 5:30 in the afternoon and think that you have won many voters. You have to run lots of them. You have to do mailouts. You have to do some radio. It was hard to get any identity when there were six Republicans running—twelve people when you considered the opponents. They were all vying for media attention, plus you've got governors and senators and congressman and everything else in there. It's terrible.

If you haven't got the stomach for it, you shouldn't get into politics. This is what I tell people all the time. If you can't stand the thought of losing, don't do it because you've got a 50 percent chance of losing. If you can't take that, then don't do it. You see a lot of these people just crushed and humiliated for life because they lost. You've just got to grow up. You have to be prepared to take a win or a loss. You don't know what is going to affect the voters. You don't know what makes them stay home or go to the polls.

Those lobbyists, bless their hearts. They are all in Austin. They all know each other. They have lunch together once a week. They are all buddies. What they do is, they want somebody who will vote right on all issues affecting, say, malpractice, doctors, and insurance. So they get together, and they all decide whom they are going to support. They send out their "push" cards to doctors, nurses, hospital administrators, pharmacists, psychologists, psychiatrists, and therapists. Most of these people don't know and they don't care, but their professional associations say, "We should vote them."

The guy out in the middle of nowhere, who will not hear the candidate, is going to rely on what his state association tells him to do.

The lobbyists got mad at one of my opinions. They didn't know me. I didn't have any stroke with them. I had been a judge for twenty-five years, and I had never had anyone interfere with any of my decisions. I wouldn't have been a good team player. It was a wonderful experience to be on the supreme court for one year. It was the climax of my career.

How did you put together your campaign organization when you ran for railroad commissioner?

CAROLE KEETON RYLANDER, AUSTIN

The Texas Federation of Republican Women was a vital ingredient. I am not independently wealthy. I don't have my own plane. I am a working mama and grandmama. We had to go out and raise the dollars and build the grassroots base. There is no question that the TFRW is a great grassroots base. Republican Women were very helpful. Back when I couldn't afford to fly, I had to drive. There would be a TFRW woman there who would keep me overnight and get me to activities. Now, it is still the TFRW women who will meet me when I walk off the plane. I had friends that donated to the campaign and lent their airplanes. It is like campaigning in five or six different states. Texas has nineteen to twenty-two different media markets.

When I ran for comptroller in 1998, I was the only statewide officeholder who won and was out spent. We raised more dollars than had ever been raised for a comptroller's race, but I was out spent. My opponent could write his own check, million after million after million, and he did so. But we weren't out hustled. I had that grassroots base built running for the railroad commission. I am a real believer in TFRW, precincts chairmen, county chairmen, and other groups. When I was running for comptroller, the Texas Classroom Teachers Association members were very supportive, though the organization does not endorse. Grassroots is so important. I have got many, many friends all across this state. Obviously, you have got to raise big dollars to have a successful statewide race, but I defeated an incumbent on the railroad commission with less dollars. We raised them and used them wisely. And, as I said, I won this time when we were out spent but not out hustled. The grassroots effort pays off.

JANE NELSON, FLOWER MOUND

Before I ran for state senate, I was in Austin often because I was on the state board of education. I would come over and watch the legislature if I had some free time. My own senator was an incumbent Democrat, very liberal. He was carrying some workers compensation legislation that I, as a businessperson, knew was detrimental to business. I went to talk with him as a constituent. He didn't have time to talk to me. He never talked to me. I ran against him because I was so angry that he wouldn't even take the time to talk to me. Then when I decided to run, I started talking to people and found that more and more people had had that same experience with him and were willing to help me. Looking back, my gosh, I ran against a powerful incumbent with a boatload of money.

How did you beat him?

A lot of help from a lot of people. Of course, financially you don't get any PAC money if you run against an incumbent. My money came in $50 and $25 contributions. I had a huge number of volunteer workers that you couldn't buy. The district that I ran in was a 50 percent Democrat district. My base was Denton and Tarrant Counties where there were lots of Republicans. I was told by a lot of political consultants, "Don't waste your time out in those rural counties. They have never voted for a Republican, and they are not going to." I took it as a real challenge. They called me the "Dairy Queen candidate" because I would go to every Dairy Queen in every one of those towns. I would get up at three o'clock in the morning and drive four hours and be there when the dairy farmers came in from milking. Those were the most conservative people in the world. One man sticks out in my mind. I talked to him, and he looked at me after listening to my bit. He said, "Ma'am, I have never voted for a Republican in my life, and I have never voted for a woman in my life, but neither has ever come asking me for my vote. I'm going to vote for you." I won six of the eleven counties a Republican had never won. It is because I went to them and said, "This is what I believe." Yes, they were traditional Democrats but hard workers. The Republican philosophy is the philosophy that they arm themselves with.

Why did you decide you wanted to run for Congress in 1992?

DOLLY MADISON McKENNA, HOUSTON

I got into it because my husband and I started a small company. We were trying to get health insurance, which is almost impossible for a company that is under ten people. We were in a regulated industry and were having a lot of hassles with regulations.

My campaign was sort of unique in a way because I wasn't coming from a history of grassroots Republican activism in Texas. I was involved with arts organizations, the symphony, and the museums. Having worked with those organizations, I encountered a lot of people who were interested in politics and had some money and put money into my campaign. My first fundraiser was a women's fundraiser. Everyone said you couldn't raise money from women. It is more difficult, but I had a fundraiser and raised $35,000 from women. All of these people had been perfectly willing to write a check for $1,000 for the symphony. Somehow I convinced them to support this campaign. We were just really calling one-on-one. A lot of them were wives of husbands who had given a lot of money to Mike Andrews, who was my opponent. In fact, the fundraiser was at the house of someone who was one of his big contributors. It just threw him into a tizzy. He started calling people saying, "Get your wife in line." It got a fair amount of attention.

In 1996, I had not planned to run. At that point, I knew it was a Democrat district. Gene Fontenot, [*the Republican*] who ran in 1994 against [*Democrat*] Ken Bentsen, spent $4 million and didn't get any different percentage than I did [*when she lost*] in 1992. Then the supreme court came down with a decision to throw out a lot of the primaries, in effect having to do with segregated districts, racial balance, and so forth. They threw out the primary and held open elections on presidential Election Day. By this point, I had determined that it was clearly not a good thing for a moderate to run in any Republican primary in a pretty conservative district. You're not going to have a shot. But in open elections, the more people who vote, the more moderate the determination is going to be because the general population is fairly moderate. It worked. There were eight people running as Republicans, and I beat them all. I would not have run the first race any differently, but I would have run the runoff differently.

First of all, I was the recipient of the Republican Party wanting to pick up a Republican seat. So they sent down all of these campaign managers and strategists. Some of them were very talented, and some of them were not doing things the way they should be done. They put time and money into direct mail. It should have been to put on a get-out-the-vote effort. They should have spent four times as much money identifying the households in the precincts that I had done very well in to start with—for a very targeted get-out-the-vote. I didn't have the choice because I wasn't spending the money, the Party was. There were a couple of positions that I had not taken strongly. I think one was minimum wage. The national party people said, "If you're going to get the right-to-work people [*the anti-union vote*], you're going to have to take a stand on this issue." That was used very heavily against me in ads. I never would have done it of my own volition. The people that supported me probably would have taken my position, but not in such a strong way that it would mobilize them. Whereas if you are going to unions, which my opponent was doing, and using a lot of union money, that kind of issue is a mobilizer. So that is the one election I would have handled differently. Would I have won it? That was a pretty heavily Democratic year and even more Democratic district. I don't know. It is hard to say.

How many points did you lose by?

It was probably something like 45 to 55 percent, maybe even a little more. But when you're talking about a runoff, that is only 6,000 or 7,000 votes. Could I have found 6,000 or 7,000 people who voted for me before and get them out to vote? That is the question. The opposition had a much more sophisticated get-out-the-vote effort. They were doing daily get-out-the-vote fliers to only the identified voters. They weren't blanketing blocks, whereas our people were forced to go to targeted precincts where I had done well before and give them to everybody. You have 60 percent of the people that support me and 40 percent of the people that support him. That is not necessarily the best way to spend your money. I think that direct mail is often useless. Particularly blanketing it to lots of people in that kind of a circumstance. That is when you look to precinct chairmen [*to help identify and get out the vote*]. Effectively, the precinct organization and the party organization had been taken over by people who disagreed with me philosophically and were working against me.

Wouldn't you be better than a Democrat?

The fact that I would agree with them on 90 percent of the issues and not on 10 percent, I have been told right to my face time after time, doesn't matter. It is the 10 percent that we care about. We would rather have someone that we disagree with 100 percent and throw them out next time than have someone entrenched on those issues with which we disagree in our own Party. What I also found out, after the fact, was that they were running underground ads and radio against me based upon pro-choice issues. A lot of that was paid for by Ken Bentsen's campaign. I only found out because the campaign consultant who did it, in retrospect, had a falling out with the people he did it for and felt badly. He came and told me. He gave me copies of the checks from Bentsen's campaign.

PATRICIA LYKOS, HOUSTON

I received a call when I was in trial in court. They said, "There is a bench opening. Would you like your name to be considered?" The strong feminist that I am, I replied that I needed to talk to my husband and my mother. "May I call you back?" My mother and husband said, "It is really an honor to receive a call like that, so you should say yes. You are not going to get it, but that is the courteous thing to do." When I was in trial, my whole focus was my client and I forgot to return the call. I got interrupted in trial again. They said, "What is your answer?" At noon, the judge called a recess and asked me to approach the bench and said congratulations. I was appointed to County Criminal Court No. 10 to take effect January 1, 1980. It was exhilarating for the first few days, and then six people filed against me in the Democrat primary. They had never elected a Republican to a trial bench in Harris County. In fact, I was the first Republican elected to a county court at law. We didn't have any contested primaries because, who is going to contest a losing ticket?

The man who prevailed in the Democratic primary raised over $100,000. I raised $48,000. None of it came from lawyers. I always gave speeches for the Party, professional groups, academic groups, and all sorts of nonpartisan groups on significant issues of the day. So I was fairly well known in the community to Republicans, thoughtful conservative Democrats, and Independents. I tried fifty jury trials that year, all of the time that I was running for office. I would give 7:00 a.m. speeches, I would do luncheon speeches, and I made two or three appearances every night and did the same thing on weekends. I told them my philosophy and educated people on the three branches of government.

Did you have a campaign manager or any kind of campaign organization to help you?

Yes, I did. I had a Republican woman who was my unpaid campaign manager. Every single penny went to the campaign for radio commercials, yard signs, and brochures. Jim Culberson did my graphics work for me. Dr. Richard Murray from the University of Houston plotted out the precincts and told me which precincts were most likely to be Republican or Independent or swing precincts. That is where I concentrated my efforts as far as the paid media went, pushing cards on Election Day, and having clean-cut youngsters wearing my T-shirts, so if people didn't want a card they saw the name. We won. In fact, I went to bed thinking that I had lost. A friend from one of the newspapers called me up and said it looks really bad. We were used to the Democrat votes coming in last. But in 1980, there were precincts on the west side of town that didn't shut down until ten at night. That meant those people were in line before seven. Our votes came in last. I woke up a relatively substantial winner. There is no question that Ronald Reagan got that vote out. That is one of the keys to winning an election, turning that vote out.

BEVERLY KAUFMAN, HOUSTON

I was nominated for county clerk in May. [*Kaufman was appointed county clerk after the death of the officeholder but was required to seek the nomination of the Harris County executive committee because the deceased county clerk's name was already on the ballot*]. Then I started campaigning. I was on page twelve of a twelve-page ballot. I got 61 percent of the vote—more than the governor. I had a lot of training, through my political activities all those years, in nurturing the news media. The smartest thing that you can do as a public servant is to be a better spokesperson for the election process and let voters know what they need to know about elections and when early voting starts. So I put out a lot of press releases that helped the media. If they didn't call me, I called them and said, "Friday's the last day to vote early." They would do an interview. I was all over the press. I bet I got a half-million dollars worth of time. The day of the election I spent on the phone answering voter calls for information. I left to go to the Astro Hall to count the early vote. I ran into my old boss, Jon Lindsay, and Commissioner El Franco Lee, who is a Democrat. I said, "I've got to go count votes, and I need a hug. This has been the longest day of my life." I didn't know if anybody even knew that I was running. The judge said. "Are you kidding? They were talking about you on the radio." Commissioner Lee hugged me. So we counted the early votes, and I had 70 percent of the early vote. I just screamed. I couldn't believe it. I guess you get too close to the trees to see the forest after a while.

NANCY JUDY, DALLAS

When I ran for the school board, I had a lot of people who volunteered to help me. When I ran for commissioner, I had volunteers. When I ran for the congressional seat, I had people who wanted me to be in Congress—influential people here. Some of them had agendas, like oilmen, others did not. They were willing to raise money and have offices staffed for me. I had phone banks where volunteers would come. Dave Fox, who was the president of the firm Fox and Jacobs, was my finance chairman. A law student who had worked for Congressman Steelman gave himself to my campaign for one year. He would pick me up in the morning and take me to all the places. That was the greatest help of all.

Did you find it difficult to raise money as a woman?

It's just hard to raise money, period. I sent out letters. I got some PAC money. I returned some money that I didn't want. They were playing both sides against the middle. They gave to Jim Mattox [*her Democrat opponent*] also. I didn't want their money. I didn't go into debt. I am not a wealthy person. I had to do it through contributions. We would have to plan everything in terms of advertising, mailings, etc. based upon the budget. You could never get caught up in the moment and go into debt. So many people do. It is nervy of you to have fundraisers to pay off your debt if you have been defeated or, if you are elected, to come back asking for more money to pay off your debt.

I called a press conference right after the Democratic primary. I read all of my opponent's out-of-state labor contributions, and he interrupted my press conference and tried to takeover. Then he made disparaging remarks about me on Channel 13 KERA. They thought he was completely out of line, which he was. In high school assemblies when I spoke, he would make very disparaging remarks and appeal to the Baptists in the crowd. He was unbelievable.

The most difficult thing was to go to Washington on these congressional briefings with other congressional candidates from around a country. The Republican National Committee televised your speech. They would give you a subject, and then two seconds later you have to get up and speak and it would be televised. Then everyone in the room gave you feedback and criticized you in this room of thirty men. That was a challenge.

CAROLE WOODARD, HOUSTON & GALVESTON

I campaigned [*for county clerk*] with very little money. After everyone got me involved, I had very little support. I lost by about 1,000 votes. I ran against Patricia Ritchie, who worked as the assistant under the county clerk, who had been there for thirty years. She had been her assistant for all those years. I really thought that I was going to win. I campaigned with about $1,200. It was mainly with the work of my husband and my church that we were able to make our own signs. Steve Stockman ran for Congress, and he helped me. He included me in his mailers because I didn't have money to do my own. I carried all of north Galveston County. It was really the black people that did not vote for me. We were hoping that I could have gotten a small percentage of the swing votes from blacks, but I didn't get it because I was a Republican. That is what they told me in all of the churches I campaigned in. "We don't vote for Republicans." It didn't matter that I was the most qualified candidate, both in education and experience. What mattered was that I was a Republican, and they would not vote for a Republican whether they were qualified or not. The more vicious part of my campaign came from black Democrats. And I am black.

When I was running for county clerk, I went to a June 19th celebration. June 19th is a celebration that black people have in Texas because that's when the slaves were freed here. There are celebrations all over, and politicians use that time to make all of the picnics and the big gatherings where they talk to people about voting. All of the candidates go and try to reach blacks. A prominent black woman elected official stood up and said that the Democrats freed the slaves. I was appalled. I went there to speak, and they would not even let me speak. They let all of the black Democratic candidates speak, but they would not let me speak because I was a Republican. So I pushed my cards, and I spoke to people and said, "That is not true." Think about it—Abraham Lincoln was not a Democrat. Then when you brought it to their attention, it was like, that is right. He wasn't. But with her there saying what she did, they believed it. If you don't go back in your brain and pull up history, it is never even questioned. It is done so subtly. I was able to make it through the crowd. I stopped and talked to people and said, "With all due respect, she lied to you."

Candidates Helping Others

NORA RAY, FORT WORTH

When Betty Andujar ran for state senate, she was real supportive of other candidates. She helped them raise money and advised them, particularly the younger ones, about how to get the precincts organized, how to get out the vote, and where to look for support.

JULIA VAUGHAN, MIDLAND

Barbara Culver Clack ran and was elected as a Republican to the position of county judge, then was a district judge, and then was appointed to the Texas Supreme Court. She was a perfect example of how you overcome the gender barrier at the same time you are overcoming political party barriers. People like her, who were willing to put their reputations on the line, get their friends involved, and really turn it into a grassroots movement were very, very important. That was one of the things I learned from her. A lot of people were surprised when I ran for office in '94 that there were so many people nobody had ever heard of being a sponsor of a political event. They did it because I asked them. I'm sure it was the same way for her. That's the way she taught me. She said, "You have to be willing to ask people for help. Very rarely will they turn you down if they know you or if they really believe in what you stand for even if they don't know you."

How do you think your run for office in 1964 affected your ability in the future to work with candidates?

NITA GIBSON, LUBBOCK

I knew right where they were. Understanding things really helps you be successful. If you understand the role of the other individual or if you empathize with them a little bit by having been there and done that, you can talk their language.

SYLVIA NUGENT, DALLAS & AMARILLO

I learned two very important things running for state legislature. One is, you can't run your own campaign. Two, I like running campaigns better than I like being a candidate.

KATIE HECK, MIDLAND

I realized how hard it was to be a candidate when I ran myself. I ran for city council and had no objectivity at all. I couldn't even pick out a photograph of myself. My children just finally tore all the photographs out of my hands and said, "Mother, hire somebody." For all of the campaigns I had managed, I could not do it for myself.

Money

SHIRLEY GREEN, AUSTIN & SAN ANTONIO

As recently as maybe ten years ago, I think that nearly all women candidates and people that worked for women candidates acknowledged that the most difficult thing for them is to raise money. However, I found when I ran for state legislature back in '64, there were also some offsetting advantages that I don't think political operatives usually recognize because operatives usually think more of money and TV buys. For instance, when I ran, there were four state representative slots and we all ran countywide. I got many, many, many more speaking engagement requests, for instance, than the three guys who were running did. It was because I was a novelty. Organizations that were having a forum would have one Democrat and one Republican. Almost anytime someone meets a woman candidate, she is more memorable because she is different. So there are pluses and minuses to being a woman.

As a legislative candidate, how do you balance the need for money with the need for volunteers?

ANNA MOWERY, FORT WORTH

Raise your money early so that you're not having to in the later stages when you need to make contacts. Early money is very important. From the time you decide you might want to run, tie up good people and get some committees. What happened with my legislative race was Bob Leonard announced that he was going to step down right before Christmas. He had promised that he would call me since he knew I wanted the spot. He called me over the Christmas holidays on a Thursday or Friday night. I immediately hung up and started calling. I called the precinct chairmen, and I got 88 percent of the precinct chairmen committed to me. I called all the downtown people that give money or have influence. Being county chairman was invaluable.

GWYN SHEA, IRVING

The transition from being an administrative assistant to a candidate running for the office [*state representative*] is a real eye-opener. When I was the administrative assistant to Bob Davis, I knew where he stood and what he thought. It was real easy for me to be the spokesperson and say Bob Davis believes 1, 2, 3, and 4. It wasn't Gwyn Shea saying that. When I became the candidate, what did I think? What did I propose? What did I bring to that arena?

It was easy to raise money for my former boss. You were asking for somebody else and not asking for you. But when you have to ask for money yourself, that is still, after twenty-five years, the hardest, most unpleasant, most undesirable thing I do in politics. Having said that, it was really interesting in 1982 to go to the business community. You always know that if people will even give you a dollar then you have got their vote because they have confidence in you. I started out with the premise that if I couldn't raise enough money or have enough money pledged to run the race, then I did not deserve to have my name on the ballot. I was able to do that. That encouraged me, but the business community was real reserved. They really, really didn't want to do much, so they didn't do much. Of course in 1982, it wasn't as big of an expense as it is today. It was real interesting because then in 1984, I won by over 70 percent of the vote, and I have never had a problem raising money since. I would say that for Republican women, and it is probably the same for the Democratic women too, if you can instill confidence in the public that you are competent, that you are not an airhead, that you can do things, then they really get behind you. You have got to prove yourself first. That is basically what I did.

How were you able to raise enough money that first campaign?

I had an awful lot of help from my former boss, Bob Davis, who had been in the legislature for ten years. Anybody like that in your corner is going to give you a head start because people respect that person and their judgment of people. I had one or two in the community that were really, really supportive of me. But it was the Republican supporters, as opposed to a broad base of support. I want to give that credit to Bob Davis and to those people who were right there in my corner.

I Won!

What did you feel when you won a place on the school board?

SITTY WILKES, AUSTIN

It didn't register with me. I am not accustomed to losing. So it just didn't register with me, the impact of what happened. There was a guy on the school board named Roy Butler. He was a big LBJ man. He had to make up his mind to get along with me. Of course, I was younger then, and I hate to say I was more attractive. The reporters in the paper said, "The other candidates didn't have a chance when the comely Mrs. Wilkes walked in the room." I had to look up the word "comely" because I had always thought of myself as homely, and so that helped. I was something like thirty-eight, and that was an advantage. They were all shocked. They usually handed these positions down. They handpicked somebody to run.

MARY DENNY, DENTON

Winning! I can't believe they really do want me!

CHAPTER 14

Candidates' Wives

"They decided to send me out on the trail, too . . .
other wives weren't doing it then." —LOU TOWER

*T*he role of candidates' wives changed through the years.
In most cases, wives were surrogates for their husbands, traveling
to remote areas of Texas to which the candidates' time schedule
would not permit a visit. They made speeches, generally avoiding
policy statements, and shook hands, making the electorate feel a part
of the campaign excitement. Although they won votes as they went,
in the early years it was often a lonely job, without many Party
faithful to support their husband's candidacy.

Some women were their husbands' campaign managers. They
did not let inexperience stop them and eagerly worked to do whatever it took to mount a campaign. As the years passed, they used
statewide contacts developed through Party work and Republican
Women's Clubs to provide the backbone for their husbands' statewide campaigns. In some cases politically better known than their
husbands, wives made meaningful contributions, complementing
the campaign efforts of the candidate. Wives sometimes reached out
for support in nontraditional areas, taking risks their husbands
could not afford to take. This teamwork made a difference in many
campaigns, and it began to pay off with electoral success.

Wives Have Guts Too

MARTHA CROWLEY, DALLAS

My husband, Frank, was reelected as county commissioner in
'64 and then in '68. We decided to move up or out. They [*the Demo-*

cratic state legislature] just gerrymandered the Thirteenth Congressional District from Northwest Highway in Dallas north and central all the way to Childress. It was [*Democrat*] Graham Purcell's district. It took in Wichita Falls. We both went into it with full knowledge that it was going to be a tough race depending on whether the little tail of Dallas County could wag the dog. It darn near did. Dallas carried by a huge majority, but Wichita Falls carried for Graham Purcell. Of course, Frank was not known that well in that part of the state. The race itself was a great experience.

ROBBIE BORCHERS, NEW BRAUNFELS

My husband, Jack, ran for state representative in 1970 and again in 1972. Fortunately, we had so many terrific volunteers and friends who helped. Comal County was one that he was able to carry. Floresville in Wilson County was in the district at that time, the home of John Connally, the Democrat governor. It was just incredibly tough sledding. You just stayed in there. I spent many, many hours knocking on doors in Schertz and Seguin in Guadalupe County.

Was it hard to go and knock on doors when you expected an "iffy" reception?

You are all wrapped up in the campaign, and you know you have so many hours and so many days. You are just out there spinning as fast as you can go, trying to get things turned as far as you can in your direction, knowing that even if it doesn't work out you are planting some seeds for later on because he was a fine candidate. People were happy to have supported him—win, lose, or draw.

You convinced your husband to be a Republican?

BEBE ZUNIGA, LAREDO

Yes. I started telling him that our points of view were more in tune with the Republicans. We worked very hard for a job. We hated to give money from our paycheck to some people who did not even work. I think he saw the way that I truly believed. I started getting him involved in every meeting that we had. One day, he just woke up and said, "What if I ran for commissioner as a Republican?" I said, "Are you sure?" That time he got 47 percent of the vote, which was unheard of here.

Wives as Campaign Managers

SURRENDEN ANGLY, AUSTIN

They could not believe that a Republican was running [*for state legislature*]. We were in our twenties. I have often thought that we were so dumb. It never occurred to us that we would lose. There were very formidable candidates against us. We formed our organization from people that I had never met who came forward and helped us. Someone went through East Austin and said that all of the welfare benefits would go away if Maurice was elected. Of course, it had nothing to do with us because it was a national issue not state issue. We got hold of the letter and sent it all over what we considered our areas, verbatim. We turned catastrophes into neat things for us.

When Maurice won in the runoff in December of 1967, Lynda Bird was being married at the White House. I have it on very, very high authority that Lyndon Johnson was so mad that he flew home from the reception and arrived here about six in the morning. He had the county chairman, who was Mr. Snead, find out what in the world had happened. I remember the *Chicago Tribune's* headline the next day was "Republican Elected in Lyndon's Backyard." I find it very interesting that three months later Lyndon decided not to run for the presidency again. I also think it was interesting that in his bailiwick strength a Republican had been elected.

JAYNE HARRIS, SAN ANTONIO

The county organization, John Wood and others, were looking for lambs to run for state representative. They came and asked my husband, Bill, to run. At that time, you ran at-large. Being the freewheeling spirit that he was, he decided that he would run. He was a lamb.

A friend of mine, Nelda Hawkins, and I decided that we could run the campaign. We went at it full bore. In those days we didn't have computers. We worked with the advertising agency. We drove around town with signs. We drummed up endorsements. It's like anything else you organize. You go to your base—your friends— then from your friends to their friends. That's what we did. We probably had a whole lot of holes in our buckets and didn't even know it. Primarily, we worked our people who were going to vote with us anyway. That's just about it.

Did his loss discourage you?

No. In fact, that is when I met a lot of other people and got involved locally in our Bexar County organization. It was the genesis of involvement in the actual elections and judicial races, because I became co-manager for an associate supreme court justice, Will Garwood. Suddenly, it clicked in my mind that what had happened in South Texas [*election fraud*] and what was happening in Texas was going to have to be changed, not from the top. We were always saying, "We want to take over from the courthouse to the White House." We were always working nationally, but we weren't getting anywhere locally.

TONY LINDSAY, HOUSTON

When Jon was going to file for state representative in 1970, he said something about filing in the Democratic primary. I said, "Democrat?" He said, "Well, yes, you have to be a Democrat in this state to get anywhere. If you ever want to do anything more than just represent this little area, then you have to be part of a bigger picture. You have to be a Democrat." So I said okay. He said that we were conservative Democrats. I said that I really wanted to be a Republican but since there weren't any Republicans, I guessed it was logical to be a conservative Democrat. So that is the way he filed. Well, lo and behold, we had enough people who moved in from out of state that didn't know you had to be a conservative Democrat, and many were Republicans. My husband ended up losing that race by only a few votes. We had worked very hard. We had done it on our own, financed it ourselves, and formed our entire political organization.

As 1974 was approaching, it was time for state reps to run again. Husband was planning to run again. Nancy Palm, who was then chairman of the [*Harris County*] Republican Party, approached him to run for county judge. Well, that was really a bolt out of the blue. It went along with what we had been saying to each other. As county judge, you have a responsible position and can really make a difference, but you don't have to leave home to do it. But that was a countywide position and just ordinary people like us couldn't finance it. We didn't have any organization, power, or backing. Who were we to think we could do a thing like that? From the very first, after Jon got the phone call, I just felt wonderful. I thought, this is it. Yes, do it!

In that election, we did the same thing that we did in 1970 only we had some people helping us this time. We got out and went door-to-door constantly. I would go day after day. Both of us got a lot of exercise that year. I really loved it. All the people were, with very few exceptions, nice even if they disagreed with you. However, for those two elections, the county judge election and the one before that, we still didn't have very much money. One of the few things that we could actually afford to go to were barbecues. We ate so much barbecue that I have never liked barbecue very well since. I was Jon's campaign chairman and volunteer chairman in both of those races and was on the phone from dawn to dark.

How did you work with the Harris County Republican Party in the county judge race?

Nancy Palm was very instrumental not only in getting Jon to run but in getting him Republican support and shepherding him through the whole election. When Jon said he would run, there was a meeting at someone's house—it may have been Charlie and Pat Alcorn's. There were probably a dozen people there. They were very active Republicans back when there were not all that many. This meeting was for us to be comfortable and know that they were going to support us at least a little bit. After that meeting, we were sure that we were going to do it. From there, we went to Republican Women's Clubs. There were not as many of those as there are now, but the Republican Party pretty much operated through the clubs and the precinct chairmen. The clubs held various events, which in those days did not draw huge crowds. They would do a little hoopla and encourage you, build you up and give you some confidence.

We tried to contact the precinct chairmen individually. A few of them we actually went and knocked on their doors. The rest of them we tried to call. We asked for their support. In those days, the precinct chairmen were expected to do their best to get all of the Republican candidates' material out in their precincts and hold parties or somehow get their candidates introduced to their neighbors. Many of them worked very hard for us.

We did scrape together a little bit of money, which I think Nancy Palm was largely responsible for getting. We got a little bit of TV right before the election. I remember the first ad I saw on TV, part of it was cut off. We only had money for just the few spots, and here this one didn't come out right. I called our media guy all upset because this ad had not run right. He knew that the station would run it over again. He kind of laughed at me a little bit for being *so* upset. Every tiny piece of media that we could get was so precious. Every bumper sticker and yard sign was so important.

There was a lot of tension between factions in the Harris County Republican Party in the 1960s. Was everyone working well together by the 1970s?

As far as I am concerned they were because they helped us. Everything that went before we didn't know about, and we had no reason to think that people weren't working together and just assumed they all were. So as far as we were concerned, they were.

Jon getting elected county judge in 1974 gave the Party a status, a way to build, and an access to the courthouse that they had never had before. We had Republicans there before but never in the kind of position that Jon had. I feel certain that was a big step in building the Party.

When your husband ran for railroad commissioner, you helped coordinate his campaign?

JUANDELLE LACY, MIDLAND

Polly Sowell, who was the vice chairman at that time, called out here and said, "Hey, Juandelle, would Jim run for railroad commissioner?" She said, "We're really trying to get a strong top of the ticket." That was when Bill Clements and Jim Baker ran [*for governor and attorney general*]. I was his campaign manager. I was his scheduler. I did all the washing and ironing. We ran a very low-budget campaign. I had done this before for other candidates, but I had not done a statewide campaign. It's a different ball game entirely. So we worked out a strategy. Out of 254 counties, we targeted 60 counties where there was the bulk of the population. We came close to winning the race. He broke the curve. Republicans in the state of Texas always used the railroad commission as their baseline. I drew from a wide range. I drew from the oil industry. I drew from the Republican Women. I drew from the Party itself. I drew from the Southern Baptists. Many times I would have a coffee in the morning, a luncheon at noon, a tea in the afternoon, a dinner or a picnic in the evening.

We were gone for ten days at a time, and then we came back to recoup for a few days. When I asked people to do something, they knew I expected it to be done. We had great response. We kind of went through an analogy with Jim Baker. He spent, I don't know, a million dollars on the race, and we spent about $90,000 and there weren't two points difference [*in the voting results*]. A lot of that depended on getting back to the basics. We picked up endorsements. Bill Clements won, and that could have helped. We had a friend in the Fort Worth-Dallas area that loaned us a motor home. We had it painted. Jim would drive, and I would try to get things all coordinated. When you are a candidate, you've got to walk out like you're fresh as a daisy with no problems at all.

MICKEY LAWRENCE, HOUSTON

In 1980, there was a position open as a justice of the peace for North Harris County. Tom ran. Five candidates ran. He won the Republican primary and prevailed in the general election. Through that experience, I got my feet wet in politics. That campaign was the most basic grassroots campaign that we have ever run. We didn't have that much money and were pretty much outsiders to the then existing Republican Party. So we started building our own base.

What kind of role did you play?

From getting volunteers, doing literature, and making sure that literature got printed to hosting suppers for numerous campaign workers, organizing block walks, helping Tom with his speeches, billboard design—you name it. You could effectively call me his campaign manager. We didn't really have anyone designated as such. People have made comments to us that it was such a well-organized campaign. We know our community, and we basically reached out and asked them to do things. They were always willing and supported us. We kind of knew what areas they liked to work in—whether they liked to get on the phone or whether they liked to endorse. It is a matter of building your data base and energizing your people to get out to vote.

Hitting the Campaign Trail

RUTH MANKIN, HOUSTON

In 1960, my husband, Hart, just completed law school, and he had a new job. He took it upon himself to run for the legislature. His employers would not let him take time off from work to run. I wonder why? I was his surrogate. I spoke at coffees and at luncheons and at rallies. How did I do this with two little children? My best friend was the Democratic precinct chairman. She was a conservative Democrat from Virginia. She was happy to help my husband because he ran as a forthright conservative. So she took care of the kids when I was on the stump. Hart used to say, "Look for Nixon at the top of the ballot, but you have to bend over and find me. I am Hart Mankin at the bottom of the ballot."

BARBARA FOREMAN, ODESSA & DALLAS

There weren't that many known Republicans. Ed ran basically an independent campaign. He had Republican help, but in a district that is predominantly Democrat you can't depend on the Republicans. We went to all of the Republican events, but we also had to court the Democrats. You would go into a little town, and you would go to see the newspaper editor and then check out the mayor. Then one person would say, you need to go and talk to so-and-so. So you'd go talk to so-and-so. Then you'd go to the cafe and have coffee at the right time. Everybody comes into town to do that. There are so many small towns out there. Ed had been in an oil field related business so he knew a lot of people in the oil field and where to find them. The first mailing, a friend and I put out.

What was it like being the candidate's wife in 1962?

It was pretty lonely. There was a lot of the district that didn't even have a Republican to run the primary. We had a two year old and a four year old. We would load them up and haul them around. We had an old Model T Ford. We would haul it on the trailer. When we got to the edge of town, we got out, unloaded the car, put the kids in, drove to town, and campaigned. I just went along and met people. I wasn't called on to speak. I went along and tried to keep the kids looking presentable and to put forth the picture of a nice family. Most of my traveling was done with Ed. A lot of sitting around and waiting while he was being interviewed by the editorial board.

What did they think when they found that you were Republicans?

We sort of soft-pedaled that. The Democrat out there was the one involved with [*convicted Texas promoter*] Billie Sol Estes and [*agricultural storage*] tanks that didn't exist. We had a sign on the back of the Model T that said "Cars go out of style but honesty in government never should." So that caught everybody's eye.

CHRIS HOOVER, CORPUS CHRISTI

My husband was encouraged to run for Congress in district fourteen in the 1960s. It was necessary that he have petitions signed by thousands of people in order to have his name appear on the ballot. We started a grassroots revolution to get his name on the ballot. We ran and lost, but we feel that we helped to build the Republican Party through that election. We tried establishing precinct chairmen in the 101 precincts in order that people might have a choice. If you don't have a polling place, then you actually don't have a choice. We felt that everybody needed a choice of whom he or she wanted to elect and from which party. We got voter lists and opened a small office with phones. Most of our first primary elections were held in garages. We did it mostly by phone and personal contacts, by saying we really needed to have a voting place and getting someone to serve. We got out the vote. We got people to man phone banks the day before the election and the day of the election to make sure that all of the Republicans got to vote. We had to secure volunteers and set up schedules.

The district included Duval County. We all went over to San Diego to a rally. We were all frightened because it was such a Democrat stronghold, but we had to go over there. Our stage was a flatbed truck. We were across the street from the county courthouse. We had to give a Republican message there. "There is a choice. You don't always have to vote Democrat." We didn't really ever have anyone angry with us except for some phone calls. We would get anonymous phone calls. They would say, "You really shouldn't be doing this." You just hang up and go on, as long as you are doing the best that you can.

"When I look at the old photos from 1961, I realize Lou and the kids did much to get me elected to the Senate. The girls then aged four, five, and six were so dear in their best Sunday dresses and pearls. Lou was the model helpmate to use a word that the

*newspaper feature writers were fond of back then. She could
have stepped off the cover of the Saturday Evening Post. We
exploited the photo opportunities in the best campaign tradition.
Mom and Dad Tower reading to the kids. Dad driving the
brood to school. It was good imagery."*
    —A passage from *Consequences* by Senator John Tower

Describe that 1961 campaign.

LOU TOWER, WICHITA FALLS & DALLAS
    Big surprise! I didn't know they [*state party officials*] were go-
ing to nominate him. We didn't have any money. They decided to
send me out on the trail, too. I don't know who really decided that,
but other wives weren't doing it then.

*Why was it such a surprise that they wanted the Senator to run
in 1961?*

John always thought that, sort of by osmosis, I knew everything that he did. I would read something or find out about something, and he would say, "Oh, you knew that." I would say, no. He
thought I knew about it because he did.
    The state was divided into five sections. Whoever was in
charge of an area, a woman, would go out and drive the route they
thought I should take and time everything. I mean to the minute.
We did most of the trips by bus. They had banners on the bus and
a loud speaker that they used when they were allowed. John traveled all the time, but there was no way that he could get every
place. People wanted to meet me without him. In some cases, it
was sort of the biggest social affair that little town had had in
almost forever. Often, it was a totally Democratic town. Let's say
the mayor's wife had a coffee for me in her home. Then everybody
could come, and it didn't have to be political. It was the mayor's
wife giving a party for the people that lived in that town. It really
was great fun. I was fortunate. I really didn't have to make speeches.
I'd just get up and talk a little bit. Since John and I talked every
day, I would tell them where he had been the day before and that

day and where he was going tomorrow. It was just a closer connection for them to have a contact like that. They really were lovely to me. It was just great. People would do a broadcast from the radio station, or I'd get in the car with them and they'd sit in front of the house and interview me.

What kinds of questions did they ask you in the interviews?

I don't think it was like something anybody would get asked today. I don't remember that anything was of great importance. I didn't say what John believed because one little thing and I could throw the whole campaign off. It didn't usually get very deep. They found out that my life was very much like theirs—taking care of the kids, seeing that they are clothed, and going to the grocery store.

After the death of John Kennedy and the huge victory of Johnson in the presidential race of 1964, there must have been an enormous amount of pressure on you both to run successfully in 1966. Did you ever have second thoughts about that?

I don't think it would have mattered very much if we had. That group [*of Party officials*] had decided he was going to run. Of course, that group included him. But the Kennedy time was one of the worst I will ever know in my life. One of the worst. The press succeeded in making Dallas feel guilty. I remember one article that I was just furious about. It said, "at the time of Dallas." It wasn't Dallas! It was the time that some nut—he wasn't even a Dallas person—killed Kennedy. They just started out, "in the time of Dallas." People would act like Dallas was all right-wing nuts. Of course, we had some. I wouldn't say that the Democrats were free of them. John was in the air going someplace to make a speech when it happened. His office started getting calls from other nuts saying it was, in a way, John's fault. You know. His office called and said for me to meet the girls at school. Isn't that a wonderful thing to have to tell your kids? We spent a couple of nights with friends. It took people a long time here in Dallas to realize that Dallas really didn't have anything to do with that. It wasn't the right-wing nuts. It was a particular nut.

Describe the 1966 campaign.

Buses for Lou. Each town organized. Each hub had volunteers. Tower Belles. They had navy blue skirts and shirts with "Tower Belles" on them. It was a big hoopla.

So you actually rode a bus?

You don't think John would do that, do you? We would go, and somebody would take charge of the bus. This one gal said, as we pulled into a town and reviewed our assignments and agreed on a meeting time, "Okay, let's circumcise our watches." Of course, she meant synchronize our watches. Everybody knew exactly what was supposed to happen and at what time. The Tower Belles handed out campaign literature while I was at the coffee, party, or whatever they had lined up for me. John could do one visit to a big town with some television coverage what I could do in twenty or thirty little towns, but it was that touch. He wasn't going to be able to go there. They seemed real pleased that I went.

When you married the Senator, did you know that it was his aspiration to run for office? Did you know what you were getting into?

Somebody in Washington sent all of the congressional wives these questionnaires. I showed it to John one time. He was amazed that I had written that he had never discussed being a Senator. He knew he was going to be nominated, but I didn't know that. It was just one of those things that he thought I knew because he did. But there wasn't any arm-twisting. It wouldn't serve any purpose. I felt the same as so many people who worked so hard on this—that he would be a good senator. He was a very good one.

I didn't even know that much about politics. I had always voted. Members of my family were Republicans but not active about it. My dad was a businessman, and it probably would have been bad for his business for people to know that he was really a Republican. He also had a cousin who ran for governor against Ma Ferguson. Dad drove the car all over the state for his cousin. This cousin and John got to know each other real well. His name was Orville Bullington. They went together to the Chicago Republican convention.

John had one grandfather that really decided his fate. This grandfather—of course they were all Democrats then—talked Republican politics. When John was elected, his dad said, "Well, son, I'm real proud of you. I think most of the family voted for you." He wasn't kidding.

What did you do in 1972 as a Tower staff member?

VIRGINIA EGGERS, WICHITA FALLS & DALLAS

I was co-chairman with a girl from Victoria, Gloria Lee of Women for Tower. John by then was such a national figure that we didn't have to go in and introduce the candidate and do the same kind of work that we did in the early years. Our job wasn't emphasized as much in that particular campaign. We tried to provide the counties with whatever they needed. Most of the time they wanted the candidate. The Senator couldn't be everyplace. We went back to the bus trips. It just helped to bring the campaign to the counties. We emphasized the smaller counties. We would bring Lou into those counties and let people feel like they were a part of the campaign. They were really working, and we wanted them to have some of the fun. You could take Lou into all of the counties that John was not able to reach, and she would charm everybody.

How was Lou Tower as a campaigner?

She was just fabulous. She was just so congenial. She was so fun. She is the wittiest person in the whole world. She had some way of drawing something out of everybody she shook hands with, and they would have a little conversation. She would look them all straight in the eye. She never spoke to the issues because it wasn't necessary in those days. It was more "we want you to meet Lou Tower and see what a gracious lady she is." She wrote thank you notes every night. She enjoyed meeting all the people. She was so grateful that they came out on John's behalf. It really did spread the word.

DOTTIE DE LA GARZA, DALLAS

Of course, I wasn't working for Tower when I covered the 1966 race. I covered Ernestine Carr [*wife of Waggoner Carr, Tower's opponent*] and Lou Tower on the campaign trail for the *Dallas Morning News*. Lou was so superior to Ernestine Carr as a campaigner. I covered bus tours, and I flew on planes with Lou and Ernestine. Lou Tower was just unbelievable. Lou Tower had the people personality that John Tower never totally developed with strangers. He was wonderful with staff, but Lou Tower would get out on that stump and would win people over. Republicans did not have a country-club stereotype when she campaigned. She was herself. She had a total interest in whomever she was speaking to. She had a wild sense of humor that, of course, she had to temper when she campaigned. She has a humor that touches people wherever they are. She campaigned more in the smaller towns where he could not necessarily go. She won over editors of papers and she won over the ladies clubs and she did fine with men because she was so direct.

If she had not been out there campaigning, what difference would it have made?

You hate to say that she was a critical factor, but not only did she loosen the Senator up but she made inroads into small rural places. Even though he said he was from Wichita Falls, and he was the son and grandson of circuit-riding Methodist ministers, I think she had the rural touch, even though she was a Bullington from Wichita Falls. She had the rural touch and the small-town warmth that he did not project. I think she helped cut into the traditional Yellow Dog Democrat, lock step, small-town image. She made the difference in small towns.

Since your husband ran for Congress, you have the experience of being both a candidate and a candidate's wife. What is important about the role of candidate's wife?

ANNA MOWERY, FORT WORTH

I don't like it. I hate to say this, but we had a candidate's wife in Oklahoma and her slip showed all of the time. All of the time I was the candidate's wife, I thought about that. As a candidate, you're so busy that you don't feel like you have to worry about that slip showing. But as a candidate's wife, it's something you need to worry about—it's going to reflect on your husband—and you do feel like you're only going to be a negative and not a positive. When you are campaigning as a candidate, you're so intense about getting your message across.

PAULINE CUSACK, HOUSTON & WILLOW CITY

Callie Robertson and I put together a charm school for candidates' wives in the late '60s with one of the local, well-known modeling schools. It was several sessions over a period of several weeks. We tried to get them to wear pantyhose, which were brand new. They had to sit on podiums and the shorter skirts were prevalent then. These garter belts peeked through on rare occasions, and we didn't want that to happen. We taught them how to rise and sit gracefully in a chair on a podium when there was not a table and how to cross their legs so that they would sit in the "S" curve and all of these little goodies.

RUTH MANKIN, HOUSTON

When George Bush moved down from Midland and was considering a run for county chairman, we were told by Jimmy Bertron, the then incumbent party chairman, that he had a good friend he played tennis with at the Houston Club named Poppy Bush. We all kind of laughed. It was kind of preppy for us. Jimmy said, "He is going to be our next county chairman." There was a group on the executive committee that said, "Let's meet this fellow before we put this to a vote." So I volunteered to have a little picnic for him in our backyard out in the precinct in southwest Houston. He and Barbara came. Our cynicism was overcome, and Barbara said to all of us, "Well, you had better elect my husband because some day he is going to be the president of the United States." We didn't know if she was omniscient or a dreamer. Of course, like most things she said, it was indeed true.

Did you work on George Bush's run for the Senate in 1964?

I did some limited public relations work for Barbara Bush. The Republican National Committee sent down an "experienced" public relations person from Washington to accompany Mrs. Bush. I was escorting her to a coffee out in the Pasadena area, which at that time was very blue-collar. It was quite an unusual place for the wife of a Republican candidate to go campaign. We came to the house where the coffee was to be held and only saw two cars in the front. The "professional" from Washington said, "We can't let you go in there; it would be humiliating." I had made arrangements with the *Houston Chronicle* for photographers to be there because they thought it a very newsworthy story. I said, "Let's go around the block once." We went around the block once, and there was one more car. I looked at Barbara and I said, "Mrs. Bush, we really need to go in there. These people expect to see you." She agreed with me. We went in and there were eight or ten people. That wasn't what really mattered. What really mattered was it showed Mrs. Bush reaching out to a part of the population that we might not have considered talking to in earlier years. Secondly, I got my brownie points because there was a very big picture in the *Houston Chronicle* and an interview the next day, which reached hundreds of thousands of readers. Maybe there were only ten people at that coffee, but everybody learned who Barbara Bush was.

SHEILA WILKES BROWN, AUSTIN

Rita Clements supported Bill Clements 200 percent. She was right there campaigning with him, making speeches just like he was. I never remember seeing Janie Briscoe [*wife of Democratic governor Dolph Briscoe*] on the campaign trail. Rita Clements was either campaigning for him or she was campaigning with him and speaking at the podium with him. It wasn't just a "Hello, I'm Rita Clements." It was making statements.

What role did you play in recruiting your husband to run for governor in 1978?

RITA CLEMENTS, DALLAS

I didn't recruit him [*laughing*]. Bill Clements made up his own mind about it. Unlike a lot of people who think about running for office, he didn't fool around and conduct his own private little poll about whether he should run. The whole thing started right here in this room with Jack Schmidt, who was U. S. Senator from New Mexico. Bill had known him when he was in the Department of Defense. He had been an astronaut, and he was a geologist. He was here for a national seminar on energy. Bill was coordinator of the seminar. Since we knew Jack personally, we invited him to stay with us. After the seminar was over, we came back here and were visiting. Jack had caught a bad cold, and we told him we wouldn't keep him up, but he said, "There's something I want to talk to you about." He had recently studied or was familiar with enough Texas politics that he went through a litany of how close all of these Republican gubernatorial candidates had come to winning. He said, "It is a winnable race." And he turned to Bill and he said, "I've decided you are the one who can do it." Bill just shook his head and kind of laughed. He said, "Oh, Jack, they have tried to recruit me to run for the Senate, and people have mentioned running for governor, but I don't think so." Jack kept pushing him and discussing it and how it was winnable. Then he said, "Well, I had better get to bed."

Bill and I moved upstairs to our study, and we must have stayed up another hour and a half discussing it. The more we discussed it, the better the idea seemed. A couple of weeks later, we made a decision that he would do this. Really, the only person we talked to about it was Peter O'Donnell, who is a very good friend in addition to having the close alliance in politics. We really respected his opinion. Bill announced. It caused quite a stir because the Republican Women were having their convention. Ray Hutchison was the anointed candidate. Polly Sowell, who had been Republican state vice chairman when I had been Republican national committeewoman and was a real good friend, called me up and said, "Rita, what is going on? I have committed to Ray Hutchison.

Can't you talk Bill out of this? This is ridiculous," or something to that effect. I said, "No, Bill is going to do it, Polly, and I'm sorry but we are going to beat Ray. You will be with us in the fall." She said, "Oh, sure I will." She said it had caused a real uproar down there. I think Republicans were kind of used to candidates going around and feeling them out and seeing whether they might be acceptable instead of just announcing out of the blue that they were going to run.

> *It must have been an unusual experience to have a contested race, especially at that level. Was that a difficult situation to be the "outside" candidate?*

Not really, because Bill brought a lot of people into the primary that might have otherwise voted in the Democratic primary. Word kind of leaked out when they were having that women's federation meeting, and Ron Calhoun of the *Dallas Times Herald* did an article speculating. So Bill decided to have a press conference and announce. The first question out of the box was from Ron, "Was it true that you voted for LBJ in 1964?" Where Ron had gotten that information, I don't know. Bill said he didn't really remember. Of course, he probably did tell some of his close friends he did, but he didn't remember. He just took a gulp and said, "Yes, that's true. I thought it would be good for Texas to have a Texan president." As it turned out, it was a one-day story. It wasn't exactly the way he wanted to start out with the announcement.

The time was ripe to really broaden the base for the Republican Party. Bill was able to raise the money. He used television very effectively and did win that primary pretty dramatically. He said, "I won't run out of cash in the fourth quarter"—or whatever football term he used—or run out of gas.

It was very helpful to have the political experience I had. A lot of the people in the Republican Party—the workers, the Republican club members—said, "Who is Bill Clements?" They really didn't know. A lot of them knew me better than they knew him. I sat in on all of the strategy sessions. During my door-to-door canvas in the Goldwater campaign, I had gotten to know

Nancy Braddus from Minnesota. So I immediately recommended that we get Nancy aboard, which we did. She helped with all of our telephone bank efforts in all of our campaigns. It was real helpful. I enjoyed campaigning with Bill, and I enjoyed campaigning on my own.

You had your own tour, didn't you?

We decided after he won the primary to spend the summer in the rural counties organizing. There were many counties that didn't have a Republican Party chairman. Our original plan was to rent two Winnebagos. I would go in one direction, and he would go in the other. The Winnebagos kept breaking down, and the young people that were helping drive didn't know what to do. I finally ended up with a station wagon, which suited me better, and with a couple of young people, which sometimes included my children. In one case, my two future sons-in-law went over to East Texas with me as volunteers. I guess my first foray up into East Texas was Greenville. We made several stops on the courthouse square and went into the coffee shop to talk to people. We would always visit the courthouses. We would hit some of the business places in town. We usually had interviews set up with the radio stations. There usually wasn't a television station but a radio station and the local newspaper. We had people working in advance planning. I probably ended up spending more time in West Texas and the Hill Country because I had grown up in the Hill Country and knew that area. It was a busy, busy summer, but it paid off. John Hill [*the Democratic candidate*] thought he had been elected governor when he beat Dolph Briscoe [*in the primary*] and acted accordingly through the summer. We spent almost three weeks in Austin doing intensive briefings on state government. Obviously, Bill did not have the knowledge of state government that most candidates who had run for governor had. We met with highway department people, and on down the long list of major boards and commissions, and were brought up to date on the issues.

Did you participate in those meetings?

I did. When I was on the campaign trail, I gave many political speeches about what he was doing. I tried to stick to evening events where both men and women were. As far as daytime events, I stuck to the downtown areas. I didn't do many coffees or anything like that. The real impact you made in those communities was when you got a radio interview and a newspaper interview and there was some kind of event, but we usually tried to hold it where it included both men and women. Campaigning is very tough, I will tell you. We made it very clear that Sundays were our day to be here at home and go to church and see the family. It was six days a week nonstop.

Wives Are an Asset

Have you seen candidates' wives make a big difference over the years?

BETTY RUMINER, SEABROOK

Oh, yes. They are in contact with people, and their overall activities just make a difference. You have got to have support from your spouse. I don't care if it's a man running for office or a woman. It just makes a lot of difference.

How have you helped your husband, State Representative Tom Craddick, stay in touch with the people in the district?

NADINE CRADDICK, MIDLAND

I have always been active in my community, volunteering. I served on a lot of boards and volunteered in schools when my children were at home. I was president of their PTAs and always involved. I now serve on a Midland-Odessa initiative for better transportation called MOTRAN—Midland Odessa Transportation Alliance. I was one of the founding members of that. It puts me in touch with totally different people than what he is in touch with. It gives me a pulse on what is going on within my community. I care about it. I am a Midlander. I want a better way of life out here for the people who live here. I didn't volunteer to enhance his career, so to speak. I did it because I wanted to do it.

You really didn't have a model since you were the first Republican first lady. What did you see as your priorities after the election?

RITA CLEMENTS, DALLAS

I decided I would limit my priorities. I have so many interests that it is hard to concentrate on a few. In fact, Bill counseled me on this. He said, "You need to think about a few things you are going to concentrate on." During the first term, education was certainly one of my priorities. Volunteerism was another, which was a natural for me. Then, restoring the Governor's Mansion, I got real involved in historic preservation. I helped on some historic preservation programs, like helping launch the first Main Street program we had in Texas, which is restoring small-town downtown areas. Then, during Bill's second term, the economy was down and we needed to really promote the economy in Texas. I took on tourism as my major project and added that to the other three. They still have pretty much the same ads on television that we developed—"Texas is like a whole other country." It really caught hold.

CHAPTER 15

Campaign Strategy and Management

"... if you have a good campaign plan that is well thought out
and you stick with it, then you're going to be successful."

—MARY DENNY

*P*arty leaders developed political strategy in the 1950s
and 1960s, discovering with each campaign what worked
and what did not. In many cases, Republican Women's Clubs
provided the starting place for candidates to recruit managers and
volunteers. Both formal and informal kitchen cabinets formed to
advise candidates in all aspects of campaign strategy, from volunteer
recruitment to fundraising and media relations. These loyal supporters could be counted on for honest feedback as the campaign
progressed. Campaigning in a state as large and diverse as Texas
often required finding new ways to take candidates out of the
comfort zone of Party regulars to meet and present their platform to
all types of likely voters.

Some women started out as managers for local candidates
while others became area managers for regional and statewide
candidates. Women then began to manage campaigns at all
levels as volunteers. They graduated to the ranks of paid campaign managers in part to command the authority they needed
and deserved. For many candidates, paying for advice meant
listening to it.

Convincing candidates to stick with a plan in the heat of
the campaign, despite the second-guessing of friends and family,
proved challenging at times. Even with effective planning and
management, events beyond the control of the team sometimes
detrimentally affected the ultimate success of their efforts.
Through the years, Republican women perfected the art of

*bouncing back after disappointment and happily celebrated their
rare victories.*

*In the early days, women did whatever they could to raise
the visibility of their candidates. They learned to use new
methods of contacting voters as they became available. With the
large campaign budgets of today, it is difficult to imagine the
transportation problems of yesterday. One of the biggest challenges
was finding the money and people to get the candidates from
place to place, especially in rural areas.*

*Whether paid or volunteer, managers learned to use their
instincts wisely. With the rise of paid managers and staff, motivating and managing volunteers became a more important challenge.
Volunteers viewed the campaign as a mission, devoting energy,
time, expertise, and will power that paid staff, in some cases, did not
have. If tension between volunteers and paid staff developed and
went unrecognized by the candidate, campaign manager, or volunteer
manager, the campaign suffered.*

Strategy

Developing a Plan

SALLY McKENZIE, DALLAS

Campaigns are not that complicated. You identify your support. You're sure they're registered. You get them to the polls. I
don't care how you do it. You can do it very simply or you can have
a big fancy headquarters and lots of activity. That's ideal—baubles
and balloons.

How do you approach developing a campaign strategy?

JANE ANNE STINNETT, LUBBOCK

You have to look at your district and know what will motivate
the voters. Also, you have to look at the opposition and see what you
think they are going to do. Then you have got to fashion a campaign
that will put out the message that you want to put out but is realistic

for your candidate. You can't have a candidate saying something that he doesn't deeply believe. I like to run positive campaigns.

POLLY SOWELL, McALLEN & AUSTIN

Living in the Valley [*in South Texas*], I knew that a vote was for sale. I tried to buy it myself. I know how hard it is. The laws may have changed, but what they used to do is pay somebody to take people to the polls. You give them however much, $50 or $100 for the day. That's all there is to it. However, it's very hard to find people who will do it for Republicans. We finally worked out a way of hiring people who worked for friends that we knew were trustworthy. We gave them a quota. We said, "If you can get fifty people to vote for our candidate in this precinct, we'll give you $100." It worked except that we could never do it in enough places for it to make much of a difference.

BETSY LAKE, HOUSTON

I have spent many, many hours talking to individuals who wanted to run. We had campaign manuals we would give them on how to run a campaign. You have to target. You have to look at your own finances and decide how much money you can raise. Mail-outs alone cost a tremendous amount of money, and you can't afford to send a lot of mail to all of the Republican households in Harris County. When I was county chairman, I rated precincts on the number of Republican voters, and I would tell a candidate, "Here are the top 100 precincts out of 1,200." We knew our swing precincts. In the primaries, you need to work with the Republican Women's Clubs because they volunteer. Most of the candidates who run in the county have to depend on volunteers.

SUSAN COMBS, AUSTIN

There is a difference in running for local office versus state-wide. If you run for local office you really do a more vertical, more intense race down through the community because you have time. You do a lot of door-to-door walking and neighborhood association meetings. It's smaller scale, but it is thicker and deeper through the community. When you're running statewide, especially in a huge state like Texas, you can't do effective door-to-door walking or neighborhood associations. Now, I try to go to every small town that I can and hit every newspaper editorial board. You work with groups that have a way of informing their members. You try to go to Republican Women's lunches so that they will get the energy up. You try to talk to some of the industry groups or chambers of commerce.

I have been on the road a lot for the last twenty-one months [*as the successful candidate for agriculture commissioner*]. What you can do is, you tell people "I'm going to be in Stanton," let's say. You tell somebody "I'm going to be there for an hour. Can you get me people?" They may get somebody from the school board, there may be a local mayor, there may be a neighborhood association, a farmer or rancher, and Republican Women. You work harder in getting representatives or people from various groups. Maybe you only go to Stanton once or twice as opposed to ten times. Days are longer generally because you're flying back from someplace or are driving back.

MARY ANNE COLLINS, DALLAS

Helen Harris's candidates won. She knew how to tell them to target—what areas they should target and how to target for what they were doing. She would even figure out a budget for them—an "A" budget and a "B" budget. If you have "B" budget, you can do this, but if you have "A" budget, you can do up to this. She knew by instinct what to do.

GLORIA CLAYTON, DALLAS

A kitchen cabinet is the backbone of the campaign. You would have someone in charge of canvassing, getting out your vote, fundraising, mailings, volunteers, and publicity. They are all volunteers. It is six or seven people who meet on a regular basis with the candidate and keep the campaign together and moving forward. How are the telephones going and what kind of results are you getting? Maybe we should send a mailing for that.

Let me give you an example. A candidate recently ran a television ad for his campaign. I was struck dumb when I saw it. It was so bad. If he had had a kitchen cabinet look at it and advise him, he wouldn't have run it. He pulled it after one day.

Sometimes the hardest part of the campaign is keeping the candidate out of it. They should be out making speeches, getting their rest, and shaking hands. Let all of the nitty-gritty be done by the volunteers. But they want to get in the act, too. If you can get the candidate out of the way, you can move forward. It is not just my thinking, it is a known fact.

BARBARA JORDAN, KINGWOOD

A kitchen cabinet is made up of the candidates' best friends who will stand by them until the very end no matter what. Then they have to look for a good campaign manager. Not necessarily somebody they really like but someone that they know can organize and stay on top of everybody and make sure that they are doing their jobs. The manager is focused on getting that person elected. The campaign manager has to be a mover and very aggressive but not offensive. Sometimes the candidate is not the same personality. They want to get elected, but they are timid in some ways about going about it. You have to have a manager that is going to move the candidate past the "I don't like to ask for money" or "I don't like to do this or that." If they are going to run, they have to do it.

CAROL REED, DALLAS

Oftentimes the frontal attack just does not work. That is the way women have had to do things. I don't care how you get from A to Z as long as it is ethical. I've seen a lot of people in this business, both on the volunteer side but mainly on the professional, that would rather lose than give up their position. It is an ego thing. If you look at the men I have had to deal with in the business over the years, everything is either a war or a football game. You just have to work not to giggle when they get their big map up and say, "We've got a frontline down here and this coming in." You'll say, "Well, maybe we ought to concern ourselves with what the average Joe out there is thinking about what we're saying."

What's their reaction when you say that?

Usually laughter, although some of them have not taken it that way, and they don't last very along. I spent years and years on the board of the American Association of Political Consultants. There are just twelve of us on the board—six Republicans and six Democrats. I think the reason they had me on the board was there were very few women back then who had their own companies outside of the Beltway [*Washington, D. C.*]. Roger Ailes was on there. Bob Squire on the other side. You talk about huge, giant egos. It would just amuse me the wars that they would have over internal stuff.

What is the most important thing to do during the last few weeks of the campaign?

ANNA MOWERY, FORT WORTH

It wouldn't be the last two weeks anymore. We have all switched because everything has to peak before early voting. The campaign is a lot like putting on a dramatic production. There's preparation, there's preparation, there's preparation and then there is the performance. Everything has to come together at the point that you want the highest visibility. You need to have completed the phone calls and disseminated your postcards. Everything in your arsenal needs to come together at that point. The main thing is to turn out the vote. It is not who your voter is, it's who your voter is that votes. You can have 40 percent of the vote committed to you and your opponent can have 60. If you turn out all of yours and he only turns out half of his, you win. It is mathematical.

Sticking to the Plan

NITA GIBSON, LUBBOCK

There are a lot of people in politics that just do what they want to do. That's not the way you are successful in politics. I agree wholeheartedly that you should be a part of the planning. But once a plan is in motion, I believe in going right down the line and keeping it and implementing it, not reinventing it along the way. There are a lot of people in politics that get to be like little Napoleons in their own county.

MARY DENNY, DENTON

When I was a county chairman, I used to give the candidates advice. Very few of them would take it. The last two weeks before election day, whether it is the primary or Election Day, candidates just go crazy. The tension is just unbearable. They have spent so much time and so much effort to get to where they are that they don't always think clearly. You really have to resist doing that because if you have a good campaign plan that is well thought out and you stick with it, then you're going to be successful. Throwing more money into buying more newspaper ads or trying to do something else is really futile. Candidates get short-tempered with themselves, their spouses, their volunteers. It is really, really tough. I swore to myself that I was not going to let that happen. Well, it's human nature. You can't help but go through all that. It was good to know that it was going to happen and to be ready for it. I still go through that now as a candidate. It is just the way it is.

Knowing Your Electorate

JUNE DEASON, SAN ANTONIO

You never know when to say, boy, do I think that old so-and-so is a dodo. You may be talking to his brother. When Tom Loeffler ran for Congress, Mary Lou Grier went out to every county seat. I've still got the book. It's a masterpiece. You flip to Menard and you see who the city council was, who they were related to, who they married. So when Tom went out, he knew not to do this or that. Not many campaigns have someone who is willing to get in that car and drive the Twenty-first Congressional District, which at that time was larger than the state of Pennsylvania. Hitting these counties cold was awful. If you get someone to walk in with you and say, "Hey, guys, I want to introduce you to Tom Loeffler here." That's a difference.

Planning Isn't Everything

FLO KAMPMANN CRICHTON, SAN ANTONIO

Politics changed a lot just by circumstances. The candidate can control some things, but sometimes there are circumstances that change everything.

GLENNA McCORD, DALLAS

Congressman Bruce Alger had been coming back to town and making speeches about what was going on in Vietnam. One speech after another, he was saying we are at war, an undeclared war. He said, "I see all of these newspaper clippings from all over the U. S., and they have notices that a private was killed in a jeep accident." He said, "You might hear about one or two of them, but I hear about all of them and they are being shot at." He said, "We are at war, and the people are not being told." For this he was labeled a warmonger. The other point was that Bruce had been elected and reelected on the premise that we can do it better in Dallas than they can in Washington. His votes were cast on what he called his yardstick. Do we really need it? Can we really afford it? It worked until all of a sudden a lot of the so-called influential people in town realized that they wanted a congressman that would bring some bacon home. We tried to get the point across to Bruce that he had to quit talking about Vietnam so much.

After the state convention in Austin, the campaign committee went into a room in the Driskill Hotel with Bruce and presented the results of a survey. Vietnam was at the bottom of the list as far as public interest was concerned. He said, "Look, I don't care what the survey shows. I'm the one who the morning after the election will go in and look in the bathroom mirror. I want to be sure I told the truth." That was Bruce. He was a man of principle, and he stuck by those principles through thick and thin.

Management

JUNE DEASON, SAN ANTONIO

I discovered that nobody paid any attention to you when you were a volunteer and said, "I think we ought to do this and I think we ought to do that." Even if you're supposed to be the campaign manager, you're a volunteer. So I started socking it to 'em for money. When somebody pays you, they do listen to what you say. They may not do it, but at least they listen.

JAYNE HARRIS, SAN ANTONIO

When you, as the campaign manager, interview the candidate, you have to ask the really hard questions. Hopefully, they will answer them totally honestly. You have to know if it is a stable marriage, not getting into the personal things like they do right now. Can your wife take the adoration that goes with this sort of thing? Is there anything that someone can start a rumor about so that you are prepared? In other words, it's no one's business but, at the same time, if you are going to have that kind of relationship with the candidate you have to know what is going on. There are some people who run for the salary. You never want to work for those.

MARTHA WEISEND, DALLAS

You help candidates by settling them in and by being realistic with them. You say, if you think you are going to work five hours a day—forget it. This is a ten- to fourteen-hour day. You need your shoes polished and all of that. It is the simple things that get your candidate elected. It's not rocket scientist stuff. It's grungy, hard work. I try and keep them from going to the same meetings month after month. I say, reach out and make new friends. Every day I expect them to make a minimum of fifteen calls and not leave a number on an answering machine but one-on-one calls to ask for votes and money. You give them guidelines that this is what you do on Monday and this is what you do on Tuesday. I don't work candidates on Sundays. It is family time.

Our candidates don't want to embarrass their grassroots supporters, their families, or themselves. They need someone with whom they can bare their souls. I try to have a relationship with them so that they can say, "Look, I'm afraid." I try to smooth the way. It's necessary because we campaign for a year to a year and a half and there's no one who would not become afraid or down about all of this. They meet all kinds of people from all walks of life.

They need to know their issues by doing background and research. If they're going to talk about a shortage of water, why, when, how do you fix it? Once they know their issues, they are comfortable with the substance of their speech. Then the more people they know, the more comfortable they are going to be because friendly faces help. When you have a campaign theme, whether it is more jobs or better education, you stick with that and give them the basic ingredients that make them secure. It takes thought about the message, and then you back up the message with facts. I insist on integrity. If you don't know the answer, say "I'm sorry, I don't know the answer, but I will have it the next time I see you" or call the campaign, but please don't act like you know when you don't. It comes back to sting you.

In the early 1960s, when you went from envelope stuffing to running campaigns, what did you do right and what mistakes did you make?

SHIRLEY GREEN, AUSTIN & SAN ANTONIO

What we did right was work very hard and learn the craft. We never had any money. Everyone learned to do a little bit of everything. The first thing you do is start trying to build support with a steering committee. If the campaign was going to be big enough to justify headquarters, try and find someone who would donate the headquarters. You had to build a schedule. Think of good speaking opportunities. Learn to write a press release. We were all just kind of teaching each other, actually. Certainly, there were some people around who had been involved long before I had. At this time, in the early '60s, Marion Findley was the county chairman in Austin. He and his wife had been active for many years. You learn from watching the smart people who made it work.

Experiences as Campaign Managers

POLLY SOWELL, MCALLEN & AUSTIN

I wanted to work on the 1960 Nixon campaign. So I called Robert N. Clark, and he was an old, old man. He remembered marching in a parade for William Howard Taft [*Republican president elected in 1908*]. When I called him he said, "Okay. You're in charge." I didn't know what to do. There was no Party structure. There was nobody to help. There were no big campaign gurus that said, this is what you're going to do. You had to do it all yourself, which is more fun than you can possibly imagine. When you run the Nixon campaign in your local area, you raise the money, write the ads, and put them on TV or in the newspaper, whatever it is that you want to do. The downside of being a total amateur and having nobody to help is you make big goofs.

ANNA MOWERY, FORT WORTH

Campaign management was mostly people skills—making people enjoy what they are doing and feel part of the process. What motivates people to really enjoy it is the feeling that they are part of something bigger than they are and that they are going to make a difference. You have to make it fun to come and work for twelve hours.

POOLIE PRATT, VICTORIA

I was George Bush's area chairman when he ran against Ralph Yarborough for Senate. I was his chairman in nine counties. I would go around to all of my counties and try to get women's clubs in every county and did in most of them.

There were so few of us. For instance, when John Tower would come to town he would come into Victoria. The candidates didn't have money back in the early days. We would give him $20 to get him to Goliad. I would have Dorothy Ramsey meet him at Goliad and whoever Dorothy would send him to in Beeville, she would give him another $20. That is how he got around the state. Nickel and diming it. It was important to have a women's club in each town so that there would be some sort of reception for him and he could meet some people. The women's clubs ran all of the headquarters.

NITA GIBSON, LUBBOCK

I became John Tower's Lubbock campaign manager. You've got to realize that back in the old days of the Republican effort in Texas, I was the only one to do it. It wasn't necessarily talent. The person that really made me determined was Charles Guy, the publisher of the *Avalanche Journal.* John Tower wanted to come to town. So they called me and they said, "Can you get some stuff going?" I took him to the *Avalanche Journal,* and Mr. Guy leaned back in the chair and put his feet up on his desk—he could hardly see us for his feet. He said, "Tell me, Mr. Tower, do you think you'll come in fourth or fifth?" I determined right then that this man will be elected Senator. It was certainly not what you would think would come from an unbiased newspaper.

People came from headquarters to tell us what to do. For the phone bank, we rented a building, put in the telephones, and got our message, telephone numbers, and people's names to call. I couldn't find enough volunteers to call. I hired girls from the business college to telephone. We began having a little money come in because people would drop by the headquarters and they would make a little contribution. We started having some fundraisers with Tower out here. We invited Barry Goldwater for a breakfast. Lou Tower came in with John. I picked them up at the airport. They asked how many we thought would be there. I said, "Well, maybe 400." There were over 1,000. Who in the world in Lubbock, Texas would have thought that at six o'clock in the morning at ten dollars a plate we could have 1,000 people for a Republican "John who?" We asked Ronald Reagan, and he came and spent an entire day.

GWEN PHARO, DALLAS

In 1962, Mary Anne Collins and Dorothy Cameron got a guy

named Bill Hayes for lieutenant governor through the primary process. They said, "You get to do the general [*election*]." I said, "I've never done a campaign." They said, "That doesn't matter. We'll help you." I was too dumb to turn them down. I got this brilliant idea to attract some media attention and get some free media— fortune cookies! I called around the yellow pages in San Francisco and found a fortune cookie factory. One day a truck drives up in front of my house. For a day and a half, they unloaded the truck. I called all of my friends' kids, and I said, "On Thursday we are going downtown, and it's going to be Fortune Cookie Day in Dallas." I went to a costume place and bought coolie hats, white cotton gloves, and shopping bags. I got some parasols, too, not knowing they were Japanese, but who cared?

I thought, "I have got to get some coverage on this." So I went down to the TV stations with some of my girls and their hats and their white gloves. Eddie Barker, the news director at Channel 4, said, "Oh, Jesus, what has she done now?" They read the fortune, and they thought it was wonderful. The fortune said, "Good luck those voting Bill Hayes Lt. Governor."

There were probably twenty of us. Millions of people crossed Main and Akard at high noon every day, and we were stationed on all corners. As people came by, we would ask them, "Would you like a fortune cookie?" Then out of the Baker Hotel walks John Connally, who was running for governor, and Clifton Cassidy, who was an old friend of mine. Cassidy said, "What are you idiots doing?" We said, "Oh good fortune. Have a fortune cookie." Connally opened his and said, "Listen to this, C. W." He read it, and Cassidy said, "Mine says the same thing." Everybody laughed. They said, "All right, girls, see you later." He was running against Jack Cox for governor that year, but he thought that was very funny. We got on the national wire.

Now I am panicked because I don't know what to do with all of the fortune cookies. We didn't make a dent. But then I started getting phone calls when everybody in the state saw the coverage. They said, "Would you send us some?" And I said, yes, I would send them for $100 a box or something. I paid all of the money back that I had borrowed for the campaign. We carried Dallas County by quite a nice margin.

SHIRLEY GREEN, AUSTIN & SAN ANTONIO

Every year that I was in San Antonio I would be somebody's co-chairman for a race. In '68 and in '70, I was co-chairman for Paul Eggers' race for governor. It was always a man and a woman that were co-chairmen. In 1978, I barely knew Jim Baker, but I had been so impressed with the job that he had done for [*President Gerald*] Ford in 1976 [*as campaign chairman*]. I saw him at the Republican Women state convention. I said, "You know, rumor is you are thinking about running for attorney general, and I'd love to help you in San Antonio if you need any help." A while later I got a phone call. He had been checking me out and wanted to know if I would be his San Antonio chairman. I said, "I would love to. Who is going to be the co-chair?" His response was, "Well, I hadn't planned to have a co-chairman. You can have one if you want it." The way to endear somebody forever, and it's one of Jim Baker's great strengths, is that anybody he authorizes to do a job he gives not only the responsibility but the authority to do it. My attitude was now, finally, I can do it the way I want to. I don't have to wait for my co-chairman to get around to calling back or authorizing me to spend money. It was one of my favorite campaigns ever.

RUTH COX MIZELLE, CORPUS CHRISTI

I was addressing envelopes and spending thirty minutes at the telephone bank. I went to a reception one day, and a neighbor of mine walked up to me and said, "I want you to meet this gentleman, Mr. Bush, from Houston." She turned to Mr. Bush and said, "This is the lady that I suggest for your campaign chairman." Well, I will tell you the truth, I really didn't know what a campaign chairman was. My family talked about it at dinner, and I told them sometime later that's the last good dinner they had cooked for them. I started in 1963 for the 1964 campaign. He was running for the Senate against incumbent Ralph Yarborough.

The first thing I did was go to the person that I had addressed envelopes for because there were three men in the race. They thought that enough people were in the race, and we did not need another strong candidate. They didn't want to give me the list of addresses I had been working on. That served a good purpose because I started from scratch. I started asking everyone. We rented a fire truck one time and brought Bush home from the airport. The kids would say, "Mom, vote for George Bush so I can ride the fire truck." We had a Neiman Marcus style show. We gave the models hats with "Bush for Senate" on them to wear with each costume. Their pictures were in the paper. Some of the men called me and said, "I am a registered Democrat. Quit having my wife's picture in the paper with a Bush sign on." We just organized the campaign the way we would organize something for the school or the community.

We had to have a runoff with Jack Cox, who had made a valiant race for governor in 1962. I remember learning a very valuable lesson from the Bush family. The advance man came to town and said, "How is everything going?" I said, "Everything is going just great. I'm having a reception after work. I sent out an oriental invitation. It says, 'Take a second lookee' and it has George Bush's picture. I'm going to serve fortune cookies, and I have written the fortune." I proudly told him that the message said, "Vote for a Republican tried and true instead of a loser of '62." Well, this man just turned red in the face and said, "Ruth, I will eat every cookie if you won't serve them." So I canceled the order. I learned that you never go for the jugular. George Bush taught me no matter how much I want to win, it just pays to be decent.

Another thing I remember about Barbara was when someone walked into a reception we were holding for them, and I said, "Barbara, these people have contributed a lot of money." She said, "Ruth, don't tell me about who gives money." I really found out that they were public servants. They were people you could always be proud of whether you win or lose. We lost that campaign.

I went to Houston to watch the returns. I was sitting next to Barbara. I didn't understand things too well. I said, "Well, that's okay. He's losing now, but he's really going to win." Barbara turned around and looked me square in the eye and said, "Ruth, in your eyes he will always be a winner, but I want to tell you, honey, he's losing now and he is losing big."

IDALOU SMITH, WACO

I was disappointed when George Bush wasn't elected that first time because we had worked so hard. Jean Lupton and I put that together with our own money. We just did whatever needed to be done. We didn't do a drop in the bucket, but we thought we were. We were both young and idealistic.

What did you do to organize the campaign committee that got Ron Paul elected in 1976?

MARY JANE SMITH, HOUSTON

In '74 we had a special election. The universe was smaller and easier to target. Our universe was three counties totaling 200,000 voters. I knew that only 15 percent was going to vote, which was 3,000 people.

If we can get 1,501 votes, we win. I know where the 35 percent that are Republican primary voters are and where the 35 percent that are Democratic primary voters are, so there are 30 percent in the middle. That totals 900 people. I need to get 451 of those people. So we have gone from 200,000 to 451.

How do you find those 451?

I know they lean Republican. It is very easy to target precincts. I prioritize the very best Republican precincts with the 35 percent primary voters. I need to turn them out, but I don't need to put the candidate there. Then I get to the other "leaning" precincts. That's where I send the candidate to walk. I had a clipboard for him. He knew who to talk with. He checked them off the list. If no one was home, he would leave a signed piece of literature saying "sorry I missed you" and go on to the next house. I tried to get the precinct chairman or someone who knew the neighborhood to walk with him. When someone comes to the door, they say "Hello, I'm working for Ron Paul" and introduce him as he walks up to the door. As the conversation winds down, the volunteer goes on to the next door. After a while, we would only do one side of the street because the word travels.

In the next election, someone called me and said, "Let's do a telephone bank." The place had a boiler-room effect. About this time, John Connally switched parties. We said, "We want Ron Paul elected. Would you help us?" We got John Connally to record a message. It was something like, "Hello, neighbors, this is former Texas Governor John Connally. As you know, I just switched parties and I am a Republican now. I am happy to endorse my good friend, Dr. Ron Paul. He is running for Congress in district twenty-two. I hope you will vote for him. Thank you so much." We had a recorder, and the worker had to dial the phone. We had light bulbs. It was real primitive. You had five different little recorders. You would sit there, and as soon as you heard a voice saying hello you punched the button. You had to get a rhythm flowing. The newspapers came out because it was so gimmicky. He won. We called into each primary voter household and into the 30 percent in the middle, too.

KATIE HECK, MIDLAND

I was always on Tom Craddick's campaign committee. The first time he ran for state representative in 1968 was difficult because he was so young and the opponent was a well-known local guy. The second time was the hardest because he had been there long enough to make an enemy or two. So it is the most fragile time to run.

The first race he had some issues, fairly general kinds of things. He knew so much about what could be done, so we were never worried about that. What he needed was name recognition. He had lived in Midland for a long time, but he was untried. We pushed him as a person and the choice that voters would have. We did everything that we could do to put his name in front of the people. We designed campaign materials so that if people threw it on the ground they could still read his name. We picked up on the colors that John Tower had used because they were highly visible—navy blue with a fluorescent yellow. Everything that he did had his name on it. It was reinforced on TV and on radio. But mostly it was the visual reinforcement. We had yards signs. We had four-by-eight plywood signs. The second time around, pretty much the same. By the third time he had a record and could run on the record.

What position did you hold in the first campaign?

Payton Anderson, George Conly, and I were the three that were Tom's committee. One of them was a money raiser, the other one signed checks, and I did the campaign material design and took care of all the advertising, placing the ads, that kind of thing. They never questioned any of my expenditures. I called Payton and said, I want to place radio advertising in the amount of such-and-such and we've only got such-and-such in the bank, can you get more? So he'd call up George, and they would go hit up whomever they hit up. We all trusted each other, and we didn't interfere in each other's area of expertise. My area got a little bit bigger, and gradually those guys kind of faded out.

MARTHA WEISEND, DALLAS

We had Clements people in all 254 counties. It was a first, if I remember correctly. We knew that we needed 1.8 million votes to win. That's why we had such a passion about it. We knew that we needed a businessman for governor because our five major building blocks were on their knees—savings and loans, banking, high-tech, farming, and the oil business. We did not want Clements to lose. We had been very sad about his first loss [*Governor Clements, who was elected in 1978, was defeated for a second term in 1982 and ran and won again in 1986*]. We did not want a repeat performance in 1986. So we had an absolute drive about us. We were to do our work and to do it expeditiously. We had wonderful, wonderful volunteers.

How did you communicate the urgency of the campaign through such a huge organization?

We were very structured. For instance, there were certain people I called on certain days so that I knew what was going on in their districts. South Texas is different than East Texas, and East Texas is different than Houston and Dallas and the bigger cities. We needed to know what the message was, what had changed. I needed to be in touch with the volunteers because they were our producers. I wrote job descriptions so that there would be absolutely no doubt of what they were supposed to do and what their time line was. We relished being structured, but it took a lot of night oil to get the organization set with that much structure in a state as big as Texas. I was available, night and day. We didn't know what time it was until we found 1.8 million people who said they would go to the polls and vote for Bill Clements. We found them the last of September. But we kept working to be sure our numbers were good. We had get-out-the-vote and phone banks that worked beautifully. We identified our voters and then, prior to the election, we asked them to go to the polls. We did as many as three calls to a person until the person said, "Yes, I have voted."

JANELLE McARTHUR, SAN ANTONIO

In John Tower's last campaign, I was his state deputy chairman and did a lot of traveling with him, setting up events. We went to all of the marginal counties where an appearance would pull just enough votes to put him over. Those were wonderful experiences in that you learn. John Tower was the master.

There were about eight or ten of us that met every Sunday afternoon the last two months of the campaign. He had refused to shake hands with Bob Krueger, his opponent, in Houston and there was a photo taken. That Sunday the polls went down, way down. Each one of us gave our "should you" or "should you not" apologize opinions because that was the big deal. The majority said you need to apologize. He said, no, I'm not going to apologize, and he was right. He made a big issue about his daughters and his wife and that a gentleman does not extend his hand when another man makes statements against your wife and family.

As a politically interested, young, up-and-coming person, did you find that longtime campaign manager Nola Gee had some

qualities that you could use in your own political development
and career?

SHEILA WILKES BROWN, AUSTIN

She was able to sense the exact kind of reaction that was
needed.

I don't remember Nola ever being the person that was up-
front at the podium. She worked behind the scene, and she knew
exactly what needed to be done. I admired that because it was
more my nature, too. I saw it, as my career progressed, as being my
role. I certainly learned from her how effective it was to be that
way—not to toot your own horn or to let your ego get in the way.
At that point, we were all there to do the best we could in order to
see that Senator Tower remained in office. She was very tuned in
to details and follow-up. Her communication skills were excellent.
She always knew in terms of the chain of command who to call
first so that toes didn't get stepped on and feelings hurt. Whatever
her personal thoughts may or may not have been about various
issues, you wouldn't have known them. She truly was in there to
represent the Senator and to do the best for him.

RUTH MANKIN, HOUSTON

We elected Bill Elliott to city council. At the beginning of
the second term, he decided he wanted to be a county commissioner. He lost that election, but he stayed on the city council. He
ran again in '67. I managed his campaign. It was a rip snorting,
tough race because the last thing that the Harris County court
wanted was a Republican commissioner. It was challenging for me
because I had never run a countywide campaign before. I had only
worked my husband's legislative campaign. There was a lot of skull-
duggery. Signs were cut down at night.

Something almost tragic happened to my family. My oldest
daughter, Margaret, was sitting at the piano in our home out in
Memorial. She got up and walked in the next room. At that moment, we heard a bullet come through the window and pass over
where she would've been sitting and lodge in the wall. We called

the police, and they came out to investigate. We talked about the idea of it being a random shooting, but we personally believed that it was done to scare us off. That made me angry because no one scares me off. I am an old Montana girl. We requested some help from the county police, and they guarded our house for the remaining ten days until the election. Bill Elliott won. That was a great, great triumph for all of us. That race was the beginning. We had to take little steps before we could take big steps.

Why did you entrust your campaign for Congress in 1978 to a woman campaign manager?

TOM LOEFFLER, SAN ANTONIO

I never have had a gender preference or prejudice with respect to my first congressional campaign. Mary Lou Grier had shown the leadership and the skills for managing the campaign. That coupled with the fact that she, Janelle McArthur, and Jim Lunz really knew the congressional district. She worked in other campaigns outside the greater San Antonio area. Mary Lou had an inherent understanding of West Texas, the Hill Country, and San Antonio. She was also a real friend for Tom Loeffler. I could totally rely upon her. Her loyalty and dedication were absolutely steeped in doing whatever was necessary and correct in the direction of the campaign and following up to make sure it was done.

Urban vs. Rural Campaign Management

FRAN ATKINSON, LUFKIN & SAN ANTONIO

As a regional campaign coordinator, first, you find a campaign chairman in each county. This has nothing to do with the Party; this is for the candidates. They give you some leads on names, and you check them out and tell the candidates what you think. In some counties it's, who can we get? Then you go on to get a finance chairman and you set up the organization. The finance chairman will raise money, the chairman will solicit assistance in the election and in doing the mundane day-to-day things. If the candidate comes to town, it's the candidate's chairman who puts on the function.

What was it like to run campaigns up in the Panhandle?

GAIL WATERFIELD, CANADIAN

If you believed in the candidates, it was very easy, which is probably a universal statement for the state. If you had a campaign, let's say for example, that had thirteen counties—piece of cake compared with Houston or Dallas. By the time I actually did it seriously, there was a chairman in every county, there was a Rotary club, a chamber of commerce, a newspaper, and sometimes a radio station. You set up a day in that town and reached everybody. You walked Main Street and got yourself in with the key people. Now, whether they agreed with you or not was not too important because they were going to be fair with you until you stuck your foot in your mouth. The press and radio might make remarks. The Rotary, the chamber of commerce, the Lions club—all of those organizations want speakers. They want to be informed. So you actually had an easier set-up than in the big cities where they could have the president of Phillips Petroleum come and speak to them. After we got county chairmen, they were always willing to head up the campaign.

LILA McCALL, AUSTIN

My mother, Margaret Luckie, was the county chair in Wharton County, which has a significant minority and Democrat population. When Kay Hutchison ran, Wharton County carried for her. Mother was a very dynamic person with very strong opinions and a great politician. Many of those Democrats crossed party lines to vote for Kay.

Staff—Paid and Volunteer

DOTTIE DE LA GARZA, DALLAS

I left the federal staff to work in the Tower campaign and worked out of the Dallas County office with Carol Reed. I was pregnant with my fourth child. I think a lot of women who built the Republican Party in Texas were doing it in between babies. Carol Reed was so energetic and so funny. She attracted volunteers to the campaign with her personality. In 1978, on election night, I was at the Tradewinds Hotel. We couldn't get the results fast enough. It was so close, that was one reason. The Senator sent Shan Pickard and me to Dallas to the Associated Press Bureau. I don't know why it was so bad. I guess because we didn't have all the communications that we do now.

The turning point of the campaign was the grassroots organization. You have to credit Republican Women's Clubs. Having the support of Republican women and having really good women staffers kind of subliminally helped play down some of the rumors about the Senator. You had women like me, a straight-arrow Catholic mother of four, attesting that the man was a good man and statesman. Carolyn Bacon, his administrative assistant, and Molly Pryor, who ran the Houston office, and others were credentials for the fact that there was a lot more to John Tower than what the rumor mill might have engendered about his womanizing. Reaching into the Hispanic electorate made a big difference in 1978. We had Lionel Sosa and those guys doing Hispanic media. That was one of the constituency groups that he worked with the best.

In addition, Cyndi Krier going to the San Antonio office and running the campaign in his opponent Bob Krueger's backyard probably turned the corner there. The Senator gave a lot of credit to the fact that he put one of his sharpest staffers in Krueger's backyard. He put that woman there for a specific purpose because that also deflected a lot of rumor mill stuff. She was very masterful at dealing with Senator Tower's second wife, Lilla, and also reaching the Hispanic vote there.

JUNE DEASON, SAN ANTONIO

I start out telling candidates I don't even want to talk to you about strategy or numbers because we both know why you're running—your opponent has done thus, thus, and thus. Your qualifications are givens. You start out with that—otherwise what are you doing in this race? You don't do anything except shake hands and raise money. No, switch that, raise money and shake hands. Money, money, money. It has to be the first thing. I'd get that basset hound elected over there if you give me enough money. Well, he's photogenic and probably as smart as some of those we've got in office already.

How would you get your basset hound elected?

Well, first of all, you have his honest countenance. Isn't that right, Clyde? The sincere look and the fact that he loves children. Because he's got short legs, he's really closer to the people. He's right down to the ground on all the issues. He was bred to be honest.

CAROL REED, DALLAS

I had a unique situation because I was on staff but I didn't need the job. Consequently, anytime anyone did something that I thought was inappropriate, dumb, or not the correct strategy for the Senator, I would state my case. The worst thing that could happen to me was to get fired and I'd go back to playing tennis. It was nice being able to start in this business without needing the money. The campaign was pretty much controlled out of Austin. Ken Towery and that whole gang. I'll never forget going down to Austin for the first time with my new briefcase, all dressed up, and getting on a plane. That was a big deal for me then. Well, you know, you walk in and after the meeting you think, these guys don't know what they are talking about or they do but it is still a bunch of smoke and mirrors. Everything that I have done, I've thought, "Now I'm going to meet the ones that really know." Then it finally dawned on me that I know as much as all these people do.

I would go to Austin to the meetings, and they would set strategy and we would agree. If Tower was in North Texas then it was my responsibility. Dottie De La Garza would handle the press portion of it. I would handle the political side of it. That meant if they decided that they would schedule him for a meeting out at a defense plant, I would make sure it was set up and advanced properly. Of course, there would be these times where they would dream up something down in Austin, and they'd call up here. They'd say, "Now, Carol, we decided to have a rally in downtown Dallas on Friday afternoon next week." I'd say, "You did?" They'd say, "Well, yeah, and the Senator can go around and pass out materials." I'd say, "I don't think I have a picture of the Senator doing that." They'd say, "What do you mean? We have decided we want to have these rallies all over the state." I'd say, "First of all, he's horrible in a crowd. Why would you do that to him? He's fabulous when we can drop him into an auditorium and have him give his incredible speech." He was a great orator and horrible on the handshake deal. John was a statesman. That's how he viewed himself, from his suits to his gold cigarette case and his very expensive taste in brandy or anything else. It did not transfer to the little guy on the street. But, yet, if they saw him on TV that night or they read what he said in the paper, they would think, well, this is a Senator. We would have these constant wars.

Finally, I'd say, "I will get right on it." I've always not been afraid. I'd call Tower on the phone, call Washington or wherever and just say, "Have the Senator call me when he's got a minute." He'd call back and say, "What do you need, Carol?" I'd say, "I'm so excited that you are going to be here next Friday for this big old rally in downtown Dallas. I want to let you know it's kind of hot right now, so you probably want to cut down on what you are wearing. I have set stuff up, and we will go door-to-door and meet some of the shop owners." "Who's idea was that?!" I'd say, "Well, I don't know. I just got this call from Austin, and we're going to have a great day. We can get a little sack lunch and go down on the Trinity River." Well, the call would come from Austin in about an hour saying, "We've had a change of mind." I'm not sure that they ever knew what the deal was.

LINDA UNDERWOOD, HOUSTON

I got a job in Youth for Nixon. From there, I went to work for John Erlichman in the Committee to Elect Nixon. In '68, I went to Miami Beach to open the convention headquarters for Nixon. When we were finished with the convention, John Erlichman said, "What would you like to do?" I said, "I want to travel with him on the campaign trail." He said, "That will not be possible, but I can probably get you on the Chuck Percy plane." This was before the vice presidential nominee had been selected, and we all thought that it would be Charles Percy from Illinois. As it turned out, Spiro Agnew was the nominee, and I remember John Erlichman looked at me and said, "Spiro Agnew?" He didn't even know. We were all shocked. The day before we were leaving to go on the first leg of the campaign trip, John Erlichman said, "Okay, I will take you with us on this leg and you can help out and see how things go, and we will take it from there." I went and I stayed. I got along with everybody.

We went all over the United States. It was the most exhilarating and the most exhausting time. Since I had been in the Young Republican National Federation, I knew people from all over the U. S. So every time we landed somewhere I had a whole group of people that would be there. John Erlichman was like the advance director. I was assistant to John Erlichman, working on all of the logistics for the next stop. Although we did have advance men, there would be a lot of changes, and we called ahead and made plans. Rosemary Woods and everybody else wrote speeches. We would type. We didn't have faxes and all of those wonderful things.

Ever since then, campaigns have tried to copy that one because it was so well managed. It worked like clockwork. We put out a schedule every day and a list of everybody that would be on the plane. There were two planes. One was the main plane with Nixon, and I traveled on that one. Then there was a press plane. We did six or seven cities a day.

LOUISE FOSTER, AUSTIN

I worked at Tower's 1978 campaign headquarters here, which was his statewide headquarters. Of course, I knew absolutely zilch. I was doing grunt work. I didn't know why I was putting all of those stamps on a mailing. It all had its purpose. Having worked in many, many campaigns now, if you put a dollars and cents value on it, it is surprising how many volunteer hours our ladies do give. There would be no way that our candidates could afford to pay for these services.

There is a lot of difference between a busy Republican headquarters and a Democratic headquarters. Years and years ago when Ronald Reagan was running, the television stations here came and took pictures and then they took pictures of the Democrats. Ours was very busy. Nobody was paid. Yet we would go down and spend an eight-hour day. Sometimes I brought work home and spent another four or five hours and took it back the next day.

Is there tension between volunteers and paid staff?

ANNA MOWERY, FORT WORTH

Yes. It is usually when the paid staff is aggressive and does not work as hard as the volunteers. It doesn't always cause a problem. Sometimes it works out very well. It just depends upon the people involved on both sides. You need volunteers that are not resentful and paid staff that knows how to handle the problem. Quite often you do get paid staff that are young and less experienced, shall we say. They really don't realize the necessity of being appreciative. I will say, too, that some of us who have been around a long time think we know everything, which is not necessarily true.

BECKY DIXON, WACO

I was able, with my background in working with volunteers, to bring in all of the support groups that the political consultants needed. We had the money guys, who brought in the money, pay for the big guns to bring in the ideas. Then they came to me to put those ideas to work by calling on my contacts out in the district.

In a rural area, you cannot go on TV around the clock because people are not going to see it. You need a good grassroots county organization in each county. You start with Republican clubs. That will be your core group for contacts. Then work with them to get a county chairman in that area. The network and the word-of-mouth gets out saying, "Look, this is a great candidate." Then they start putting together little groups. The grassroots element is still there regardless of the other money that you pour into a campaign.

Media

BARBARA NOWLIN, HOUSTON & FRIENDSWOOD

Des Barry was running for Congress. One time he was invited to go to Channel 13 in Houston to appear on a question-and-answer show. Callers could ask questions that were going to be more or less scrutinized by his campaign manager. He invited me to come down. We would look at the questions together. This was before the day of videotapes, or I would have a funny videotape. I had on a dress and high heels—that was back in the days when everyone was all dressed up, in the '60s. The campaign manager was very tall, so I was standing on my tiptoes to see a question and all of a sudden I lost my balance and started falling backwards. I hit the backdrop. It didn't fall over, but it went "boing, boing, boing." Des Barry and the people sitting at the table with them were looking like, what happened? I have never been so embarrassed. I said to the people at home, "Did you hear a loud noise?" and they said yes. I said, "That was me."

During the 1960 presidential campaign, Lyndon Johnson made an appearance with Lady Bird in Dallas. Before he arrived, a Kennedy-Johnson ad ran, which included the names of prominent Dallasites. Many who read the ad, to their surprise, found themselves listed as Kennedy-Johnson supporters. The visit also coincided with a scheduled "Tag Day" for Congressman Bruce Alger. The events of the day provided fodder for the conflict-driven press and resulted in unflattering publicity, which benefited the Kennedy-Johnson ticket.

Efforts continued to communicate effectively with the media through better preparation and knowledge of the issues. Sometimes, though, women found the portrayal of Republican candidates so inaccurate that they formed new campaign organizations to educate the voters.

MARTHA CROWLEY, DALLAS

Tag Days had become a traditional thing in campaign years for Bruce Alger. The Tag Day Girls were known for their red vests and beanie-type hats. The girls were almost without exception cute young girls, very gracious, nice, and fun. After we had our coffee and put on our little hats with "Vote for Bruce Alger" tags, we hit the streets. We had assigned corners, bank buildings, lobbies, or whatever. After people got to their offices, we all went back to the Adolphus Hotel on the mezzanine and had another cup of coffee before the lunch hour. We got our bags refilled so that we could tag everybody. Then we went back and hit our corners again when the lunch crowd came out.

What happened the night before the infamous Tag Day when LBJ and Lady Bird were present?

In the newspaper the night before there was an endorsement ad for Kennedy and Johnson in one of the papers. My husband's mother's name was in that ad. The list of names was like a telephone book. People couldn't believe their names would appear in this ad. A lot of those people were mad enough about it that they apparently came downtown to greet Lyndon Johnson.

JOY BELL, DALLAS

I remember being inside the Adolphus behind one of the brass rails. I think John Tower came through first. After Tower came in and went up the stairs, that is when Johnson came in. We were in there cheering for Tower, but I don't remember anything against Lyndon. I'm sure it was pretty quiet. It wasn't that big of a deal. It was made to be a big deal. Everyone was so far away from him. It was just LBJ and Lady Bird and maybe another person or two plus the news cameras. She stopped, and I don't remember exactly what she said. I think she said, "You know you are on the wrong side," or something to that effect.

Accounts say the women in the crowd physically assaulted Lady Bird. Was that true?

No. If she was, I wasn't there because there wasn't anyone inside that center lane. I guess that's why I was so amazed how they could turn it. I don't think there was anything bad about it at all! I just couldn't believe that the press could do that. They call it spin now. There are a lot of people who believe everything that they read and go through life that way. It hurt, what they said about us. I just kept quiet and let it go.

FLO KAMPMANN CRICHTON, SAN ANTONIO

I had been active in George Bush's campaign for Senate in 1964. I remember going with him and Fred Chambers to Dallas to meet with Felix McKnight, who was publisher of the *Herald,* to introduce George to him. He had been a friend of my family. The *Dallas Morning News* people had been friends, and so they were very helpful to George.

MARY LOU WIGGINS, DALLAS

The Buddy MacAtee newspaper ad when he ran successfully for the state legislature was kind of a big deal. I don't think people had done something quite on that scale before, with hundreds of names in a full-page ad. That was pretty impressive. That, of course, cost money. A lot of it didn't cost money. You'd go to the newspaper in Rockwall, for example, and try to get free press. You had to pay for ads of course.

GLENNA McCORD, DALLAS

Republicans probably had more strategy exhibited in state legislative races because of Ann Good and Dale Yarborough. They took the legislative candidates as a group and drilled them on issues. You can do strategy to the "nth" degree but if you can't get your message across to a newspaper, forget it. We had this fellow who worked for the *Dallas Morning News* as a reporter. He left the paper and came to work for the Republican Party to do research. We had volunteers who ate up this stuff—Bonnie Hurst and Vic Robertson in particular. They did clipping and filing, and it got to the point that in about two years time when any issue or political problem came up, he could pull it right up out of the files. Ann and Dale used his knowledge and expertise because he knew the political writers, what they looked for, when you would get something across, and when you wouldn't. He tried his best to convince people that the paper was going to have the last word—you would never have the last word. Be careful what you say. There are a few people who should have listened to him more closely.

JUDY CANON, HOUSTON

It was after the 1980 election, actually about midterm. The media started this mantra about Reagan doesn't do enough for women. The National Organization for Women [*NOW*] attacked him in the media about what he hadn't done for women. You looked closer at them and realized that those women were not nonpartisan women. They were Democrats who were going under the nonpartisan banner trying to attack Reagan for their own purposes. I was working at the Republican headquarters in Harris County. I had listened one day too many to the morning news.

It just came over me that somebody ought to do something about this and somebody ought to do it the same way they are doing it. Ann Lee was the Republican Party secretary for Harris County. I talked to her and a couple of other buddies of mine who were all in the Magic Circle Republican Women's Club that Barbara Bush helped found years ago. Why can't we do something in some way to counter this and form a nonpartisan organization too? Our agenda will be similar to theirs, but we are going to show the positive side. We believe the glass is half full and not half empty. No president has done it all. We have to be practical about it. That was our whole theme.

Republican campaigns will have women for whoever the candidate is within the Republican umbrella. This was outside of the umbrella. It was not paid for by or a part of Republican politics. It was supported by individual contributions, and it was nonpartisan. We started out with four or five women. Penny Butler had our first organizational meeting. It was Penny, Ann Lee, Marie Clark, Senya Lemus, and Stephanie Milburn.

First, we had to make everyone aware of what we were doing. The National Federation of Republican Women was about to have their meeting in Louisville. We thought that was the best way to go nationwide with it. We devised a brochure "Women for Reagan." We got a logo—"American Women Supporting the President" with a woman's profile in the middle of it. There was a blue and white bumper sticker that said "Women for Reagan." Our brochure spelled out all of the things that he had done and was doing for women. We designed a button that said "Women for Reagan."

We got on the plane and went to Louisville. We got a table and started selling our buttons, brochures, and bumper stickers for two dollars. Our organizational meeting was on the agenda. I got up and talked about what we were doing. Women could take our idea back to their precincts, their hometowns, and set up Women for Reagan there. All they had to do was send us names and a dollar, and we would send them a button, brochure, and bumper sticker. Darn if these people didn't start ordering our materials. People ordered from all over the country. Everyone felt some relief—okay, we are doing something. NOW and the media mantra are not just going unanswered. We were just amazed at the number of people that came along who were Democrats that wouldn't have done anything because they were not going to follow along the Republican line, but because it was a nonpartisan group they participated. I would say around 25 to 30 percent were Democrats. We worked not to be connected with the Republican Party. We were in about 30 states. When he won, that was it. People would say, "Aren't you going to do something else?" We said, "No, that is all we wanted to do."

So many times people sit around and complain about the media. What made you decide you could make a difference?

I guess I was young enough to be idealistic. I felt like there were enough people out there like me who didn't find the facts were there to support the way Reagan was being presented. The hypocrisy! I couldn't stand any more, and I wanted to do something. I don't think that I have ever felt that strongly about anything before or since.

CHAPTER 16

Campaign Nuts and Bolts

"Campaigning is really hard work, not only for the candidates,
but it is hard work for the workers."   —KAY DANKS

*W*ith the strategy formed and the managers in place, the
time came to execute the campaign plan. Most plans
incorporated two basic parts: identify the voters and get them to
the polls on Election Day. There were two types of voters, those
who enthusiastically sought the opportunity to become informed
and even worked on campaigns and those who went to the polls
on Election Day. Ideally, strategies maximized the motivation
of the first group to reach the second.

Each campaign established a headquarters as its nerve
center. The headquarters also served as a meeting place and
raised the candidates' visibility in the community. Developing
enthusiasm and sustaining it through Election Day was critical.
Campaigns brought the candidates to the voters whenever
possible by holding rallies, hosting coffees and teas, and taking
bus tours. When it was not possible for candidates to reach each
voter personally, surrogates went out to campaign—most often
their wives. Loyal followers also sent postcards to friends and
associates, called on local media outlets, put up signs, and
creatively helped generate enthusiasm.

Campaign headquarters, phone banks, and get-out-the-
vote efforts have all become more sophisticated through the years.
In the early days, calling a page from the phone book was a
common method of both identifying voters and pulling crowds
together for political rallies. Women turned the vote out on

Election Day by relentlessly calling identified voters until they said their ballots had been cast and by giving voters rides if necessary.

In the beginning, most campaign workers knew they did not have a prayer for victory. They hoped to hold on to the few seats they held and make strides toward a higher percentage of votes than the last election. Women often developed their own definition of the word "win" so that they could keep motivated and look forward to the next election. Regardless of their objectives, women all worked toward fair and honest elections in which Republican candidates received the benefit of the votes from their followers and could expect a proper vote count after the polls closed.

Campaign Headquarters

CLAUDETTE LANDESS, AMARILLO

People were interested in coming by Nixon headquarters and picking up the literature in 1960, which is the reason you wanted a very prominent location. Knowledgeable people were behind that desk and talked to people as they came in.

JANELLE McARTHUR, SAN ANTONIO

Every Tuesday I went downtown to the little Bush headquarters by the Milam Building. Around the corner from us was the Goldwater campaign headquarters. We were kind of in competition with one another. Lillian Schnabel taught me how to stuff, seal, and stamp envelopes. I don't know how many hundreds of women since that time I have taught. They are always amazed that there is a way to stuff hundreds of letters.

ANNA CLAIRE RICE, HOUSTON

When David West was running for a district judgeship, we didn't really have a headquarters for him. Often I would use my house. We sat around the table and did mail-outs.

FRANCIE FATHEREE CODY, PAMPA

Headquarters helped get things going in Pampa. When we had the opening, the radio stations came and the newspaper came. We let people know that we were alive. We staffed it for two months, and we lost the election.

RUTH McGUCKIN, HOUSTON & WASHINGTON COUNTY

Usually, the candidates wanted to run their own headquarters. They got their own volunteers. That was better because the county headquarters couldn't do all of that. Most people don't know what the county does. When I was vice chairman, it was my job to run the headquarters. My biggest job was to prepare the financial statement for the cost of the elections. Everything was listed, including clerks, judges, and polling places. It was several hundred thousand dollars. Headquarters contracted for about 400 polling places. We had to write to the schools, talk to them on the phone, go and look at the facilities. We had to talk to the people who were in charge of the voting machines and tell them how many voting machines we would need and at what address, what time, on what day.

The hardest thing besides the financial statement was figuring out which names to put on the ballot. It would be the same for every precinct as far as president and vice president and state offices, but then it would start changing from state representatives on down. We would go to the printer, sit down, and go over all of the ballots with them. We did mailings occasionally for the Republican ticket, but we weren't supposed to take sides in the primary.

JACQUE ALLEN, WICHITA FALLS

My first campaign was for George Bush. Paul Eggers was running for governor. We had one little room that was campaign headquarters. When Eggers was coming to town, his chairman, Mary Jane Maxfield, would call and say, "Come on down and help me pull all that Bush stuff off the wall." So we would take the Bush stuff down, and we would put all of Eggers' up, just like it was his headquarters. He would come in. Well, then Mildred Staley would come in and say, "You're not doing anything for George." So we would take everything down and put up George's stuff. There were so few of us that we all worked for every candidate. Most of the candidates thought, "Gee whiz, they are really for me."

FRANKIE LEE HARLOW, DEL RIO

People liked the fact that they could come down there and express their opinions, get some free literature and a cup of coffee. It was a small town, and it was easy to get people in. I won't say that all of them that came in and got bumper stickers and coffee voted for us right at the moment, but we kind of put a bug in their head about why are you voting for those Democrats?

CINDY BROCKWELL, BOERNE

Betty Nuss had been here in Kendall County Republican Women forever just doing the grunt work. She wasn't interested in doing more. She was interested in stuffing envelopes. Just the basics that are important.

Why is it important to have people like Betty Nuss around?

The basics never changed no matter the size of the campaign. With the size of the campaign, the candidates have more money, but your local candidates don't have the budget to pay a mail house to send out their direct mail pieces. Volunteers do it. So people like Betty Nuss were dependable. It saves the candidate money so they can spend their money on things that you can't do with volunteers, like newspaper ads.

SHIRLEY GREEN, AUSTIN & SAN ANTONIO

In those early days, volunteers did almost all of the work. I was never paid until I went to work for George Bush for president in 1979, and then we were paid pittance wages because Jim Baker can stretch a penny further than anyone.

I developed and always used a little device of day chairman

for the campaign. Very few people could work every day of the week, but a lot of people would give a day. So someone would be the Monday headquarters chairman, someone else the Tuesday headquarters chairman, and so on. It was a matter of learning to apportion your resources. One hour you'd be cleaning out the potty in the headquarters, and the next one you would be trying to learn to drive in a motorcade, and the next one you would be trying to get ten dollars out of somebody. We just had to do it all. There were people that worked campaigns who really weren't that active in the clubs. But the Republican Women's Clubs did the bulk of the work in the early '60s at least.

NADINE FRANCIS, ODESSA

I had strict instructions on how to run a headquarters. I always had something for the people to do. There was a saying, "if you don't have something for the volunteers to do, make up something and throw it away." That was not my philosophy. By this time, I was holding a full-time job. I would take my kids to school then go to the headquarters and get things lined up. I always had a headquarters chairman, Willie Shortes. She was a former office manager for a title company. We would lay out the work, and then when people came in we had it there for them to do. It was run like a business office. We eventually had to have a set of rules for how people dressed when they came to the office. No curlers for example.

DEE COATS, HOUSTON

Sometimes you worried about people infiltrating. We did have one of those during the 1988 primary. She came in saying she wanted to volunteer. She wasn't anyone that I knew. She was a reporter who was not on our side. I don't remember how we figured it out, but we did. She was trying to sabotage our campaign. We had her typing up volunteer cards. She was changing one number in each telephone number so that we couldn't get a hold of them. We discovered it when we were merging a list. We realized that on all of the cards she had changed one number.

Let's Meet the Candidate

Personal Contact

ANN HARRINGTON, PLANO

In 1961, [*Speaker of the House*] Sam Rayburn died. Our cousin Conner Harrington ran for his seat in a special election. We went to McKinney, Texas to campaign around the old courthouse. There were benches that the older men sat around on. We called them the Spit and Whittle Club. They would sit and talk, and Conner was giving out brochures. This man looked at him and said, "Boy,"— Conner was probably thirty-eight at the time—"are you a Republican?" Conner said yes, and the man threw the brochure down on the ground and spit on it. When we went to Wylie campaigning for Goldwater we had tomatoes thrown at us, but we were glad they weren't bricks or rocks.

BEBE ZUNIGA, LAREDO

We have *pachangas* here in Laredo, which are very, very popular. Someone in a neighborhood decides they want to get together. So someone says "I'll bring the meat," and somebody says "I'll bring the beer," and somebody says "I'll bring the mariachis." There are no strangers there. The minute you meet them you automatically become their friend. This is where the Republican Party has had problems in the past getting to talk to people and telling them what we are all about. The people were afraid to invite Republicans because we have the reputation of being snobbish with so much money (I wish). My house has been a railroad station. We have had parties for many statewide candidates. Coming to the house, they know it is not an elaborate house and the minute you walk in the door you are one of us. It has really helped. We have a very popular restaurant here named Cotulla, and every morning, especially on Saturdays and Sundays, you literally have to wait in line—and sometimes the line is a block long—but every single person goes to Cotulla for breakfast. We have taken George Bush and Kay Bailey Hutchison there to go around the tables and shake hands with everybody.

JESS ANN THOMASON, MIDLAND

One thing that works in campaigning is the candidate him or herself goes to the main post office in the morning and the afternoon, takes material, and shakes hands. You will not believe how well that works. Is that country or what?

Rallies

FRANCIE FATHEREE CODY, PAMPA

We had this big rally and a barbecue at the rodeo ground. All of the people running as statewide candidates were coming. Jack Cox [*who was running for governor*] didn't want to be with any of them, which made it a real problem for those of us that were holding it. Finally, we said, "You have to do this. This is the way it is billed." So he did do it. He didn't want to be seen with them because those other people had no chance of winning

GLORIA CLAYTON, DALLAS

George Bush was running for the Senate in 1970. Anne Nicholson, who was the president of the Dallas County women's assembly, called me frantically mid-afternoon and said, "Gloria, I have just had a call. George Bush's plane is coming into Love Field. We have got to have a rally." I said, "When?" And she said, "Tonight." We called women's clubs and put phone committees into action. We went to the dime store and got red, white, and blue crepe paper. We went out to Love Field and decorated—very little but enough that it looked a little festive. I got a call that said the staff has not had a bite to eat and they don't have much time. Could you pick up some Colonel Sanders chicken and bring it out to Love Field? My station wagon smelled like Colonel Sanders chicken for a week. I had boxes and boxes of Colonel Sanders chicken in my car. The rally actually came off pretty well. He spoke for a few minutes and got back on the plane, and the staff grabbed all of the chicken and went running out to the plane. We were just so eager to do what we could.

KAY DANKS, GALVESTON & AUSTIN

Campaigning is really hard work, not only for the candidates, but it is hard work for the workers. We worked in '80 and '84, we worked probably fifteen hours a day in headquarters doing whatever needed to be done. Linden Heck [*Howell*] ran the '84 campaign. Linden called me into her office one day and said the president and vice president are going to be here next Thursday. The advance team will be here tomorrow. We will need to pick them up at the airport and have five sites in mind. She said, "You'll need a bus." So I called the Kerrville Bus Company, and they said it was almost closing time for them. I said, "We have to have this. I know we're supposed to have a check for you up front, but if you will send the driver with the bus in the morning, I will walk straight out to the bus and hand him the check." We picked up the advance team. It was July, and it was hot. They came in their three-piece suits. So the first place we stopped was the baseball field and it was so hot. We got there, and they started taking their ties and jackets off. We ended up using Auditorium Shores.

They said, "We have to have 10,000 people." I said, "Ten thousand people? There are not 10,000 Republicans in Austin. I don't know how we are going to get 10,000 people." So we gave away tickets, and we acted like it was a big deal. We had hundreds of people who made signs. I called a woman and said, "I need some help, the president and vice president are coming." She said, "Why did you call me? I've never been on the same side as you." I said, "Well, we have to have everybody." She did her job beautifully. We had to get people from San Antonio to come and set up the stage. It was frantic because when the advance team comes the Secret Service comes and so do the communications people. They all set up in a suite in the Hyatt Regency. They go inspect the tops of the buildings downtown. Most people are not aware of how much it takes to move these people from one place to another. You have to have cars. You have to have a bus. You have to provide food and drinks for the press on the bus. We had to have a press platform built. I thought, "Why are we doing this? They are not ever nice to us." They came, and it was really exciting. We were really hot.

Postcards and Letters

MARTHA CROWLEY, DALLAS

Frank and his supporter would have their picture taken to-gether. A "Vote for Crowley" sign was somewhere on the wall. It would be put on a postcard. "Hope you will support Frank Crowley" was printed on the back, and there was a space left for the sup-porter to write and sign his name. We encouraged these people to send postcards to places they traded, like the gas station, the clean-ers. We did it for Bruce Alger. They would do the addressing, then we would make them bring the cards back and mail them to be sure that they would get out.

DEBORAH BELL, ABILENE

You need to make an effort and not assume that people know. Very intelligent businesspeople don't read up on issues. They de-pend on word-of-mouth. My goal is to reach the people I know or I meet. I send out postcards giving them my opinions about who they should support. It means a lot to them because no-body else is doing it. We had a city treasurer who came to me. I said, "The best thing that you can do, Lisa, is to do a postcard telling your qualifications. City treasurer is kind of low on the to-tem pole. Get people to commit to mail so many and stamp them for you. If I send it to people and say "this is who you ought to support" and they like me, that might help sway it.

PENNY ANGELO, MIDLAND

When my husband, Ernie, ran for mayor, I set up a telephone list and gave volunteers areas to call. We sent letters every night. Ernie would wake up in the morning and say "Now, we need to send a letter." By night, they would have them printed, and the next day he'd say, "We need to send another letter." We must have done that ten days in a row. We were running against a popular incumbent mayor pro tem.

We had to do it all by hand. First, we didn't have the money to do it any other way. Second, frankly the technology had not caught up with the way that we wanted to do it.

Bus Tours

MILLIE TEAS, DALLAS

We were Pioneers for Reagan. We went in Pat Jacobson's motor home. Jane Bergland, Betty Ambrose, Sharla Moore, Pat Jacobson, and I were going to travel all over these little counties and reach out to people that were away from the campaign. Right before we left on a trip, the *Dallas Morning News* said that East Texas is a landslide for Carter and that Reagan probably wouldn't be looking for any assistance in that area. Well, we went down through Central Texas and all over East Texas.

We had the bus decorated, and we were all in red, white, and blue with hats with streamers and buttons all over them. We went up and down the street asking everyone to vote for Ronald Reagan. We stopped once, and there was a crew of telephone workmen. A picture should have been in *Time* magazine of Pat hanging out of the motor home handing this guy a Reagan flyer. We had a ball doing it, and we made an impact.

CATHERINE SMYTH COLGAN, DALLAS

In 1974, I was appointed by state chairman Jack Warren to chair the Candidates Caravan. It was the first time that we had candidates for all of the seven statewide offices. We had a motor home motorcade and went to sixty-nine towns in thirty days. One day, we got off to a fifteen-minute late start, and we were fifteen minutes late everywhere we went. But the other days, we were right on time. There were two fascinating things about that trip. Number one, most of the candidates traveled with us the whole time. Polly Sowell, the state vice chairman, traveled part of the time; Barbara Lewis, president of TFRW, was off and on; and I missed a few days. But most of us traveled the full month. One of the young staff people at Republican headquarters who had just finished at the University of Texas helped arrange our logistics. He was Jeb Bush.

In a number of towns, particularly in West Texas, many people had never laid eyes on a Republican. We would pull up in front of the newspaper office and walk in unannounced. This, I am told, paved the way because the next time we had statewide offices four years later a trail had been blazed. They knew there was such a thing as a Republican.

The other interesting thing that happened is that we were all together on the tour the night Nixon resigned. That was absolutely riveting. We were dumb struck, but the man who was the lieutenant governor candidate stood up and proposed a toast to President Ford. We carried on from there. We were supposed to fly the next day to El Paso. We called ahead, as we did every time, to make sure that they were ready for us, and they said, "Are you really going to come?" We said, "Absolutely!" But we knew that literally sealed the fate of all seven of our candidates. They were determined to proceed. Promises made, promises kept. People had made arrangements, spent money, and planned parties. We completed the tour with style.

Coffees and Teas

NADINE FRANCIS, ODESSA

When Jack Cox ran for governor, it was back in the days of the coffees. Coffees, coffees, coffees. They were in people's homes. Of course, it was mostly women. I would often try to set up a luncheon for men if I could, but for the most part, it was coffees. I was at the airport lots of times at eight o'clock in the morning. We would have a couple of coffees, even three, before lunch and then have lunch. The instructions out of Austin were to keep him as busy as you can. Then we would go call on individuals and businesses. When you don't know how difficult a job is, you just kind of go do it. I was very naive. If Peter O'Donnell sent something out that said "do this," I would have gone to the end of the earth practically to get it done.

LOU BROWN, MIDLAND

Barbara Culver Clack basically ran her campaign for county judge. That was before the times of campaign chairman and campaign treasurers and filing all these papers. Katie Heck was helping her and her husband. She would call somebody and say, "Would you invite the people that live on your street?" They would basically have cookies, punch, and coffee. The candidate would be there to greet everybody. The candidate at that point did not walk in the door and everybody was there to greet her. Barbara was there greeting everybody at the front door. Maybe she even brought the cookies. She would tell them why she wanted to run for county judge. She was very articulate and convincing, and she was very warm. A lot of people would go away shaking their heads saying, there's no way they are going to elect a woman to political office in West Texas. She's got good ideas about running a county, and I like what she says about ad valorem taxes. I might vote for her, but I don't think there's any way we're going to do this. Sure enough, that was the first win that gave the Republicans that first breath of life.

ROBBIE BORCHERS, NEW BRAUNFELS

The Tom Loeffler campaign took about a year of my life. We were absolutely determined that this was our chance to get a Republican congressman. So here in Comal County I started in '77 inviting people to events for him here at home. It would be breakfast or cocktails or something just for people to come in and meet him. When he came to town, I would take him place to place for days. He stayed sometimes two or three days. We would just hit everybody that we could think of to visit. He was a delightful candidate. I never will forget that after the parties he was always there to help with the cleanup and always insisted that he'd take the garbage out.

BECKY CORNELL, SAN ANGELO

Congressmen Collins from Dallas ran against Lloyd Bentsen for the Senate. I was his chairman for ten or twelve counties in the area. One time, Mrs. Collins came and there was a tea party for her in Murchison out west of town. I dreamed the night before that I was late and had to pick her up at the airport in my bathrobe. I said, "Oh, don't worry. We will take the shortcut by the Boys Ranch, and we will be in Murchison in plenty of time." I was up at the crack of dawn the next day so I would be sure not to pick up Mrs. Collins in my bathrobe.

Car Caravans

MARY ANNE COLLINS, DALLAS

We would ride around in these caravans for "Bruce Alger for Congress." I had my first baby then and put her in the car seat. We'd have big signs on the car and ride all around neighborhoods and shopping centers.

MARTHA CROWLEY, DALLAS

Rita Clements was Rita Bass then. She was very, very active in the early days. We used to do car caravans. She and I were pregnant at the same time and could barely squeeze behind the steering wheel. We used to get antique cars, and if that didn't work we got convertibles. We went to shopping centers and drove slowly around with the candidates. I don't think that we could blare too much music. It was a no-no. Get little kids and hats. Red, white, and blue everything. Something to draw attention to the candidates.

MARION COLEMAN, PASADENA

I got a motorcade together when Nixon was coming into Herman Park. I went before the city council and asked if we could get motorcycle police officers. They laughed at me. They said, "Oh, we will give you a car. How many cars do you think you'll have,

Mrs. Coleman?" I said probably about 75 to 100, and they all laughed. We had 257 cars. The Houston Police Department met us on the Gulf Freeway and led us into Herman Park. I had a little boy who brought a bicycle, and he decorated it because he thought he could go with us. I just stuck him in my car. We really made a mark in Houston and Pasadena.

Creating a Presence

JOCI STRAUS, SAN ANTONIO

In 1960, they asked would I head up the Nixon Girls? I got every high school and college signed up, and I got a group from each one. We met every Saturday at a parking lot at one of the malls. We got permission from the mall keepers to be at the parking lot, and we would stop as a car would pull up and ask if we could put a Nixon bumper sticker on the car. We always had to ask. We had training sessions on how to ask and how to take a "no" nicely. We were at every function that was possible with our uniforms on.

One of the most fun things was when John Wayne came to open the new Alamo movie. My husband and my father-in-law were out of town. They had tickets to the opening of the movie. What an opportunity to have my Nixon Girls there outside the theater giving out bumper stickers and buttons. First, I called the chamber of commerce who was sponsoring the opening, and I said, "Would you mind if I came to the reception at the St. Anthony. I have a ticket. And would you mind if I wore my Nixon Girl outfit?" I asked Theo Weiss, the president then. He said, "No, I wouldn't mind. Of course not! You go right ahead." So I did. I picked up my mother-in-law. It was pouring rain, and I had on my raincoat. I walked into the party, and everyone in there was dressed to the teeth in their furs and jewels. I took off my raincoat and everyone said, "OH!" It was the first time you could tell your real friends from the people who were embarrassed for you. It was really interesting.

I was approached by this young man. He said, "Miss, would mind taking off your hat?" I said, "It's part of my outfit. It's okay.

John Wayne is a Republican. Who are you?" He told me he was his press agent. "Oh, fabulous. Let's go over and meet him." So I locked arms with him, and he took me over to meet John Wayne, which was the most wonderful moment. Then all my girls were standing outside of the theater. There were six on each side as people came in. We had a presence. Somebody had to know we were out there, and we had to have a chance.

SITTY WILKES, AUSTIN

I was on a Bush Belle committee. Rita Clements was involved with that in 1970. She had us go down on Congress Avenue and do "Buttonhole for Bush Days." You would feel like a prostitute if you did it now. I went down there and stood on Congress Avenue. We put a campaign button in the men's buttonholes. You could never do that today. I still have my Bush scarf that she had us wear.

Anything to Generate Enthusiasm

MARGARET BAIRD, HOUSTON

I had a little toy Pomeranian dog back then. We made a campaign outfit for him, with the candidates' names on either side of the outfit, and on top we had a small piece of wood, which had a little hole for a flag. When he ran, the flag would wave. He also had a little hat, which had campaign buttons all over it. However, he wasn't as willing to wear that. The first election in which my dog campaigned was the Nixon-Agnew race against George McGovern in 1972. We always hoped that the candidates' names would not be too long. Every election, we would update the campaign outfit.

When my youngest child was born in 1973, I used my baby and her baby carriage to campaign. The carriage was covered with bumper stickers. Later, she helped me campaign using her wagon covered with bumper stickers, and she would cover herself with them. As my little Holly grew older, she would entertain at the polls. She and friends would dance and sing political songs, some of them original. My feeling was you had to generate enthusiasm. Animals and babies will always attract attention, and attention is the name of the game.

What is your sign strategy?

First of all, you need to get a lot of signs up. Signs are extremely important psychologically. I try to find visible corners on busy streets first of all. You make sure you have every other block covered. Some people would allow me to put any sign up. They'd say, "If you are supporting them, then I trust you." Signs, particularly all over the important big streets, have a positive impact on voters. I can remember elections where all of a sudden, overnight, dozens of signs disappeared. It was so depressing. Psychologically, it is really important to have signs to generate a good voter turnout and enthusiasm.

BILLIJO PORTER, EL PASO

In 1980, when George Bush ran for president against Ronald Reagan, I was going to support George Bush. Of course Patty Bruce did, too. We were the chairmen for the Sixteenth Congressional District. I said, "Let's get it going because there's no organization in some of these little counties, like Hudspeth." There weren't any Republican county chairmen. I said, We're going to go out in our Levis and be one of the group." We went everywhere west of Odessa including Pecos, Valentine, and Fort Hancock. We spent three or four days getting Bush chairmen. We took the material and told them what we wanted to do, and we met with them and drank beer with them. Whatever we had to do, we got these people. I remember the Bush people were so proud of us because we even had a chairman in Loving County with only 300 people.

I understand that later on when the Reagan chairman in El Paso found out what we had done they were mad because we had organized. We had gotten all of the people. In some of these counties, there were only two Republicans. I talked to them and said, "Now, George Bush is a Texan and we have got to support our fellow Texans." I had done some organizing when John Connally had run for president. I already had some contacts there. Here was a chance to really sneak them into the Party. That was my main motivation. Here was my chance to say, "You are going to have to make a commitment. You are going to have to vote in the Republican primary if you are going to vote for your guy." We had these people committed. Some fell by the wayside early on, but I had their names. By god, I supported Connally. You are going to support my guy now.

Phone Banks

REBA BOYD SMITH, ODESSA & ABILENE

In Taylor County, we got out the vote. We did what Nancy Braddus said. If you follow instructions, you get the job done. There were four steps. You identified the voter. We zeroed in on the undecided voter. We sent them information. We called the undecided voters back to say, "We hope you received the information. Could you join us now and support Bill Clements?" Then we got out the vote. We called every one of those people.

BARBARA NOWLIN, HOUSTON & FRIENDSWOOD

Running those phone banks back in the early days when volunteers were hard to come by was challenging. It is an absolutely grueling experience to be there every day. You get the location, set it up, staff it, and then are there all the time. That experience, that teamwork, that camaraderie is probably the best. You learn their names and that was not hard with someone there day in and day out, but we had 600 volunteers. Looking back on that experience, working together really drew us together. There was a bond. It was a wonderful experience. Very rewarding, very gratifying.

JANIE BROCK, SAN ANGELO

In spring of '84, we were getting ready to set up the phone banks. A friend of mine accepted the chairmanship of the phone banks and asked me to be a captain. They were having training in Midland, so she took me to Midland for the training. By the time we came back, I was the assistant chairman of the phone banks. She got sick two or three months into the campaign, and I became chairman. I was brand-new to Republican election procedures. Gladi Wright was my right hand. I put in about sixteen hours a day at the headquarters, and Gladi was usually down there to help. Before the election was over, I had been completely indoctrinated in the procedures.

BARBARA PATTON, HOUSTON

Phone banks are one of the best ways to reach out and connect with the voters and show some excitement about a real opportunity to elect someone to office. The other thing they are, is an opportunity to get volunteers involved in working for the candidate. A lot of times you found a volunteer that came in and wanted to help with one aspect of the campaign and do the telephones, and you found out they had all of these other marvelous skills— perhaps being a surrogate speaker or writing press releases or being a field rep for the campaign or eventually going to work for that particular candidate. Working on the phone and other volunteer positions in a campaign can be a wonderful training ground for a career or for being called upon to do another job.

PENNY BUTLER, HOUSTON

If we don't have a personal touch at phone banks, we are going to lose our vital nerve. It is simply amazing what kind of stories and information you can gather if you get on the phone and talk to some of these people. I think that is part of what is really missing these days. Some people feel so foreign about campaigns and about leadership because candidates are not getting good feedback. They're looking at polls that "high-powered people" are doing, and we are not really talking to people on the ground. That is a real mistake. We need things that volunteers can do and that will bring out some of the younger people.

PATTILOU DAWKINS, AMARILLO

Martha Weisend was Bill Clements' overall campaign chairman in 1986. She was a general if there ever was one. She would call and bark "Pattilou Dawkins!" I would say, "Yes, ma'am?" "Now tell me, what were your numbers today? How many calls did you make? How many were Clements'?" We had to report into her every morning by 9:00 a.m. So of course it was very important that the people who worked at night got all the numbers correct. Invariably, they didn't. I'd get over there by 7:00 a.m. and make sure that the numbers were all correct because she scared the pooh out of me. I lived in fear that Martha Weisend was going to call, and my numbers wouldn't be accurate. I tried not to fabricate, but there were sometimes that I would lie on those numbers to make sure I didn't incur the wrath of Martha Weisend because you didn't want to do that. She was a general, and it worked. We had the number-one phone bank. We got out 98 percent of all of our identified voters.

How in the world did you do that?

I had drivers. Everybody had a Suburban. We would go to rest homes. We would go everywhere. Our phone bank kept working. We called people until they said that they had voted. We would maybe call people two or three times the day of the election. We would ask had they voted and they would say, "Quit calling me. I'm going as soon as I put the wash in the dryer." We would say what time do you think that might be? "Well, in another fifteen minutes, I guess." We would call them back in fifteen minutes and we would say, "Have you voted?" We had people working from their homes. We probably had 100 phones working that day calling people to make sure that they had voted.

Voter Identification

MARY ELLEN MILLER, AUSTIN

All of the campaigns that I have been involved with I have always felt that voter identification was extremely important. Without it, a manager can not use money or the candidate's time to the highest degree of productivity. You need a guideline for where to put your volunteers, where to schedule your candidate, and where you spend your bucks. So the first thing that I do in every race is all of the arithmetic for the campaign. I get all of the statistical information on past voting patterns and know what is a reasonable expectation of votes, the ones that you can forget about and the middle ground—the savable. I set the vote goals before we ever start. I want to know where we are every single day, what we need, and where we are going to get it.

What was your role in John Tower's 1978 race?

They wanted me to be in charge of voter I.D. Phone bank results plummeted after Tower refused to shake hands with [*Democratic opponent Bob*] Krueger. I'm surprised the photo didn't win the Pulitzer. Polly Sowell and I cornered John in a limousine in Dallas and said you are in big-time trouble. He said, "I know it." I said to him, "I have an idea, but we will never get the money from finance to do it." I will never forget what he said. He looked at me and he said, "Do what you have to do, Darling." So Polly and I went to southwest Harris County because that is where most of the new people were. We sent out some teams door-to-door asking if the election were held today who would they vote for. We found seven or eight out of ten were Republican. That is one of the times that we didn't turn out the vote by identified vote. We called everyone and turned them out by the percentages. That was a turning point in John Tower's election. There is no question about it. Later I did a total, just like I would do before an election. County after county after county, Krueger beat Tower. If they had had a turn-out, Krueger would have beaten John Tower.

Do you think that it would have been as successful if it had not been for the volunteers who were willing to get on the phones and make those calls?

No. John Tower was so well loved by party members, and you see how that shines through in conversations with other people.

Volunteers were fundamentally important because it was like a holy crusade to them to reelect Tower. He and Lou were both so well loved, and anyone would do anything for them. That was the ingredient. You couldn't put a dollar value on it. There is no way you can put a dollar value on that.

If you don't have a phone bank you are inviting defeat every time. We wouldn't have known what we had to do if we hadn't had a phone bank. Maybe it doesn't matter if you have a real popular person who is going to win by 70 percent of the vote and has been reelected three times. When you are serious about it, it's more than just winning. It's getting the best investment of their time, spending your money where it will do the most good.

Get-Out-the-Vote

GWEN PHARO, DALLAS

No job was too dirty for any of us. We were on a crusade. We would sit at the headquarters on Lemmon Avenue, and they would give us a phone book. They would say "you call this page," and we would sit there like idiots and call every number on the page in an afternoon. We would pretty well get the phone book covered before Election Day. We would just say, "Is this Mr. Jones? Mr. Jones, this is Gwen Pharo at Republican headquarters. We'd like for you to vote for our candidate, Mr. X." They would say yes or no, and we put a little mark by their name. That's how we developed lists for phone calls.

KRIS ANNE VOGELPOHL, GALVESTON

The first phone banks that really stand out in my mind we did in our house. We brought in eight extra lines. We had phones in all of the different parts of the house. We had women who were taking their children to school, dropping them off at nine o'clock, and coming back here to phone. Then they would go and pick up their children at noon. Then a group of women who didn't pick up children until three or four o'clock in the afternoon came at noon and called until three o'clock. Then we had a group of widows who came in about three and worked until six on the phones because they did not have to prepare an evening meal. I would prepare an evening meal so that before these widows left we would sit down and have a hot meal. Then we would have a hot meal ready for young couples coming home from work who would come by here and call until nine. We had a real system going, and we kept all phones full at all times.

Some women could not walk into a Republican headquarters as they can now. The people who helped us with our early phone banks were the parents of our children's friends. The groups that came in the evening were our friends' mothers. It was through friendships. Recruiting is the hardest thing we had to do.

GLENNA McCORD, DALLAS

[*County Chair*] Harry Bass took our strongest precincts and figured out where all of the known Republicans lived distancewise from the polling place. He put these phone lists together and brought them up to headquarters on Election Day. Bobbie Biggart and I were at headquarters. He came in around six o'clock. He said, "Are you two the only ones here?" He said, "We are going to call all the people on these lists. These are our strongest precincts." He said, "I have figured out how long it takes them to get from their house to the polling place. We are going to call until five minutes to seven." The three of us sat there with the phone lists. He had listed all the people that lived the farthest away first, so we would call them first. When you talk about getting out the vote, that was getting it out until the very last minute.

MARGARET BAIRD, HOUSTON

In my neighborhood, people started voting without having to be reminded because they became interested and felt like their vote counted. I would tell them how many elections have been won or lost by less than one vote per precinct. It all adds up to victory if you make sure that you get those votes out.

THEO WICKERSHAM, SAN ANTONIO

I found that one way to help get more people interested in your Party was a ride to the polls. As we are riding along to the polls you are hoping that they are not going to vote for a Democrat. There was one old couple in Cibolo. They said, "We just appreciate you so much for coming way out here in the country and picking us up." I said, "Well, you are adamant about getting to the polls. I could tell that when you called." They said yes. Come to find out, they were Democrats. I said, "I want to show you my ballot before you get out of the car. I want to tell you about each one of these people—which ones I know and why I want to vote for them." They were so interested. From then on, they'd always call me to take them to the polls. I am sure by word-of-mouth they have a lot of their people turned.

CAROLE RAGLAND, LEAGUE CITY

Turning out the vote is very difficult now. I have enough Republican voters in this county to make a difference in any race—4,000 or so. I sent a letter out before the last election, and in Galveston County none of our candidates won. In our precinct, we only had 1,500 votes. Only our precinct commissioner in our gerrymandered precinct won. The letter said, "Gov. John Sharp. Think there's no way? Think again. How would you like to wake up the day after the election and have John Sharp elected Lt. Governor? John Cornyn is trailing in the polls because Jim Mattox has name ID. This can happen if you don't vote. Did you know that there are three candidates that live right here in our precinct? Please go vote."

Ballot Security

PAT MCCALL, HOUSTON & UVALDE COUNTY

Ballot security is making sure that those people who come in to vote have the right to vote. We had poll watchers. Men. As you know, this is ranching and farming country. We had a lot of big farmers and ranchers who went down to poll watch. It was a small county so it wasn't difficult. Everybody knew everybody else. If they came in and they weren't legal, they would look at one of the poll watchers who knew them and turn around and leave.

How did you figure out that you needed a good ballot security program?

Because of what I had gone through in Houston and Harris County. People had always said we would never carry one side of town, and I said, "Well, if we get ballot security, we might have a chance." We put it together and it worked.

BARBARA PATTON, HOUSTON

Back in 1965 through '67, Mildred Fike would always be in charge of ballot security for any election. She was a very meticulous person. She was very talented mathematically and very distrustful of people [*laughing*]. She was perfect for the job. She analyzed the election returns—the demographics. It helped to plan for the future for another campaign.

MARY ANNE COLLINS, DALLAS

We had a very good ballot security program. Helen Harris was a prime mover. She was one of the brains of this Party—our little old lady in tennis shoes. She knew political strategy and was a meticulous person. Candidates like Ike Harris would go to her for advice in their campaigns. She also would figure out the number of delegates per precinct, and she was just meticulous. She ran one of our first ballot security programs. She had regional poll watchers in Dallas County before we were able to get election judges.

GLENNA McCORD, DALLAS

We became aware that we were going to have to do something about poll watchers at an early stage. Democrats weren't accustomed to having anyone look over their shoulders. The evidence of vote fraud was all around us every election day. We had to devise some way to try and counteract that. You could have affidavits galore and people willing to go into a courtroom to swear what they saw, but if you didn't have a judge in place to hear the case you could forget it. We're talking about the days when there wasn't a Republican judge in Dallas County. Maybe there were one or two in the whole state. So we couldn't get the cases heard, but something had to be done. If it hadn't been for the women who gave their time to volunteer, we would not have been able to do what we did.

Volunteers took the obituary list, and as soon as the voter registration list came in from the county for the election of 1968, they went through those voter registration lists and made notations as to who was dead. In so doing, they also found a lot of duplications. So we put all our data together on three-by-five index cards, and then we put them in alphabetical order according to precinct. When I was vice chairman, I had a call from a lady in Dallas who was a liberal Democrat. She was trying to find polling places for the Democratic primary in precincts where there weren't very many active Democrats. We were having a hard time finding a place to vote in areas of Dallas that were her precincts. She said, "Do you think that we can work together on this?" I said, "Sure. I need help too."

She called me at home one night, and said State Senator Mike McKool was having hearings around the state trying to get some good information together to knock out some of this voter fraud that was going on. The conservative Democrats were doing the same thing to the liberal Democrats that they were doing to us—stealing elections. They would steal their election in the primary and steal ours in the general election.

In September 1970, as co-chairman of the Dallas County Republican Ballot Security Committee for 1970, I appeared before McKool's State Senate Committee for Election Law Reform. I presented an exhibit of the poll books from a number of precincts with the combined total number of duplicate registrations from those precincts, which totaled 791. I also pointed out that in 59 precincts of commissioners district one there were 681 voters listed in the wrong precinct. I also informed the court that volunteers at Republican headquarters had checked the obituary lists in the daily newspaper. The deceased voters were listed by precinct on slips that, upon request, would be available for the purpose of purging the list. Judge Sterrett and the commissioners agreed that it would be impossible to purge the list of convicted felons unless every person in the state were fingerprinted. I turned to him at that point and said, "Judge, we just sent men to the moon and back. If computers can do that, then I think they can purge these lists." He almost swallowed his cigar.

We requested that some guidelines be drawn for precinct election officials to determine qualifications of the voter who has lost his certificate and whose name is not in the poll book in his home precinct. We had one report after another of people who had registration certificates but got to the polling place and their names were not in the book. My sister was one of them. In October, we were given permission to talk to the tax assessor-collector and to his assistant in voter registration. We discussed using the computer to delete the duplicate social security numbers. We purged the list of 7,048 duplicates. This is the possibility of 7,048 people voting twice. Then, physically scanning the list, we deleted an additional 7,438 for a total of 14,486 names. We printed Dallas County's first master list of registered voters in alphabetical order so that if an election judge had questions about a voter's qualifications he could learn if a voter had been listed in the wrong precinct. In addition, we shared the list of deceased voters. With the addition of the 1987 deceased voters, a total of 16,473 names were removed from the poll books.

BERYL MILBURN, AUSTIN

I think the Clements election for governor was fair because we watched the ballot boxes. I remember meeting at the Clements headquarters, and the vote was so close. They said, "You've got to go back, and you've got to contact all of your county chairmen to be sure they know where the ballot boxes are and stay with them." So we did. All through the night, people went and found the ballot boxes and stayed with them. We guarded that ballot box, and that's what made it a fair election, and Clements won.

ESTELLE TEAGUE, HURST

In the early '60s I started doing early voting for the county clerk. I was known as the token Republican. We had chief deputies that we used to chase down the stairs to get the ballots. The deputies would say, "I've always sent loose ballots out. Now, why can't I take one to these old friends of mine?" We sat on the cans all night long in the basement of the courthouse to keep people from getting into them. We've gotten it cleaned up, but it took us a good while.

We had a precinct judge who got mad at one of our poll watchers and slapped her and told her to get out. The poll watcher sat there and said, "I'm entitled to be here and I am staying." We had nursing homes that voted 75 percent of their patients when I was in charge. The handwriting didn't compare so I threw them out. When they took it to court, the opponent won the election by fifty-five votes. That is the only time in the history of Tarrant County that the ballot box was ever opened to match up votes. The judge ordered that all of the mail-in ballots be matched up to the stubs. That's when he declared that they were illegal, just as I said they were.

FRANCIE FATHEREE CODY, PAMPA

I guess it was 1962. The state party wanted us to get poll watchers. The poll watchers were to be there to make sure that the elections were being run correctly. We had a cantankerous little guy who was the presiding judge. They counted the ballots all by hand. There was a big precinct and it was late. He decided he was going to quit counting that night, take the ballots home, and start the next day. The poll watcher called me. I said, "No, no, he can't do that!" I said, "Tell him to meet us at the courthouse." I called Clayton, the county chairman, and said, "We have got to go to the courthouse." There was the sheriff, the deputy sheriff, Clayton, the judge, the poll watchers, and me. I said to the judge, "I understand that you're tired, but you can not take the ballot box home with you. How about locking it up in the sheriff's office?" He said, "No, I am in charge of these until they are counted, and I am taking them home." I convinced him that I didn't write the Texas election law, but I was just trying to go by the law. I got the sheriff to chime in with me. The sheriff said, "She would like to lock them up here. Will you do that?" This poll watcher had already missed one day of work so he had to miss two days of work.

RUTH McGUCKIN, HOUSTON & WASHINGTON COUNTY

I believe it was 1968, soon after Nancy Palm became the county chairman. We got in the election returns from several precincts in the west part of Harris County, which we knew were Republican precincts. But the vote came in overwhelmingly Democrat. So we knew something was wrong. Nancy Palm got a court order to go to the storage facilities and inspect the voting machines. She went with a marshal and a screwdriver and opened up the machines. They had rigged from the straight Republican lever a wire over to the Democrats. If you pulled the Republican lever, it would vote straight Democrat. She went throughout the warehouse unscrewing the machines and changing them. The county judge was furious. He was not elected after that.

ESTHER BUCKLEY, LAREDO

All of the hoodwinks of voting, we had them. There was the folded ballot, where a guy would come and ask for a ballot and have a folded ballot in his pocket. The folded ballot was voted. He would drop the folded ballot in the ballot box and take the new one and put it in his pocket for the next voter. The trick with the string. Strings were cut the length of the ballot. They would line them up to the side of the ballot and tie knots on the squares where they were to vote. All of these things that they would do because the people were illiterate in many cases. In a lot of cases, we knew they would come up from Mexico. In one of the 1972 elections, there was a truck that had forty people in it. This truck would drive up to a polling place. They would get out of the truck and get their voting cards, go in to vote, come back, and the driver would pick up the voting cards. We could never prove corruption.

One of the things that helped a lot is when we could pay poll watchers. It made them [*the Democrats*] nervous. We have documented something like 500 cases of things that they did. Like a voter would come in and they would say, "What is your name?" "Juan Gonzales." "Oh, which Juan Gonzales are you? The one that lives at 1302 or the one that lives at 101? Oh, 101." Of course it wasn't him. There'll be a Juan Gonzalez or Juan Rodriguez in every single polling place. They never ever asked for I.D.

ANNE SHEPARD, VICTORIA & HARLINGEN

In 1984, I was running ballot security in the state. We called all of the Republican County chairmen to make sure that all of their precinct chairmen were on target and knew exactly what they were supposed to do during the election. One part was the legal side. You have your attorneys lined up with what to do in the event of irregularities. Then we had the organization side of it. The poll watchers had to be organized and trained.

In my opinion, most people didn't want to break the law. They just didn't know the law. In some cases, they had been election judges for years. They just didn't know the law, and we just had to help them out. Then there was intimidation. If you have a voting booth in someone's garage or a volunteer fire station and you go in and say "I want to vote Republican," and the Democrat county chairman is sitting there looking at you, and they say, "You want to do what? Vote in the Republican primary? You have to walk through five of us here and then go to the back of the room." It would be intimidating. There were pictures taken. That was tough. Both parties have frankly done a better job of letting their election judges know what the laws are.

MARION COLEMAN, PASADENA

In the 1960 Nixon race we had poll watchers because there were no Republican judges. I had canvassed every member of my precinct. Every single door I went to, whether they were registered or not, and asked for support, even a dollar, or gave literature. On Election Day, all of a sudden, this bus load drove up. All black people. They went to the voting booths and were instructed, "See that lever? Just pull that." I went up and said to the election judge, "I have to challenge this because these people do not live in this precinct." "How do you know that, young lady?" Then I opened up my portfolio and said, "I canvassed every one of these houses, and there is not one black person living in Pasadena, never mind my precinct." He said, "Well, honey, I don't want to disappoint you; we just love you to death. We wish you were a Democrat." He said, "We have this election already won. Right here in Texas and in Illinois." No sooner had they left than another bus load drove up, and they all voted a straight Democratic ticket. That was shocking to me. Of course, I took all of this down, but it didn't mean anything. I know that it sounds unbelievable, but I witnessed it.

FRAN ATKINSON, LUFKIN & SAN ANTONIO

Our women's club studied the Texas election code ad nauscum. We wanted to get poll watchers because we could not get clerks appointed by the commissioners court, which were all Democrats. So the only way we could get our people into the polls was to appoint poll watchers. I learned it so thoroughly that I could train poll watchers, and I did, frequently in other counties. Angelina County was written up in 1960 for voter fraud. There were boxes that came in doubled in votes. There were all sorts of shenanigans. There were indictments. *Look* magazine, which was popular at the time, was one of the magazines that mentioned Angelina County along with Cook County in Illinois as high points of voter fraud. The only way you can cure that is to have both parties represented at an election.

The poll watchers were there to observe and report any wrong-doing or ask the judge to correct it on the spot. You had to know many points in the law. For instance, a judge is not allowed to pick up a ballot and hand it to a voter. The voter picks up his own ballot. They used to just stand there handing them out like a deck of cards. I'm not saying that there was anything wrong, but the potential was there to hand out pre-marked ballots for people to cast. In those days, you were not allowed to carry a list of who you were going to vote for into the polls. Husband and wife could not vote in the same booth. I had one old fellow tell me one time, "Well, why not? We sleep together." And I said, "Mister, I didn't write the law, the Democrats did." "Oh, it's bound to be a good law then," he said. We had one precinct where there was a lot of suspicious nonsense going on. So we put five poll watchers on duty, the absolute limit of what we could put in, and the judge never came back. It was not our intent to run her out. It was our intent to make it clear to her that we expected an aboveboard election.

LIBBA BARNES, SAN ANTONIO

I went to poll watching school. Arthur Seeligson and Fred Wright and I went to this precinct way on the West Side. It was when Lyndon Johnson ran against Barry Goldwater. Arthur Seeligson had sent out all of these registered letters to everyone in the precinct. They came back no such address, no such person, a variety of reasons. So when these people would come to vote we knew that they were not legal voters, and we would challenge them right there. The election judge herself was saying in Spanish when they went in, "Pull the left lever." She called Democratic head-quarters, and their lawyer told us that if we caused any more trouble he was going to throw us in jail. When we left at eight o'clock that night, a cheer went up.

GAIL WATERFIELD, CANADIAN

We were beginning to get a little more professional and a little more organized in Hemphill County. Francie Cody called up one day and said, "You have got to be a poll watcher." I hate to admit this—I said, "What is a poll watcher?" She told me, and I said, "Well, Francie, that's like telling people you don't trust what they're doing." She said, "It is not. You need to get down there and get yourself registered and your papers turned in to be a poll watcher." I said, "Okay, Francie, I'll go do that." The morning I had to go down, I was actually trembling. I thought these are all my friends. I am here as a poll watcher, pretending to watch for something to be done wrong. I spent the whole day and learned a bunch. I found out that day the only way you are going to learn the ropes is to climb them. From that year on, I had poll watchers at every single election. It was no big deal.

Transition between Primary and General Elections

How do you bring the campaign volunteers together behind the primary winner so you can win the election in November?

FLORENCE NEUMEYER, HOUSTON

The first thing is winning over the opponents to endorse the winner. If they come out and endorse, then usually their volunteers and supporters will take the lead from that. Now, sometimes they don't endorse and let everybody choose for themselves. Sometimes the winner lets it been known that it is time to close ranks and continues to try and win those people because you don't always know who they are.

You just have to put your best foot forward. You find out who the key players are. The candidate goes to them and says, "You know, I would like your support. Tell me what can I do. Tell me why you chose my opponent over me. What can I do to convince you I am really the person that you can support now?" Chipping away at it. Of course, at your first speech, the very night of the election, you reach out to everybody that supported the other candidates and say, "Now I want your support."

What Makes Campaigns Fail?

FLORENCE NEUMEYER, HOUSTON

A lot of things can make a campaign fail. Lack of enough funds to get your message out. Candidates do have to have the right balance of money, commitment, and knowledge of the electorate. They can fail due to mismanagement of volunteers, bad campaign management, or lack of a candidate that is really dedicated.

A lot of times candidates would be great and could be elected, but they are a bit lazy or get shy about mixing with people.

Bad strategy might be a better way to put it. It doesn't have to mean that it is the campaign manager. It can be the candidate's advisory committee. The whole committee can take the wrong stance. For example, they run a campaign like they are running for something in Washington and they are really running for the school board. They never really get down on the local level where the people are. Candidates can side on the wrong issues. Their message is not quite right. They don't choose the right management of volunteers, supporters, and information that they pick up from the grassroots. You would be surprised how many people who run for office really are reluctant to mix with the average Joe in a precinct. Sometimes people are telling candidates a certain thing is wrong or they are concerned about an issue, and candidates don't pay attention. If you go to several civic club meetings and you hear the same thing, then maybe you just need to do something with that information in those precincts. You really have to be in tune to what you are hearing.

Some candidates choose the wrong campaign to get in. That is one of the biggest things. They are set up for a fall from the beginning. We had people that would file against Congressman Bill Archer. You can build up name I.D. for something in the future knowing that you can't win. But in this case, you can make people mad just because you file against someone that they love and respect so much. Are you going to win friends and influence people or make people mad so that they are never going to forgive you? Sometimes you have a lot of good people running in the same race. Then it gets down to who can run a well-funded campaign, choose the right issues, and be articulate in conveying to the public what their concerns are and what they are going to do about them. So it can be choosing the wrong race at the wrong time.

In the general election, any number of things can happen. Those failures come from higher up. For example, when [*Republican gubernatorial candidate*] Clayton Williams made the remark that he made [*a joke about rape*], I was doing a state rep race and we picked it up on the phone bank. My guy was an incumbent, and he had won in a special election. It was a slightly Democratic district, which was always difficult to overcome. Our guy was very popular. We were going great guns. When that statement was made, we began to hear from the women on the phone bank, "I am voting for the woman"—meaning Ann Richards—"and I am voting straight." We knew in our district that if they turned out and stuck to that attitude our guy was done. It wasn't anything to do with him because he had a good record and was well liked and supported by a number of Democrats. If we had had a million dollars, we couldn't have done anything.

Staying Motivated in the Face of Defeat

FLO KAMPMANN CRICHTON, SAN ANTONIO
Victories, I have discovered, were not achieved or accomplished. They were built step by tiny step. Just don't leave a stone unturned. Take every opportunity you can.

VERA CARHART, RICHARDSON & HOUSTON
I went to Del Rio one time when Tom Loeffler was running [*for Congress*]. It was a night meeting and involved a lot of men. They were upset because Tom had not been there. I said, "Well, I know he is coming, but don't expect candidates to spend all of their time here, and don't be upset when I tell you why. They have to go where the votes are. You just told me how many votes you have here. Set goals and start working to develop the potential you have." I quoted some election where a Republican lost by half of a percent, which equated to so many votes. I said, "If Del Rio, El Paso, and some other towns could have all contributed about twenty more votes, we would have won those elections. So if you turn out a thousand more votes than what you normally have, you are making a big contribution toward electing Tom Loeffler and Bill Clements." Several of the men came to me after the meeting and said, "Thank you. You said something that makes sense. I have never thought about it that way."

ANNE BERGMAN, WEATHERFORD

Shirley Green said one time, "We all worked so hard back in the years when we didn't expect to win but we wanted to turn out our vote." If we got 47 percent of the vote, we thought we won because we turned out our vote. We'd sit around after the elections in this little county and just go over those votes and all of the voter I.D. calls. We'd say, "Well, we turned out our vote. That's all we can do."

ANN WALLACE, FORT WORTH & AUSTIN

We lost so many times. You would just think, "I'm not going to do this anymore." But then here would come a good candidate, and you'd think, "I'm going to give it one more good try." We lost so many more than we won. All and all you made a lot of good friends that you still have. It's kind of like the old dalmatian dog at the firehouse—when the bell rings you get up, shake yourself off, and get ready to go again.

CHAPTER 17

Money

"Money could not have been all-important, thank goodness, or the Republicans never would have won."   —ANNE ARMSTRONG

*P*olitics used to be a low-budget endeavor, but as campaigns *became more sophisticated and the role of the media grew so did the need for money. Early on, volunteers conducted low-key fundraising efforts to pay their candidates' expenses and buy a few ads. An effort was also made to collect as little as five dollars from as many people as possible in the hope that this would raise the stakes for those individuals and motivate them to go vote on Election Day.*

As expenses grew, so did the magnitude of the fundraising effort. Women planned events, asked for money, and followed up, in many cases developing an admirable list of contacts. They learned to ask for a lot of money from those with a lot of money. Throwing a fundraiser became an art—in planning a party, getting the word out, generating enthusiasm, and collecting the money. The state party created the Key Republican program to support its operations. State Republican Executive Committee members and others were expected to raise $1,000 each year. Some women also became prominent national fundraisers.

Women worked hard to learn to ask for money. Some thought they did not have the personality or the contacts to be successful. Developing a system that worked for them personally and following through with it became the key to success. Overcoming the fear of rejection was sometimes the least of their fundraising problems. Most members of the business community did not find it politically expedient to give to Republicans, and it was not unusual for donors to remain anonymous for fear of retaliation from the Democratic machine. Once people were persuaded by philosophical appeals and convinced of the potential impact of their contributions, wallets started opening and money came into the Republican Party and Republican campaigns.

Role of Money in Politics

The Early Years

FLO KAMPMANN CRICHTON, SAN ANTONIO

Fundraising was confined to a few occasions. When you talk about dollars then and dollars now, it's just unbelievable. We had a loyal bunch of small givers. People didn't mind sending five or ten dollars. We worked with very little money. When John Tower was first running [*for Senate*], we ran that campaign on a shoestring. Probably the whole statewide effort cost $200,000.

KATHRYN McDANIEL, BORGER

Campaigns didn't cost as much as they do now because so much of the campaign was done on a volunteer basis. For example, instead of having to run newspaper ads or television ads people would just go door-to-door and ask everybody on their street to vote for that candidate. Many times that was more effective but took time not money.

ANNE ARMSTRONG, ARMSTRONG

Money could not have been all-important, thank goodness, or the Republicans never would have won. It's hard to remember now that the Democratic Party was weak except for labor. Labor was never as strong in Texas as, say, in Michigan or Pennsylvania although labor money flowed in here at times when there were important races. The Democrats had a pretty good noose around most of the money in those days because at that point it was largely a conservative party. The main campaign cry of the conservative wing of the Democratic Party was, if you vote for those Republicans they are never going to win and you're going to put in the Ralph Yarboroughs and the labor lovers. Very rarely were we able to keep up financially with the Democratic candidate. Money was not all-important but as Phil Gramm said in the 1996 presidential election, "Money is the mother's milk of politics." We made up for the money we didn't have in enthusiasm and drive. We really had a feeling of mission. Women were much more apt to be at home. They were the civic backbone of the small towns and the big cities. They turned a lot of that effort to the Republicans and to the Republican Party.

LIZ GHRIST, HOUSTON

Media is very, very expensive. It has become a major business. When we first started, everyone volunteered. Someone was a research person—that was a volunteer. Someone was an administrative assistant that handled all of the correspondence and the calendar—that was a volunteer. Now, we pay people to do all that. In order to have any hope, you hire "the best people." The best people are identified by their previous successes. You have to set up the office, the staff, the equipment, the technology. Raising money becomes paramount. A candidate for Senate now has to raise $10,000 a day in order to plan for his reelection. Not only do they have to raise money but they have to spend it effectively.

How can you be an effective fundraiser but not leave anyone expecting favors?

What I fall back on in every bit of fundraising that I do is the personal philosophy of the candidate or the party that I am raising the money for. There are so many people who give money in this community with no strings attached. They just want the person that they support to be elected and do a good job. I know that is not true universally. There are those who every time they pick up the phone and call they want a response. Every time they want a meeting or special favor they expect to be handled. They are money givers, too. The person that is the recipient of the money has to learn how to handle that, to not offend, and to not violate his personal convictions.

JUDY JONES MATTHEWS, ABILENE

The way things are now money is 75 percent of it. Sweat equity is important, but money buys the publicity. That's what counts. That's what they all tell me anyway. I never thought of money as being as necessary to politics in the early days. It has grown exponentially in the last few years. Too much really.

RITA PALM, FORT WORTH

In those days, fundraising was not done by third parties. It was usually the candidate himself or a friend of the candidate or a friend of yours. Not many people had that kind of money or thought it was politically expedient to give money. You had contractors that wanted state contracts, and there were a few big boys. But most fundraising was much more personal. When Bush ran for the Senate in 1964, you would go to a party and people would just hand you a check. You would just make kind of a slight comment like, "George is really doing a good job. I hope you can find some change for him." It was really low-key.

JANE JUETT, AMARILLO

It is important to get funds whether it's big dollars or little dollars. If somebody donates even five dollars to the candidate, they are probably going to vote for him. They want to protect their investment. So I think that fundraising is good.

GLENNA McCORD, DALLAS

We never had enough money! When John Tower ran the first time, it was the funniest operation, as I look back. The women made all of the yard signs. Stuart Tears was precinct chairman. He and his wife, Fran, both worked so hard in the Party. There is nothing those two wouldn't do to help. Fran was a public school art teacher. Stu built two silk screen frames for us. We put these silk screens in the garage out back of the headquarters. The women would go out there during the day and make the signs. The men would come at night and nail them on the stakes and get them distributed.

Can't Do It without Money

LOU TOWER, WICHITA FALLS & DALLAS

You can't do without money. So you have to get people to believe in you enough to put some money into the campaign. Campaigns just got wild as far as what they cost.

ILLA CLEMENT, KINGSVILLE

When you are giving money to the Party to help them get a person elected, it's not really for self-dealing. You want that person elected because the country needs them whether it's the president or a state office. We are lucky that we are a free country and can have a choice in an election.

You need an organization that helps people get elected. It takes money, like anything else. If you are building anything, whether a company, a store, or a school, it takes money. People may think it's terrible that money makes a difference in an election, but that's life. Sex makes a difference in marriage. You are not going to change some things.

LINDA UNDERWOOD, HOUSTON

We used to say, it takes three things to win an election. Number 1 is money. Number 2 is money. Number 3 is money. It was true then, and it is true today. Money bought exposure—travel, television, and billboards. Now it is an electronic age but then it was billboards, yard signs, and walking a precinct. People wanted to meet the candidate or speak with somebody. This is what women did more than anything. They were advocates who were going out and talking to people and telling them about the candidates. The importance of human contact should never be diminished. You can't just do it by television.

MARTHA WEISEND, DALLAS

You don't get there from here unless you get on TV. Anything that has to do with print and electronic media is expensive. There is some earned media [*free*], but in relationship to every bit of earned media you get you have to pay big bucks. It takes money for travel, bumper stickers, yard signs, postage, and staff. If you're running statewide in Texas, you need an airplane because it is such a vast state. It gets expensive to run in Texas. It takes both money and volunteers. Televisions do not vote. They certainly will carry the message, but once they have, your message is dead unless somebody picks up on it. So when I see a campaign without people there on a daily basis who believe in the candidate, I'm very afraid. Candidates need people. It's where the enthusiasm is, and it's where the vote is.

DEBORAH BELL, ABILENE

Fundraising is important for a city. Abilene was known years ago as not giving money. Yes, they would vote Republican. I am not saying that candidates look only at that because at the same time you have got issues, but you need to show that you are working to contribute your part.

Who Is Effective and Why

Were there many women involved in fundraising in the early years?

PETER O'DONNELL, DALLAS

Not very many. There were a few and Flo Kampmann Crichton was one and she was awfully good at it. By and large, they weren't. You don't get a big, long line of people standing at your door asking to raise money. We had to recruit people to do it. You could ask them, and they would say, "Oh, I will work, but I'm not any good at raising money." It was hard to recruit them to do it. You can't make them. It is all volunteer. We had our needs, so we had to just keep moving and find someone who was able and wanted to do it. There were a few. In San Antonio in addition to Flo, Irene Cox Wischer was effective, but they were few and far between. There are more than there used to be. Nancy Brinker is a terrific fundraiser today.

Why was Flo a good fundraiser?

In the first place, she could make a substantial contribution herself and that is important. She was charming and persuasive.

GWEN PHARO, DALLAS

I was privileged to sit in on the Saturday morning Marching and Chowder Society. I was included in that as was Rita Clements and I believe Dale Wigley and Bobbie Biggart. There you were given a sounding board. I saw that the people who either contributed money or could raise money had a louder voice than people who didn't involve themselves in fundraising. I decided I could become a good fundraiser. I did.

ELLIE SELIG, SEGUIN

You have to work very hard to get that inside track. Don't misunderstand me, I don't think everything that was accomplished cost money to get there. I think it helps. Money is a way of getting into the inside of politics. If you can do that, you can talk to somebody that knew somebody. You got a little higher up. You could get an invitation to a party. It sounds hokey.

Just Do It

FLO KAMPMANN CRICHTON, SAN ANTONIO

Fundraising is something that I learned. When you first get involved in politics at age twenty-one, you are so starry-eyed and think everything is going to work. Then I discovered the most important and first lesson of politics is that just being right doesn't necessarily mean you're going to win.

You have to figure out the way you do it best. Whether it is writing letters or going to see people, the main thing is to do it. Most fundraising committees are a lot of talk. They could talk about how they were going to do something or how something should be done, but the point is they never did it. So you had to get behind them and say, we have got a deadline on this. We have got to raise so much money because every campaign has a budget.

JUANDELLE LACY, MIDLAND

All women have to do is ask, and if they say no you can't fall off the ground floor. Women can raise money as easily as men. If you really and truly want big contributions you go to the person eye to eye. If possible, the candidate should go. A lot of candidates are reluctant. It is not easy to raise funds. It is probably one of the most difficult things to do. Women are prone to say, "I just can't ask for money." It's no worse than asking for something else. That's a cop-out as far as I am concerned.

Know Your Target

LIBBA BARNES, SAN ANTONIO

I think I have the reputation that, if I have not given, I'm not going to ask you to give. I knew on a very personal basis a lot of these people. It got there toward the end they'd see me coming and say, "Now what do you want money for? That's all you want." After a while, you get tired of doing that because people think, "Do you really like me for me or is it because you know I'm going to give you some money?" I really limited myself to whom I would go ask for money, and they would know that I had checked the candidates out.

Strangely enough, not a lot of people like to do it. Working with Joci Straus made me realize that there was a real need because we did not have any strong men back then. We did not have people like Red McCombs, Lowery Mays, and Gene Ames. Raising the money was left to us to do.

LIZ GHRIST, HOUSTON

You have to know your case. You have to get in to see the right person to present your case. Sometimes you have to convince people that they feel the way you know they feel, but most often they are ready and you just have to ask. When you bring closure, you get out of there. It is business. It is a consistent, organized campaign you put yourself on to get the job done. There is nothing grandiose about it. It is just hard work.

BARBARA BANKER, SAN ANTONIO

It takes time and it takes persistence. It's just like a dog with a bone. You can not give up. Once I identify a little softening that you might consider a contribution, then I'll call you tomorrow. I will stand in that door to keep you from going out if I have not had the opportunity to tell you what I came to tell you. I am assertive in that respect. It takes a determination that is almost akin to rudeness, but you can't open people's minds for them. You have to get them to a point where they're receptive to listen. That's when you've got to know what you're talking about. You can't just sluff it off saying, "Oh, he's a great candidate and he's a friend of mine." You have to spend time to know what their platform is or where they stand on issues. Friends and business associates say that when Barbara Banker calls for money it is not "if" but "when and how much?"

The first thing I try to do is to figure out a pocketbook issue that they support because you're only going to get a person's attention for a very finite amount of time. You want to talk to them about an issue that they are going to get excited about.

HALLY CLEMENTS, VICTORIA

I have more nerve than the law allows. I enjoy calling people up and persuading them to give to a good candidate. I do not enjoy working with any professional fundraisers. I much prefer volunteers. Victoria is small and you also get the "you scratch my back and I scratch your back" sort of thing. Truly, it is a round-robin sort of a situation. I think that it is important if you want to be a fundraiser that you go to these public functions and be seen and get to know people by their first names.

To be a good fundraiser, you need a bunch of easy bullshit. Make a person feel comfortable even if he is not going to give anything. Make it a pleasant experience. Let's forget this business about idealism. People think of the pocketbook first. The men do. Education is always a safe bet. Mainly, try and stay away from anything controversial. You don't want to get in any type of argument with people.

Match Them

KATIE SEEWALD, AMARILLO

In 1962, Dr. Tom Duke and I were co-chairmen of the Jack Cox [*gubernatorial*] campaign. Tom was a very busy doctor so I did a good deal of the work. I raised a lot of money just by going in and staring people in the face and saying, "Look, I've given a thousand dollars. You're giving a thousand dollars." I knew that was the way that Johnny O'Brien did it. He was our chief fundraiser for the Party. One day the president of the bank called and said, "I hate to tell you, but the Cox account is overdrawn." I said, "It is not." He had me mixed up with one of the Democratic candidates. So I said, "Well, I just feel so bad that I think you're going to have to give me a big contribution for the campaign to make up for this." So he did. I used every angle.

SHIRLEY GREEN, AUSTIN & SAN ANTONIO

In my experience, most of the women who were successful in raising money were of a social or economic class themselves that they could lean on their friends who had money and raise money as much through personal friendship and loyalty as through any real commitment to the Republicans. Certainly in the early days that was true. We had some very good women fundraisers, not many but there were some.

BECKY CORNELL, SAN ANGELO

Some friends were very generous when I had to ask them for money. Sometimes the businessmen who have helped one another were able to raise more money than a volunteer. That is very effective, certainly more so than the volunteer saying, "We would love it if you would give us $10,000." I told one person how much I had given, and they gave that, too. I thought, "Wow, this is great."

Don't Be Afraid

PENNY BUTLER, HOUSTON

A good fundraiser is not afraid to ask. You have to ask and then follow up quickly and say thank you. A person just wants to be acknowledged. Enthusiasm and a lot of persistence help. Unless you ask, you will never know. The worst they can say is no. That happens a lot.

SYLVIA NUGENT, DALLAS & AMARILLO

People are afraid of fundraising. Everybody thinks that fundraising is some magic. Fundraising is just work. It is very simple. You identify your universe. You contact them by letter and then you contact them in person. You make sure that the best person asks them. Then you collect the money. Then you have the party.

Believe in It

SALLY MCKENZIE, DALLAS

I've been on the national finance committee and the state finance committee for just about everybody. I always said, "I'm not a good political fundraiser, but I can raise money for George Bush until the world looks level." You can do it if you believe in somebody.

GWEN PHARO, DALLAS

I learned to go ask for money for candidates by getting it in my head that this money was not for my personal gain. It was for a greater cause. I really believed in what we were trying to do, which was to give the people of Texas a choice politically and to get rid of the back-room deals and to force the Democrats to have to work to maintain their party. If something isn't for your personal gain, it makes it a whole lot easier to beg. They would say, "Give her what she wants so she will get out of here."

JUDY JONES MATTHEWS, ABILENE

Good fundraisers like people. They have a light touch. I am convinced that people aren't good fundraisers unless they are doing it for something they really believe in. I do not think people who raise money professionally are nearly as effective.

JOCI STRAUS, SAN ANTONIO

Joe and I had Desmond Barry, the candidate for lieutenant governor in 1962, to dinner. We both thought, "Wow, this guy is worth working for." I put together a luncheon on the telephone and talked to every single person that came. We had 150 people. He gave such a good talk that people were just mind-boggled. I got my finance chairman from that luncheon. We got free headquarters downtown. We raised so much money that we had more money than we could use. We went door-to-door. Got $100 here, $100 there. If I came home without $1,000 a day, I had a bad day.

I walked down the street and attacked a building. I called ahead, and I knew who was in each building. I said, "Can I come by and see you?" It was pretty scary the first time. My palms were really perspiring, and I was really nervous because I had never asked somebody for money before. But if you believe in something, you can do anything. I believed in this person. So it wasn't so painful after the first day or two. It became kind of fun.

Fundraising Methods

Candidates Raising Money Themselves

JANELLE MCARTHUR, SAN ANTONIO

One of the things Joci Straus and I would do when Senator Tower came to San Antonio was meet at her house and dial for dollars. I'd get the phone number and Joci would say, "All right, Senator, this is a man that you met thirty-five years ago. He was the best man at your wedding." You know, that kind of thing because the Senator was not good at names. When he walked into a crowd, he always felt like someone wanted something. They did. This is how we would get him to make phone calls.

BARBARA BANKER, SAN ANTONIO

Candidates sometimes show weakness when they make calls because sometimes people perceive that they are getting panicky that the money is not coming in. So they are sitting down and dialing the phone themselves. I've had calls from people and wondered, "Why are you calling me? Are you out of money?"

You have been an effective fundraiser. What advice would you give to candidates, both men and women, on how to develop a good fundraising effort?

KAY BAILEY HUTCHISON, HOUSTON & DALLAS

I did different things according to where I was positioned in a particular race. When I ran for the legislature, my fundraising was very grassroots oriented with small fundraisers. Women were very instrumental in helping me with little donations. I also gave the impression that I was going to win. I was able to show the numbers of people in the district that were Republican. I had six opponents in the Republican primary, so I had to get through that first. But I looked like a winner. I think that is very important in fundraising. I was supported by businesspeople. As I went up the ladder and ran for Senate, I was at a disadvantage in fundraising because I was running against an incumbent Democrat and two incumbent Republican congressmen. All of the big money went to them. I was unknown in Washington, and none of the PACs [*Political Action Committees*] or business groups supported me. So I was very grassroots oriented in my Senate campaign. I was able to raise about a million dollars in the first race with people I had worked with who knew me and thought that I had a good chance to win and that I would be the right candidate for the Republican

Party. I put together a good solid team of men and women in that race. Once you are an incumbent, people think you're going to win so it makes it easier.

Dialing for Dollars

LINDA UNDERWOOD, HOUSTON

It seems like every time I called and said, "This is Linda Underwood in [*National Committeeman*] Albert Fay's office," I was calling for money. I was so naive at the time. I would call anyone. I will never forget in Des Barry's campaign [*for lieutenant governor*] they had such a hard time raising money. They would put a list in front of me, and I would just go down the list and call people in Houston. I raised a lot of money because I didn't know it couldn't be done. People were just amazed that I had no fear. Albert Fay would say, "You call. You get more money than I do."

ISABEL GRAY, PASADENA

One time my husband, Fred, was out of town when he was precinct chairman. He was supposed to raise so much money. I got on the phone, and I raised more money than he did. He would call two or three of his old pals. They would give him the money, and he would turn it in. Well, I called everyone that voted and asked them for money. I just asked them for whatever they could afford $1 or $15. Some sent $50. It was not big money, but I raised it.

So We Need to Throw a Fundraiser

POLLY SOWELL, McALLEN & AUSTIN

I realized that we had to raise some money. I had a friend from McAllen, Kay Wharton, who had actually worked in Washington and was a Republican. She said to call Peter O'Donnell in Dallas—it was before he was state chairman—and she gave me his number. He said, "Yes, I'll be glad to come down and help." He told me exactly what to do. I needed to get somebody's house, invite people to come, and serve dinner. He would come down and talk to them about money. So I did everything just like he told me. I asked Marian and Forest Finch, who had a nice pretty new house, if we could use their house. I called people. The women stayed in the kitchen. We cooked. Even me. I was the one who organized the whole damn thing, invited the men, got them all there, did the whole thing, but I stayed in the kitchen with the women while Peter talked to the men about giving money. Nobody thought a thing about it.

When did women get out of the kitchen?

Shortly thereafter. It was all gradual, an evolutionary thing.

JAYNE HARRIS, SAN ANTONIO

Some fundraisers fail because they put too much into them. At a lot of the fundraisers that I have done, the hosts furnished the food. Our costs were wine, invitations, and postage. When you do not have that situation, you try and go to the simplicity of it. If you get into dinners and things like that, you get into a lot of money. If you do it with finger food from five to seven o'clock and catch people going home, you can have something very nice. The presentation is everything in my book.

I have seen fundraisers that are total busts. It is poor planning and in some instances it is the candidate. It takes in-depth planning right down to who's going to work your table. You have the name tags ready. You make it as efficient and as lively as you can. I am not talking about giddy stuff. If you have someone who knows the guests when they come in, greet them by name. Being real is very important. People know when you are not real. They pick up on it in a minute.

MARY BODGER, CORPUS CHRISTI

We held the Pachyderm Polka. A union leader called me and said he was upset because we hired a nonunion band. I said that was too bad because that was the price and the kind of band we wanted. He said, "We just may come out there and picket you." I said, "Please do. It would help us." But he didn't do it. That dance was a huge success.

PAULINE CUSACK, HOUSTON & WILLOW CITY

In 1970, Bill Archer asked me if I would be special events chairman, which was for fundraising. At that time, he was a state rep. That was a wonderful job. One of our events was a box supper out in the Sharpstown area and Senator Goldwater came in. We charged twenty-five dollars per person. The place was full. There were other events along the way. In 1972, it was kind of a repeat of the same thing. We didn't have as much fundraising then because it wasn't as needed. He was taking something like 80 percent of the vote in those days. Bill was elected [*to Congress*] in 1970. It was not until 1994 that he became chairman of the House Ways and Means Committee. Had I thought "I am doing this because some-day he is going to be chairman of ways and means" I would have worked even harder than I did. I just wanted to get him into office because I trusted him.

Key Republicans

MARY JESTER, DALLAS

When Peter O'Donnell was state chairman, he made all of the people on the state committee sign notes for $1,000. Sure enough they did. They all raised their $1,000 to pay off their notes and become Key Republicans. We would use any way to get the money.

POLLY SOWELL, MCALLEN & AUSTIN

When I got elected to the SREC, our state chairman was Peter O'Donnell. He made us all sign a pledge that we would raise $1,000. I thought I would die! A thousand dollars was a lot of money. I thought, "What in the world am I going to do?" I worried about it for six months. I'd wake up in the middle of the night in a cold sweat. What if my husband finds out that I have signed this pledge? What if I can't raise the money? I was just beside myself. I finally decided that I would just have to go try. There was only one person I knew who had $1,000 and might even remotely consider giving it to the Republican Party. I circled the block around his office about ten times trying to get up the courage to go in and ask him. Finally I did. Quivering I said, "I'm here to ask if you would give the Republican Party $1,000." He said, "Sure. How do I make the check out?" I almost fell out of my chair!

LIBBA BARNES, SAN ANTONIO

When Joci Straus and I were working together, we would go downtown and call on ten or fifteen different people. Joci would say, "We're coming with our hands out. We want a little contribution for the Republican Party of Texas." She was raising her Key. Finally, she turned to me and said, "Now we've raised my Key, we'll start on yours." I came home and I thought, that's hard work for $1,000. So I picked up the phone, and Tim Hixson was the first person I called. I said, "Tim, I'd like for you to give me $1,000 for the Republican Party of Texas." He said, "When do you want the check?" I got my Key before Joci got hers because I went down and got that check right then and sent it in.

Then, of course, you get so paranoid about your list. You really don't want anybody else calling on your people. Well, that didn't last for very long. Ace Mallory was another one of my donors. All of a sudden, I saw that Diane Rath had a Key on her lapel. I thought, "How in the world did she get that?" Well, when I called Ace, Diane had gotten there before I did. I said, "Where is your loyalty?" He said, "Well, it's all going to the same place." It is but it isn't.

THEO WICKERSHAM, SAN ANTONIO

Rejection doesn't bother me. All they can do is say no. One of my old mentors years ago back in the late '60s or early '70s taught me one of the things that works best. If you tell somebody how you are going to use the money, they will help you. For example, "we're going to use $300 for a mail-out" or "2000 signs cost so many thousands of dollars." You always ask for a little bit more than it takes. When I was on the SREC, George Strake would say you must raise so much money per year. He used to tell this story at our meetings. "You know we have got to raise this money. Why not do what Theo does? She sends me these tacky $15 and $25 checks every month." I was getting them from widows on fixed incomes. I'd tell them that I was on the SREC and we raise so much money per year. I sent a copy of my quarterly report to the people who had contributed for that quarter. I circled things that their money helped buy. By getting people involved, they're going to trust you and believe in you and your candidates.

BETTY STERQUELL, AMARILLO

I had trouble because when I volunteered, they would hand me the $25 and $50 contributors. You have to call a lot of contacts to raise $1,000. I would rather they give me the $100 cards because it is just as easy to ask somebody for $100 as it is for $10. I had to overcome that. In that phase of my life, I couldn't contribute $1,000 for a Key. I earned mine.

Letter Writing

FLO KAMPMANN CRICHTON, SAN ANTONIO

For me, letter writing is the most effective. The people that you want to reach, their time is fairly valuable. You have got to have respect for other people's time. So rather than make a phone call or ask if you can come by and visit, they've got something on paper and they can look at it and read it and decide what they want to do. Of course, you can have a follow-up phone call. But I believe in giving people time to think about it. That's not everybody's way of doing it.

Make fundraising letters short and personal, and write a little extra P. S. at the bottom. It takes a lot of work, but it is worth it. You simply just spell it out. Generally, when you have a committee, you divide up the names and people take people they know best. It's done a thousand different ways.

Candidate Fundraisers

PATTILOU DAWKINS, AMARILLO

Emmy O'Brien organized "Babysitters for Ike." We would babysit for people. The money they paid us, we gave to the Eisenhower headquarters. Well, they wanted to support Eisenhower and gave us a lot of money—certainly more than we were worth. We spoiled the kids. We would take them to the country club and feed them under their parents' names on the country club tab. Yet they still had us back.

SURRENDEN ANGLY, AUSTIN

When my husband ran for the legislature, we raised money mostly by direct mail. From the very get-go, he had a lot of parties at private homes. Toward the very end of the campaign, he bought thirty minutes of television. He had a call in question-and-answer show. That night was our biggest campaign contributors' party. He would leave the station and come to the big donors' party.

MARTHA CROWLEY, DALLAS

We did "Crowley Follies." It was mostly publicity. I don't know whether we raised any money or not. It was a lot of fun. Frank and his niece Peggy were really good at song parodies. They would use familiar show tunes, like "Big Spenders" and "The Country Needs a Man Like Me." We would get a hall with a stage. Kitty Harrington was the director of so many of them. A couple of them turned out to be really pretty good shows. In fact, the press club came down there. It's a shame that I had to get so old before I realized I was such a good chorus girl.

PAT JACOBSON, FORT WORTH

I ended up doing a Wayne Newton concert to raise money for Ronald Reagan. That is the hardest thing I have ever done. We sold tickets at various amounts, like $10 tickets for up in the balcony and $25 and $50 tickets and then up to $500. The difficult part of it was Ronald Reagan was there, the national press was there, but we were not sure the people would show up. I looked out at the crowd in the Rogers Coliseum and said a prayer of thanks. It was standing room only. It's a terribly frightening thing. I later called [*Reagan advisor*] Mike Deaver, and I said, "Don't you ever ask me to do a concert again."

Personal Effort

MARJORIE ARSHT, HOUSTON

You're not involved unless you're interested, and you're not interested unless you're involved. Writing a check is a way to get someone involved.

They credit me with being the originator of the neighbor-to-neighbor drive because in the '50s, [*party activists*] Albert Fay and Dudley Sharp and Ted Law had funded the Party. I kept saying, "Get people to give you a dollar." Of course, it would spread out the Party and bring people in. If they are going to give you a dollar, they are going to vote. When George Bush became county chairman, he said that he wanted everyone in the Party.

CAROL REED, DALLAS

I raised money for Senator John Tower. Tower and Fred Agnich [*state representative and national committeeman*] used to just take great joy in sending me places that no one else would go. I didn't know it. Here I am twenty-nine or thirty and kind of cute back then. They would just howl, I know. They would send me over to get money out of Joe Staley. He was drinking a lot. Well, so was everybody. I would call Joe and say, "It is that time of the year to make your contribution to the Senator." He'd say, "Great, meet me for lunch at the Cipango," which was across the street from where the Mansion is now. It was "the" private club in Dallas—"the place." So I'd show up at lunch and at four o'clock in the afternoon I would crawl out of the place with a check. Women's groups would just have a heart attack. But this was all part of the dance. I thought there was no way I could make it through an-other lunch with those guys.

Tower and Agnich would say, "You go see Herb Schiff." They used to love this—you don't have to do this to me but once. I'm pretty bright. But then it got to the point where I kind of enjoyed it. Herb Schiff, he was oil and gas; he is now dead. The first time they ever sent me to Herb's office they said, "Now, Herb gives big checks." They said, "Don't leave there until you have your $1,000 check" or whatever was the most ludicrous thing they could come up with. Herb used to tell the story about the first time I marched into his office and he said, "So glad to see you. Here's the check." He slides it face down across the desk to me. I thought, well, this is much easier than I expected. Then, doing what a man would never do, I looked at the check. It was like $50. I thought, well, he is teasing me. I thought, what the heck I have nothing to lose. So I said, "Mr. Schiff, I can't possibly take this back." He said, "What's the matter? That's what I normally give." I said, "No, that's not what you normally give." I realized that I had been had. "Tell you what," I said, "I'm just going to tear this little check up, and I'm going to give it back to you because if I were to take this check back, word would get around Dallas that you're having financial difficulties. It will just be our secret that you can't afford to give but $50. So why don't you just keep that check?" Well, he looked at me. I'll never forget it. I wasn't sure whether he was going to go ballistic, but he just burst out laughing. He said, "How much did they tell you I was going to give?" I said $1,000. He took his pen out and wrote me a check.

When I got back to the two clowns that had sent me on that little mission, they were just dumbfounded. They always sent me to the ones that were their good friends. They always gave me terrible information.

The bottom line is, I wasn't ever afraid of asking for money. I could get away with stuff that no man could. There was nothing wrong with it. There is an ego thing that goes on, and so I always assumed that they would love for me to call on them and ask them for money. I don't always get what I want, but I get closer to get-ting what I want.

RITA PALM, FORT WORTH

When Phil Gramm came into the Party, he was still a Johnny-come-lately. In 1983 and '84, he was running for reelection and needed some cash. I asked some of my real estate guys, "You have been making deal after deal after deal. How about giving Phil Gramm some money?" For years, I had taken Shaklee vitamins. I met the Shaklee government liaison at the convention in 1984. I said, "You know, Shaklee needs to give to the states that contribute to their well being." She agreed with me. They had a Political Action Committee. She gave Phil Gramm $5,000. It was just because I asked. Then, I was so successful with my one real estate guy, I asked the next one. I raised probably $60,000 or $70,000 in one afternoon, just asking. I couldn't believe it. It was so easy. We did that some for Bush. They can say no, but you have to be willing to ask.

SYLVIA NUGENT, DALLAS & AMARILLO

It's like a game. You just take one person and you follow to the next person. You call one person and say you want to have a fundraiser. You go to your Republicans first and then ask, "Who in your town would be good for that?" Who are the presidents of the banks? Who has the most money in your town? Who is the most respected? Who would want to do this? Then you guide that person to maximize your dollars.

ANN WALLACE, FORT WORTH & AUSTIN

In 1960, I decided we needed an airplane with "Tower for U. S. Senate" on it to fly over the TCU [*Texas Christian University*] football stadium. It was going to be $250. I called ten people and asked them for $25 apiece. It was something that they could see. So you nickeled and dimed it. You didn't dare ask anybody for $250. In those days, if anybody gave you $1,000 you would think they were trying to buy you.

JUDY JONES MATTHEWS, ABILENE

The most effective way to raise money is to ask people who have a lot of money for a lot of money.

National Level Fundraising

FLO KAMPMANN CRICHTON, SAN ANTONIO

When you operate on the national level, so to speak, you do not get involved so much in individual fundraising as in the setting up of benefit lunches and dinners for a cause. The Republican Boosters was a congressional committee that made direct gifts and donations to a candidate. They held booster lunches all around the country. We worked on those. We worked on the Senate-House dinner they have in the spring.

I was going to be appointed to the national finance committee in 1965 or '66. There were one or two women on it. I asked John Tower and told him I was thinking about resigning as national committeewoman because I wanted to be with my children a little more and the finance committee wouldn't be as demanding. I ended up on the executive committee of the finance committee, which was fine with me. The congressional committee and the congressional boosters, particularly, raised money for Party candidates and for the incumbents. The national committee raised money and would divide it up. We had to select cities for fundraising dinners or luncheons, and we had to get a chairman for it. That was my job.

I had to get a chairman for the boosters in Houston. I got George Bush to get Jim Baker [*Bush's eventual secretary of state*] to head it up. I think that was the first time he had done something politically. He may have been involved somewhat on the local level, but I don't think that he was involved nationally. He did a superb job.

The trouble was, when Nixon was running again for president and I was on the finance committee, he arbitrarily moved it into the Committee to Reelect the President—CREEP. All of a sudden, I found out I was no longer on the national finance committee. It was nonexistent. It worried me a little bit. Of course in an election year, the function of the national finance committee is to elect the President.

Later, I worked as a founder of the Republican Eagles. We met with President Ford. There were about fifteen of us. It was really Jerry Millbank's idea. He got us invited to the White House. We listened to President Ford's ideas and organized it. We tried to recruit people into the Eagles. Amazingly enough, there are quite a few people. We started out at a $10,000 contribution, now it's $15,000 a year. I would rather give to individual candidates than do that. I still think that's a good program for those corporations and PACs that can do it.

Fundraisers as Recruiting Opportunities

THEO WICKERSHAM, SAN ANTONIO

We would tell Democrats in the '70s what wonderful candidates we had, and we would also question them about who the opponent was. Joe Sage was a Republican who ran against Al Brown [*for state representative*]. When a friend of mine said I'm voting for Brown, I'd ask, "Do you know him well?" "Well, I know that he's a good Democrat." I would say, "I'm giving a fundraiser for Joe Sage at my house. I'm having a backyard party with lots of cold margaritas and barbecue, and it's all free. I'm sending out 2,000 invitations, and you are going to be one of them. Not only did they come, but two years later when Alan Schoolcraft ran against Al Brown those people all came and helped me.

BILLIJO PORTER, EL PASO

The first thing I ever did was go with my husband to a fundraising dinner with Spiro Agnew in 1971. We went to that, and then I became involved. I was a real fan of John Tower and so was my husband. In 1972, when he ran, I volunteered. I guess they were really glad to see a volunteer because everybody else was working for Nixon.

MARY TEEPLE, AUSTIN

The women I watched doing fundraisers were really good at recruiting people to help. It was opening up the arena and involving as many people as you could to help you make the telephone calls, write the letters, visit the people that you know want to give the money. Women are good at enlisting people and convincing others that causes are important. They make it a lot of fun to work. Women have no fear of going to their peers or even people that are outstanding in the community and asking.

Once, we had a goal of raising $20,000 for Senator Gramm. It did not occur to me that perhaps I could get that from twenty people. So instead, we formed a team and worked very hard at getting two hundred people to give $100. Nancy Braddus was always talking about how important numbers were in politics. The whole Hyatt Regency was full of people wanting to give Gramm $100. He raised his goal, but it took a lot of time and we enlisted an army of people to do that. It is very necessary to ask people who can contribute large amounts to get involved, and it's also fun to involve people who give $50. It just takes longer and you work harder.

Who Gives and Why

JUDY JONES MATTHEWS, ABILENE

I think it is so important to be involved in fundraising for candidates that people want to be elected—to get money behind them for publicity, the mailings, and particularly television.

Why would somebody want to give money to a political fundraiser if they could invest the same money or give it to a tax deductible charity?

Don't you feel really strongly about politics in this country? Don't you feel really strongly that we need to get rid of the people in the White House now? Well, I think that's it. I think you find people that feel really strongly about a particular candidate or a particular party and think it is important that we get things done. Of course, there are people who give a lot of money and expect something in return, and I am sure that they get it.

Do you think that politicians have a big problem with that?

It seems to me it should not be a problem. I don't believe a politician should let himself be blackmailed. That may not be the right word. I think men like Ronald Reagan or Dwight Eisenhower wouldn't do it.

ILLA CLEMENT, KINGSVILLE

I was willing to donate money to the Party to get things done that I believed in and that I felt the Party was right about. Or for the person. But I think if you are donating money, well, there may be certain people who have things they want in return. Maybe somebody wants a road built, and somebody in local politics will do it for them. But mostly I was just thinking of the leadership of the country. Of course, getting the people elected that are really good—that is the most important thing.

DONA BRUNS, NEW BRAUNFELS

When Craig Enoch and Tom Phillips were running for the Texas Supreme Court, they came to town several times. One thing about New Braunfels, we can get them to vote but they are not very generous about giving money. For the first time, we were getting people to give more money to those offices because they were really concerned and wanted very much for those people to be elected. They felt that we had such good candidates that we needed to support them.

Associated Republicans of Texas

FRAN ATKINSON, LUFKIN & SAN ANTONIO

Associated Republicans of Texas [ART] is a funding organization. When the Party changed hands back in the Reagan years, the people who came in were not fundraisers. So we set up this organization to raise funds and dispense them according to our formula. Our formula is this—first we target races. We don't put a Don Quixote to tilt at windmills in a totally hopeless district. We target races, say, for the state house or senate or some judicial races.

We don't give money to candidates who won't work and who won't raise their own funds. We do not ask them for their political ideology. If they are running as a Republican in a target race and they are working, we will fund them. For instance, at the state convention anybody that runs for any party office is grilled on his or her political ideology. We don't do that. We just figure if they are running as a Republican they are going to be better than the other guy. Plus we need the majority.

We have given money to good candidates and were involved in recruiting candidates back in the days when you couldn't find them. Now they are coming out of the woodwork. We do not take part in primaries at all. We don't endorse one candidate over another. The winner of the primary comes in and makes a presentation to the candidate committee of ART, which is quite large, sometimes fifty or more people. Then we vote on how much money we want to give each candidate.

Obstacles

Please Don't Use My Name

ANN WALLACE, FORT WORTH & AUSTIN

It was either 1959 or 1960. I would go to luncheons and events for Nixon or for Tower. I would be seated at a table and feel a tap on my knee. The first time, I kind of wondered what was going on. I put my hand down, and here was a hand with folded money. In those days, it didn't matter because it wasn't against the law. No one wanted to be known to be against Lyndon Johnson. But here was a little money, and I had a notebook where I would very carefully write this down. It was always cash. They would say, "You know what this is for?" I did, and that is where it went. They didn't want a paper trail. We ran that entire campaign in Tarrant County on less than $3,000.

I kept those records for I don't know how long. I did relay to John who had given after he was elected. He needed to know. I would write just a note that said "it was so good to see you" and copy John on it. I was scared to death that, if Lyndon really got fired up, he would track me down and I would be the source revealing where all of the money came from.

SITTY WILKES, AUSTIN

I had a list—it was years ago—of the millionaires in Austin. It was only like twenty-something. We had a Lincoln Day dinner, and we would sell tickets. I remember even going to Mildred Moody—she was former Democrat governor Dan Moody's widow—upstairs to her bedroom. Sometimes, there would be $500. She would buy a ticket from me. She was a conservative. There were people who were hidden that didn't like the socialist ideas of the Democratic Party but who couldn't afford to be a front person.

NANCY LOEFFLER, SAN ANGELO & SAN ANTONIO

People weren't used to giving money to candidates, particularly Republican candidates. That was the biggest challenge.

FRAN ATKINSON, LUFKIN & SAN ANTONIO

A lot of people gave money as long as I didn't use their names. That was before the days when you had to report everything. I couldn't do that now. Back in those days, I could cash checks and just turn the money in. People would give me cash.

> *Secrecy assisted you when being a Republican was not acceptable. If you were required to report contributions then as you are today, it would have been a deterrent?*

Oh, yes!

The Candidate

FRANCIE FATHEREE CODY, PAMPA

I got a whole room full of people to pay $50 to have lunch with Tower after he got elected. As soon as he finished talking, he went straight to his room. I had told them they would get to meet him and shake hands. I was furious with him. I went down and pounded on the door and said, "Now, Senator Tower, you have got to come back. I have already told them that you are going to visit with them." He did, but he wasn't that thrilled. It hurts you in your fundraising. It hurts you when you drag these people out and make them pay. Back then $50 was a pricey luncheon. These were people I was counting on for money for other elections.

Competition for Fundraising Dollars

JANE JUETT, AMARILLO

One thing that hurts locally is every week we get maybe two requests from the state party and two from national for money. I am sorry, but what I can give to them is such a drop in the bucket. We support our local candidates. In a way, they have made people so mad with all of their letters and phone calls. People consider it wasted money to do that. If I received a letter a few times a year rather than one every week, I would be a lot more inclined to donate. We get one addressed to W. E. Juett. One addressed to Mrs. Jane Juett and one to Mr. and Mrs. W. E. Juett, and then sometimes we get one addressed to Mr. Juett. We have told them about all of these duplications. They say it is cheaper to send them than it is to correct the list. That does not leave a good impression.

RITA PALM, FORTH WORTH

When Bush ran for Senate in 1970, we had John Tower over to our house one Sunday afternoon. We invited people over and got him a little money for his next campaign. We also made sure he knew that in Tarrant County, at least, it was going to be balanced if Bush won. It was not a threat to him.

When Bush ran for president in 1988, I was chairing that campaign. The sheriff candidate came down with a couple of the legislators and judges that needed help. The swell was going for

Bush pretty heavy here. I said, "Listen, if you all would get behind us to get Bush 61 percent of this county, you all will go in without having to spend a lot of money." They had never thought about that. We sold the coattail effect. There was no bickering or complaining that, "I didn't get my share." We had everybody out at all of the big sports events and outside the fence at General Dynamics. They could hand out their literature, but they had to hand out Bush literature. We had somebody out there handing out literature three shifts a day for the fourteen days prior to the election. We had to have the help of the local candidates because there were not enough of us. We had parades, and they all carried Bush banners. It was a joyous campaign with minimum antagonism.

NANCY PALM, HOUSTON

Let's face it, the fact is the state party is an absolute necessity, but in the major metropolitan counties they are not as necessary as they are out in the rural counties. I objected to them coming in constantly and raising big money out of Harris County to be used in other counties.

How did you balance the need for money in the late 1960s and early 1970s?

There wasn't much balance. They were able to collect large sums of money out of Harris County. We went with direct mail to small donors, which was sort of innovative. Volunteers made up for a lot money. We did our own polling. Why couldn't they see that a local person running locally helped the individual running a statewide race?

HALLY CLEMENTS, VICTORIA

The thing I dislike the most is the Republican National Committee running in and sending out all these little flyers first, before you get an opportunity to work your traps. I could name people who would give $1,000 or $500, but they receive a letter asking for, say, $500, $200, or $100. I think they need to let the individual workers do their bit and then pick up the pieces later on.

CHAPTER 18

We Won! Now What?

"Lots of candidates have high aspirations and expectations that
they are going to change the world." —MARJORIE VICKERY

*Fighting uphill battles year after year, longtime Party workers
could easily see an election victory as an end in itself. Yet, after
each victory, the now-former candidate had to find a way to
make the transition to the new role of elected official. Election
day victories were a new beginning not only for the candidates
and workers but also for Texas. Republicans now had an
opportunity to put their philosophy into action.*

*As newly elected officials or as their staff, women made a
lasting imprint on Texas and the nation. They found that, as
with elections, passing new law was not an end in itself. Laws
needed proper implementation and revision or repeal if they were
not producing the desired results. The boards that run Texas government required conscientious men and women as members, and the
newly elected or appointed Republican boards worked to wrestle
power from the entrenched bureaucracies that administered
programs on a daily basis. Some women from Texas also served
on a national level in the legislative and executive branches.*

*Beginning in the 1960s through today, women politicians
tried to make government operate with the best interests of all
citizens in mind. Women also found a new source of power.
After years as credible, loyal, and trusted campaign and Party
workers, they became both informal and formal advisors to state
and national members of both the legislative and executive
branches. At last, women influenced the Texas and national gov-
ernments in the ways they had so humbly worked for since the 1950s.*

They helped secure a two-party political system in Texas and, as either Republican elected officials or their advisors, women endeavored to assure that our governmental bodies be honest, responsive, and fiscally responsible.

What was the responsibility of those early Republicans once they got elected?

ANNE ARMSTRONG, ARMSTRONG

We always hoped they would help give a boost to other Republicans. Most did. There was a great feeling of camaraderie not just among the women but also in the whole Party. Senator John Tower was a model for helping other Republicans. He was not the world's best glad-hander, but he did believe in the Republican Party of Texas and the two-party system. He would help other candidates. Frankly, and I won't name names, there were even times when I and other state leaders didn't want certain local candidates to be associated with some of our stronger candidates. We felt that they were so weak they would drag other candidates down. This is one of the eternal problems of politics. You make hard decisions.

Elected Officials

What did it feel like the day after you won a seat on the city council and reality set in?

KATIE HECK, MIDLAND

It was amazing. All of a sudden I was one of the "stupid set" — elected officials. It was discouraging. I can see why good people tend to have better things to do than run for office these days.

The day after the election for county judge that you weren't supposed to win, what did you do?

BARBARA CULVER CLACK, MIDLAND

[*Party official*] Payton Anderson gathered up Bill Davis, who won a seat in the legislature, and me and took us to Dallas for an

SREC meeting. There was a handful of Republican local candidates who won that year. We were there for the SREC to look at successful candidates.

During the campaign—I wouldn't say it was a dirty campaign—the state district judge here, being a partisan Democrat, sort of got caught up in the race toward the end. Some things that he reputedly said, of course, got back to me. I wasn't in the mood to go down there on January 1st along with the other Democrats and have him swear me in. So our little campaign organization got Julius Neunhoffer, the Kerr County judge, to come out from Kerrville. We had a luncheon and a celebration, and he swore me in. That was sort of my revenge or something. I don't think that got me out on the right foot, but it felt good to celebrate with my constituents this occasion of being the first Republican in the courthouse.

How did you build a consensus with the Democrats on the court?

They realized that I was going to be there four years, and we might as well work together.

When you look back on it now, what was the difference for the county to have you, a Republican judge, as opposed to another Democrat?

I don't think any. I just probably brought a few little new ideas, but everyone does. Nobody likes officious females so I didn't try to boss them around. I tried to make sure that the county commissioners got all of the glory and all of the blame. I presided and did not take an active part in the deliberations unless they asked me. They finally realized that I wasn't on a glory ride and that they could trust me. I was a lawyer, which helped.

MARJORIE VICKERY, COPPER CANYON

Lots of candidates have high aspirations and expectations that they are going to change the world. I had those expectations, and I do think I was able to accomplish a lot of things, but I didn't accomplish all that I wanted to. All I needed to do was take a speed-reading course. We had mountains of things to read to be ready for each state board of education meeting. One of the goals that I was able to accomplish was, I wanted mandatory kindergarten for children. At that time, it was optional for school districts to have kindergarten. Another thing I wanted was for every child to learn a second language from kindergarten on up. If a child learns that from six years on up, it is not as difficult. I was co-chairman of the curriculum committee. We went all over Texas having hearings on this. As it worked out, we got a second language to be optional.

CYNDI TAYLOR KRIER, SAN ANTONIO

I am a classic Republican in the south, who Governor Lamar Alexander from Tennessee identified in the '80s as running for office for the first time because they were against whatever the Democrats in the office were doing. Then they got elected and realized they couldn't just be against everything. They were responsible for governing. That took programs that worked and commitments and philosophies of how to build things up, not just tear them down. I felt fortunate that Lamar and some other national Republicans at that time organized a group that invited local legislators and local officials from states across the south to Tennessee twice a year. We focused on local and state issues and how we could come up with legislation, and we exchanged ideas. I became committed to how we could control state spending and control the growth of taxes that had just exploded right before I got to the state senate.

I filibustered in the senate in 1991. I called attention to the fact that Texas was ignoring the constitutional amendment that limited the growth of state spending to the growth in the state population and the inflation rate. If they wanted to spend more than that, they had to disclose to the public what they were doing and they had to take a vote specifically to exceed that cap. The amendment had been adopted at a time in the '70s when we had more money than the legislature knew what to do with. The case ended up being taken to the Texas Supreme Court. While the court ruled that we were too far down the way in the budgetary process, I think it is significant to every taxpayer in Texas that in every budget since, the law has been followed. It is important for Texas and state spending, but I think it is more important for good government. If government doesn't follow the rules and play by them, it's hard to expect the public to.

The differences that I have made aren't the big differences, such as the bills that were passed—like reforming the workers compensation system, which was absolutely about to die, or casting a decisive vote on indigent health care, which now needs fixing again. Those aren't the things I think of when I look back. I think of the one-on-one personal differences I've made through constituent casework. For example, the little girls who had PKU, a disease that I had never heard of. It is really a dietary problem where they couldn't digest normal food and had to live their lives on a dietary supplement. With it, they could live fairly normal lives. The state didn't treat that dietary supplement as a medication. It's very expensive and the family couldn't afford it. So I worked with the health department in getting medical professionals involved and getting the rule changed, not just for that family but for all the families. That's what makes me feel good.

I keep these boxes that I call small harbors. It's after a poem I read one time that goes loosely "we all have small harbors in our soul where we may go and rest a while." Whenever I am really frustrated and think I'm not accomplishing anything, I just go and open one of those boxes and pull a note out, and I am reminded of all those little things that made a big difference in people's lives.

MARY DENNY, DENTON

The first week or two is just so awesome. Truly awesome. Just walking into the state capitol and realizing, my gosh, I have been elected to the legislature. Am I really going to be up for the task? I had some self-doubt and insecurity starting out. It is not the warmest, friendliest place to just go into. Republicans in the house and senate don't have a mentoring program in place for new members. For real basic stuff, there is an orientation, but it doesn't tell you a lot that is real practical and that you need to know. Members themselves, because of the very nature of the competitiveness of dealing with legislation, don't share a lot. The Democrats, on the other hand, have put in place a better farm club. We Republicans have been watching them over the past four to five years to see how they do with the new freshman. You'll see that happen this next session when some of the more senior members will take new ones under their wings. We will give them pieces of legislation, something that we know is going to pass, and shepherd them through the whole process so that they learn how to do all this. I'm not sure that women haven't helped speed the process along or bring it to full service, and now the men even realize, well, yes, we could do a bit better job of this.

NANCY JUDY, DALLAS

The main thing as a public official is to think defensively every minute of every day. Before you ever open your mouth, every time you are asked a question you think, "What can somebody make of this?" It makes a difference in how you phrase your response. It is instinctive if you want to prevail. You think about what you're going to say and how it will come out in the paper.

I had very good press coverage. I had good rapport with the reporters. If I ever felt they were not getting in the story the proper reflection of what I had said, I would never hesitate to call them. They respected me. I was not intensely political. I had to ask for people's votes, but when I had the job [*as Dallas county commissioner*] I addressed the issues at face value. I did my homework, and I voted my conscience.

LIZ GHRIST, HOUSTON

I was asked to fill a one-year vacancy on commissioners court. I wish people understood the power of commissioners court. I could have probably gone into the office with the intention of just holding the seat until the election, but I was an activist commissioner. My attitude was, "Let's find out what we think should be done, and we've got eleven months to get it done." I hired three women and one male. I said that I wanted everything wound up by the time I left office.

Was one of the people you hired Molly Pryor?

Yes. Molly probably could have run this county with one hand tied behind her back. I asked her to be my administrative assistant. She knew how to reach people and how to make people feel good about doing their jobs correctly. She could also take factions and make them work together. She had been John Tower's executive assistant here in Houston.

You can't do it without a good staff. If everyone doesn't pull his weight, you are defeated before you start. The secret to success is finding people that are smarter than you are. My philosophy is never compromise on quality.

SHAROLYN WOOD, HOUSTON

The federal courts were going to take over the state judiciary. The Democrat officeholders at the top were going to let it be done. In September 1988, the attorney general's office [*of Democrat Jim Mattox*] called a meeting of the judges in metropolitan counties, and a lot of us were Republicans. They looked around and said, "I don't know if any of you guys are going to be here, because there is this suit in federal court [*for voting rights violations*] and they are going to win." Of course they had a grin on their faces, telling all of the Republicans their days were numbered. Dallas judge Harold Entz, Houston judge Bill Powell, Vinson and Elkins partner John Golden, and I started looking into it. We found that maybe it was not that clear-cut. In lawsuits about voting rights, there is a [*state*] violation and then there is the [*federal*] remedy. The remedy was to put judges into the state rep districts. We knew exactly what would happen there. We felt we were fighting for the independence of the judiciary. In February, it was very clear that we had things in place, including the support of Governor Bill Clements. As soon as Jim Mattox found that out, all of a sudden the plaintiffs dropped the Governor as a party in the lawsuit. When they dropped him as a party, the judges lost our only champion.

My husband and I talked it over and decided that if I didn't do it, nobody would. There was no judge in Dallas that would agree to put his name on it. I decided to do it and called the law firm that I knew to have a fantastic federal court securities litigator, Porter and Clements. Senior partner Gene Clements agreed to handle it. They hoped they would be able to recover their attorneys fees somehow, and I committed to raise the money to pay the $150,000 in expenses. I did raise that, but the $750,000 in attorney's fees it took for my lawyers to prevail in that lawsuit were totally unpaid. Vinson and Elkins assisted with the expenses. Bracewell and Patterson assisted with manpower. When we got to trial, the attorney general's office didn't argue. Everyone thought we lost. We won on appeal. We won it twice in the Fifth Circuit. We half won in the Supreme Court, and it came back and we won it again twice in the Fifth Circuit. It took us a lot of years. The reason that there are Republican judges today in Texas is because we did that.

GWYN SHEA, IRVING

My district elected me to the legislature not to pass another law but to kill all of the bad ones that we could. They also wanted me to correct the legislation that was not working. It was basically a conservative philosophy.

Agendas happened to wind up on your desk because of your committee assignments. I was the first female to be appointed to the ways and means committee, which put me right in the middle of every business issue in the state because it deals with taxes or revenue. I served all five sessions on the house insurance committee and was the only female elected to the national conference of insurance legislators. I also served on the county affairs and house administration committees.

In 1987, the largest tax bill in the history of the state was proposed. We did not need a tax increase. We had a surplus, but the Democrats were in control. We were able to not pass that tax bill out of committee when it came. The speaker, who was of course a

Democrat, took the tax bill out of the ways and means committee and put it in one of his friendly committees. They didn't pass as large a tax as they would have, but they did pass a tax bill. That was probably one of the biggest battles that we have ever been in. Of course, the next session, myself as well as all of the rest of us were eliminated from that committee and didn't sit on it again.

Later, in 1993, I was appointed by commissioners court to fill an unexpired constable term. I thought of all the things that I might do after I left the legislature, this certainly was not on my radar screen. After I was there six months, I thought I may have something to contribute. So I enrolled in the police academy. It was an intense study of all the codes—the alcohol beverage code, the family violence code, the vehicle code, the code of criminal procedures, the penal code, and all of those things that we deal with in law enforcement. I remember thinking, "Gee, I was there when we wrote this. We meant for it to do this but in the real world of application, it is not working."

So interestingly enough, in 1995 I went back to the legislature as a quasi-lobbyist. We spoke to those things that needed to be changed. We changed five areas of the codes in order to make them serve the public better and help law enforcement at the same time. My professor at the police academy said, "We have never had this perspective. You can tell us what was happening at midnight on the floor of the house when this crazy bill in the vehicle code was passed regulating roller skates." I have been back on occasions as a guest adjunct instructor at the academy, to give a legislator's perspective on how some of this crazy stuff gets done.

PATRICIA LYKOS, HOUSTON

After I became a judge, I had no friends who were lawyers. It is terribly isolating to be a judge if you behave appropriately because you are cut off from your friends. You can not ever have a sense of impropriety. I demanded the lawyers be prepared. It is appalling to me that lawyers think they can walk into a court with criminal jurisdiction, when you are talking about life and liberty, and be very cavalier in their approach.

I was able to do a lot in the way of policy. Judges have a tremendous responsibility. We don't just sit there and say "sustained" or "overruled." If there is a problem out there that you ascertain from your presiding, then it is your duty and obligation to do something about it. For example, I got the first residential center here for probationers. It took a long time to get twenty-some other judges into agreement and to get the funding for it. We also got community service and required urine analysis for probationers. I asked them when the plea was over when was the last time they used drugs. If they used the night before, I wasn't going to punish them for telling me the truth, but I needed to know what their problem was so that we could create these programs. There is a lot a judge can do to make the world a better place and not violate any ethical standards.

DORIS WILLIAMS, LAKE JACKSON

Everyone knew that I was a Republican when I was mayor. I still participated in my partisan politics on a regular basis. It never hurt me. You can not bring partisan politics into city politics. About the only thing that you can bring there is your conservative philosophy. I really took care of people's money, probably better than I took care of my own money. I believe in not raising taxes. All those things in your Republican beliefs are good with local politics.

ANITA HILL, GARLAND

You have to prove yourself as a woman member of the legislature. You have to prove that you are not emotional. As long as you carry part of the load and you don't fall back on "poor little ol' female me," they respect and help you. One time, I went to the Citadel Club at the Driskill Hotel. I was told to go up to the second floor and wait outside the door to the Club. I sat there and sat there and sat there, and finally I was going to go in. I started in, and this woman rushed up. I told her I needed to meet with members of the Garland city council. She wouldn't let me go in. We moved the meeting downstairs. I was just boiling and steaming inside because my people were being punished. I believe in the private club concept, but not when it receives tax benefits and public officials, male or female, can't come in. I was furious. When I got back to the capitol, I went right up to the press table. A lot of the well-known names, like [*liberal commentator*] Molly Ivins, were there. Word got out to my colleagues, and one of them got up and proposed a resolution that no one use the Citadel and the Driskill until I had been apologized to and everything had been resolved. On Friday night, MCI [*telecommunications company*] had a dinner and reception scheduled for the Driskill Hotel and they cancelled it. I didn't do anything aggressively at all except to get it out of my system, but the Citadel did offer an apology.

At the time that it happened, the president was asked about it and he said that women were a distraction and they sounded like a gaggle of magpies. I still don't know how a gaggle of magpies sounds, but the day after I was kicked out there was a luncheon held. Carole Kneeland with Channel 8 in Dallas passed the mike around the tables, and it was very loud. There were only three or four women and all of these men. They played that back on the late news, my publicity machine was working by accident. After I calmed down a little bit, I got to thinking, "What about my colleagues who are minorities?" One of the most outstanding members of the house was Wilhelmina Delco from Austin. I asked her about getting inside the Citadel. She said she would have to go up the fire escape just to get in.

But the episode did give some attention to that issue.

KAY BAILEY HUTCHISON, HOUSTON & DALLAS

In the '70s and even in the '80s, we still had to prove that we were credible, tough, capable of handling the job, and reliable. When I ran for the legislature in the '70s, I ran as and was a conservative woman. I was told later, after I served a term, that everyone was so surprised because I was really conservative. They had never had a conservative woman so this was a new phenomenon.

How did that help you when you came to the U. S. Senate?

Each experience certainly helped me succeed in the next experience. Certainly my legislative experience made me able to cope with the ebb and flow of politics. But it also helped that I knew state government and that I knew enough to be able to have a platform. Legislative experience allowed me to make a smooth transition into the Senate because I understood the give-and-take and the rough-and-tumble. I understood losing. I understood compromising. I understood, pretty much, parliamentary procedure because it was similar.

In what areas have you been able to have the biggest impact legislatively or otherwise as a public official?

In each of the positions I've held, I have had a different kind of impact. In the state legislature, I focused on a few big things and I won those. I passed the first mass transit bill for Texas. I reorganized the highway department to include mass transit in the highway system. I created county historical commissions because I thought it was so important to preserve our Texas heritage. I, along with the other women members together in a coalition, passed the bill that would put Texas in the forefront of fair treatment for rape victims, which was the forerunner for addressing violence against women. We also passed equal credit rights for women in Texas.

In the state treasurer's office, I was successful in holding the state income tax back, which I think will have far-reaching consequences for Texas. We passed a 5 percent ceiling on state debt. I think that will keep us in a good financial situation. Then in the Senate, I feel I have been effective for Texas, but I have also had an impact in the foreign policy arena. In national defense issues, I have been very active and now serve on the Helsinki Commission. I have also allowed homemakers to have equal IRA's [*individual retirement accounts*] with those who work outside the home. I have been able to pass anti-stalking laws. I broke the impasse in welfare reform by getting a formula that was fair to all of the states. In each area where I have served, I have picked certain issues that were important to me and tried to make an impact, and I think that I have.

Staff Members

MARTHA CROWLEY, DALLAS

I volunteered in Bruce Alger's Washington office in 1955. My husband, Frank, was his administrative assistant. They kind of split the duties. Bruce did the homework. He studied issues thoroughly, and Frank handled the office for the most part. They would consult if it was a controversial issue coming up for a vote. Pretty much I think they were in agreement.

In the office, I learned how to use the roto-typer. I just did the nit-picking things that no one else wanted to do. I was pretty much acting as the hostess. I would take constituents sightseeing and tour the Capitol. That way, it gave him some time. He didn't have to stop and do the same things over and over with constituents. I had them for dinner. I just did unofficial entertaining. If they needed any work to be done themselves, I would often help. If they needed to contact somebody, I would write and find out where.

CAROLYN BACON, DALLAS

I was the first woman administrative assistant. To be honest, I really didn't face any obstacles. Before Senator Tower named me, I thought I would. When he told me that was what he wanted to do, I said, "You ought to think very carefully about whether or not you should have a woman in this position." In fact, there were three men in Texas to call and see if they approved. He told me that he called and they all approved. It wasn't long before there were other women named administrative assistants.

How did you develop the expertise in the various committee areas that the Senator was involved in?

I had worked for Bruce Alger. It is amazing how much legislation is the same year after year after year. I worked in Tower's state office with Honey Alexander. I did casework and some legislative work. Then, when I went to Washington and was working directly with his administrative assistant, I got involved in all of the different areas.

So many have said John Tower voted right. What importance did you have as his administrative assistant to keep him on that track?

When you look at his legislative career, he was a man who worked from a very strong philosophical base. On the big issues he knew exactly what was the right thing. There were always many smaller issues, and that is when the role of the staff is to make sure the Senator has all the data he needs to make the right decision on that vote. So it is in some ways a research operation. Gathering the data, presenting it to him in the most objective fashion as possible, and then looking at it and making a decision.

Why do you think Tower was willing to hire you to be his critical staff person and Nola Gee to be his critical campaign person when it was uncommon to hire women?

It was the mark of Senator Tower. He was really a wonderful person to work for because he delegated very well and yet was always the first one to step up and take responsibility. When you look at his staff, you will see that it was really remarkable; he had very little turnover. When people left the staff it was because they were going to a higher position. He had no gender bias. He had no ethnic bias. We always had a good mix of women and minorities in the top positions. When I left he named David Martinez, a Hispanic, as administrative assistant. He looked for ability, loyalty, and dedication. Gender and other things were not a part of his criteria for making decisions. When you look at the Tower staff, he launched many wonderful careers by being an exceptional mentor to his staff.

JOANNE POWELL, SAN ANGELO

The job that I have working in Lamar Smith's office is getting to meet the constituents. Of course, it doesn't matter who walks through that door, whether they're Democrats or Republicans, Congressman Smith is their representative if they live in the Twenty-first Congressional District. Lots of times, the people who come to this office for help are on their last leg. They don't know which way to go and maybe have had the door slammed in their faces before. If it's something that deals with a federal agency, I will tell them up front that we can't change or influence a decision but we can make sure that they have been given every proper consideration. Sometimes their problem is just bogged down in red tape. Sometimes they just want people to listen.

CINDY BROCKWELL, BOERNE

As chief of staff for State Senator Wentworth, I am responsible for the capitol office and the San Antonio district office and the office in San Angelo. I am responsible for everything. I hire and fire. I am much more involved in the legislative process in Austin. The district offices don't get involved at all in legislation. We have only three legislative staff members in the capitol office. Some of the bills were mine. When you work a bill, it means it's yours. You work with the constituents or lobbyists whose idea it was. You go to the hearings. The Senator has bill books, and you write his remarks to lay out the bill before the committee. You answer possible questions the committee might have. You have to think of what objections or what questions they might have, then come up with answers. If you get it through the committee, you write his floor remarks. If it passes, then you coordinate with the house member who's going to carry that bill. Give them your bill books so they have every bit of information on that bill and do not have to reinvent the wheel. You coordinate with the house member's staff to get the bills through the house. Then if it passes and it is a big bill and you want a bill signing with the governor, you coordinate with the governor's staff to get a time and slot.

Every morning when I walk in the capitol, I think I am the luckiest person in the world. They are paying me to do this! I like Texas government. There are only thirty-one members in the Texas Senate. In Congress, there are 435 House members. Surely you can make more of an impact as one of thirty-one than in Congress. I just like to be a part of it.

CATHERINE SMYTH COLGAN, DALLAS

I worked in Jim Collins's congressional office in Dallas for years. I ran the volunteer program there, keeping up with the mailing list. We had what we called our hotline. There was another lady named Tera Mae Carson. We kept up the mailing list. We worked one day a week in the office for a number of years. He used it for his newsletter, where he communicated and corresponded with all of his constituents. From that list we pulled volunteers and campaign workers. We did solicitations for funding. It was primarily a communication line with his constituents for all purposes.

Appointees

RUTH SCHIERMEYER, LUBBOCK

We had sixty-some appointees from Lubbock County under Governor Clements. It doesn't just happen. You have to be very proactive. As county chairman, I worked very closely with the chamber of commerce. Every time I had someone that we wanted to have or wanted an appointment, I would call the chamber and get their support and contact our senator and both of our state reps. The chamber organized a committee on political affairs with an appointments subcommittee. They met regularly and looked at all of the appointments that were coming out, and I served on that committee. That helps the governor and the senators or state reps if people are out there actively looking for people that represent the views of the governor. You know then that his philosophy is being carried through those boards and commissions. If the people being appointed do not represent that philosophy, then the governor is simply a figurehead and has no strength.

JANE ANNE STINNETT, LUBBOCK

From my perspective in watching the Bush appointments, they have been extremely diligent to make sure people have a real interest in the position that they are being appointed to, know something about it, and are dedicated to show up at the meetings and take an active role. Clements did the same thing. The people who were on the task force that I was on were all people who were leaders in agriculture. I think that both Bush and Clements were more into—of course, I'm probably prejudiced because I'm Republican—appointing people because of their abilities. There are plenty of women and plenty of minorities who are extremely capable and do a great job.

All Kinds of Influence

SHIRLEY GREEN, AUSTIN & SAN ANTONIO

A wonderful opportunity came to be appointed Director of Public Affairs for NASA at headquarters in Washington. I went to start my space career, which was three unbelievable, wonderful years except the [*space shuttle*] *Challenger* blew up in my first month on the job. It was the biggest public affairs disaster of the century.

The first week that I got to NASA, I had a meeting with the fellow immediately above me. NASA is a very nonpolitical agency. There were only five political appointees in the whole structure nationwide. He was looking at my resume and he said, "Well, I see that you have been deputy press secretary for the vice president, and I am sure that was very heady stuff but it was a very small office. NASA is known for managing big programs. You will be judged at NASA on your management abilities. Do you feel like you have that kind of background?" He asked this in the most patronizing tone. I looked at him and I said, "You're right, we do come from very different backgrounds. I am sure that the things from my political life don't have very much meaning for you. I ran a headquarters with all volunteers where I kept ten phones manned, three shifts a day, and had more than 100 people working for me everyday. And they were all volunteers. They could all leave if they didn't like my management style. You learn something about managing people."

*How in the world did you hold it together when you were
watching the Challenger lift off that day and continue to do
your job?*

It was unbelievable. At the launch control center down at the
Kennedy Space Center, there is one console for the agency's director of public affairs and the Kennedy Space Center's director of
public affairs. We had monitors of the three network television
stations and NASA television and headphones where we could
talk back to the press center on our own loop as well as hear the
mission commentary. The console was by big glass windows. Chuck
Hollingshead, who was the director of the Kennedy Space Center,
was sitting by the window.

I can still see it. I had only seen one other launch. When the
big puffball of smoke and flames happened and then the boosters
started falling off, all I could think was, I don't remember this happening before. Surely, it's just because I'm so inexperienced that I
don't know. There was not a sound in launch control. Finally, I
realized as Chuck turned around that I had been gripping his shoulder. When he turned back, of course we both had on our ear-
phones. We couldn't hear each other, but I said to him and he
could read what I was saying, "Is it gone?" I have never seen a look
of such horrible sadness in a face in my life. He was just shaking
his head and said, "Oh, yes, it is gone." Then as I looked back
through the tiers of consoles in launch control, everybody was just
staring at their blank computers. It was just dead quiet. It was just
the most shocking, sad, and difficult situation.

Every part of the NASA family, every element of its management structure, has contingency plans. I would always sit and read
my contingency plan carefully all night in my hotel room the night
before. The first thing on my mind was that, if the administrator
was not there, get in touch with the administrator. On our console, I had one outside line. I grabbed the phone to place a call to
Washington immediately to get him on the line, at which point,
all of the other contingency plans started kicking in. One of them,
for the whole launch control center, was to cut all outside phone

lines so that phone calls couldn't come in. This one phone line that I had open was the only phone line that we had open for several hours. By the time I had gotten through to headquarters, they were saying that [*spokesman*] Larry Speaks at the White House was trying to reach me. So they patched him through and I told Larry what we knew, which was of course absolutely nothing, because he had to go out and file a brief. It was just unbelievable.

That day we had credentialed over 650 reporters for the launch. It was the largest one for a long time because of the teacher [*on board, Christa McAuliffe*]. By that night, we had nearly 1,100 reporters at the Cape not counting the ones in Washington or Houston. By the next morning, we had 1,300 reporters. Our phones at the press center recorded nearly 4,000 lost phone calls because of busy signals. Every news organization in the world was either calling or getting on a plane and arriving. We put our public affairs people on 24-hour duty at both Kennedy Space Center and Johnson Space Center in Houston and at headquarters and Marshall [*Space Flight Center in Huntsville, Alabama*]. We had around-the-clock shifts for six weeks because some news agency from somewhere in the world on some other time frame was on filing deadline all the time.

> *If you can make it through that as a public affairs officer, you can make it through anything?*

I had several gripping moments before, which were good preparation. When Bush was elected vice president [*in 1980*], I was his deputy press secretary and was with him in Fort Worth the day President Reagan was shot [*in Washington, D. C.*]. We had only been in office two months. I had not been traveling that much. That kind of attention was new, and we had a lot of press on the plane that day. That proved to be an interesting dry run for one of the things that I learned—anytime things start happening in a crisis, start taking notes because later you can't remember the times and places. Reporters always want to know what time did Alexander Haig call? What time did the Vice President get the word? What time did you all land?

I did that the day of the *Challenger* accident. I immediately grabbed a yellow pad and started jotting down when I first talked to the White House, when I talked to the administrator, when we said we'd set a briefing. I've gone back and looked at some of those notes and can't read them. Obviously, I was just scribbling like a mad woman.

When the Marine barracks was bombed in Lebanon and killed 250 Marines, the Vice President went over on a secret mission. We were smuggled out of the White House. Nobody even knew that we were out of town. That was, I thought at the time, probably the hardest day that I would ever spend working professionally. They had recovered all but I think thirty-five or thirty-eight of the bodies when we got there about thirty hours after the bombing.

So I had several very, very difficult and dicey times. The thing about *Challenger* that was so extraordinary was that as gripping as the first twenty-four hours were, it didn't end for six months. The evidence was all buried under three hundred feet of the Atlantic Ocean. As soon as they got the salvage operation going, it was every day and every night—what have the ships found? The leaks about where we were in the investigation, the impounded material that you couldn't get out of impoundment—the press was killing us, charging us with hiding evidence and not being straightforward. The presidential investigation was doing its thing and the Congress wanted to do its thing and NASA was trying to do its thing. It was just around-the-clock horror stories for six months.

How do you keep your integrity in that kind of situation, with the endless contact and all of those different groups asking questions and making requests?

Well, you try and do the best you can. Our record was pretty spotty. There have been a lot of books written about the *Challenger* accident and round tables addressing how you plan for crisis, how you build a good contingency plan, and what should be included in the plan. We did a lot of soul searching, and we did a better job than we were given credit for at the time. There was a rush of the media to want answers and want them now. It led to the assump-

tion that if you didn't give the answer now you must be withhold-
ing evidence. I used to say to public affairs groups that scientists
and engineers are not like you and me. They are accustomed to
subjecting everything to peer review to ascertain its authenticity.
If they brought up a piece of what they thought might be the right
solid rocket booster, which is what blew up, reporters with their
long camera lenses would think, "That is the booster." We couldn't
confirm that it was part of the booster, and they would put the
story out about what they thought "but NASA won't confirm it."
They would take another hit on us, but the scientists and engineers would want to take that piece of debris and examine it and
ascertain for sure. So it was a push-pull between the scientific need
for accuracy and the public affairs desire to tell what we knew,
even if we weren't sure. There was a lot of internal conflict that
made it very difficult.

BERYL MILBURN, AUSTIN

Governor Clements appointed me to be the chairman of the
University of Texas coordinating board [*now the Texas Higher Education Coordinating Board*]. I was the first woman to do that. I didn't
even know what it was when he asked me to do it. He had already
promised me that he would name me a regent when the time came.
To him, being on the coordinating board was a more powerful
position. Well, he just didn't have any idea what a plum a regent
appointment was. So more than a year later, when I was serving as
the chairman of the coordinating board, he appointed me to the
board of regents. At the coordinating board you were a referee,
and nobody likes a referee. Being a regent was just fascinating, and
I loved every minute of it. It was a lot of work, and I gave it a lot of
time because I had the time. I was chairman of the land and investment committee for four years, which was in charge of all the
millions of acres out in West Texas, the Permanent University Fund,
and the investments.

After I retired as state vice chairman of the Party, I was appointed vice chairman of the Texas Constitutional Revision Commission in 1973. We did all the research, rewriting, and recommen-

dations. Then we presented that document to the constitutional convention, which was composed of the legislators and the senators sitting as one body. They did not adopt any of it. It turned out to be an exercise in futility. Who knows why? I think they had high hopes that it was going to go, but it didn't.

GWYN SHEA, IRVING

My first appointment after I left the legislature was as a member of the Texas Workers' Compensation Insurance Facility. The Governor's instruction [*George W. Bush*] at that time was get in there, clean it out, and shut it down. I said, "Yes, Sir." You get in there as a governor's appointee with a board that has been appointed by the former governor. It doesn't take a brain surgeon to count votes. I sat there quietly like all good freshman should and learned the program and process. When I said yes to this appointment, I had already said no to four others. I knew the workers' compensation insurance facility because I was there when it was created in the legislature. I knew that it had a date it was supposed to go out of existence. I couldn't remember exactly when, but I said, "I can say yes to this because it'll be a short-term deal."

Finally, we got enough board members that we had enough votes to exactly follow the instructions that had been given. In the meantime, I realized that instead of cleaning it out and closing it down, why don't we privatize it and sell this piece of business to the private sector? So I went to the Governor and said, "What would you think about it?" He said, "Sounds great to me." We privatized that facility and sold it to the largest reinsurer in the world. That was a real feel-good kind of accomplishment.

One of the things that everybody talks about is that the governor of Texas is a weak governorship. What they fail to realize is that government really rests at his appointees' feet. His appointees are probably the most powerful thing that he has going for him. The philosophy that you bring to the arena is paramount because they make major, major decisions not only about how state dollars are spent but about the day-to-day mechanics of how that agency ought to respond to things. That is one of the things both Democrats and Republicans give George W. Bush big marks for—making really meaningful appointments to boards with people who are very grounded in what their responsibilities are going to be.

ANNE BERGMAN, WEATHERFORD

Governor Clements appointed me chairman of the community development board in Austin. The first year, we worked with capital development grants and loans for sewers and water supplies, infrastructure that people needed in small towns. There's a certain amount of federal money that comes to the state and is administered within the region. We had oversight of the grants. Staff did most of the work. Appeals came to our board. Sometimes cities appealed when they got ranked below another. The Democrats were political. They would cave in to somebody because they liked him or because of a consideration that shouldn't be given. It was supposed to be on the merits only. It was all ranked. It never occurred to me to be political.

DEBORAH BELL, ABILENE

I was appointed by Governor Clements to the Brazos River Authority. I was the first woman ever appointed. I kept saying, "What do I know about water?" He said, "You are going to learn about water." The river authorities in general had had a bad name. The way we're structured at BRA is that we get $100 for a meeting, which is not a fortune, and we get reimbursement for our expenses. I spend about forty days a year either in committee meetings or board meetings or going to a national water resources meeting. When I came on the board, the median age was like sixty. There had been people on the board that had been serving twenty-five years with no turnover, no fresh ideas, and no new thoughts. River authorities are very arrogant because they are quasi-governmental. We get our revenue from the municipalities, counties, and individual customers. We don't have to come to Austin begging.

When I came on this board I was in my thirties, and men were in shock. It was a very "yes" board. They would stay within their own confines and committees. I went to every committee

meeting even though I was only a member of the lake management committee. I could see the workings of the board rather than
having them come to me at the quarterly board meeting and give
me the lowdown. When Clements started making appointments,
we changed the BRA from a "yes" board to a "wait a minute, is this
the best thing for the Brazos River?" board. Now the board is active and forward thinking. What I was doing with Governor
Clements was changing the way river authorities are run. It was
going to be the board telling the general manager what to do and
not the other way around.

DEBBIE FRANCIS, DALLAS

Governor Clements appointed me to the Texas Developmen-
tal Disability Board Planning Council. I served, I guess, ten years.
I have worked over the years on disability-related issues because
our youngest son was in a near-drowning accident when he was
almost two. Bo turned twenty last week. He is severely brain dam-
aged and handicapped. For a number of years, I have also done
political work, but I really had somewhat of a more specialized
calling. But that's also taught me a lot about government—state
government, federal government, their programs, and how money
really filters down. I don't think there is a person alive that pays
taxes and minds helping somebody who can not help themselves—
particularly somebody with mental disabilities. Part of my goal is,
if everybody can be more responsible and better educated, then
hopefully they will need less government dollars and more government dollars will be spent on a child who will never be able to
function as an adult.

Both elected officials and citizens have a responsibility. I have
the responsibility to pick up the phone and call their office and ask
the legislative aide who deals with the issue. I have done some of
that. They have a responsibility to have a staff that is going to
cover all areas of government and be knowledgeable. I will tell
you, if there was a book put out that had nothing but one page that
said, "You won't believe the difference you will make if you will
take the time to write or call"... Most of us never write, and most

of us never call. We never give any input other than to vote if we vote. Because I'm close to certain legislators or certain other government officials, I know the impact. Officials will tell me they received a letter, and they didn't know anything about the issue. It may have been one person who wrote, called, or went by the office. They are more moved by that than a lobbyist. It's just that lobbyists are mostly who they hear from. When an individual does do it, they are very moved because not that many individuals give sincere input on issues.

NADINE FRANCIS, ODESSA

I worked for the Governor's Office for Volunteer Services. I was the field coordinator. I helped various departments learn how to recruit volunteers. I had contacts all over the state. Our secretary was a holdover in that office when we went in. After I had been there for a little while, she came in one day and she said, "I don't understand why people would volunteer like you are asking them to. Why don't they get out and get a real job if they are going to give their time like that?" When I went to Austin, I didn't know people didn't know that you volunteer or how to use volunteers. They were afraid that if a volunteer could do their job then they would lose their job. I couldn't see why they didn't know that when they needed somebody to help out in Timbuktu and didn't have anybody out there, they could call. Well, we had somebody in all of these places.

PATTILOU DAWKINS, AMARILLO

I went to Austin and so many times I would think, "What's a little girl like me doing in a place like this?" It was an ego trip. I'll tell this story—it was a part of me I didn't like. The mental health and mental retardation department had a commissioner. He was an M. D., a psychiatrist. It takes someone with business experience to run a department like that. The previous legislature had realized that we needed a business manager and had changed the law saying that the head man did not have to be an M. D. I was appointed in June of '87. It took a lot of time to come up to speed.

Clements appointed me chairman in November. He called me into his office. James Huffines, his appointments chairman, was there. He said, "I want you to be chairman. Can you handle it?" "If you are asking me if I have the ability to be chairman of an organization, the answer is yes. If you're asking me if I know or have the knowledge of MHMR, the answer is no. I can learn it, though, and I can be a good chairman." Clements said, "Well, I want you to be chairman, and there is one thing that I want you to do." He said, "James has done your work for you, and we've got the votes to fire the commissioner. You are the swing vote, and you've got to vote against him." In MHMR, the chairman only voted to break a tie. He said, "Can you do that?" and I said, "Sure, I can do that."

I got back to my hotel room—I get emotional every time I think about it. I thought, that's not right. You can't vote against that man. You don't know him that well. I felt like the most un-Christian person on earth. I felt like, "This is what power has done to you, Patti." I hated myself. The governor's office is the most awe-inspiring place. The whole ambiance is so powerful. I was in there and I was caught up in it and I hated myself. I knew it was wrong. It was *wrong* for me to vote against that guy.

The next morning I called James Huffines and I said, "James, I can't vote against him. I don't know of anything bad that he has done. Let me go talk with him and see if I can get him to resign. Let's go at it another way." He said, "You told the Governor that you would." I said, "Well, I can't, James." He said, "Can you get him to resign?" I said, "I don't know. What can I offer him?" He said, "Well, I don't know, maybe three months severance pay." I said, "Let me go visit with him." So I went in and said, "I'm sure that you have gotten wind the Governor wants you replaced." He said, "Yes, I know." I said, "I think that he has the votes. If I can get you a good severance package, would you resign?" He said, "Yes, I'll do that." I said, "What do you want?" He said, "Six months." So I called James back and I said, "James, he wants six months, but he will resign." He said, "Well, let me talk to the Governor."

We had a board meeting that Friday and this was like Tuesday. He called me back Thursday. He said, "The Governor wants to talk to you." I talked to Governor Clements and said, "Governor, the man has young children. He probably can get a job back in Houston, and I think it's even going to take six months to find somebody to get transitioned. Please do six months." He was real disappointed with me and said it often. Finally, he said, "Okay, you have six months." I called the commissioner that night and said, "You've got six months. Please write a letter in the morning." So that Friday at our board meeting, I presented his letter of resignation.

I look back and I will never forget the power that people have over other people's lives. I thought, I will never, ever again do anything like that. I hated myself. I think of it whenever I think of power—the abuse of power there would have been if I had voted against that guy. You just feel omnipotent. Several years later, James and I discussed that conversation. It was a very defining moment in my service to my government. It made me so aware. I see that happening with people when they get elected or get appointed to something. It's so easy.

CAROLYN PALMER, SAN ANTONIO

In the '80s, the commissioners mostly let the organization tell them how they should work. That was the way it was on the library commission [*Texas State Library and Archives Commission*] in 1989 when I first started. They didn't have a clue as to what was happening in the libraries, and I don't think they even really cared. When I was appointed by Governor Clements, I didn't know a thing about libraries. But I did want to serve on a commission. So as we would go around to various cities, I would call the library and go and talk to whoever would talk to me and learn the language. One time I was in Houston and I finally realized they were rolling out the red carpet. I talked to the head librarian and said, "What is going on? I can't give any speeches. I am trying to sneak in the back door and learn something." He said it was because I was the only commissioner that had ever stepped foot in the library that they knew of. Now, you can't keep the commissioners out. They work very hard with the legislature. I think that appointments are no longer being made as a reward for having given money or your time for helping the governor get elected. You only get appointed if you are going to work.

One would think, as I did, that getting appointed to a commission like the library commission is going to be very quiet. I could not have been more wrong. One of the rules that we set is about who handles the records and how, and where and which records of state government are kept—which ones can be destroyed and which ones can not. Sometimes we don't help the governor. For instance, I got a call when Ann Richards was governor from the state librarian. He said, "I need some help. I got a call from the Governor's representative from Houston. They want me to write a letter saying that it was okay to destroy some of the records that she had destroyed." I said, "Don't write the letter. Let me find out what is going on." What had happened was the Governor had destroyed some telephone records. This was right before Kay Bailey Hutchison was going to go to trial [*on charges of misuse of state employees*]. It was a Monday. I talked to my husband about it. He didn't react like I thought he should react. I thought, well, maybe I am just over reacting.

It was now Thursday. Rick Perry [*then agriculture commissioner*] joined us for hunting, and I said to him casually, "I want to tell you this story." He said, "You are kidding me, of course." I said, "No. This is happening right now. The Governor is in Houston. She wants us to okay that she did this." He said, "What have you done?" I said that I had been trying to get somebody to give me some advice and to react the way I think they should be reacting because I thought this was wrong. Then he called [*political operative*] Karl Rove and all of these phone calls and faxes started. It was just an unbelievable experience. The newspapers got a hold of it and, as a result, the following Monday Kay Bailey Hutchison's trial was dropped. It was because the Governor had just done what they were trying to say that Hutchison had done. The Governor did not get the kind of letter that she wanted. She got a letter, but it stated that there had to be some further investigation. So in that respect, a commission can help or not help the governor.

CLAIRE JOHNSON, ABILENE

I don't think I am nearly as partisan as I may appear. As Governor Bush says, we work for the people of Texas not for either party. In doing that, you have to be willing to listen to what the other side has to say. There are certain issues where the person you expect least likely to agree with you will show you that he is right. You may be wrong because you didn't have the right information. You have to learn to put your ego away and listen to what people have to say.

JANIS LOWE, FRIENDSWOOD

I was appointed to the Board of Pilot Commissioners for the Ports of Galveston County. According to the statute, the pilots work directly for the governor. The governor has got to have the board in order to ensure safety in the ports. He expects the commission to make recommendations as to who are the best qualified pilots.

We have been a hands-on commission, and with all respect to the gentlemen I think it is because there are three women on the commission. We went out on the ships to see what in the world we were setting policy for. I have boarded many a ship at sea when it is ten miles out. You go out on the pilot boat and the boat and the ship run right together. A very talented pilot boat operator will just kiss the big ship and never stop. You climb up a ladder sixty feet in the air that can swing. To let go of the boat and put both hands on the ladder and climb—I was so exhilarated that I had done it. I appreciate what pilots do in inclement weather because I am a fair weather commissioner. It was really scary, but it gave me an appreciation for what they do. The skills they have to possess—because when they are called, they don't get a choice of not going. It is a male world, and the three of us women have pushed our way into it.

CAROLE WOODARD, HOUSTON & GALVESTON

When Bush was elected governor, he appointed me to the Texas Board of Human Services. I feel like we have been able to accomplish some things that have made a difference. We brought out the Lone Star Card—it's used to purchase groceries like a credit card. We implemented programs to bring mothers off welfare. We supervise welfare, the elderly, Medicaid, food stamps, nursing homes, and homeless care agencies. We try to push forth Bush's agenda—every citizen being held accountable and those people that are able to work having opportunities to work. We also push his agenda for welfare to work.

CYNTHIA TAUSS, LEAGUE CITY

When I got in there, I quickly realized that the perception of the parole board as dealing only with violent murderers and pedophiles is incorrect. The really violent offenders are only a small, small percentage. The rest is drugs, credit card theft, and burglary. Back in the early '90s, they were letting everybody out. The Governor has changed a lot of the laws. Those truly violent people do not get out. The State of Texas, whether it be through mandatory release or discharge of sentences or parole, has to maintain a 15 percent release rate or we will be back in court. Fifteen percent every year! No matter how full the prisons are, I know that the Governor is never going to ask us to release anybody that we are not ready to release.

Victims' groups used to despise the parole board. Now the parole board is supported by all of the victims' organizations. Contrary to what the media says about us being a secret organization, we are not. All of the members meet regularly with the victims groups, with family members, and even with inmate groups. We try to communicate with everyone in the process.

Did you seek this appointment?

After the election [*of Governor George W. Bush*], everyone talked about appointments. When I was in high school, I made a list of goals for myself. One of them, and I don't know where it came from, was to be on the Texas Board of Pardons and Paroles. So when this opportunity came up I applied. I worked very hard for it. I got letters of recommendations from my senator, some police departments, the NAACP, and Democrat elected officials. I went everywhere to show support and to get the position. Some of the people that I work with on the board who were Ann Richards' appointees said, "You applied?" There didn't seem to be any application process at that time. When people ask me, I tell them to call the appointments office and have them send you a green sheet. Fill it out and send it in. It is very open.

What kind of goals were set by the president when you held an appointed position?

ANN WALLACE, FORT WORTH & AUSTIN

Actually, you are pretty much left without anybody saying "this is what you must do." When I went to Washington, I sort of sat there thinking, "Okay, where's the word? What do I do as director of the United States Office of Consumer Affairs?" I found out after about a month that there wasn't a guidebook. Concern about privacy issues had started at this point because of the ability of computers to compile data. So that was one of the things we dealt with. We published a handbook and gave the name and address of almost every major corporation in the United States, along with who to write and a sample letter of how to complain. We dealt with various complaints. You try and serve the president as best you can.

I was head of the delegation to go to the Organization of Economic and Property Development—OEPD. The headquarters were in Paris. You'd go to these meetings and come out in the hall and all these people were saying the Bush administration doesn't pay any attention to us. It would really irritate me. I told the White House one time, "I've got a woman, an ACLU [*American Civil Liberties Union*] lawyer, who is pretty reasonable, and I'm going to put her on my official delegation to go to the OEPD meetings." There was dead silence. I said, "Check it out, but I think this would be a wise thing to do." Finally, somebody called me back and said,

"Well, it's your game." I almost had an ulcer over the thing. I did that two or three times with people who were really very vocal against the administration. All of them thanked me for being included in the delegation and thanked me for allowing them to speak. They would bring up their issues, which was all right in my opinion because at least I was giving them an arena to express things, which sort of somehow had the blessing of the President. They couldn't very well bad-mouth him.

When I first got there I said, "Give me the name of everybody that is out there against us." The top person was Ralph Nader. I sent word out to all of them that I wanted them to come over for a brown-bag lunch. My staff thought I'd lost my mind. I said, "I don't want any of you all there because I don't want to be able to pull on a resource. I want one person there to take notes." Ralph Nader did not come but Joan Claybrook did. They all came because they were very curious about this. We had a very good meeting. They wanted to know what my agenda was. I said, "I don't have one. I want to know what your agenda is." I said, "I've got somebody over here taking notes because at my age I don't remember everything." So at least I was on speaking terms with everybody and knew where our enemies were, so to speak.

BERYL MILBURN, AUSTIN

I served on the U. S. delegation that observed the El Salvador elections. We rode with armed guards everywhere we went. I remember taking a helicopter ride to go to one of the remote villages to observe the election. We flew high enough that we couldn't be hit by a rifle but low enough to be able to see the countryside. While we were gone, there was a firefight in the mountain behind our hotel.

It amazed me that you would see people walking for miles to go and vote. Then they would dip their finger or thumb in some kind of ink to show that they had voted. They had to walk home knowing that some of their neighbors might shoot them. The opposition was very vehement about trying to stop the election. People stood in line for hours to vote, and they had walked for hours to get there. But the trouble with an official delegation like that is there are really three parts to an election—registration of the voters, casting the ballots, and counting the ballots. All we observed was the voting. The first part and the last part we didn't participate in, so how could we tell whether it was an honest election? You really couldn't.

ESTHER BUCKLEY, LAREDO

My husband told me on a Friday that on Sunday we were going to Washington. On Monday I went through interviews all day long. At the end of the day, they told me to go back to my hotel and "we will let you know." That night, they called me back and said that I was going to be appointed to the Commission on Civil Rights.

My job was to enforce the Bill of Rights, to study the issues of discrimination as to race, color, creed, ethnic or national origin, and to look at all laws and all agencies. We had monitoring responsibilities on all the agencies. The commission is an advisory board to the president. We met once a month except for July or August. It could be either two days or four days, and we would have hearings all over the country. I was very lucky because my school superintendent was extremely progressive. When I got appointed, I came back and said, "They want me to travel maybe two to four days a month." My superintendent said, "Every time you go, you do more for the 22,000 children in our school district than if you stay in the classroom."

Did it make a difference that you were appointed to the commission as opposed to a Hispanic Democrat?

It was of value in the community in the sense that the Democrats had been here for so long they really didn't have a Laredo Hispanic woman out there. I was on the stage with Reagan at the rallies in Dallas and in Austin. It made Democrats look again. It made them think, maybe we are in the wrong place. Plus, I am convinced that a lot of women got recognition in the Democratic Party because they had to compete with the Republican Party for a change. If Clements or Tower appointed somebody, they needed to do something to match it because they were losing. For a change, they were actually having to do something for this area [*South Texas*], whereas before they were taking us for granted. It's the way the system works. We were getting discretionary money from Clements for this area so the Democrats were going to have to do something. They were going to have to deliver some of what they had promised because now there was somebody else who could deliver. Having money coming in during the Reagan years, we got a lot of things done with housing grants and urban development grants that wouldn't have come in otherwise.

As a member of the commission, I did not get what I wanted as far as putting out reports on Hispanic issues. But I read every single report that came out during my nine years. I did a lot of editing. We looked at some issues that I think were important. In 1988, we were looking at the fact that the minority population in Texas is going to be a majority, and we had better do something about their education and work skills. If 40 percent of our Hispanic kids are dropping out of school, and they're one of the larger groups, it doesn't take a very efficient mathematician to know this is serious. There will be 40 percent unemployment and more in the Hispanic community. A lot of what I learned I brought back. Education is the answer, and anything that we do for education is going to make a difference.

Influencing Public Policy

As a woman dedicated to politics and agriculture your whole life, did you ever have an opportunity to affect public policy?

NITA GIBSON, LUBBOCK
Have you ever heard of the PIK program? That was my idea. In 1982, the first part of Reagan's administration, we were in a very, very serious economic slump. Farmers were going broke. Every time I'd walk, my mind was full of agriculture. What can we do? Everything you can point your finger at, we have a surplus. Prices

are zilch, and here we are getting ready to raise another bin-buster.

We lived out of town a couple of miles, and I used the Hobbs Highway to go into Seminole to the cotton co-op office. It was a four-lane highway, and the side going into town was torn up. Have you ever seen these machines that tear up the old asphalt and run it through a little deal, then they run it back through and press it and it is brand new highway? The second day I watched this I thought, why can't we recycle our crops back to ourselves? Why do we want to just keep producing when there isn't a market and go further in debt? It was a custom of mine to try my wild ideas out on friends and some enemies every once in a while. You know you have got to get the truth. I asked about five farmers that were big in Gaines County. What if we agreed to set aside 50 percent of our land this year and not plant? In lieu of that, we get back an equal amount from last year's crop. They said, "You know, it might work." As it happened, a friend called me and said, "The National Cotton Council is having a producers' steering committee meeting in Lubbock. Are you going to go?" She said, "I wish that you would."

The meeting started at nine o'clock. I was the only female, which was not unusual, except for the reporter at the *Avalanche Journal*, Kathleen Harris. She and I sat at the very back. They knew who I was, and at coffee-break time, I went up to the chairman of the committee and said, "I've got an idea. I have a copy of it here. Would you like to see it?" So I gave it to him and to the others that were standing around. After the coffee break, I sat down with Kathleen. First thing you know, I heard my name. The delegate from California stood up and said, "This cotton pool, what is this cotton pool?" So I explained it.

I said the whole idea is PIK—Payment In Kind. Instead of us raising 100 percent of our production capability, let us produce only 50 percent of it and receive equal amount from storage—because it is in the bins—as a payment in kind. Old Charlie Cunningham was in the audience from the USDA [*U. S. Department of Agriculture*]. There were some soybean and corn people there. That was like 9:30 or 10:00 in the morning and by noon that idea was in Washington D. C. Within ten days time, I was called to come to the White House because President Reagan was going to announce this program. I said, gosh darn, I don't have the money to fly up there. So Charles and I drove to Dallas, and Reagan came to Dallas and announced it at the Farm Bureau convention.

How do you think that your involvement in politics helped you have the confidence to present your idea?

People need to realize that their involvement in politics is one of the best ways to grow. I remember the first time I had to introduce somebody I was shaking all over. Just scared absolutely to death to make any kind of public announcement. You have the challenges, the opposition, the confrontations, and you grow. You don't get cynical and get mad and get all bent out of shape. You just work with it and roll with the punches.

Have you seen women have an impact on policy on an informal basis?

DORIS WILLIAMS, LAKE JACKSON
Sure. Once they get to know you, they listen to you. I've had many candidates call me up and ask me about my opinion on things before I was elected mayor. They believe in your judgment and if you say things, you're going to follow through. Republican women through the years have a very good reputation and get very much respect from the elected officials because they realize that these people have helped them in many ways. Maybe they want to just call and get some grassroots information on what is happening. Through the years you do get to know people real well, and you are important to them.

LUCILLE ROCHS, FREDERICKSBURG
The people that I have supported, like Jeff Wentworth, Harvey Hilderbran, and Lamar Smith, are people that I have checked out and gotten to know personally. I was in Washington this March with the Child Welfare League of America. We spent an afternoon on Capitol Hill. I was in nine congressional offices and talked to aides. I have gone up for the last three years to do this. We have

been able to get legislation through Congress to improve the lives of families and children. We got new legislation passed this year for children who are in foster care and will be graduating from high school and becoming independent. They were not allowed to have more than $1,000 in assets. What were they going to live on? We got that changed from $1,000 to $10,000. We have gotten other benefits for kids who do not have family to support them but who really want to get an education or a job or vocational training.

My advice is to get to know the elected officials' aides. Attend their functions and introduce yourself. If there are bills before the House or before the Senate, get people involved in letter writing and phone calling so they know that we out here in the grassroots know they are there and have some things that we would like for them to consider and support. I have not done this alone. I have done this because I know a lot of people and am very involved in the community. I am just the spark plug.

CHAPTER 19

Where Now?

"A lot of other people just say, oh, politics is a dirty game.
It's very sad. They are giving up their right to control their own
destiny by not participating!"   —MARY LOU WIGGINS

The Texas Republican Party now has the opportunity to take advantage of the organization and victories of the past fifty years and develop into a party that can dominate the Texas political landscape for the next fifty years. The Party must find ways to attract youth and minorities to the Republican philosophy the way it did in years past. To rid the state and nation of apathy, the Party must effectively communicate the ways in which politics affects our daily lives. People of all generations can fulfill their dreams and breathe political life into their ideas through their actions and with their money.

The Changing Role of the Party

ANNE ARMSTRONG, ARMSTRONG

Things have changed a lot since I was so active in politics. The Party is far less important now. I remember the columnist in Washington, David Broder, who I came to respect even though he is much more liberal than I am. When I went up to Washington as co-chairman of the Republican National Committee, I was proud that with the help of others we got the female part of the pair designated as co-chairman, not vice chairman, and I was elected instead of just appointed by the male chairman. It gave me my own constituency and my own strengths for the women. David

Broder told me and subsequently wrote often on how the parties were diminishing in power. He was very sorry about it. I was sorry then and a little miffed to think that the Republican National Committee was going to diminish in importance, but it has and so have the state parties.

I say that media is the main reason. With television now, the candidates can build up their constituencies in a way that was impossible before. But the main thing, I think, is that the media has taken the place, in many ways, of the state party and its importance in backing candidates. It's more like a referendum now than it is a regular election. There is not the filtering anymore of a party. In some ways, that is bad. We make mistakes. Maybe if we had had a larger, wiser Democratic Party, it would have checked more on William Clinton. But he was awfully good on the tube, and the public liked him. There weren't the old back-room party checks and rechecks on candidates they were going to offer to the public.

It's fun to relive the Party the way I saw it was, or wished it were, in the past. We need to face reality about the campaigns of President George Bush or Senators Kay Hutchison or Phil Gramm. They want the Party. They need the Party. They treasure the Party. They don't want to get at odds with the Party. But their clout today, compared to what it would have been in the '60s, is far greater than it was back then. The individual candidates whether a legislator or a Senator—and the higher up the rank you are the more clout you get—have independence from the Party because they can command the media.

Organizational Priorities

Passing the Torch

THEO WICKERSHAM, SAN ANTONIO
Mary Morton Jackson [*precinct organizer and SREC member*] told me you can never retire until you have someone to follow in your footsteps.

GAIL WATERFIELD, CANADIAN

My bottom line thinking, and I tell my kids this, is that I worked during my younger years and I have contributed and now it's *your* turn. You're the ones that are going to have to go through the educational system with children. You're the ones that are going to have to go begging on the streets for medical care. I'm financially secure, and I've got insurance. You go solve it. I think that the forty-year-old and younger generations are very disillusioned.

I think there are so many people who truly say to themselves, "I can't do anything about it. I can't make a difference." Whereas my generation never thought we couldn't make a difference. We weren't smarter. We weren't brighter. My children are both very successful. They just don't have any interest in politics. I think they will one day, maybe. I hope so.

SURRENDEN ANGLY, AUSTIN

One of the deepest concerns that I have is watching my children and their families and their friends. They are all married, and they all live in Austin. Even when the mother stays at home, the husband doesn't get home until 7:30 or 8:00 o'clock at night. There are a lot of driven and well-educated people with good ideas that can't possibly take on a political role in anything. They can barely take on a PTA meeting. It is very disturbing to me how much this generation, let's call it thirty-plus, works. Many of them have fabulous ideas, but they are exhausted. We were not that way. I am concerned that this is going to cut down on good potential candidates of any kind.

MARTHA WEISEND, DALLAS

I will spend my time to help groom the younger generation. We have some very bright young men and women, young professional people who are very capable, to lead our party by being elected to office or just by simply giving of their time and energy. I think that will be my challenge. What I've learned I can put in a thimble, but I want to share that thimbleful of what I know with younger, wiser people who are coming along. They care about Texas, and they care about what is happening to our country. When you look at the television, we are very blessed to be Americans. If that's silly or a little weird, I don't care because I believe that, and unless we keep telling our story it is going to fade.

Challenges of Governing

ANN LEE, HOUSTON

It is easier to be knocking on the door trying to get in, because you mind your p's and q's more, but when you get in and dominate things it's scary. We have to be very careful. It is very disheartening for me to realize that not all Republicans wear a white hat.

MARJORIE ARSHT, HOUSTON

The Republican Party has to learn how to govern. They are learning it at the state level. But the fact of the matter is that today, with the wealth of elected people that we have, it's up to them now not to be intimidated and to stop feeding the kitty with money. We have a man here [*a political consultant*]. He intimidates people. "If you don't give me $10,000 or $25,000 then I will run someone against you." They have all fallen for it. With the 1998 Republican sweep [*of statewide offices*], I hope that they are not going to be as intimidated as they have been in the past. Our future lies with our elected officials now. I used to believe in the power of the people, but I don't anymore because well-rounded people have lost interest. We were after the Holy Grail. We were idealists. We were going to change Texas, change the world. I think people have lost faith in that.

Minorities and Youth

NANCY PALM, HOUSTON

We have got to find some way to deal with the ethnicity that is here. One of the media came to me about the Asian community not too long ago. They said, "Nancy, you are the only one that I remember back in the '70s who was talking about the fact that the Asians had to be brought into the political process." We did have an Asian candidate, and she is now on the council and ran for countywide office and we almost elected her—Martha Wong. That to me is the biggest problem this Party faces—that and not allowing litmus tests. I will be blunt about it—the homosexual situation and the abortion situation. I am about as firm against abortion as a human can be. My husband [*a doctor*] would come home and talk to me about these little babies. He came close to thinking that it was murder to kill one of them. That affected me a great deal. But we can not let two issues determine the future of this party.

RAQUEL GONZALEZ, LAREDO

We have to go to the grassroots to reach Hispanics. We have to educate people. We have to have leaders who are willing to go out there and, like anything else, start converting people, like a religion, and start communicating what Republicans stand for. It's going to be a big effort. We have to invest money in the process.

BILLIE PICKARD, RAYMONDVILLE

We tend to lump Hispanics as though they are a homogenous group. I would go after the better-educated people because they have more in common with the Republican Party. Their goals and aspirations are more like the Republican Party. I would not pursue the vote of the Hispanics who are used to having their vote bought, being carried to the polling place, and being told how to vote. That was one of the mistakes that I saw during my time of involvement. There were Hispanics who were desirous of getting into your pocket. So they would go to the campaigns and say, if you will give me money to do this and money to do that then I will put on this event for you and we can bring x-number of votes. History shows that they couldn't and didn't. Yet it was a natural thing for the candidate or the organization of the candidate to want to believe that they could deliver.

If I were building the Party, I would contact people like our upstanding local federal judge and ask him for names of young, promising Hispanics who have similar conservative views and work with them. Whether Anglo, Hispanic, or whatever, they need to be people that can be respected. They will bring other people along with them.

ANNE SHEPARD, VICTORIA & HARLINGEN

Give Hispanics opportunities for fundraising and helping. Give them opportunities to come into the Party and be a part of it as far as organization. When you are having a fundraiser, invite new people to help. When you're having a Republican function and have different officeholders to town, be sure and include them in the organization process. Include new people. It doesn't matter if they are male or female, old or young—you just need a mix of people working. When you have the same old group, whether it is five of you or twenty but it is the same people, you have a clique and people are uncomfortable in a clique. It is common sense and it is courtesy.

CAROLE WOODARD, HOUSTON & GALVESTON

The best way to reach African Americans is to constantly keep the education process going among the black professionals who think for themselves and are basically Independents. There are many, many, many blacks in Houston that are independent thinkers. They don't vote party, but they vote who is going to do the best for them. Those are the people that you have to target and pull into the Party. The more information that you give them, the more knowledgeable they become about the two parties and candidates. There are poor candidates in both parties. There are some Republicans that I would not vote for, but overall the Republican platform and the Republican Party is where you'll find most of the professional people and that is where most of them are voting. The problem is you can't count them because they live in neighborhoods where the boxes are predominantly white. Unless you're out there doing an exit poll, you do not know that black people are voting Republican. If the polls show that you got 27 percent of the black vote, it is probably much higher. The neighborhood that I live in is mostly white. I'm probably counted as a white vote.

How can you reach black children?

It has to be done through the churches and organizations like Jack & Jill and Links. Organizations and churches where children are taught to be independent thinkers. I don't think you tell them to be one party or another but just not to be brainwashed.

JAN CLARK, HOUSTON

The Greater Houston Council of Republican Women has gotten involved with immigration and naturalization. We just had a day passing out the Republican philosophy in six languages. I put a welcome sheet on there with my phone number. We actually got our first phone call. We are trying to put together things that these people really need when they become new citizens or come to a new country. Of course, some of them have been here for a while. We're trying to pull together some things that they really are interested in to get them involved with us. Job opportunities, health, doctors they may need to know about, that sort of thing. We have an outreach chairman, and she has six people under her—a Filipino, a Chinese, two blacks, and a Hispanic who has been through immigration herself. The Filipino does a radio program every morning. She works to get them to vote. They will call her and ask who to vote for. They opened a Hispanic Republican headquarters here in town. They try to pull them in and get them active. Get them to vote. Make them Republicans.

DIANA RYAN, SAN ANGELO

The young people probably don't see themselves as contestants at all in the arena because they don't think they have what it takes. Words are cheap and unless you have the money you can't buy a place in it. One thing that may be good is the computer age. People can bypass high-dollar giving and get to issues and someone's position. The information superhighway may prove to be able to include people across the land like we have never been able to do before. It's getting so you can get any kind of information you want, and it is not jaded by what ABC or NBC says. Television is kind of a catch-22. People turn on the TV, and if it is broadcast it is believable. We as a nation have not learned to say, "Wait a minute. I don't believe that." People are the key to everything. People caring about one another.

CINDY BROCKWELL, BOERNE

Young women can form school clubs through the schools' government classes. Some take field trips to county commissioners court so they can see personally what kind of decisions elected officials are making. When I talk to kids, I just remind them that government affects everything you do. What age do you get your driver's license? Do you have to wear a helmet riding a motorcycle? What age can you drink alcohol? How fast can you go on the roads? They can see, yes, it does affect me.

CATHY McCONN, HOUSTON

I see the future of the Republican Party growing brighter because the young people who I meet, particularly in the Young Republicans—the young marrieds and the young singles—are very enthusiastic about our message. They are every bit as conservative if not more than those of us who have been at it for a longer time. They understand that it helps the family. There was a recent survey that identified the Republican Party as the Party of family values. It is about individual freedom and letting people do what they know they can do if the government would just get out of the way and stop taxing them so heavily. All those things the young people understand.

LAVERNE EVANS, EL PASO

I taught for a quite a while and worked to get young people involved in the political process. I always stressed that it was a privilege and a responsibility to be involved in the political process and to know what is going on. If you know where a candidate stands, you have a pretty good idea of what they are going to do once they are elected. You need to follow up to see if they fulfilled their promises. I even got to take them to the airport when President Reagan came. When Congressman Jim Collins came, the students interviewed him. They got to go to several of the election-night campaign headquarters and see what the process is of winning and losing. It was just a process that I got them involved in so that when they got older they would vote.

ANN HARRINGTON, PLANO

I read patriotic stories to my grandchildren that you can hardly find anymore, if you are not an old book collector like I am, since they have changed the history books. We put out a flag, and we respect the flag. I think it is just being a good citizen in general. You have to start treating people the way you like to be treated.

What advice would you give a girl today who wonders if she could be an outspoken woman of principle?

PATRICIA LYKOS, HOUSTON

First of all, search for a virtuous life. You are going to die, and you know it, so you have got two choices in life. You can live a life of honor and dignity or you can make it an existentialist absurdity. Then you make the decision that you're going to live your life with honor and you're going to be in search of a virtuous life. You determine what your principles are. You live them. It is sort of like religion. I subscribe to Saint Matthew's theory that you pray in private. Or like they say in Texas, that you walk the walk because there are a lot of people who talk the talk. You have got to be able to look in the mirror and respect yourself. I despise the word self-esteem. That is such an oxymoron anyway. How can you esteem yourself? You esteem others, but you can respect yourself.

So the first thing is to live your life so that you have self-respect. You start out with that as your premise and your foundation. You gain as much knowledge as possible. I encourage girls to be as athletic as possible. Not only is it healthy, but competition hones those skills. Whatever you decide to do, be passionate about it. Politics manifests itself in many ways. Some people are campaign managers, others are strategists or run for office. There are just so many ways to participate in politics, but the important thing is that you do participate. If you care, do something.

SUSAN WEDDINGTON, SAN ANTONIO

The Republican Party has got to take a more serious look at today's technology, especially to reach our young people. The Internet is a wonderful vehicle for accessing the youth. The other thing is to increase our visibility on the college campuses. It is hard to keep a consistency to that organization because young people move in and out of school. In the near future, the state party needs to take a more active role to be sure that that auxiliary is more consistent and more active on the campuses. Our leaders need to spend more time going into classrooms. We need to be more actively engaged. We also need to cast a vision to the local communities, either through the local Republican Women's Clubs or through the county organization or both, to develop outreach programs that will include younger people in various activities and events. There is so much we can do at the local level to include young people. The vision and emphasis need to come from the top leadership.

How about the minority community?

The model of the last four years is fairly good to continue, which is personal outreach. In the past, outreach programs have consisted of touring the minority areas just before the campaigns and establishing a Hispanics-for-whomever and really never hearing from us again. Governor Bush along with our other statewide candidates in '98 really went all out going to areas that had been traditionally Democrat and spending a lot of time there. The fruit of that was the number of Hispanics voting Republican was substantially increased, with the Governor winning some counties that had never been won before by Republicans. What it takes is commitment. The SREC followed up on that and took our meetings out of Austin for the first time in twenty years. We went to McAllen, El Paso, and Beaumont. We got great coverage because the question was, "Why are you bothering to come to areas that are Democrat strongholds?" To show people that we truly want them to have an opportunity to participate in our Party and get to know us. It is important for us to go to where the people are and not ask them to come to us.

How did Jacque Allen influence you when you were young and thinking about getting involved in politics?

CAROLYN NICHOLAS, WICHITA FALLS

Jacque was the Republican Party not only in Wichita County but also in the entire area. When I first became interested in the Party, Jacque had been the county chairman and on the state committee. She commanded the respect of people because she had knowledge and she was effective. Even when we were young, she was always a political mentor. She didn't exclude us. She made a special effort to invite us to special things. It was fascinating to see her interact with people because it was always about the issues and the races. It was never a front for her to promote herself. But for me, especially, it was the respect that Jacque seemed to command from everybody.

Get Rid of Cynicism and Vote

MARY LOU WIGGINS, DALLAS

It is so important to vote. A lot of other people just say, oh, politics is a dirty game. It's very sad. They are giving up their right to control their own destiny by not participating! They don't have that sense of mission. They are willing to compromise and let it happen.

CAROLE RAGLAND, LEAGUE CITY

People are complacent and don't want to be bothered. They don't want to rock the boat. They'd rather stay home and watch television than go to the precinct conventions, or go sail than go to the county conventions.

JUANDELLE LACY, MIDLAND

I know and I hope that others realize how important politics is—the process of it, not necessarily politics itself. Without it we would not have our freedom. I don't think that so many young people or baby boomers realize the price that has been paid and what we've got. All wars are political. I have been all over the world, and there is truly nothing better. We have lots of faults, but our process is the best there is.

LOIS WHITE, SAN ANTONIO

You are in politics whether you know it or not. It is a part of life. Dirty people make dirty politics. I learned way back when that you always voted. Even when you didn't vote, you voted, because by not voting you helped whoever win. You helped the bad guys win by not voting so you have voted. It's hard day after day to keep on doing what people see as change. But if I had been in a state that was all Republican and there were no Democrats, I would have said, maybe we need a second voice here.

I am accustomed to being a minority. It taught me some things, too. I know how you have to survive in a majority. Republicans here don't know that—how to survive as a minority. They have never been a minority in anything else. There are certain ways a minority has to survive. You believe in your righteousness—I am on the side of right. Even though there is one person here, I am worth more than 2,000 or 3,000. It doesn't get you the office but it doesn't stop you from trying to jump on out there.

Openness

BETTE JO BUHLER, VICTORIA

I don't think there is a question but what we all have the responsibility to maintain openness, morality, and conservatism without a capital "C." We've got to maintain our interest in the entire population. We get the reputation for being kind of a closed party for only the elite. I don't know how we earned that.

Every piece of mail that I get stresses how serious they are in getting your opinion. We all raise our eyebrows because down at the bottom there it is—the question, will you give $100, $500, or $1,000? You feel that that is the ultimate purpose.

You have got to choose a candidate locally that convinces people. We have to have people working for the Republican Party on the volunteer staff and the women's clubs who are totally open and not discouraging and unwilling to listen.

CAROLYN NICHOLAS, WICHITA FALLS

There is always a group that comes along and thinks they invented the Party. About every decade it seems. The biggest thing is to co-opt that group. So often they come in as an opposition group. Get them interested in, not a single issue and not a single candidate, but in the Party. I have been told that those days are numbered, but to survive as a Party, that is what we have got to do.

BILLIE WHITEFIELD, HOUSTON

They can not squabble and get too compartmentalized. Some of the women would be diametrically opposed to each other on certain issues and yet if their candidate got the nomination I worked for them because he was Republican. If we can continue to keep that as our objective, we will grow. In other words, sure, I'm going to work for a candidate that reflects my views and others will work for another candidate, but philosophically we agree 75 percent maybe 80 percent. Decide that winning the election is the main thing. I feel like, if after the primary our candidate is elected, and I helped elect him, then even though we may not agree on every-thing I have more influence and more input. He is still more likely down the line to vote my way on something than a Democrat.

GAYLE WEST AND ISABEL GRAY, PASADENA

West: Disagree, have your differences in your precinct, but don't hold grudges.

Gray: We had to work with all different kinds of people. Any Republican would be better than a liberal Democrat as long as they aren't immoral. You can't win if you are fighting each other. We had battles in the SREC, and after it was over we didn't dislike each other, we worked with each other. Some people think that there is just one issue and they will stick with it no matter what. We are losing our country! They can't see the forest for the trees. I'm not for abortion, but some people just can't understand. The only thing they think about is abortion. There is more than one issue—taxes, crime, and national defense. I truly don't believe that you can legislate morality. If a person is going to have an abortion, they will find a way.

West: It's definitely power. We have a lot of that in the local organization.

Preserve the Grassroots

PAT JACOBSON, FORT WORTH

You have to get people involved to get them to the polls. When [*President Bill*] Clinton won, very few people went to the polls. That means not very many people were involved. When Reagan won, just look at the people that he drew. Ronald Reagan was the grassroots guy. He believed in people being involved. I think that's why he won. I'm not saying that you don't need money. That would be foolish to say. But it is more important that you have people involved. You can't win a race unless you have people voting.

ESTELLE TEAGUE, HURST

The biggest responsibility Republicans have is to listen to their constituents. If you don't listen to your constituents, you don't know what is going on. As long as they continue to listen to their constituents, they will continue to be reelected.

JESS ANN THOMASON, MIDLAND

I have had some disappointing fundraisers for incumbent candidates where donors felt "we got them elected and they've forgotten us." I would put things together the next election, and people would say, "Well, I have already supported him. He has forgotten who I am, and I was his best friend the last time." So the candidates don't stay in touch with their donors and contributors. That really hurts worse than anything.

They need to come into Midland or other cities, like Senator Teal Bivens does. He will bring different candidates in and have a luncheon. It's called the 31 Club. Then you follow that with a little reception say at five o'clock and serve Diet Cokes and Sprites. Just spend thirty minutes telling them what is happening in Austin or Washington. You have the Republican Women on the phones calling people to get them out for it, or you send postcards. They show up. They want to be remembered.

MICKEY LAWRENCE, HOUSTON

We have got to get back to grassroots campaigning, and we have got to get back control of the grassroots in the Republican Party. It belongs to big-money interests and special-interest PACs. Different PACs are trying to get the word out and recruit candidates. One thing we are trying to do is to get information out to the Republican activists about this process. I have been giving talks on how PACs work, how they get their money. I accumulated all of the different articles that have been written in the last three or four years. Usually, when people walk out of my talk and are active Republicans, they say, "We didn't know all of this was going on." It is a matter of educating people about how this system really works.

The bottom-line message that I am trying to give is grassroots Republicans have to take back control of their Party. Now, it is large-money interests, and a lot of the large-money interests are nothing more than candidates on a slate pooling all of their money into a PAC, which is nothing more than a political consultant handling twenty-five different candidates who are contributing to the political consultant's action committee. The literature all comes out as if there is a PAC endorsing all of these candidates. Really, it is not the support of individuals like you and me. It is from the campaign funds of all of these candidates that pool their money.

People don't even realize that. People need to know the truth. The truth is not getting out. A lot of times, when people do hear the truth, they are very uncomfortable with confrontation. They hear the truth, but it is sort of a silent truth.

Role of Candidates

ANDY BEAVER AND NANCY STEVENS, CORPUS CHRISTI

Stevens: It might take longer for Nueces County to be a two-party county, but we carried for Governor Bush last time.

Beaver: Even in my precinct. In 1968, seven voted in the primary, but in the 1998 general election we carried it. Now we can be the election judges.

Stevens: If your precinct goes Republican, then you get to be election judge. We went from 20 election judges to 63, and there are 122 precincts in Nueces County. When you have an election judge, you don't have to pay a poll watcher. You know the election is going to be run better.

JAN KENNADY, NEW BRAUNFELS

Having qualified candidates who will run is our next challenge. We have a real dearth often of candidates who are qualified. It's from the local level on up. The life of a politician is not very easy. I know so many people who would be wonderful elected officials who wouldn't touch it. That is certainly true on the local level. That is one of our greatest challenges.

RUTH SCHIERMEYER, LUBBOCK

I ran a campaign for an Independent. Our sheriff died, and because of the timing the parties had to put someone on the ballot. The executive committee met and put someone on the ballot that had been forced to resign from two other counties. I had the man that I knew needed to run put his name on the ballot as an Independent. Then I volunteered to run his campaign. Everyone said that you could not win a campaign as an Independent. The Republican vote was too strong. Roughly 35 percent of the people in Lubbock County vote straight party. We won with 87 percent of the vote. Everything that could be against us was. Straight party votes did count, so we had to educate voters that they could vote for him. From the party side, he is a Republican. He voted Republican thirteen years and is a Hispanic Republican.

They asked him if he was going back to the Republican Party the night he was elected. He said, "I never left." The other Republican had not voted in one of our primaries. It was just a power play. It puts a lot of responsibility on us. I am Republican through and through, but as Republicans, if we become as strong as the Democrats used to be, it is our responsibility to be absolutely certain that the Republican candidates are the best candidates. That is not what we had done in this case.

Role of Volunteers

ANNA MOWERY, FORT WORTH

I really do dislike the fact that we're using paid phone banks, even away from the state. We're having people that can not pronounce the names of the candidates making the phone calls. I realize that it is very difficult to get the volunteers necessary to run a phone bank, but Mike Waldron, my phone bank chair, never has had a problem with it and I have never had a problem. The fact that you have a dedicated person making the phone call for their friend [*the candidate*] is very effective to me. I hate that we're getting away from it. Politics is local—everybody knows that. Anytime we replace volunteers with paid staff, there is a problem. Volunteers defend you at the coffee shop. When you're having coffee and people start saying that the person who's running for office is a stupid idiot, you have someone who will say, I don't think so. I know this person and they have bright ideas. You have armies out there, going where they go everyday besides being at the headquarters.

BILLIE PICKARD, RAYMONDVILLE

TV is now the dominant factor. I look back at Clayton Williams, and his [*gubernatorial*] campaign was primarily a TV campaign. The first one I can remember. They made some effort locally but did not have the state and county organization that candidates like Bill Clements had. So when Williams stubbed his toe, he didn't have people in a local area that had made the commitment to his campaign there to say, "Oh, he shouldn't have done that, but . . ."

JANE NELSON, FLOWER MOUND

In today's world, you need money to win a campaign. There is no doubt about it. The beauty of volunteers is that these are people who know you. They live in your community. They each have their realm of people that they live with and go to church with and work with. No message that comes across on television relates to people like somebody in their community saying, "I know this lady and she believes in what we believe in and she will make it happen." The value of volunteers is immeasurable. I could never have won my election without dedicated volunteers. But you still need some money.

CATHERINE SMYTH COLGAN, DALLAS

If you take the people out of politics, you lose. There is an old saying that involvement breeds interest. When you involve the people, they become interested in the candidate and interested in the race. They will get out and work.

Special Interests

Do you think you made a difference being elected as a Republican rather than as a Democrat?

SHAROLYN WOOD, HOUSTON

Yes. I don't know if it is true for people coming in today because of a more mature Republican Party. But definitely in the '80s, we could come in without special-interest groups wanting a piece of us. I have watched my Democrat judge friends have to go out to the special-interest groups in their Party and stand up and eat all of their principles and try to walk a tightrope without compromising their principles to stay in office. Their special-interest groups are pretty well known and identifiable. It concerns me that I see Republican special-interest groups following the natural paths.

In my election speeches, I have said repeatedly that the most wonderful thing about running as a Republican was that you didn't have special-interest groups wanting to litmus test you. I think that is changing today. There are a lot of people on the bench today to whom I said, "Run as a Republican—it is not like being over there in the Democratic Party where there are all of these people that you have to kowtow to. Come to the Republican Party because the Republican Women are there and they will not hold you up for money. They are good honest people that just want good honest public servants." That is our selling card, and it is what we ought to stay with as a Party. We have been successful and should not forget that.

Stay True to the Mission

PATTILOU DAWKINS, AMARILLO

The TFRW has been a real influence. That is a wonderful organization if they'll stick to their knitting. One of the most influential books in my life was *What We Must Know about Communism,* [*former FBI director*] J. Edgar Hoover's book. I read that book, and one of the questions asked of Mr. Hoover was, "How do we know if our organization is being infiltrated by Communists?" That was real important in the early '50s. Of course, now we do not have the Communist threat, but his answer was to make sure that your organization sticks to its mission statement and its purpose. If somebody starts wanting your organization to move away from its mission, be leery. It would be like going to a ladies' golf association meeting and somebody standing up and wanting the ladies' golf association to get involved in a bicycle run to cure lupus. It may be a very worthy project, but it's not the purpose of the ladies' golf association. Well, that is the way I am looking at TFRW right now. We had better really stick to our mission statement or we're going to be off on some tangent that has nothing to do with electing Republicans and women in politics.

Civics Education

DOLLY MADISON McKENNA, HOUSTON

What I have seen from my last ten years in politics is that you really have both parties pulling very much farther to the right and to the left in terms of the activists within the organizations. The people who are working in primaries, who are volunteering, and who are choosing the candidates are the ones that are coming from some issue-oriented group. Now, in the Democratic Party, it may be unions or environmental groups. In the Republican Party, it may be the gun people or the anti-abortion people. Those are the ones that have gone out and taught their people how to participate in the political process—that have had training sessions on going to precincts, taking over meetings, organizing ways to get issues on platforms, and that kind of thing. Meanwhile, the average person doesn't even know that this process exists.

I think in the whole state of Texas maybe 75,000 people participate in both parties' precinct meetings combined. They are the ones that are determining the issues that will go to the platform. People are so turned off about politics because they see harshness from these groups running the parties and they don't want to participate. And yet when they don't, the parties are more like these groups that they don't like. So the more they participate, the more they will like the process because the process will look more like them.

Don't Sit on Our Laurels

What do you think your mother, Henrietta Armstrong, would

say if she were alive today and could see how far the Republican Party has come in Texas?

ILLA CLEMENT, KINGSVILLE

I think she would be very pleased but would say it is never safe to think that just because it is this way now it's going to stay that way. There are a lot of places in the country that are not this way. Maybe we ought to be giving them money. Maybe the Republican Party leadership ought to be saying, you know, the place that needs your money is so-and-so; if you are satisfied with what is going on in your state, if you have any money, you can send it to these people. It's going to take money to do anything.

JAN CLARK, HOUSTON

The Republican Party rests on its laurels and gets over confident. This is our greatest danger. Okay, we have all of this success—let's sit back. That is when you need to worry. When you're on the top of the hill, somebody wants to knock you off badly. Now we have to start working harder than we ever have and keep this together because it is not going to be easy.

The Role of Women

POLLY SOWELL, McALLEN & AUSTIN

We see more women holding office. They're usually a little bit older and have kids at least in college and not under foot. So this gives them something to do with the second half of their lives. I think it's great, and they ought to get into politics because they know a lot.

SUSAN WEDDINGTON, SAN ANTONIO

There is nothing but good news for women in the Republican Party. In the last two years, the Republicans have had more females on the general election ballot for statewide office than the Democrats. We currently have more female officeholders statewide than the Democrats ever had in their strongest years. We have women in positions that are traditionally held by men, for example, agriculture commissioner and comptroller. The fact that my election as the first female state chairman of either major party in Texas speaks volumes about the Republican Party being a party that is looking for leadership first, whether it is male or female. When I talk to the press and tell them the facts—that the Republicans have actually had more females on the general election ballot and we have more women in office today than the Democrats ever did—it shocks them. Women have changed. They have a more diverse group of interests. Our Party has got to be able to meet the interests of women today. No one-shoe-fits-all.

CAROLE KEETON RYLANDER, AUSTIN

Women have a very bright future in the Republican Party. You hear talk of the so-called gender gap. There is a gender gap in Texas, but it is in the Democrat Party not the Republican Party. We now have nine women in statewide elected office in Texas. The Democrats have none.

I can remember when I switched parties some very outspoken Democrats said you will be leading women in the opposite direction. I said I will be leading women in the right direction. We are role models for others. Bottom line, women are concerned with families, budget, paychecks, jobs, education, and all of the same things that men are concerned about.

Fundraising

PETER O'DONNELL, DALLAS

First thing they have to do is write their own checks. Many of them are well able to do it, but they are not used to doing it. Then call on others. No one is stopping you from going out and raising money. If you think you can do it, why, saddle up. I don't know of anyone saying we don't want you raising money around here because you are a woman. That is crazy. We have some outstanding women that raise money for charitable purposes, but I haven't seen them utilize that talent for political purposes. Nancy

Brinker is a good fundraiser for both. Women, in my opinion, are still not drawn to fundraising. Not too many people are.

PATRICIA LYKOS, HOUSTON

Women need to open up their checkbooks. I have been at functions where women were discussing going to Tony's for lunch, then they turn around and write a check for twenty dollars and think they have done something big. I also know people who are on very modest incomes that when they write out a twenty-dollar check it is something extremely significant for them. So if you care and if you believe, then you write that check.

Money gives you access. If there are issues that you care about, how are you going to get your candidate to address them rather than just give them lip service? The media is, I would say, 90 percent liberal Democrat. It takes money to get those critical ads out there, which is free speech. Free speech in the media is very expensive. It is like a war. It takes money to buy the materials, the uniforms, and the troops. You need a treasury to finance it. If you don't have great financial resources then give what you can and volunteer your labor.

DEBBIE FRANCIS, DALLAS

We were having a fundraiser for Susan Combs, and it was less of a fundraiser than getting people out to see her and get that vote out. I made the comment to Susan that I was glad she was having another fundraiser that was going to be a bigger hitter, because all of the women I asked to come to this luncheon were also being asked to work the phone banks, get out the postcards, and attend volunteer activities. Most of the men are not being asked to do all that. They have just been asked to give some money. But you're asking all of these women to do all of this stuff. There is kind of a limit on how much money you can also hit them for. With most of the men, you are not asking them to do five things. You're asking them to do one thing, write that check.

She said, "Oh, gosh, do you think we should do the event at all?" I told her we would have no problem having a wonderful event at a lesser price. But if we're going to go up into the hundreds of dollars just for a woman's event in the middle of the day it's not going to fly.

POLLYANNA STEPHENS, SAN ANGELO

It is kind of a joke out here. People always tend to visit my husband, Steve, in his business to get his support. He will come home and tell me so-and-so came by today and I gave him such-and-such. Never once did they ask for *my* vote or *my* support. A lot of times, if it was somebody that I knew, I would say, "Well, tell him that he's going to have to ask for my vote or my support before he gets it." I've had some call me and talk about it. Of course, it was all done kind of tongue in cheek. But I find that interesting. They would always go to him, and they would always expect that I would support whatever he supported.

Now, people really do realize that women voters have a lot of say-so, a lot of strength. They have a lot of money to contribute, and candidates are out seeking their support now a lot more than they used to. I did it jokingly for a long time, but in the back of my mind I'm thinking, "I wonder why they just take it for granted that whoever Steve supports I'm going to support."

DIANE RATH, SAN ANTONIO

Fundraising is the next step we have to conquer in politics because that does get you into a different level of decision-making and a different level of appointments. You do have governors or senators with national appointments and governors with state appointments where the major appointments usually go to men, and I think we are seeing that change. They're being much more diverse with those appointments, but they normally go to major donors and women just haven't been there.

JANE ANNE STINNETT, LUBBOCK

A few years ago, mostly the men raised the money. That was the deal. Women did the work—the invitations, nametags, and refreshments—and men raised the money. I don't think that's true today. Our mayor, Wendy Sitton, raised $90,000 to run, practically by herself. I think women now, particularly women in business, are more in tune with asking for money themselves. Women will give money. I don't think that they give it as well as men. In the old days, you always sent the fundraising letter to the man's office because you didn't want the wife to open it and say, "Oh, that would be a new dress for me." Women can raise money and do raise money. Certainly, the big fundraisers around the state are women. Sylvia Nugent and Jeanne Johnson Phillips are two.

CATHY McCONN, HOUSTON

There is a feeling among women, if you don't own your own business and you are a mother and a wife, it's almost like it's the man's job to give money. The school asks for money for a fundraiser, and they will write out a $50 check or a $100 check, no problem. But when it comes to a candidate, they either feel like "my amount is too small," which of course no amount is ever too small to make a commitment, or it's not something they focus on. As a couple we give, but I sign the checks. My husband lets me decide who we should support. I have gotten thank you notes back several times to my husband. Not even to me. I signed the checks! The very least they could do is figure it was from both of us and send a thank you note to both of us. I would write this nice little note and say, "If you ever want to get money from me again, you ought to thank the person that sent you the money."

DEBORAH BELL, ABILENE

Women can raise more money than men can. If I believe in a person, I am not afraid to call anybody and try to raise money for that candidate. I really think women have a leg up on men. The polls show women are playing a bigger and bigger part in the elections. Women can bring other women in. It is important not to overlook other women and just go straight to men. Women are in business now and have just as many contacts and different kinds of contacts that men can not touch.

KAY BAILEY HUTCHISON, HOUSTON & DALLAS

When I first started running, it was very difficult to get women to give money because they weren't used to it. Women have come into the system, and they have come into the system of giving money. Not as much as men because they are not used to writing the big checks as much, but it is a lot better than it used to be. It *is* important because if you care about an issue, the way to have an impact is to get *your* candidates elected. That takes elbow grease and money. We do have to encourage women to get involved.

Communicating Our Message

MARY DENNY, DENTON

You know, generally, when women are involved in politics people assume that they are Democrats or that they are liberals or moderates certainly. But that is just not true. I am really pleased that Republican women are getting more and more involved because it helps break that stereotype. We have worked with our Democrat counterparts to enact a lot of good legislation dealing with women's issues. I even hesitate to call them women's issues, although when they are about women's health, that's really what they are. I would like to be successful in breaking the stereotype that women in elected office are moderates or liberals. It's amazing to me that, across the country, when I'm sitting on an airplane and people ask me what I do and I tell them [*a state representative*], they assume right away that I'm a Democrat and then are somewhat surprised to find out that I am a conservative Republican. I've never been in a "class" that fit a stereotype until now. We have some work to do in that area.

BECKY FARRAR, HICO

Republicans don't do a very good job of making their case to the people. They need to package their message in a better way. The Democrats are masters at that. They have the message of the day. If Bill Clinton says something one day, you hear that same message coming from congressmen, Democrat chairmen, office-holders, legislators, and candidates. The Republicans are not like that. People are listening, and if they hear the same message over and over and over, they begin to remember it. This to me is why the Democrats have been so successful. This second level is where we have got to get to—the heart not just the brain. The Republicans are cerebral and academic. Our message is often directed to the brain not the heart. Voters who are not activists respond to heart messages not brain messages. So we have to learn somehow to talk about the heart issues, whether it is safe children or good schools or protect Social Security. It is hard for Republicans because we are not offering the moon. We're not offering them free health care or government giveaways. Republicans have to have the right message and we have got to package it in such a way that it hits the heart. We need to learn how to campaign with integrity but still win the election and the war.

CHAPTER 20

The Legacy

"Women of that generation have left a legacy of having accomplished
a great deal, but don't stop there. Keep going. The sky's the limit."
—DIANNE THOMPSON

*O*ne must only look at the election results of the late 1990s to
realize the legacy left by the thousands of women working in
Republican politics through the years. The election of Republican
candidates is not the only legacy they leave us. Their work in
Texas is a model for grassroots political organization in the U.S.
as well as in former Eastern Block countries and Latin America.
It also shows us that anything worth accomplishing is worth
whatever time and effort it takes to accomplish it. In today's
hurry-up world, these Texas heroines show us that patience,
hard work, and determination remain character traits to be
admired and instilled in future generations. They also prove
that good government does not develop independently. It exists
only when the citizenry actively involves itself in government,
works to elect qualified candidates, then holds them accountable.
Simply put, participation protects the American system of
government and ultimately our way of life.

Created Something New

JOCI STRAUS, SAN ANTONIO

It's a challenge to build something from scratch. It's people oriented and I love people. It's been a learning experience the whole way. I have learned so many things that I have been able to apply elsewhere. I couldn't begin to tell everything I have learned about people or about how to be convincing about something that you believe in strongly, how to raise money, and how to write your own press releases. The successes were so beautiful that you forget the times that you have not been successful. We had an opportunity, which I think is critically important, to build from the bottom up a competitive system which is the root of our whole American philosophy.

> *You've got a daughter who is in her early teens. What do you think that your mother, Bobbie Biggart, would want her to know about what she and her friends did for Texas?*

LEE BIGGART, DALLAS & AUSTIN

She would be the proudest about the odds they were up against. They started off organizing, supporting candidates, making phone calls, and getting their groups organized. They didn't expect to win. When they finally pulled off a few victories, they were upset victories. They never had the consensus on their side. They took such a long view. Nobody's going to win this year or in the next decade. It was an incredibly patient approach. What they decided was, if you didn't have a Republican governor of Texas you couldn't win the national election. Talk about a stretch—to say "We're going to elect the first Republican governor so we can get the president." That's moving pretty far uphill. That's what they were doing when everyone was saying about Bill Clements, we're going to win this one. From that base, we are going to elect Reagan. Texas Republican women got to see it go from nothing to the full banana in their careers. Some died ten years before it happened, and their kids got to see it. But these women, by and large, got to see finally the fruits of their labors. I think they were all politically satisfied because when it was finally said and done, whatever they contributed, they saw success in ways they couldn't have believed. My mother was enthusiastic about politics and had enough good victories, I think, there at the end. She saw plenty of defeats too. But they just kept plugging away. The result was the statewide slate of Republican candidates that we elected in 1998. How did this happen? Well, it didn't happen over night.

Made Texas a Role Model

ANNE ARMSTRONG, ARMSTRONG
Our state from the beginning gave women true leadership roles in finance. I remember the patronage committee, early on, that I was put on. The powerful things that counted in politics—Texas women had those jobs. All states are glad to have us lick the envelopes and put out the yard signs, but in Texas we were right at the fulcrums of power. I felt that it was a very good example to set. I use John Tower as an example. Nola Smith ran three of his campaigns. We put a woman up for the Texas Supreme Court, Barbara Culver Clack from Midland. Then Tower had a woman as his chief of staff, not as a constituency person or liaison to women or something like that, in his office. Carolyn Bacon ran that office. Many Senators still haven't gotten that message. We set examples not just for the rest of the South but for the nation.

Someone said you used to say, "Okay, girls, let's go save the country."

GWEN PHARO, DALLAS
Everywhere I would go in the country I would run into Republican politicians. They'd say, "You have got to tell us how you all do it." We would sit down and say there is nothing pleasant about it. It is just hard work. Step one leads to step two and two to three. It is just a standard way that you win elections. Number one, you go and ask for the votes.

CATHERINE SMYTH COLGAN, DALLAS
In Texas, it was, "Why not try it?" Many of us who learned in

Texas have carried our knowledge on to other places. Shirley Green, Mary Lou Grier, and I all ended up in Washington at the same time. We had a fantastic old-girls network on the national and international levels. I can remember talking to Jim Baker on the phone one day when he was chief of staff [*to President Reagan*]. We were talking about the questions of the day on the phone. My comment to him was that international politics was a piece of cake after you have survived the back alleys of Texas.

Sense of History

DIXIE CLEM, PLANO
Our children need to know history. Our people need to know that the state of Texas did not always have a Republican governor and our county did not always have a Republican county judge, or our city a Republican mayor. They need to know what the Republican Party stands for. They don't really know. The kids need to know what they're standing up for. What they believe.

Provided Inspiration to Other Women

SHEILA WILKES BROWN, AUSTIN
The women who were involved then have stuck with it. The Anne Armstrongs, the Rita Clements, the Polly Sowells, the Beryl Milburns. They are still doing it. Bobbie Biggart did it till the day she died. I guess maybe that is the generation of the '50s as opposed to the '60s or the '70s. Once they got started down that path, they just never gave up, and they are still doing it today. I think that is probably why they have been successful. Persistence. They have it.

DIANNE THOMPSON, BOERNE & HOUSTON
Women of that generation have left a legacy of having accomplished a great deal, but don't stop there. Keep going. The

sky's the limit. That's the legacy. It says, "You can do this. Don't stop here. Reach for the stars."

*W*here are the stars that you want to reach? What do you want to accomplish for your family, education, or business? How does the government affect your life? Women asked these same questions in 1952 before they got involved in Republican politics and the Texas Republican Party. Instead of saying "we face insurmountable odds" they said "this is a challenge we need to embrace," and they persisted until the job was done. Did they get discouraged when their friends and family thought them foolish for pursuing their political interests? Perhaps. But they did not let these reactions dissuade them from their ultimate goal of honesty and responsiveness in government and a two-party Texas. Their dedication gives us all a real example of the power of grassroots political action.

Each of us has the opportunity to face the challenges of today with the same long-term, optimistic approach that our mothers and grandmothers, friends and neighbors used yesterday. Their legacy to us is a grassroots model which will help us make things happen in politics. Let's use it!

Acknowledgments

*T*he women featured in *Grassroots Women* and those they represent provided a constant source of motivation. Many times when facing an obstacle I asked myself, if these women faced the same challenge, how would they approach it? Their examples of creative problem solving led the way.

Research would be almost impossible without access to public libraries, and we have one of the best here in Boerne, Texas. Louise Foster, Library Director, and John Powell, Reference Librarian, helped track down even the most obscure fact or figure.

Just like many grassroots women who were influenced by their parents, I am a better person because of mine, Sue and Dave McKain. They taught all five of their children—Carolyn, David, Kathy, John, and me—our responsibilities as citizens. In addition, Mother's sharp eye and Dad's view of the big picture made immeasurable contributions to the book.

Grassroots Women would not have been written without Mary Lou Grier. From the moment the book was envisioned, she did whatever she could to see it come to fruition whether recommending women for interviews, reading through multiple initial drafts and making suggestions, or acting as a sounding board. She is the true inspiration for this book. Kitchen cabinet members Fran Atkinson, Polly Sowell, Beryl Milburn, Sally McKenzie, Pam Hodges, and Susan Block, with their enthusiastic support from inception, bolstered me while I found my way through the research and book-development maze.

Shannon Davies understood the concept of *Grassroots Women* from our first conversation. She believed in fully telling this slice of Texas history and encouraged me to keep the original plan although others advised fitting it to the publishing industry mold. Shannon edited this oral history and its numerous speaking styles with ease and insight. George Lenox made this book look as graceful and full of life as the women whose story is conveyed on the pages. He is a gifted designer whose knowledge and experience enhanced the finished product in more ways than design. Thank you to Carla Giammichele for her expertise and concern for the quality of the book. Many of her ideas were touchstones for the marketing and distribution of *Grassroots Women*.

Jim Grier deserves my deepest gratitude. In addition to being a wonderful husband and best friend, his levelheaded approach to life keeps me on track. I wholeheartedly agree with Marguerite Binkley, who said, "Many husbands gift their wives with jewels; my husband indulged me the greatest gift a man can accord his wife: my time."

Finally, I thank God and my family at St. Mark Presbyterian Church for the courage to envision and complete this undertaking, and for carrying me over the bumps in the road along the way.

Photo Scrapbook

The Dallas delegation to the 12th Annual Republican Women's Conference, with Congressman Bruce Alger (*left*) and Senator John Tower in Washington, D. C., April 1964. Courtesy Babs Johnson

Joci Straus (*second from left*) takes the family to Washington to visit Congressman George Bush. Courtesy Joci Straus

Ruth Mankin and John Tower staffer Tom Cole celebrate the 1966 Senate election with a "We Kept Tower" bumper sticker. Courtesy Ruth Mankin

Dwight Eisenhower supporters at the Dallas County precinct 56 convention in 1952. Photos such as these helped seat the Eisenhower delegation at the 1952 Republican National Convention in Chicago. Courtesy Martha Crowley

A candidate for state legislature in the 1970s,
Leon Richardson (*left*) rides on Melinda Paret's
horse-drawn buggy at a campaign fundraiser.
Courtesy Leon Richardson

Theo Wickersham speaks to the
McAllen Rotary Club about the
importance of being politically
educated.
Courtesy Theo Wickersham

Barry Goldwater visits with
Mary Lou Grier before a fundraiser
in San Antonio in the early 1960s.
Courtesy Mary Lou Grier

Pasadena
Republicans pull
out all the stops
with a booth for
Jack Cox at the
1962 Pasadena
Rodeo. Courtesy
Marion Coleman

Louise and Jim Foster
register voters in Austin.
Courtesy Louise Foster

Many precinct organizations took root at neighborhood coffees. Senator Tower visits with voters as his wife, Lou, walks to greet them in a living room in Lubbock. Courtesy Nita Gibson

From second left: Babs Johnson, president of the Dallas County Council of Republican Women's Clubs; Rita Bass (Clements), state committeewoman; Flo Kampmann (Crichton), national committeewoman; and Barbara Man, TFRW president are guests of the Bruce Alger Weekly Report with Melvin Mudd (*right*). Courtesy Babs Johnson

Anne Armstrong while serving as a counselor to President Richard Nixon in 1973. Courtesy Anne Armstrong

Flo Kampmann Crichton (*left*) and then husband, Ike Kampmann, dance alongside Republican National Committee Vice Chair Bertha Adkins and Ed Mayer, a state committeeman, in 1957. The Bexar County Republican Party welcomed Adkins to a celebration of the important role played by women in the Texas GOP. Courtesy Flo Kampmann Crichton

Robin, from the TV show *Batman and Robin*, lands at the 1966 Harris County Republican Convention for a surprise respite during a long night of hardball politics. Courtesy Ruth Mankin

Polly Sowell chats with President Gerald Ford in 1975 while former Governor John Connally listens in. Moments earlier, Connally, a 1976 vice presidential hopeful, made a Freudian slip and introduced Sowell as the vice president —not the vice chair— of the Republican Party of Texas. Courtesy Polly Sowell

Opposite page, from left: Ruth Fox, Barbara Kaufman, and Estelle Teague on the floor of the 1988 Republican National Convention in New Orleans. Courtesy Ruth Fox

Barbara Culver Clack and Bill Shaner unveil the sign for Midland County Republican Headquarters. Courtesy Douthea Shaner

Babs Johnson (*left*) presents Liz Strickland, president of the Dallas County Women's Republican Club, founded in 1920, with a plaque naming the club Club Emeritus of the Dallas County Council of Republican Women's Clubs in 1963. Courtesy Babs Johnson

At the 1967 National Republican Women's Convention, Marguerite Binkley, Anna Claire Rice, Jarvis Jenkins, and other members of the Houston delegation were guests of Senator and Mrs. John Tower and Mrs. Clair Shenault at her home in the Watergate in Washington, D. C. Courtesy Anna Claire Rice

Members of the Canyon Lake Republican Women's Club participate in a Fourth of July parade. Courtesy LaVerne Cudabac

The Inner-City
Republican Women's
Club in San Antonio
hosts an event.
Courtesy
Lois C. White

Members of the West Memorial Republican Women in Houston visit State
Representative Milton Fox and his wife, Ruth, in the capitol. Courtesy Ruth Fox

Lou Tower (*far left*) and John Tower
visit with Nita Gibson (*second from left*)
and Terry Tapp in Lubbock.
Courtesy Nita Gibson

From left: Betty Cunningham,
Jodi Salzman, Alice Koonz,
and Anna Claire Rice welcome
Lou Tower (*second from left*)
to Houston as she campaigns
for Senator Tower.
Courtesy Anna Claire Rice

Bill and Ginny Elliott of Houston
celebrate his corner-turning election to
the city council in 1968. Ruth Mankin
was Elliott's campaign manager.
Courtesy Ruth Mankin

John Tower campaigns with Marjorie Arsht
in her 1962 run for state legislature.
Courtesy Marjorie Arsht

From bottom: Martha Weisend,
Congressman Steve Bartlett,
Roger Staubach, Eddie Chiles,
Cipriano Guerro, Fran Chiles,
General Dick Cavazos, and
Beryl Milburn accompany
Governor Bill Clements
(*bottom right*) as he flies around
the state during the 1986
campaign.
Courtesy Martha Weisend

Mary Lou Grier with the
other Republican statewide
candidates in front of the
"GOP Voteswagon" in 1974.
Courtesy Mary Lou Grier

Lucy Saenz (*left*) and Alicia Vela Cantu along with her children, Arnold and Leticia, pick up senatorial candidate George Bush at the Laredo airport for a campaign event in 1970. Courtesy Alicia Vela Cantu

Barbara Bush and LaVerne Cudabac make calls for President George Bush's reelection campaign at a phone bank in New Braunfels. Courtesy LaVerne Cudabac

Pat Jacobson hands out a Ronald Reagan bumper sticker to a telephone lineman in the "Pioneers for Reagan" tour of East Texas in 1980. Courtesy Millie Teas

Jean Baker of San Antonio works a phone for Clements in 1978. Courtesy Teddy Peterson

George and Barbara Bush visit with 1970 Senate campaign volunteers Teddy Peterson and Lane Vaughan in San Antonio. Courtesy Teddy Peterson

Pattilou Dawkins, with B. R. Barfield,
introduces a grateful Governor Clements
to an Amarillo crowd after a record-setting
voter turnout in the 1986 election.
Courtesy Pattilou Dawkins

An example of creative fundraising: Bob Overstreet,
candidate for state representative, and Marion Coleman
prepare for Donkey Softball, pitting the Young
Republicans against the candidates.
Courtesy Marion Coleman

New Braunfels Republican Women raised record amounts for candidates at their annual
Wurstfest food booth. Courtesy Bucky Smith (*far left*)

George W. Bush campaigns for his father in 1988 in San Antonio with (*from left*) Teddy Peterson, June Deason, and Caroline Ellwood. Courtesy Teddy Peterson

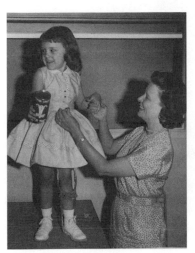

Barbara Culver Clack, as Midland County Judge, promotes an Easter Seals fundraiser. Courtesy Barbara Culver Clack

State Senator Betty Andujar is sworn in as governor-for-a-day on May 7, 1977, while her husband, Dr. John Andujar, looks on. Official program courtesy Fran and Vic King

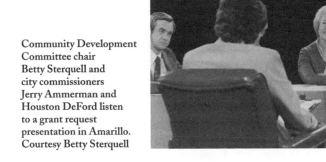

Community Development Committee chair Betty Sterquell and city commissioners Jerry Ammerman and Houston DeFord listen to a grant request presentation in Amarillo. Courtesy Betty Sterquell

State Representative Kay Bailey (Hutchison) speaks to the 63rd Texas Legislature in January 1973. Courtesy Texas State Library and Archives Commission

Henry Bonilla cuts the ribbon and opens his 1992 Campaign for Congress in Laredo. Courtesy Bebe Zuniga

About the Participants

This is a brief description of the political activities that each participant discussed in the interviews. It is intended to introduce the people speaking in the book and not intended to be a full biography detailing their years of political work. Most of the women who were interviewed held many positions in the state and local Republican Women organizations. Only the office of club president is noted when the women discussed that position. The interview date follows each name.

ART *Associated Republicans of Texas*
TFRW *Texas Federation of Republican Women*
NFRW *National Federation of Republican Women*

Nancy Abdullah, Dalhart, *March 28, 2000:* County chair, campaign worker.

Jacque Allen, Wichita Falls, *April 20, 1999:* County chair, campaign manager, state committeewoman, County Chairman Association organizer.

Helen Anderson, Houston, *March 24, 1999:* Party activist, campaign worker.

Penny Angelo, Midland, *August 19, 1998:* Campaign worker, candidate's wife.

Surrenden Angly, Austin, *March 15, 1999:* Campaign manager, TFRW president, candidate's wife.

Anne Armstrong, Armstrong, *May 13, 1999:* State and national committeewoman, co-chair Republican National Committee, advisor to Presidents Nixon and Ford, ambassador to Great Britain, fundraiser, campaign chair.

Marjorie Arsht, Houston, *February 23, 1999:* County vice chair, candidate for state legislature, fundraiser.

Fran Atkinson, Lufkin & San Antonio, *October 31, 1997:* State committeewoman, deputy state vice chair, fundraiser, ART board, campaign worker.

Carolyn Bacon, Dallas, *March 7, 2000:* Congressman Bruce Alger's staff, Senator John Tower's administrative assistant.

Margaret Baird, Houston, *August 17, 1999:* Party activist, campaign worker.

Barbara Banker, San Antonio, *August 31, 1998:* Fundraiser, campaign worker.

Libba Barnes, San Antonio, *July 20, 1998:* Precinct chair, fundraiser, state committeewoman, campaign staffer.

Andy Beaver, Corpus Christi, *June 4, 1999:* Party activist, Republican women's club president.

Deborah Bell, Abilene, *November 19, 1998:* Fundraiser, campaign worker, Brazos River Authority appointee.

Joy Bell, Dallas, *August 18, 1999:* Party activist, campaign worker.

Norma Benavides, Laredo, *April 5, 1999:* Party activist, elected school board member.

Anne Bergman, Weatherford, *September 22, 1998:* Precinct chair, campaign worker, TFRW president, Texas community development board appointee.

Lee Biggart, Dallas & Austin, *September 15, 1998:* Son of Dallas party activist Bobbie Biggart.

Joan Biggerstaff, Plano, *May 4, 1999:* Party activist, campaign worker, Texas board of health appointee.

Marguerite Binkley, Houston, *July 6 and August 2, 1999:* Party activist, rules expert.

Mary Bodger, Corpus Christi, *June 6, 1999:* Republican women's club president, party activist.

Robbie Borchers, New Braunfels, *October 1, 1998:* State committeewoman, campaign manager, candidate's wife, Republican women's club president, county chair.

Betty King Boyd, Waco, *March 1, 2000:* County vice chair.

Jayne Brainard, Amarillo, *September 2, 1999:* Republican women's club president, rules expert.

Janie Brock, San Angelo, *August 19, 1998:* Campaign worker, precinct chair.

Cindy Brockwell, Boerne, *October 9, 1999:* Campaign manager, State Senator Jeff Wentworth's chief of staff, state committeewoman.

Lou Brown, Midland, *August 19, 1998:* TFRW president, campaign worker, county vice chair, NFRW third vice president.

Shelia Wilkes Brown, Austin, *August 13, 1998:* Campaign staffer, Governor Bill Clement's staff.

Patty Bruce, El Paso, *October 17, 1998:* Campaign worker, county vice chair, state committeewoman.

Dona Bruns, New Braunfels, *February 4, 2000:* Campaign worker, party activist.

Esther Buckley, Laredo, *March 2, 1999:* County chair, U. S. Commission on Civil Rights appointee.

Jane Bucy, Lubbock, *November 20, 1998:* Campaign worker, fundraiser, party activist.

Bette Jo Buhler, Victoria, *April 7, 1999:* State vice chair, state committeewoman, fundraiser, campaign worker.

Penny Butler, Houston, *March 24, 1999:* National committeewoman, fundraiser, campaign worker.

Barbara Campbell, Dallas, *February 3, 2000:* TFRW president, campaign worker, party activist.

Judy Canon, Houston, *September 20, 1999:* Party activist, Women for Reagan organizer.

Alicia Cantu, Laredo, *April 12, 1999:* Candidate for school board, campaign worker, party activist.

Vera Carhart, Richardson & Houston, *February 23, 1999:* TFRW president, party activist, campaign worker.

Hardy Childress, San Antonio, *September 11, 1998:* Husband of party and TFRW activist Beulah Childress.

Fran Chiles, Fort Worth, *September 24, 1998:* National committeewoman, fundraiser, campaign worker.

Barbara Culver Clack, Midland, *August 18, 1998:* Elected first Republican woman county judge in Texas, Texas Supreme Court appointee.

Deanne Clark, Lubbock & Dimmitt, *August 17, 1999:* County chair, campaign worker.

Jan Clark, Houston, *May 28, 1999:* Campaign worker, Republican women's club president.

Gloria Clayton, Dallas, *June 15, 1999:* County vice chair, campaign worker.

Dixie Clem, Plano, *May 4, 1999:* State committeewoman, county executive director.

Illa Clement, Kingsville, *May 13, 1999:* Fundraiser, state committeewoman, ART board.

Hally Clements, Victoria, *April 7, 1999:* Fundraiser, campaign manager, party activist.

Rita Clements, Dallas, *June 14, 1999:* Fundraiser, national committeewoman, national Goldwater door-to-door campaign chair, wife of Texas's first modern Republican governor.

Dee Coats, Houston, *August 18, 1999:* Campaign worker, party activist.

Amelie Cobb, Beaumont, *February, 25, 1999:* Fundraiser, state committeewoman, campaign worker.

Francie Fatheree Cody, Pampa, *August 28, 1999:* State committeewoman, campaign worker, fundraiser.

Marion Coleman, Pasadena, *February 23, 1999:* County area chairman, campaign worker.

Catherine Smyth Colgan, Dallas, *September 24, 1999:* TFRW president, campaign staffer, county vice chair, appointed Canadian embassy cultural affairs officer.

Mary Anne Collins, Dallas, *September 23, 1998:* State party staffer, county vice chair, campaign worker.

Susan Combs, Austin, *May 12 and September 15, 1998:* Elected state representative and Texas Commissioner of Agriculture.

Lisa Compton, Clyde, *November 18, 1998:* Party activist, campaign worker.

Becky Cornell, San Angelo, *August 17, 1998:* Fundraiser, party activist, campaign worker.

Margaret Cosby, Boerne, *October 29, 1997:* Precinct chair, campaign worker.

Nadine Craddick, Midland, *September 20, 1999:* Party activist, candidate's wife.

Flo Kampmann Crichton, San Antonio, *October 2 and 28, 1998:* State vice chair, national committeewoman, national finance committee member.

Dorothy Crockett, Odessa & Marble Falls, *February 16, 1999:* County chair, campaign worker, Republican women's club president.

Nancy Crouch, Houston, *March 26, 1999:* Campaign worker, party activist.

Martha Crowley, Dallas, *September 25, 1998:* Party activist, campaign worker, Congressman Bruce Alger's staff, candidate's wife.

LaVerne Cudabac, Canyon Lake, *December 12, 1999:* Party activist, campaign worker, Republican women's club president.

Pauline Cusack, Houston & Willow City, *March 25, 2000:* Fundraiser, campaign worker, county chair.

Linda Custard, Dallas, *September 24, 1998:* Precinct chair, campaign worker.

Kay Danks, Galveston & Austin, *September 15, 1998:* State committeewoman, campaign worker, fundraiser.

Anita Davis, Hemphill, *February 24, 1999:* Party activist.

Nancy Canion Davis, Galveston County, *August 18, 1999:* County chair, state committeewoman.

Pattilou Dawkins, Amarillo, *July 25, 1998:* Party activist, candidate for state legislature and county judge, appointed mental health and mental retardation board chair.

Dottie De La Garza, Dallas, *September 11, 1999:* Senator John Tower's Senate and campaign staff.

June Deason, San Antonio, *February 16, 1998:* Party activist, campaign manager.

Holly Decherd, Austin, *August 10, 1998:* Campaign worker, state party secretary, fundraiser.

Mary Denny, Denton, *July 27, 1998:* County chair, elected state representative.

Becky Dixon, Waco, *February 21, 2000:* Party activist, campaign worker, State Senator David Sibley's staff.

Dorothy Doehne, San Antonio, *August 9, 1998:* State vice chair, state party secretary, state committeewoman.

Mary Donelson, Amarillo, *July 22, 1998:* Party activist, campaign worker.

Linda Dyson, Houston, *February 23, 1999:* Party activist, campaign staffer.

Virginia Eggers, Wichita Falls & Dallas, *September 30, 1999:* Campaign staffer, deputy state vice chair, state vice chair.

Wanda Eidson, Weatherford, *September 22, 1998:* County chair, state committeewoman, fundraiser.

Laverne Evans, El Paso, *February 3, 2000:* Party activist.

Becky Farrar, Hico, *February 2, 2000:* Candidate for state legislature, county chair, campaign worker.

Barbara Foreman, Odessa & Dallas, *May 4, 1999:* Candidate's wife, state committeewoman.

Louise Foster, Austin, *March 15, 1999:* Party, TFRW, and NFRW activist.

Ruth Fox, Houston & Austin, *August 10, 1998:* TFRW president, candidate's wife, campaign manager.

Debbie Francis, Dallas, *September 24, 1998:* Party activist, campaign worker, Republican women's club president.

Nadine Francis, Odessa, *September 27, 1998 and June 16, 1999:* Party activist, Governor Bill Clement's staff.

Joan Gaidos, Dallas, *August 18, 1999:* Party activist.

Gaynor Galeck, Amarillo, *July 23, 1998:* Party activist.

Mary Garrett, Danbury, *February 1, 2000:* Party activist, state committeewoman.

Liz Ghrist, Houston, *March 25, 1999:* Fundraiser, party activist, commissioners court appointee.

Nita Gibson, Lubbock, *November 20, 1998:* Campaign worker, candidate for county judge, state committeewoman.

Taffy Goldsmith, Dallas, *June 16, 1999:* Party activist, campaign worker, precinct chair.

Raquel Gonzalez, Laredo, *April 12, 1999:* Party activist.

Isabel Gray, Pasadena, *March 23, 1999:* Party activist, campaign worker.

Shirley Green, Austin & San Antonio, *August 12, 1998:* Campaign manager, Vice President George Bush's deputy press secretary, NASA public affairs officer, Governor Bush's staff, TFRW staff.

Fay Surrett Greenwood, El Paso, *August 24, 1999:* Party activist.

Mary Lou Grier, San Antonio & Boerne, *September 1, 1997:* Campaign manager, county vice chair, appointed deputy director National Park Service, candidate for Texas land commissioner.

Frankie Lee Harlow, Del Rio, *February 29, 2000:* County chair, campaign worker.

Ann Harrington, Plano, *February 19, 2000:* Party activist, campaign worker, candidate's wife.

Jayne Harris, San Antonio, *February 11, 1999:* Campaign manager, candidate's wife.

Katie Heck, Midland, *August 18, 1999:* State committeewoman, campaign manager, elected city council member.

Bette Hervey, El Paso, *October 17, 1998:* Party activist, campaign worker.

Anita Hill, Garland, *September 30, 1999:* Elected state representative.

Chris Hoover, Corpus Christi, *February 3, 2000:* County vice chair, candidate's wife.

Annette Hopkins, San Angelo, *August 17, 1998:* Party activist, campaign worker.

Barbara Howell, Fort Worth, *September 7, 1999:* Party activist, campaign worker, fundraiser.

Becky Husbands, Waco, *February 8, 2000:* Party activist.

Kay Bailey Hutchison, Houston & Dallas, *October 21, 1999:* U. S. Senator, elected Texas Treasurer, elected state representative, fundraiser, candidate for Congress.

Pat Jacobson, Fort Worth, *September 8, 1999:* Fundraiser, campaign worker.

Mary Jester, Dallas, *June 17, 1999:* President Dallas County Council of Republican Women's Clubs, party activist.

Babs Johnson, Dallas, *September 23, 1998:* President Dallas County Council of Republican Women's Clubs, campaign worker.

Claire Johnson, Abilene, *November 19, 1998:* Party activist, campaign worker, governor's appointee.

Barbara Jordan, Kingwood, *August 30, 1999:* Campaign worker, TFRW activist.

Nancy Judy, Dallas, *February 1, 2000:* Elected county commissioner and school board member, candidate for Congress, party activist.

Jane Juett, Amarillo, *July 22, 1998:* Party activist, campaign worker, fundraiser.

Beverly Kaufman, Houston, *June 12, 1998:* Precinct chair, TFRW president, elected county clerk.

Jan Kennady, New Braunfels, *December 12, 1999:* Elected mayor, TFRW president.

Vic King, Fort Worth & Boerne, *June 5, 1998:* Precinct chair, elected county commissioner.

Carolyn Knight, Austin & Marble Falls, *August 13, 1998:* Party activist.

Cyndi Taylor Krier, San Antonio, *September 29, 1998:* Senator John Tower's staff, elected state senator and county judge.

Juandelle Lacy, Midland, *August 18, 1998:* Party activist, Republican women's club president, campaign manager, candidate's wife.

Betsy Lake, Houston, *March 23, 1999:* County chair, campaign worker, fundraiser.

Claudette Landess, Amarillo, *July 23, 1998:* Campaign worker, party activist.

Mickey Lawrence, Houston, *October 1, 1999:* Party activist, candidate's wife.

Ann Lee, Houston, *March 24, 1999:* Precinct chair, campaign worker.

Tony Lindsay, Houston, *November 12, 1999:* Campaign manager, candidate's wife, elected judge.

Wilda Lindstrom, Houston, *May 26, 1999:* Precinct chair, state committeewoman.

Nancy Loeffler, San Angelo & San Antonio, *July 31, 1998:* Fundraiser, party activist, campaign worker.

Tom Loeffler, San Antonio, *June 28, 2000:* Former U. S. Congressman.

Harriet Lowe, Dallas, *June 15, 1999:* County executive committee member, campaign worker.

Janis Lowe, Friendswood, *March 4, 1999:* Elected city council member, Port of Galveston pilots board appointee.

Patricia Lykos, Houston, *October 5, 1999:* Party official, elected judge.

Barbara Man, Wichita Falls & Dallas, *October 14, 1998:* TFRW president, national committeewoman.

Iris Manes, Houston, *August 24, 1999:* State committeewoman, campaign worker.

Ruth Mankin, Houston, *October 22, 1999:* Candidate's wife, party activist.

Wendy Marsh, Amarillo, *July 24, 1998:* Party activist.

Judy Jones Matthews, Abilene, *April 19, 1999:* Party activist, fundraiser.

Janelle McArthur, San Antonio, *March 30, 1998:* TFRW president, fundraiser, campaign manager.

Lila McCall, Austin, *February 19, 1999:* Party activist.

Pat McCall, Houston & Uvalde County, *May 27, 1999:* Party activist, Pachyderm Club organizer, county vice chair.

Cathy McConn, Houston, *August 25, 1999:* National committeewoman.

Glenna McCord, Dallas, *November 12, 1998:* County vice chair, campaign worker.

Kathryn McDaniel, Borger, *July 24, 1998:* State vice chair, state committeewoman.

Ruth McGuckin, Houston & Washington County, *October 4, 1999:* State committeewoman.

Dolly Madison McKenna, Houston, *October 22, 1999:* Candidate for Congress.

Sally McKenzie, Dallas, *October 24, 1997:* Fundraiser, party activist, West Point board of visitors appointee.

Beryl Milburn, Austin, *November 4, 1997:* Candidate, party activist, fundraiser, TFRW president, university coordinating board and University of Texas board of regents appointee.

Mary Ellen Miller, Austin, *March 15, 1999:* Political consultant.

Carolyn Minton, San Angelo, *November 9, 1998:* Party activist, campaign worker.

Ruth Cox Mizelle, Corpus Christi, *October 20, 1999:* Campaign manager, party activist.

Winnie Moore, Lubbock, *November 20, 1998:* Party activist.

Birdie Morgan, Abilene, *April 19, 1999:* Party activist.

Anna Mowery, Fort Worth, *September 8, 1999:* Elected state representative, county chair, candidate's wife.

Jane Nelson, Flower Mound, *November 4, 1999:* Elected state senator, campaign worker.

Florence Neumeyer, Houston, *October 4, 1999:* Party activist, campaign manager.

Carolyn Nicholas, Wichita Falls, *April 20, 1999:* County chair.

Louise Nixon, Fredericksburg, *April 4, 2000:* Party activist.

Barbara Nowlin, Houston & Friendswood, *March 5, 1999:* Party activist, Republican women's club president.

Sylvia Nugent, Dallas & Amarillo, *July 24, 1998:* Party activist, candidate for state legislature, campaign manager, congressional staff, fundraiser.

Ana Ochoa, Laredo, *April 12, 1999:* Party activist, elected college board member.

Peter O'Donnell, Dallas, *January 27, 2000:* State chair, national committeeman.

Nancy Palm, Houston, *May 28, 1999:* County chair, county vice chair, state committee-woman.

Rita Palm, Fort Worth, *September 7, 1999:* Fundraiser, campaign manager.

Carolyn Palmer, San Antonio, *April 9, 1999:* Party activist, library and archives commission appointee.

Martha Parr, Amarillo, *July 23, 1998:* Party activist, county party staff.

Mayetta Parr, Amarillo, *July 22, 1998:* Young Republicans activist.

Barbara Patton, Houston, *March 27, 1999:* Goldwater Texas campaign staffer, county party staff, fundraiser, campaign worker.

Ann Peden, Hondo, *June 27, 2000:* County chair, County Chairman Association president, state committeewoman.

Teddy Peterson, San Antonio, *September 29, 1998:* Campaign and congressional staff, party activist, Republican women's club president.

Gwen Pharo, Dallas, *June 15, 1999:* Fundraiser, campaign manager, party activist, congressional and presidential staff.

Billie Pickard, Raymondville, *October 12, 1999:* State committeewoman, fundraiser, campaign worker.

Caroline Pierce, Houston, *August 19, 1999:* Republican Women activist, campaign worker.

Billijo Porter, El Paso, *October 17, 1998:* County chair, campaign worker.

Ruth Potter, Dallas, *September 21, 1999:* Party activist.

Joanne Powell, San Angelo, *August 17, 1998:* Party activist, campaign worker, congressional staff.

Poolie Pratt, Victoria, *April 7, 1999:* State committeewoman, campaign worker.

Ann Quirk, Austin, *August 17, 1999:* Young Republicans activist, campaign worker, State Senator Drew Nixon's staff.

Jean Raffetto, Houston & Seabrook, *May 27, 1999:* Party activist, campaign worker.

Carole Ragland, League City, *March 22, 1999:* Precinct chair, campaign worker.

Diane Rath, San Antonio, *May 14, 1998:* State committeewoman, campaign worker, fundraiser, appointed Texas workforce commission chair.

Nora Ray, Fort Worth, *September 22, 1998:* Precinct chair, county vice chair, campaign worker.

William Rector, Wichita Falls, *April 20, 1999:* State committeeman.

Carol Reed, Dallas, *September 24, 1998:* Political consultant, fundraiser, Senator John Tower's campaign staff.

Dorothy Reed, Amarillo, *July 22, 1998:* County vice chair, campaign worker, Republican women's club president.

Glenda Reeder, San Antonio, *July 14, 1998:* Republican women's club president, state committeewoman.

Anna Claire Rice, Houston, *May 26, 1999:* Republican Women activist, campaign worker.

Leon Richardson, Nederland, *February 25, 1999:* Precinct chair, candidate for state legislature, campaign worker.

Lucille Rochs, Fredericksburg, *March 22, 2000:* Party activist, campaign worker.

Doris Mayer Rousselot, Sonora, *November 9, 1998:* Party activist, campaign worker.

Betty Ruminer, Seabrook, *March 23, 1999:* Precinct chair, campaign worker.

Ken Ruminer, Seabrook, *March 23, 1999:* Party activist, campaign worker.

Diana Ryan, San Angelo, *August 23, 1999:* Party activist, fundraiser.

Carole Keeton Rylander, Austin, *July 11, 2000:* Elected Texas Railroad Commissioner and Texas Comptroller of Public Accounts.

Dottie Sanders, Houston, *May 27, 1999:* Precinct chair, campaign manager, Republican Women activist.

Ruth Schiermeyer, Lubbock, *November 21, 1998:* Campaign manager, county chair, Brazos River Authority appointee.

Katie Seewald, Amarillo, *July 23, 1998:* Party activist, campaign manager, fundraiser.

Ellie Selig, Seguin, *January 28, 1999:* Fundraiser, Republican Women and party activist.

Bill Shaner, Midland, *August 18, 1998:* County chair.

Douthea Shaner, Midland, *August 18, 1998:* Precinct chair, campaign worker.

Gwyn Shea, Irving, *September 18, 1999:* Elected state representative, appointed and elected constable, Texas workers compensation insurance board appointee, Representative Bob Davis's staff.

Anne Shepard, Victoria & Harlingen, *February 8, 2000:* State committeewomen, campaign worker.

Bucky Smith, New Braunfels, *October 1, 1998:* Party activist, campaign worker, fundraiser.

Idalou Smith, Waco, *September 7, 2000:* Party activist, campaign worker.

Mary Jane Smith, Houston, *May 27, 1999:* County party staff, campaign manager, political consultant.

Reba Boyd Smith, Odessa & Abilene, *November 18, 1998:* Party activist, candidate for county treasurer, campaign worker.

Polly Sowell, McAllen & Austin, *August 12, 1997 and September 30, 1998:* Deputy state vice chair, state vice chair, campaign manager, Governor George W. Bush's staff.

Diana Stafford, Irving & Amarillo, *July 24, 1998:* Campaign manager, fundraiser.

Pollyanna Stephens, San Angelo, *August 17, 1998:* Candidate's wife, fundraiser, San Angelo State University board appointee.

Betty Sterquell, Amarillo, *July 23, 1998:* County chair, fundraiser, community development committee appointee.

Nancy Stevens, Corpus Christi, *June 4, 1999:* County chair, candidate for county clerk.

Jane Anne Stinnett, Lubbock, *November 21, 1998:* Campaign manager, political consultant.

Joci Straus, San Antonio, *February 16, 1998:* Campaign manager, fundraiser, precinct chair, presidential appointee.

Betty Strohacker, Kerrville, *July 13, 1998:* Party activist, campaign worker, Upper Guadalupe River Authority appointee.

Cynthia Tauss, League City, *March 5, 1999:* County chair, Texas board of pardons and paroles appointee, candidate for county commissioner and state representative.

Estelle Teague, Hurst, *June 15, 1999:* State committeewoman, TFRW activist.

Millie Teas, Dallas, *February 11, 2000:* Campaign worker.

John Tedford, Sonora, *August 20, 1998:* Colleague of state committeewoman Maxine Browne.

Mary Teeple, Austin, *August 13, 1998:* Campaign worker, fundraiser.

Jess Ann Thomason, Midland, *August 24, 1999:* Fundraiser, campaign worker.

Dianne Thompson, Boerne & Houston, *November 19, 1997:* TFRW president, campaign manager, NFRW fourth vice president.

Lou Tower, Wichita Falls & Dallas, *September 23, 1998:* Wife of U. S. Senator John Tower.

Patti Rose Trippet, Waco, *March 3, 2000:* Party activist.

Linda Underwood, Houston, *March 26, 1999:* Young Republicans activist, campaign staff.

Julia Vaughan, Midland, *August 18, 1998:* Candidate for appeals court judge.

Margaret Vickery, Fort Worth, *August 25, 1999:* Party activist.

Marjorie Vickery, Copper Canyon, *July 23, 1998:* Party activist, elected state board of education member.

Kris Anne Vogelpohl, Galveston, *March 4, 1999:* County vice chair, campaign worker, fundraiser.

Ann Wallace, Fort Worth & Austin, *August 10, 1998:* Campaign manager, fundraiser, state committeewoman, U. S. office of consumer affairs appointee.

Zubie Walters, Yoakum, *October 11, 1999:* Party activist.

Gail Waterfield, Canadian, *August 14, 1998:* Party activist, campaign manager, candidate's wife, fundraiser.

Susan Weddington, San Antonio, *March 7, 2000:* State chair (a first for a woman of any major political party in Texas).

Martha Weisend, Dallas, *May 4, 1999:* Campaign manager, fundraiser, state committeewoman.

Gayle West, Pasadena, *March 23, 1999:* State committeewoman, fundraiser, candidate's wife.

Lois White, San Antonio, *June 9, 2000:* Party activist, candidate for state legislature.

Billie Whitefield, Houston, *March 25, 1999:* Party activist, candidate's wife, campaign worker.

Theo Wickersham, San Antonio, *July 14, 1998:* State committeewoman, campaign worker, fundraiser.

Mary Lou Wiggins, Dallas, *September 25, 1998:* Campaign manager, party activist.

Sitty Wilkes, Austin, *August 12, 1998:* Party activist, fundraiser, elected school board member.

Doris Williams, Lake Jackson, *October 1, 1999:* Party activist, elected mayor.

Irene Cox Wischer, San Antonio, *June 4, 1998:* TFRW president, fundraiser, party activist.

Joan Wood, Waco, *February 28, 2000:* State committeewoman, campaign worker.

Sharolyn Wood, Houston, *March 26, 1999:* Elected judge.

Carole Woodard, Houston & Galveston, *June 9, 2000:* Party activist, campaign worker, candidate for county clerk, Texas board of human services appointee.

Bebe Zuniga, Laredo, *April 12, 1999:* Party activist, campaign manager, fundraiser.

Additional Interviews:

Tom Anderson, Houston, *March 24, 1999*

Anne Crews, Dallas, *September 13, 1999*

Caroline Emeny, Amarillo, *July 23, 1998*

Mamie Proctor, Houston, *May 21, 1999*

State Republican Executive Committee Women Members, 1952–1989

1952-53

NATIONAL COMMITTEEWOMAN:
Mrs. Carl G. Stearns, Houston

VICE CHAIR:
Mrs. Buck West, San Antonio

DISTRICT COMMITTEEWOMEN:
 1 Mrs. George Hamilton, Texarkana
 2 Mrs. Charles L. Bacheller, Kilgore
 3 Mrs. Fred W. Graves, Jacksonville
 4 Mrs. R. D. Holloway, Port Arthur
 5 Mrs. Gertrude Leek, Livingston
 6 Mrs. J. M. Sloan, Palestine
 7 Mrs. I. L. Elam, Edgewood
 8 Mrs. Sam Whitaker, Paris
 9 Mrs. Jack Adamson, Honey Grove
10 Mrs. Rebecca Brune, Anna
11 Mrs. H. W. Roberts, Dallas
12 Mrs. Ben Ballard, Jr., Hillsboro
13 Miss Nettie Turner, Rockdale
14 Miss Henrietta Fricke, Brenham
15 Mrs. Elma Allen, Hallettsville
16 Mrs. R. H. J. Osborne, Houston
17 Mrs. James Hadcock, Galveston
18 Mrs. James Lawrence Wood, Refugio
19 Mrs. C. R. Guibor, Seguin
20 Mrs. Mildred F. McNab, Bertram
21 Miss Mollie Ann Nelson, Clifton
22 Mrs. E. H. Barnhart, Denton
23 Mrs. W. C. Witcher, Wichita Falls
24 Mrs. L. S. Howard, Roscoe
25 Mrs. William Schroeder, Fredericksburg
26 Mrs. Verlie H. Cowan, San Antonio
27 Mrs. Beatrice D. Frase, Donna
28 Mrs. Charles L. Renaud, Fort Worth
29 Mrs. John Darden, Midland
30 Mrs. Bertha Helen Kerr, Lubbock
31 Miss Ruthelle Bacon, Amarillo

1954-55

NATIONAL COMMITTEEWOMAN:
Mrs. John R. Black, Dallas

VICE CHAIR:
Mrs. Frank T. O'Brien, Amarillo

DISTRICT COMMITTEEWOMEN:
 1 Mrs. Sam Whitaker, Paris
 2 Mrs. Nan Bacheller, Kilgore
 3 Mrs. Fred Graves, Jacksonville
 4 Mrs. Jack Love, Orange
 5 Mrs. Travis Moore, Crockett
 6 Mrs. R. H. J. Osborne Jr., Houston
 7 Mrs. Romer Bullington, Tyler
 8 Mrs. Allie Mae Currie, Dallas
 9 Mrs. H. M. Dyer, Commerce
10 Mrs. Jack D. Brownfield, Fort Worth
11 Miss Henrietta Fricke, Brenham
12 Mrs. Miles Hastings, Jr., Waxahachie
13 Miss Nettie Turner, Rockdale
14 Mrs. Elmore R. Torn, Taylor
15 Mrs. Hargrove Smith, Eagle Lake
16 Mrs. Emmie K. Schroeder, Fredericksburg
17 Mrs. J. C. Overbaugh, Lake Jackson
18 Mrs. Richard M. Lucas, Beeville
19 Mrs. Dorothy L. Vance, Hondo
20 Lila Nichols, Kingsville
21 Mrs. Neal D. Terrey, Alice
22 Mrs. Christine Unger, Denton
23 Miss Enid Gossett, Wichita Falls
24 Mrs. Gertrude Surratt, Snyder
25 Mrs. R. S. Waring, San Angelo
26 Mrs. Tom Slick, San Antonio
27 Mrs. Paul Armstrong, McAllen
28 Mrs. Sadie Thomas, Ralls
29 Mrs. Percy Pogson, El Paso
30 Mrs. Curtis Traweek, Hereford
31 Mrs. Raymond W. Harrah, Pampa

1956-57

NATIONAL COMMITTEEWOMAN:
Mrs. John R. Black, Dallas

VICE CHAIR:
Mrs. Miles Hastings, Jr., Waxahachie

DISTRICT COMMITTEEWOMEN:
 1 Mrs. Sam Whitaker, Paris
 2 Mrs. Charles Bacheller, Kilgore
 3 Mrs. Paul Powell, Woodville
 4 Vacancy
 5 Mrs. Rachel Faulkner, Coldspring
 6 Mrs. John W. Martin, Houston
 7 Mrs. T. W. Benham, Mineola
 8 Mrs. Ralph W. Currie, Dallas
 9 Mrs. H. M. Dyer, Commerce
10 Mrs. Joseph Kennedy, Fort Worth
11 Mrs. Elizabeth B. Daugherty, Fairfield
12 Mrs. W. H. Getzendaner, Waxahachie
13 Mrs. Nettie Turner, Rockdale
14 Mrs. Elmore R. Torn, Taylor
15 Mrs. Hargrove Smith, Eagle Lake
16 Mrs. Emmie K. Schroeder, Fredericksburg
17 Mrs. J. C. Overbaugh, Lake Jackson
18 Mrs. Frank Buhler, Victoria
19 Mrs. Dorothy L. Vance, Hondo
20 Mrs. Thomas R. Armstrong, Armstrong
21 Mrs. Neal D. Terrey, Alice
22 Mrs. Christine Unger, Denton
23 Mrs. W. H. Lobaugh, Graham
24 Mrs. John DuMont, Abilene
25 Vacancy
26 Mrs. Robert Grice Maverick, San Antonio
27 Mrs. Paul Armstrong, McAllen
28 Mrs. L. H. Thomas, Ralls
29 Mrs. E. C. Bunch, Odessa
30 Mrs. Curtis Traweek, Hereford
31 Mrs. G. N. McDaniel, Borger

1958-59

NATIONAL COMMITTEEWOMAN:
Mrs. John R. Black, Dallas

VICE CHAIR:
Mrs. Frank S. Buhler, Victoria

DISTRICT COMMITTEEWOMEN:
 1 Mrs. Sam Whitaker, Paris
 2 Mrs. Charles L. Bacheller, Kilgore
 3 Mrs. Jack H. Wade, Lufkin
 4 Mrs. Fletcher Graham, Beaumont
 5 Mrs. Rachel Faulkner, Coldspring
 6 Mrs. John W. Martin, Houston
 7 Mrs. Uldene Hill, Grand Saline
 8 Mrs. E. D. MacIver, Dallas

 9 Mrs. H. M. Dyer, Commerce
10 Mrs. Peggy Floore, Fort Worth
11 Mrs. Elizabeth B. Daugherty, Fairfield
12 Mrs. George Benjamin, Cleburne
13 Miss Nettie Turner, Rockdale
14 Mrs. Malcolm Milburn, Austin
15 Mrs. Hargrove Smith, Eagle Lake
16 Mrs. Emmie K. Schroeder, Fredericksburg
17 Mrs. J. C. Overbaugh, Lake Jackson
18 Mrs. W. D. Welder, Vidauri
19 Mrs. Frank X. Vance, Hondo
20 Mrs. Thomas R. Armstrong, Armstrong
21 Mrs. Neal D. Terrey, Alice
22 Mrs. G. W. Ewing, Jr., Breckenridge
23 Mrs. W. H. Lobaugh, Graham
24 Mrs. John DuMont, Abilene
25 Mrs. Charles F. Browne, Sonora
26 Mrs. Robert Grice Maverick, San Antonio
27 Mrs. Paul Armstrong, McAllen
28 Mrs. L. H. Thomas, Ralls
29 Mrs. R. L. Waller, Midland
30 Mrs. Curtis Traweek, Hereford
31 Mrs. G. N. McDaniel, Borger

1961-62

NATIONAL COMMITTEEWOMAN:
Mrs. Ike S. Kampmann, Jr., San Antonio

VICE CHAIR:
Mrs. G. N. McDaniel, Borger

DISTRICT COMMITTEEWOMEN:
 1 Mrs. Sam Whitaker, Paris
 2 Mrs. Robert T. Reeves, Kilgore
 3 Mrs. Jack H. Wade, Lufkin
 4 Mrs. Stewart Last, Beaumont
 5 Mrs. Drew Jackson, Dayton
 6 Mrs. M. S. Ackerman III, Houston
 7 Mrs. Uldene Hill, Grand Saline
 8 Mrs. B. L. Kanowsky, Dallas
 9 Mrs. H. M. Dyer, Commerce
10 Mrs. Peggy Floore, Fort Worth
11 Mrs. Sue Hayes, Palestine
12 Mrs. Charles G. Murray, Whitney
13 Mrs. O. W. Hayes, Temple
14 Mrs. Malcolm Milburn, Austin
15 Vacancy
16 Mrs. Emmie K. Schroeder, Fredericksburg
17 Mrs. D. D. Napier, Richmond
18 Mrs. Lawrence Wood, Refugio
19 Mrs. Frank X. Vance, Hondo
20 Mrs. Thomas R. Armstrong, Armstrong
21 Mrs. Neal D. Terrey, Alice
22 Mrs. G. W. Ewing, Jr., Breckenridge
23 Mrs. W. H. Lobaugh, Graham

24 Mrs. A. K. Doss, Jr., Abilene
25 Mrs. Charles F. Browne, Sonora
26 Mrs. John H. Wood, Jr., San Antonio
27 Mrs. Virginia Armstrong, McAllen
28 Mrs. Gordon Treadaway, Lubbock
29 Mrs. William A. Heck, Midland
30 Mrs. Gilbert Lamb, Muleshoe
31 Mrs. G. N. McDaniel, Borger

1964-65

NATIONAL COMMITTEEWOMAN:
Mrs. Ike S. Kampmann, Jr., San Antonio

VICE CHAIR:
Mrs. G. N. McDaniel, Borger

DISTRICT COMMITTEEWOMEN:
 1 Mrs. Sam Whitaker, Paris
 2 Mrs. Robert T. Reeves, Kilgore
 3 Mrs. Jack H. Wade, Lufkin
 4 Mrs. Stewart D. Last, Beaumont
 5 Mrs. W. A. Walling, Jr., Huntsville
 6 Mrs. M. S. Ackermann III, Houston
 7 Mrs. Howard Hill, Grand Saline
 8 Mrs. Jo Kanowsky, Dallas
 9 Mrs. H. M. Dyer, Commerce
10 Mrs. John L. Wallace, Jr., Fort Worth
11 Mrs. George A. Hayes, Palestine
12 Mrs. Charles C. Murray, Whitney
13 Mrs. O. W. Hayes, Temple
14 Mrs. Malcolm Milburn, Austin
15 Mrs. Paul Henderson, El Campo
16 Mrs. Maxine Smith, Uvalde
17 Mrs. D. D. Napier, Richmond
18 Mrs. Frank S. Buhler, Victoria
19 Mrs. Gladys Strauss, Seguin
20 Mrs. Tobin Armstrong, Armstrong
21 Mrs. Alonzo Benavides, Laredo
22 Mrs. G. W. Ewing, Breckenridge
23 Mrs. W. H. Lobaugh, Graham
24 Mrs. A. K. Doss, Jr., Abilene
25 Mrs. Charles F. Browne, Sonora
26 Mrs. Edward T. Hill, San Antonio
27 Mrs. Richard Sowell, McAllen
28 Mrs. Charles Gibson, Lubbock
29 Mrs. H. B. Phillips, Kermit
30 Mrs. Curtis Traweek, Hereford
31 Mrs. Warren Fatheree, Pampa

1966-67

NATIONAL COMMITTEEWOMAN:
Mrs. J. C. Man, Wichita Falls

VICE CHAIR:
Mrs. G. N. McDaniel, Borger

DISTRICT COMMITTEEWOMEN:
 1 Mrs. A. C. Hoffman, Mt. Pleasant
 2 Mrs. Barton L. Owens, Longview
 3 Mrs. A. E. Cudlipp, Lufkin
 4 Mrs. Lamar Cecil, Beaumont
 5 Mrs. W. A. Walling, Jr., Huntsville
 6 Mrs. Hal Hazelrigg, Houston
 7 Mrs. Howard Hill, Grand Saline
 8 Mrs. Jo Kanowsky, Dallas
 9 Mrs. David Wells, Sherman
10 Mrs. John J. Andujar, Fort Worth
11 Mrs. George A. Hayes, Palestine
12 Mrs. Charles C. Murray, Whitney
13 Mrs. O. W. Hayes, Temple
14 Mrs. Malcolm Milburn, Austin
15 Mrs. Adele D. Larson, Cuero
16 Mrs. Maxine Smith, Uvalde
17 Mrs. Clara Slough, Texas City
18 Mrs. Frank S. Buhler, Victoria
19 Mrs. Gladys Strauss, Seguin
20 Mrs. Tobin Armstrong, Armstrong
21 Mrs. Alonzo Benavides, Laredo
22 Mrs. Oran Boyles, Wichita Falls
23 Mrs. Jack Maxfield, Wichita Falls
24 Mrs. A. K. Doss, Abilene
25 Mrs. Charles F. Browne, Sonora
26 Mrs. Edward T. Hill, San Antonio
27 Mrs. Richard Sowell, McAllen
28 Mrs. Charles Gibson, Lubbock
29 Mrs. J. T. Moorhead, El Paso
30 Mrs. E. R. Little, Dimmitt
31 Mrs. Warren Fatheree, Pampa

1968-69

NATIONAL COMMITTEEWOMAN:
Mrs. J. C. Man, Jr., Wichita Falls

VICE CHAIR:
Mrs. Tobin Armstrong, Armstrong

DISTRICT COMMITTEEWOMEN:
 1 Mrs. A. C. Hoffmann, Mt. Pleasant
 2 Mrs. Howard Hill, Grand Saline
 3 Mrs. Basil Atkinson, Jr., Lufkin
 4 Mrs. Dale Hager, Beaumont
 5 Mrs. R. A. Buchanan, Liberty
 6 Mrs. Abe Farrior, Houston
 7 Mrs. J. D. Boggs, Pasadena
 8 Mrs. Jo Kanowsky, Dallas
 9 Mrs. Blanche R. Martin, Denison
10 Vacancy
11 Mrs. Elmer Lindstrom, Houston
12 Mrs. Paul C. Coffin, Itasca
13 Mrs. Charles Hanson, Temple
14 Mrs. B. J. Smith, Austin

15 Mrs. Raymond Arsht, Houston
16 Mrs. H. K. Herbert, Dallas
17 Miss Estelle Tartt, Galveston
18 Mrs. Joe N. Pratt, Victoria
19 Mrs. Joe R. Straus, Jr., San Antonio
20 Mrs. James H. Clement, Kingsville
21 Mrs. Alonzo Benavides, Laredo
22 Mrs. John J. Andujar, Fort Worth
23 Mrs. R. L. Robinson, Dallas
24 Mrs. A. K. Doss, Jr., Abilene
25 Mrs. Charles F. Browne, Sonora
26 Mrs. Baxter R. Grier, San Antonio
27 Mrs. Richard Sowell, McAllen
28 Mrs. J. L. Pinkerton, Monahans
29 Mrs. J. T. Moorhead, El Paso
30 Mrs. Tom Suits, Petersburg
31 Mrs. Warren Fatheree, Pampa

1970-71

NATIONAL COMMITTEEWOMAN:
Mrs. Tobin Armstrong, Armstrong

VICE CHAIR:
Mrs. Bradley Streeter, Wichita Falls

DISTRICT COMMITTEEWOMEN:
 1 Mrs. A. C. Hoffman, Mt. Pleasant
 2 Mrs. Walter Judge, Mineola
 3 Mrs. W. L. Rehkop, Athens
 4 Mrs. Dale Hager, Beaumont
 5 Mrs. S. W. Kowierschke, Bryan
 6 Mrs. Abe Farrior, Houston
 7 Mrs. J. D. Boggs, Pasadena
 8 Mrs. Jo Kanowsky, Dallas
 9 Mrs. Jack Martin, Denison
10 Mrs. John S. Howell, Fort Worth
11 Mrs. Elmer Lindstrom, Channelview
12 Mrs. Paul C. Coffin, Itasca
13 Mrs. Charles Hanson, Temple
14 Mrs. Robert Farris, Austin
15 Mrs. Eugene Fike, Houston
16 Mrs. H. K. Herbert, Dallas
17 Miss Estelle Tartt, Galveston
18 Mrs. Joe N. Pratt, Victoria
19 Mrs. Joe R. Straus, Jr., San Antonio
20 Mrs. James H. Clement, Kingsville
21 Mrs. Warren Wagner, Crystal City
22 Mrs. John J. Andujar, Fort Worth
23 Mrs. Robert R. McCready, Dallas
24 Mrs. Mary Doss, Abilene
25 Mrs. Don Wolfenberger, Midland
26 Mrs. Edward T. Hill, San Antonio
27 Mrs. L. V. Mead, McAllen
28 Mrs. Jack R. Cook, Andrews

29 Mrs. J. T. Moorhead, El Paso
30 Mrs. Tom Suits, Petersburg
31 Mrs. Warren Fatheree, Pampa

1972-73

NATIONAL COMMITTEEWOMAN:
Mrs. Tobin Armstrong, Armstrong

VICE CHAIR:
Mrs. Malcolm Milburn, Austin

DISTRICT COMMITTEEWOMEN:
 1 Mrs. Bill Gaw, Marshall
 2 Mrs. Walter Judge, Mineola
 3 Mrs. W. L. Rehkop, Athens
 4 Mrs. Joe Richardson, Nederland
 5 Mrs. S. W. Kowierschke, Bryan
 6 Mrs. Abe Farrior, Houston
 7 Mrs. J. D. Boggs, Pasadena
 8 Mrs. Jo Kanowsky, Dallas
 9 Mrs. Jack Martin, Denison
10 Mrs. Richard Hewitt, Fort Worth
11 Mrs. Elmer Lindstrom, Channelview
12 Mrs. Paul C. Coffin, Itasca
13 Mrs. Charles Hanson, Temple
14 Mrs. Stuart Benson, Austin
15 Mrs. Eugene Fike, Houston
16 Mrs. H. K. Herbert, Dallas
17 Mrs. Jack Garrett, Danbury
18 Mrs. Lee Briscoe, Eagle Lake
19 Mrs. Edward Baker, San Antonio
20 Mrs. James H. Clement, Kingsville
21 Mrs. Bruce Foster, Hondo
22 Mrs. John J. Andujar, Fort Worth
23 Mrs. I. Ray Dunlap, Dallas
24 Mrs. Jack McGlothlin, Abilene
25 Mrs. Edgar Francis, Odessa
26 Mrs. Louis Doehne, San Antonio
27 Mrs. George R. Lipe, Brownsville
28 Mrs. R. S. Tapp, Lubbock
29 Mrs. John Root, El Paso
30 Mrs. Tom Suits, Petersburg
31 Mrs. Jack Hart, Gruver

1974-75

NATIONAL COMMITTEEWOMAN:
Mrs. Richard D. Bass, Dallas

VICE CHAIR:
Mrs. Richard Sowell, McAllen

DISTRICT COMMITTEEWOMEN:
 1 Mrs. Jack C. W. Martin, Denison
 2 Mrs. Walter Judge, Mineola
 3 Mrs. W. L. Rehkop, Athens

4 Mrs. O. J. Richardson, Nederland
5 Mrs. Lee Briscoe, Eagle Lake
6 Mrs. Elmer Lindstrom, Channelview
7 Mrs. Jack E. Brown, Houston
8 Mrs. Jo Kanowsky, Dallas
9 Mrs. M. J. Snell, Dallas
10 Mrs. Joe F. Teague, Hurst
11 Mrs. Lewis A. Rockwood, Houston
12 Mrs. John J. Andujar, Fort Worth
13 Mrs. Paul H. Till, Houston
14 Mrs. R. T. Roberts, Austin
15 Mrs. Charles E. McGuckin, Houston
16 Mrs. Charles A. Foster, Jr., Dallas
17 Mrs. Jack Garrett, Danbury
18 Mrs. Kenneth L. Jarratt, Edna
19 Mary Morton Jackson, San Antonio
20 Mrs. John B. Armstrong, Kingsville
21 Mrs. Edward Baker, San Antonio
22 Mrs. Jack L. Eidson, Weatherford
23 Mrs. I. Ray Dunlap, Dallas
24 Mrs. Jack McGlothlin, Abilene
25 Mrs. Robert S. Johnson, San Angelo
26 Mrs. Louis C. Doehne, San Antonio
27 Mrs. George R. Lipe, Brownsville
28 Mrs. Edgar B. Francis, Odessa
29 Mrs. John Root, El Paso
30 Mrs. John J. Kirchhoff, Plainview
31 Mrs. Jack Hart, Gruver

1976-77

NATIONAL COMMITTEEWOMAN:
Mrs. William P. Clements, Dallas

VICE CHAIR:
Mrs. Richard Sowell, McAllen

DISTRICT COMMITTEEWOMEN:
1 Mrs. Jack C. W. Martin, Denison
2 Mrs. George Pearson, Tyler
3 Mrs. W. L. Rehkop, Athens
4 Mrs. Howell Cobb, Beaumont
5 Mrs. Lee Briscoe, Eagle Lake
6 Mrs. Elmer Lindstrom, Channelview
7 Mrs. Jack E. Brown, Houston
8 Mrs. Jo Kanowsky, Dallas
9 Mrs. M. J. Snell, Dallas
10 Mrs. Bruce Jacobsen, Fort Worth
11 Mrs. Jack Boggs, Pasadena
12 Mrs. John J. Andujar, Fort Worth
13 Mrs. Paul H. Till, Houston
14 Mrs. R. T. Roberts, Austin
15 Mrs. Charles E. McGuckin, Houston
16 Mrs. Charles A. Foster Jr., Dallas
17 Mrs. Brockett Hudson, Seabrook

18 Mrs. Kenneth L. Jarratt, Edna
19 Mary Morton Jackson, San Antonio
20 Mrs. John B. Armstrong, Kingsville
21 Mrs. Burton Barnes, San Antonio
22 Mrs. Jack L Eidson, Weatherford
23 Mrs. I. Ray Dunlap, Dallas
24 Mrs. Jack McGlothlin, Abilene
25 Mrs. J. K. Dixon, Llano
26 Mrs. Louis Doehne, San Antonio
27 Mrs. Manning Dierlam, Brownsville
28 Mrs. Edgar Francis, Odessa
29 Mrs. John Root, El Paso
30 Mrs. John J. Kirchhoff, Plainview
31 Mrs. Jack Hart, Gruver

1978-79

NATIONAL COMMITTEEWOMAN:
Sen. Betty Andujar, Fort Worth

VICE CHAIR:
Mrs. Polly Sowell, McAllen

DISTRICT COMMITTEEWOMEN:
1 Mrs. Blanche Martin, Denison
2 Mrs. Juanita Broyles, Tyler
3 Mrs. Lila Rehkop, Athens
4 Mrs. Amelie Cobb, Beaumont
5 Mrs. Sue Briscoe, Eagle Lake
6 Mrs. Wilda Lindstrom, Channelview
7 Mrs. Randy Brown, Houston
8 Mrs. Barbara Foreman, Dallas
9 Mrs. Iris Snell, Dallas
10 Mrs. Pat Jacobson, Fort Worth
11 Mrs. Nancy Boggs, Pasadena
12 Mrs. Barbara Howell, Fort Worth
13 Mrs. Jacquelyn Till, Houston
14 Mrs. Mary Lee, Austin
15 Mrs. Ruth McGuckin, Houston
16 Mrs. Jennie Foster, Dallas
17 Mrs. Dottie Hudson, Seabrook
18 Mrs. Jayce Jarratt, Edna
19 Mary Morton Jackson, San Antonio
20 Mrs. Billie Pickard, Raymondville
21 Mrs. Libba Barnes, San Antonio
22 Phyllis Kay Babcock, Denton
23 Mrs. Peggy Wilson, Dallas
24 Mrs. Bette McRae, Waco
25 Mrs. Elizabeth Rohn, Kerrville
26 Mrs. Dorothy Doehne, San Antonio
27 Mrs. Peggy Rodgers, Edinburg
28 Mrs. Janelle Evans, Brownfield
29 Mrs. Patty Bruce, El Paso
30 Mary Ellen Cummings, Wichita Falls
31 Mrs. Ila Jo Hart, Gruver

1980-81

NATIONAL COMMITTEEWOMAN:
Mrs. John J. Andujar, Fort Worth

VICE CHAIR:
Mrs. Louis C. Doehne, San Antonio

DISTRICT COMMITTEEWOMEN:
1 Mrs. Jack C. W. Martin, Denison
2 Mrs. Emmitt Clem, Jr., Plano
3 Mrs. W. L. Rehkop, Athens
4 Mrs. Barbara Rush, Beaumont
5 Mrs. Sue Briscoe, Eagle Lake
6 Mrs. Elmer Lindstrom, Channelview
7 Mrs. Archie H. Manes, Jr., Houston
8 Mrs. Ed Foreman, Dallas
9 Mrs. Jack Sommerfield, Garland
10 Mrs. Bruce Jacobson, Fort Worth
11 Mrs. Jack Boggs, Pasadena
12 Mrs. John S. Howell III, Fort Worth
13 Mrs. Paul H. Till, Houston
14 Mrs. Clyde E. Lee, Austin
15 Mrs. Charles E. McGuckin, Houston
16 Mrs. Kay Bailey Hutchison, Dallas
17 Mrs. Marilyn Smith, Alvin
18 Mrs. Simon C. Cornelius, Victoria
19 Mary Morton Jackson, San Antonio
20 Mrs. Marshall Pickard, Raymondville
21 Mrs. Burton Barnes, San Antonio
22 Mrs. Virginia Upham, Mineral Wells
23 Mrs. W. W. Wilson III, Dallas
24 Mrs. James F. Wood, Waco
25 Mrs. Edward J. Rohn, Kerrville
26 Mrs. W. J. Pieper, Jr., San Antonio
27 Mrs. R. W. Rogers, Edinburg
28 Mrs. Mark Majors, Odessa
29 Mrs. H. L. Bruce, El Paso
30 Mrs. Jacque Allen, Wichita Falls
31 Mrs. Scott Nisbet, Pampa

1982-83

NATIONAL COMMITTEEWOMAN:
Mrs. H. E. Chiles, Fort Worth

VICE CHAIR:
Mrs. Louis C. Doehne, San Antonio

DISTRICT COMMITTEEWOMEN:
1 Mrs. Nancy Gordon, Avinger
2 Mrs. Emmitt Clem, Jr., Plano
3 Mrs. Jeannie Turk, Sour Lake
4 Mrs. Tommie Byrd, Beaumont
5 Mrs. Mildred Fike, Hempstead
6 Mrs. Elmer Lindstrom, Channelview
7 Mrs. Archie H. Manes, Jr., Houston
8 Mrs. Ed Foreman, Dallas
9 Mrs. Jack Sommerfield, Garland
10 Mrs. Bruce Jacobson, Fort Worth
11 Mrs. Jack Boggs, Pasadena
12 Mrs. Anna Mowery, Fort Worth
13 Mrs. Pat Black, Houston
14 Mrs. Kay Danks, Austin
15 Mrs. Ann Striegler, Houston
16 Mrs. Kay Bailey Hutchison, Dallas
17 Mrs. Nancy Canion, League City
18 Mrs. Simon C. Cornelius, Victoria
19 Mrs. Mary Morton Jackson, San Antonio
20 Mrs. Marshall Pickard, Raymondville
21 Mrs. Burton Barnes, San Antonio
22 Mrs. Virginia Upham, Mineral Wells
23 Mrs. Wanda Damstra, Grand Prairie
24 Mrs. James F. Wood, Waco
25 Mrs. Edward J. Rohn, Kerrville
26 Mrs. W. J. Pieper, Jr., San Antonio
27 Mrs. Dorothy McDonald, Pt. Isabel
28 Mrs. Janelle Evans, Brownfield
29 Mrs. Lisa Mercurio, El Paso
30 Mrs. Jacque Allen, Wichita Falls
31 Mrs. Sybil Daniels, Perryton

1984-85

NATIONAL COMMITTEEWOMAN:
Mrs. Fran Chiles, Fort Worth

VICE CHAIR:
Diana Denman, San Antonio

DISTRICT COMMITTEEWOMEN:
1 Mrs. Nancy Gordon, Avinger
2 Mrs. Jan Copas, Tyler
3 Mrs. Jeannie Turk, Sour Lake
4 Mrs. Tommie Byrd, Beaumont
5 Mrs. Katye Kowierschke, Huntsville
6 Mrs. Wilda Lindstrom, Houston
7 Mrs. Patricia Vanoni, Houston
8 Mrs. Virginia Steenson, Richardson
9 Mrs. Joan B. Wood, Waco
10 Mrs. Pat Jacobson, Fort Worth
11 Mrs. Nancy Canion, League City
12 Mrs. Anna Mowery, Fort Worth
13 Mrs. Iris Manes, Houston
14 Mrs. Kay Danks, Austin
15 Mrs. Nancy Palm, Houston
16 Mrs. Martha B. Weisend, Dallas
17 Mrs. Vicki Hapke, Houston
18 Ms. Sybil Daniel, Victoria
19 Mrs. Mary Morton Jackson, San Antonio
20 Mrs. Delores Price, Kingsville
21 Mrs. Robbie Borchers, New Braunfels
22 Mrs. Virginia Upham, Mineral Wells
23 Mrs. Ruth Rayner, Dallas

24 Mrs. Amelia Dixon, Llano
25 Mrs. Elizabeth J. Rohn, Kerrville
26 Mrs. Diane Rath, San Antonio
27 Mrs. Laura B. Duffey, Brownsville
28 Mrs. Janelle Evans, Brownfield
29 Mrs. Bette D. Hervey, El Paso
30 Mrs. Jacque Allen, Wichita Falls
31 Mrs. Lottie Eller, Panhandle

1986-87

NATIONAL COMMITTEEWOMAN:
Fran Chiles, Fort Worth

VICE CHAIR:
Diana Denman, San Antonio

DISTRICT COMMITTEEWOMEN:
 1 Nancy Gordon, Avinger
 2 Jane Yancey, Plano
 3 Marguerete Graves, Kirbyville
 4 Marguerite Foulk, Beaumont
 5 Katye Kowierschke, Huntsville
 6 Wilda Lindstrom, Houston
 7 Patricia Vanoni, Houston
 8 Virginia Steenson, Richardson
 9 Joan Wood, Waco
10 Pat Jacobson, Fort Worth
11 Gayle West, Pasadena
12 Darla Mortensen, Fort Worth
13 Iris Manes, Houston
14 Kay Danks, Austin
15 Nelda Eppes, Houston
16 Martha Weisend, Dallas
17 Vicki Hapke, Houston
18 Anne Ashy, Victoria
19 Katy Evans, San Antonio
20 Leona Knight, Corpus Christi
21 Robbie Borchers, New Braunfels
22 Vivian Millirons, Burleson
23 Patricia Taylor, Dallas
24 Amelia Dixon, Sunrise Beach
25 Ann Peden, Hondo
26 Diane Rath, San Antonio
27 Becki Olivares, McAllen
28 Janelle Evans, Brownfield
29 Bette Hervey, El Paso
30 Jacque Allen, Wichita Falls
31 Lottie Eller, Panhandle

1988-89

NATIONAL COMMITTEEWOMAN:
 Mrs. Fran Chiles, Fort Worth
VICE CHAIR:
Diana Denman, San Antonio

DISTRICT COMMITTEEWOMEN:
 1 Nancy Gordon, Avinger
 2 Jane Yancey, Plano
 3 Marguerete Graves, Kirbyville
 4 Marguerite Foulk, Beaumont
 5 Katye Kowierschke, Huntsville
 6 Wilda Lindstrom, Houston
 7 Jeanne Wilson, Houston
 8 Virginia Steenson, Richardson
 9 Sarilee Ferguson, Waco
10 Jane Burgland, Arlington
11 Gayle West, Pasadena
12 Jane Berberich, Fort Worth
13 Iris Manes, Houston
14 Holly Decherd, Austin
15 Nelda Eppes, Houston
16 Lynne Tweedell, Dallas
17 Penny Butler, Houston
18 Anne Ashy, Victoria
19 Mrs. Theo Wickersham, San Antonio
20 Leona Knight, Corpus Christi
21 Barbara Schoolcraft, Seguin
22 Vivian Millirons, Burleson
23 Patricia Taylor, Dallas
24 Helen Rutland, Belton
25 Cindy Brockwell, Boerne
26 Diane Rath, San Antonio
27 Mary Ann Rios, McAllen
28 Janelle Evans, Brownsville
29 Bette Hervey, El Paso
30 Jacque Allen, Wichita Falls
31 Bobbie Nisbet, Pampa

SOURCE:
Texas Almanac for the years 1952-1959;
1961-1962*; 1964-1989

*Although the *Texas Almanac* has consistently
been published biannually on even years, the
almanac was not printed in 1960. The biannual
publication resumed in 1964, therefore names
of some of the officeholders during this time
period are unavailable. Original state
committee rosters were unavailable from the
Republican Party of Texas.

APPENDIX 2

Women Delegates to the Republican National Conventions, 1948–1988

1948 (33 TOTAL DELEGATES)

AT LARGE DELEGATES /*Alternates*

Mrs. H. E. Exum, Amarillo
Mrs. Carl G. Stearns, Houston

DISTRICT DELEGATES /*Alternates*

1   *Mrs. Ida Watson, Naples*
5   *Mrs. H. W. Roberts, Dallas*
7   *Mrs. Minnie W. Smith, Houston*
8   *Mrs. R. H. J. Osborne, Jr., Houston*
9   *Mrs. Mary Ann Marcak, Victoria*
12   *Mrs. Sarah M. Renaud, Ft. Worth*
15   *Mrs. Helen Sargeant, McAllen*
17   *Mrs. L. S. Howard, Roscoe*
18   Miss Ruthelle Bacon, Amarillo
20   *Mrs. H. A. Cowan, San Antonio*

1952 (37 TOTAL DELEGATES)

AT LARGE DELEGATES /*Alternates*

Mrs. J. C. Overbaugh, Lake Jackson
Mrs. Jack E. Bliss, Midland

DISTRICT DELEGATES /*Alternates*

1   Mrs. Charles Bacheller, Kilgore
5   Mrs. Allie M. Currie, Dallas
8   Mrs. R.H.J. Osborne, Jr., Houston
    Mrs. Ralph Feagin, Houston
9   *Mrs. R. S. Morris, Rosenberg*
10   *Mrs. E. R. Torn, Taylor*
    Mrs. R. L. Hatchett, Jr., Austin
12   Mrs. J. D. Kennedy, Ft. Worth
20   *Mrs. William Smith, Houston*

1956 (54 TOTAL DELEGATES)

AT LARGE DELEGATES /*Alternates*

Mrs. John R. Black, Dallas
Mrs. Frank Buhler, Victoria
Mrs. R. D. O'Callaghan, San Antonio
Mrs. Tom Armstrong, Armstrong
Mrs. W. A. Smith, Houston

DISTRICT DELEGATES /*Alternates*

1   *Mrs. R. M. Head, Texarkana*
    Mrs H. F. McWilliams
2   *Mrs. A. G. Natwick, Beaumont*
3   Mrs. C. L. Bacheller, Kilgore
    Mrs. James W. Fair, Tyler
5   *Mrs. E. D. MacIver, Dallas*
    Mrs. A. E. Swenson, Dallas
6   Mrs. Eliz. Daugherty, Fairfield
7   *Mrs. Sue Hayes, Palestine*
8   Mrs. John W. Martin, Houston
9   Mrs. J. Overbaugh, Lake Jackson
    Mrs. Hargrove Smith, Eagle Lake
10   *Mrs. Malcolm Milburn, Austin*
    Mrs. Virginia Dana, Austin
11   Mrs. Goodhue Smith, Waco
13   Mrs. W. H. Lobaugh, Graham
15   Mrs. Paul Armstrong, McAllen
16   *Mrs. R. M. Metcalf, El Paso*
17   Mrs. John Dumont, Abilene
    Mrs. Gus Ewing, Jr., Breckenridge
18   Mrs. G. N. McDaniel, Borger
19   Mrs. L. H. Thomas, Ralls
20   Mrs. Robert Maverick, San Antonio
21   *Mrs. E. K. Schroeder, Fredericksburg*
    Mrs. Charles F. Browne, Sonora

1960 (54 TOTAL DELEGATES)

AT LARGE DELEGATES /*Alternates*
Mrs. John R. Black, Dallas
Mrs. T. R. Armstrong, Armstrong
Mrs. I. Kampmann, Jr., San Antonio
Miss B. Blodgett, Corpus Christi
Mrs. Jane Smith, San Antonio
Mrs. Donald Cameron, Dallas

DISTRICT DELEGATES /*Alternates*
1 *Mrs. James W. Fair, Tyler*
2 Mrs. Stewart D. Last, Beaumont
   Mrs. A. G. Natwick, Beaumont
3 *Mrs. Uldene Hill, Grand Saline*
5 Mrs. Ben Kanowsky, Dallas
   Mrs. James Biggart, Dallas
6 *Mrs. N. T. Berquist, Lufkin*
7 Mrs. George A. Hayes, Palestine
8 *Mrs. R. W. Kurtz, Houston*
   Mrs. Roland A. Gray, Houston
9 Mrs. D. D. Napeir, Richmond
   Mrs. Sid Farmer, Jr., Galveston
10 *Mrs. Gail Hill, Austin*
11 Mrs. O. W. Hayes, Temple
   Mrs. Chas. G. Edison, Sr., Waco
12 *Mrs. Peggy Floore, Ft. Worth*
13 Mrs. J. C. Man, Jr., Wichita Falls
   Miss M. MacDonald, Wichita Falls
15 *Mrs. Claude Van Renesse, Pharr*
16 Mrs. R. M. Metcalf, El Paso
17 Mrs. G. W. Ewing, Jr. Breckenridge
   Mrs. A. K. Doss, Jr., Abilene
18 Mrs. G.N. McDaniel, Borger
19 Mrs. Gordon Treadaway, Lubbock
20 *Mrs. Joy Carrington, San Antonio*
21 *Mrs. C. F. Browne, Sonora*
   Mrs. V. H. Wright, San Angelo
22 Mrs. J. W. Martin, Houston

1964 (56 TOTAL DELEGATES)

AT LARGE DELEGATES /*Alternates*
Mrs. I. S. Kampmann, San Antonio
Mrs. Richard Bass, Dallas
Mrs. G. N. McDaniel, Borger
Mrs. L. M. Cox, San Antonio

DISTRICT DELEGATES /*Alternates*
2 Mrs. Dale Hager, Beaumont
   Mrs. R. A. Buchanan, Liberty
4 Mrs. Blanche Martin, Denison
5 Mrs. Jo Kanowsky, Dallas
   Mrs. J. F. W. Hannay, Dallas
6 *Mrs. Bill McNutt, Corsicana*

7 Mrs. B. E. Atkinson, Jr.,Lufkin
   Mrs. Walter Haning, Athens
8 Mrs. E. P. Lowe, Baytown
9 Mrs. Helen May, Lake Jackson
   Mrs. Bette Jo Buhler, Victoria
10 Mrs. Malcolm Milburn, Austin
   Mrs. R. C. Barbour, Austin
   Mrs. Billie J. Pratt, Burnet
11 *Mrs. George Emerich, Waco*
   Mrs. William Lee, Waco
12 Mrs. John Howell, Ft. Worth
13 Mrs. J. C. Man, Jr., Wichita Falls
   Mrs. B. Streeter, Wichita Falls
14 Mrs. T. Armstrong, Armstrong
17 Mrs. A. K. Doss, Jr., Abilene
   Mrs. Jack Edison, Weatherford
18 Mrs. Warren Fatheree, Pampa
19 *Mrs. Charles Gibson, Lubbock*
20 Mrs. Edward T. Hill, San Antonio
   Mrs. Baxter R. Grier, San Antonio
21 Mrs Charles F. Browne, Sonora
   Mrs. Gladys Wright, San Angelo
22 Mrs. G. O. Johnstone, Houston

1968 (59 TOTAL DELEGATES)

AT LARGE DELEGATES /*Alternates*
Mrs. Bradley C. Streeter, Wichita Falls
Mrs. Barbara Culver, Midland
Mrs. Tobin Armstrong, Armstrong
Mrs. Ike S. Kampmann, Jr., San Antonio
Mrs. Malcolm Milburn, Austin
Mrs. Edward T. Hill, San Antonio

DISTRICT DELEGATES /*Alternates*
2 Mrs. B. E. Atkinson, Jr. Lufkin
   Mrs. W. L. Rehkop, Athens
3 Mrs. Jo Kanowsky, Dallas
   Mrs. Robert R McCready, Dallas
4 *Mrs. Jack Martin, Denison*
5 Mrs. Richard D. Bass
   Mrs. Godfrey Collins, Dallas
   Mrs. H. K. Herbert, Dallas
6 Mrs. John J. Andujar, Fort Worth
8 Mrs. E. Lindstrom, Channelview
   Mrs. M. Shepherd, Houston
9 Mrs. Dale Hager, Beaumont
   Miss Estelle H. Tartt, Galveston
10 *Mrs. F. X. Bostick, Austin*
   Mrs. Robert Farris, Austin
11 Mrs. Gordon King, McGregor
   Mrs. Charles Hanson, Temple
12 *Mrs. Alton Ray, Jr., Fort Worth*
14 Mrs. Joe N. Pratt, Victoria
   Mrs. Jack Garrett, Danbury

15 Mrs. Richard M. Sowell, McAllen
Mrs. J. H. Clement, Kingsville
Mrs. L. V. Mead, McAllen
16 Mrs. J. T. Morehead, El Paso
18 Mrs. G. N. McDaniel, Borger
Mrs. Warren Fatheree, Pampa
Mrs. Tom Suits, Petersburg
22 *Mrs. Warren H. Binkley, Houston*
23 Mrs. W. A. Smith, Floresville
Mrs. Marvin Selig, Seguin

1972 (52 TOTAL DELEGATES)

AT LARGE DELEGATES /*Alternates*
Mrs. Anne Armstrong, Armstrong
Mrs. James F. Biggart, Dallas
Mrs. Richard D. Bass, Dallas
Mrs. Robert C. McArthur, San Antonio

DISTRICT DELEGATES /*Alternates*
1 Mrs. Walter Judge, Mineola
2 Mrs. B. E. Atkinson, Lufkin
Mrs. Beth Jo Tucker, Beaumont
3 *Mrs. J. Kanowsky, Dallas*
Mrs. Dewitt Moffett, Dallas
5 Mrs. James Clayton, Dallas
Mrs. Charles Foster, Jr., Dallas
7 Mrs. Nancy Palm, Houston
8 Miss Ola Dee Koeppel, Houston
9 Mrs. O. J. Richardson, Nederland
Mrs. Elmer B. Vogelpohl, Galveston
10 Mrs. Beryl Milburn, Austin
Mrs. Thomas G. Price, Austin
Mrs. Lee Briscoe, Eagle Lake
11 *Mrs. Ruel Dixon, Waco*
Mrs. James F. Wood , Waco
12 Mrs. Alton S. Ray, Jr., Fort Worth
13 *Mrs. Pierce Langford, Wichita Falls*
Mrs. Ila Jo Hart, Gruver
14 Mrs. George D. Stevens, Corpus Christi
Mrs. Owen D. Cox, Corpus Christi
15 *Mrs France Lipe, Brownsville*
16 Mrs. Itha Jeudeman, Odessa
Mrs Edgar Francis, Odessa
Mrs. John Root, El Paso
18 *Mrs. Lillian B Tilley, Houston*
Mrs Dorothy Potts, Houston
19 *Mrs. James W. Lacy, Midland*
20 *Mrs. Pearl Cloud, San Antonio*
21 Mrs. Baxter R. Grier, San Antonio
Mrs. Louis Bohls, San Antonio
22 *Mrs. Toby Blumenthal, Pasadena*
23 Mrs. Marvin Selig, Seguin
Mrs. Bruce T. Foster, Hondo

24 Mrs. M. G. Burgland, Arlington
Mrs. Stan Stooksberry, Ft. Worth
Mrs. I. Ray Dunlap, Dallas

1976 (100 TOTAL DELEGATES)

AT LARGE DELEGATES /*Alternates*
Fran Chiles, Fort Worth

DISTRICT DELEGATES /*Alternates*
1 Lila Lee Rehkop, Athens
2 Betty Jo "B. J." Tucker, Beaumont
Jeanie Turk, Beaumont
3 Barbara Staff, Dallas
Lauren D. Hobbs, Dallas
Iris Snell, Dallas
Virginia S. Steenson, Richardson
4 *Betty Anderson, Terrell*
5 Jean Sommerfield, Garland
Carlota Phillips, Dallas
Beth T. Miller, Dallas
Barbara Carter, Mesquite
Sherry Allen, Dallas
6 Betty Andujar, Fort Worth
Dorothy Smith, Fort Worth
Irene Cash, Dallas
Anna Mowery, Fort Worth
Shirley Black, College Station
7 Jacqueline Till, Houston
Billie Whitefield, Houston
Ruth McGuckin, Houston
Carol E. Belton, Houston
8 *Isabelle Gray, Pasadena*
9 Nancy Canion, League City
Wilda Lindstrom, Channelview
10 Rhoda Benson, Austin
Kay Danks, Austin
Sue Briscoe, Eagle Lake
Joye Boggs Flanagan, Austin
11 Bette MacRae, Waco
Dorothy Wood, Waco
Dorothy F. Crockett, Marble Falls
Alta Ada Schoner, Brownwood
12 Pat Jacobson, Fort Worth
Helen Fitzgerald, Fort Worth
Gwendolyn C. Morrison, Fort Worth
13 Ila Jo Hart, Gruver
Kathryn McDaniel, Borger
Nadine Gregg, Amarillo
14 Sylvia Berry, Rockport
Demarious K. Frey, Corpus Christi
15 *Martha Alworth, Kingsville*
Wanda Jones, Alamo
Linda D. Montemayor, Brownsville

16 Sharon Carr, El Paso
 Bette D. Hervey, El Paso
17 *Dorothy H. Hall, Big Spring*
18 Penelope L. Horton, Houston
 Ann Striegler, Houston
 Maxine Shaver, Houston
 Mary Lou Brooks, Houston
19 Barbara Culver, Midland
20 Mary Jackson, San Antonio
 Elsie L. Franson, San Antonio
 Gladys K. Hamilton, San Antonio
 Sue Heacock, San Antonio
 Jean Bensmiller, San Antonio
21 Dorothy Doehne, San Antonio
 Elizabeth J. Rohn, Kerrville
 Helene Randolph Moore, New Braunfels
22 Marguerite Binkley, Houston
 Nancy Boggs, Pasadena
 Dorothy Hudson, Seabrook
23 Annette Matthews, Luling
 Bonnie B. Sunvision, San Antonio
 Marilyn Brien, San Antonio
 Eddy Mae Mosby, San Antonio
 Lorene Lyles, San Antonio
 Wanda Roe, Jourdanton
24 Jane Burgland, Arlington
 Jane T. (Jan) Sutton, Grand Prairie
 Nancy Johnson, Arlington

1980 (80 TOTAL DELEGATES)

AT LARGE DELEGATES /*Alternates*
Kay Danks, Austin
Beverly Rupe, San Antonio
Martha Weisend, Dallas

DISTRICT DELEGATES /*Alternates*
 1 Lila Rehkop, Athens
 2 Jeannie Turk, Sour Lake
 3 Dorothy B. Golden
 Sally McKenzie, Dallas
 Jeanne Tower, Dallas
 Ida Papert, Dallas
 4 *Jody Smith, Denton*
 5 *Laverne Moore, Dallas*
 Irene McCommon, Dallas
 6 Annabelle Farrell, Duncanville
 Ada Gibbs, Fort Worth
 Katherine McNutt, Corsicana
 Betty Getzendaner, Waxahachie
 7 Barbara Harris, Houston
 Barbara Patton, Houston
 8 Sue Helbig, Baytown

 9 Gwen Emmett, Kingwood
 Nancy Canion, League City
 Tommie M. Byrd
10 Pamela Findlay, Austin
11 Dottie Young, Round Rock
 Katrina Stone, Corpus Christi
 Helen Rutland, Belton
12 Fran Chiles, Fort Worth
 Barbara Howell, Fort Worth
 Modean Barry, Fort Worth
13 Bobbie Nisbet, Pampa
 Christina Richardson, Amarillo
 Nadine Gregg, Amarillo
 Sybil Daniel, Perryton
14 *Sylvia Berry, Rockport*
15 Delores F. Clark, Brownsville
 Pat Kline, McAllen
 Jean Bensmiller, Whitsett
16 Sara L. Robbins, Odessa
17 *Dottie Scott, Abilene*
 Mary Dulaney, Snyder
18 Naomi Andrews, Houston
 Claire Moore, Houston
19 Rosalind K. Haley, Lubbock
 Janelle Evans, Brownfield
 Corrine E. Weis, Midland
20 Mary M. Jackson, San Antonio
 Marge Kahler, San Antonio
 Sue S. Heacock, San Antonio
 Lois C. White, San Antonio
21 Dorothy Doehne, San Antonio
 Elizabeth Rohn, Kerrville
22 Adele Hedges, Houston
 Becky Orr, Houston
 Margaret Napier, Richmond
22 Florence Bennett, San Antonio
 Annette Mathews, Luling
24 Naomi Laird, Irving
 Wanda Damstra, Grand Prairie
 Jane Bergland, Arlington

1984 (109 TOTAL DELEGATES)

AT LARGE DELEGATES /*Alternates*
Martha Weisend, Dallas
Mary Ann Leche, Dallas
Anne Armstrong, Armstrong
Kris Ann Vogelpohl, Galveston
Penny Butler, Houston
Carolyn Knight, Granite Shoals
Barbara Campbell, Dallas
Ester Yao, Houston
Fran Chiles, Fort Worth
Belinda Dyer, San Antonio

Diana Denman, San Antonio
Esther Buckley, Laredo
Mary Denny, Aubrey
Dorothy McClellan, San Antonio
Nancy Palm, Houston

DISTRICT DELGATES /*Alternates*

1 Lila Lee Rehkop, Athens
  Nancy M. Gordon, Avinger
2 *Lydia Damrel, Vidor*
  Jackie Dillion, Woodville
3 Mabel Burns
  Mary Scruggs, Plano
  June Coe, Dallas
  Virginia Steenson, Richardson
4 Mary W. Whitt, Terrell
  Edith Jester, Whiteright
  Jan Copas, Tyler
5 LaVerne Moore, Dallas
  Ann Collins, Dallas
6 Naomi Godfrey, Fort Worth
  Evelyn Gustafson, Cleburne
  Shirley Rogers, Conroe
7 Kay Shillock, Houston
  Patricia Vanoni, Houston
  Billie Whitefield, Houston
8 Pat Wall, Kingwood
  Jo Helen McGee, Kingwood
  Patti Johnson, Humble
9 Tommie Byrd, Beaumont
  Vicki Hapke, Houston
  Barbara Nowlin, Friendswood
10 Ellen Garwood, Austin
  Annette Matthews, Luling
  Kay Danks, Austin
  Anne Lassiter, Austin
  Holly Decherd, Austin
11 Louise Irby, Killeen
  Audrey Corbett, Salado
  Jackie LaMonte, Copperas Cove
  Sarilee Ferguson, Waco
12 Iona Reed, Azle
  Elise Cole, Fort Worth
  Mary Conner, Fort Worth
13 Jacque Allen, Wichita Falls
  Carolyn Moorhouse, Seymour
  Jane Juett, Amarillo
14 Sylvia Maddox, Victoria
  Lynn Grebe, Bay City
  Anne Ashy, Victoria
  Patricia Leininger, Shiner
15 Peggy Rodgers, Edinburg
  Virginia Armstrong, McAllen

16 Madge Zuloaga, El Paso
17 Kathy Webster, Abilene
  Birdie Morgan, Abilene
18 Mary Jane Smith, Houston
  Martha C. Baird, Houston
  Helen Hanna, Houston
19 Mary Lou Parsons, Odessa
  Johnnye Davis, Odessa
  Janelle Evans, Brownfield
20 Dorothy Doehne, San Antonio
  Diane Rath, San Antonio
  Evelyn Ruks, San Antonio
21 Carolyn Minton, San Angelo
  Margaret Cosby, Boerne
22 Doris Williams, Lake Jackson
  Ann Lee, Houston
  Patricia Black, Houston
23 Katy Evans, San Antonio
  Ann Peden, Hondo
  Elizabeth Plum, San Antonio
  Cynthia Wood, Laredo
  Alicia Cantu, Laredo
24 Dedie Mankin, Duncanville
  Helen Parker, Grand Prairie
  Amanda Hall, Cedar Hill
  Marge Bega, Dallas
25 Anna Claire Rice, Houston
  Gayle West, Pasadena
  Izzy Gray, Pasadena
26 JoAnn Smith, Denton
  Violet Bradel, Arlington
  Vivian Millirons, Burleson
  Mary Louise Dodge, Dallas
27 Delores Price, Kingsville
  Mildred Thodos, Corpus Christi

1988 (III TOTAL DELEGATES)

AT LARGE DELEGATES /*Alternates*
Penny Butler, Houston
Kay Bailey Hutchison, Dallas
Carole Fleming, Sugar Land
Doris Williams, Lake Jackson
Sally McKenzie, Dallas
Nancy Crouch, Houston
Jocelyn L. Straus, San Antonio
Marta Greytok, Taylor Lake Village
Ruth Fox, Austin
Flo Atherton, San Antonio
Ann Quirk, San Antonio
Holly Decherd, Austin
Beth Mahaffey, Dallas
Rita Clements, Dallas
Jeanne Johnson, Dallas

Dot Adler, Richardson
Cynthia A. Garza

DISTRICT DELEGATES / *Alternates*

1 Beth Furrh
2 Betty Joe Tucker, Sour Lake
   Patti Tate, Conroe
3 Betty Doke, Dallas
   Barbara Pinsker, Dallas
   Alma Carter, Plano
4 *Dorothy Banfield, Whitesboro*
   Beverly Thomas, Greenville
5 Lynne Tweedell, Dallas
6 Faye Diamond, Cleburne
   Florace G. Kling, College Station
   Margaret W. Forehand, Fort Worth
7 Dee Coats, Houston
   Claudette Martin, Houston
8 *Jeanette Guttormson, Kingwood*
   Wanda Hudson, Kingwood
9 Lisa Duperier, Beaumont
   Carolyn Smith, Houston
   Janet Farmer, Galveston
   Letha F. Barber, Galveston
10 Mary Teeple, Austin
   Becky Orr, Austin
11 *Otha Taylor, Temple*
   Helen Quiram, Waco
12 Rita Palm, Fort Worth
   Estelle Teague, Hurst
   Elizabeth Diano, Fort Worth
   Kit Sears, Fort Worth
13 Susan Tripplehorn, Pampa
   Jane Juett, Amarillo
   Jacque Allen, Wichita Falls
   Carolyn Nicholas, Wichita Falls
14 Barbara Schoolcraft, Seguin
   Anne Ashy, Victoria
15 *Beth Brady, Edinburg*
16 Patricia D. Bruce, El Paso
   Bernice Peralta, El Paso
   Marcia Waugh, El Paso
17 Anne Bergman, Weatherford
   Lynn Oates, Decatur
   Claire Johnson, Abilene
   Marilyn Patterson, Abilene
18 *Mary Newsome, Houston*
   Alison Smith, Houston
19 Johnnye Davis, Odessa
   Ruth Schiermeyer, Lubbock
   Carolyn Powers, Odessa
   Jane Anne Stinnett, Lubbock

20 Dorothy Doehne, San Antonio
   Mary Wathen-White, San Antonio
   Diane Rath, San Antonio
21 Lou Brown, Midland
   June Deason, San Antonio
   Cindy Brockwell, Boerne
   Alene Treadwell, Ft. McKavett
   Dianne Thompson, Boerne
22 Claudine Spillos, Missouri City
   Jorene Aycock, Lake Jackson
   Marjorie Arsht, Bellaire
   Beverly Kaufman, Houston
23 Theo Wickersham, Universal City
   Carol Eddlemann, San Antonio
   Helen Marie Jones, Eagle Pass
   Elsa Guajardo, Laredo
24 Caroline Fields, Irving
25 Gayle West, Pasadena
   Betsy Lake, Houston
   Margaret Baird, Houston
   Beverly Montera, Houston
   Dorothy Sanders, Houston
26 Mary C. Denny, Aubrey
   Rosa Lopez Terry, Carrollton
   Terry Grisham, Arlington
27 *Leona Knight, Corpus Christi*

SOURCE:
Delegates to the 1948, 1952, 1956, 1960,
and 1964 conventions from Paul Casdorph,
The Republican Party in Texas 1865–1965
(Pemberton Press, 1965). Delegates in 1968,
1972, 1976, 1980, 1984, and 1988 from the
official proceedings of Republican National
Conventions.

APPENDIX 3

Texas Federation of Republican Women Presidents, 1955–1999

1955   Mrs. Robert D. O'Callaghan (Aileen), San Antonio
1957   Mrs. Dick Elam (Maxine), Abilene
1959   Miss Betty Blodgett, Corpus Christi
1961   Mrs. J. C. Man, Jr. (Barbara), Wichita Falls
1963   Mrs. Irene (Cox) Wischer, San Antonio
1965   Mrs. George Pearson (Ginny), Tyler
1967   Mrs. Malcolm Milburn (Beryl), Austin
1969   Mrs. Louis Bohls (Cleo), San Antonio
1971   Mrs. Maurice Angly, Jr. (Surrenden), Austin
1972   Mrs. Robert C. McArthur (Janelle), San Antonio
1973   Mrs. Jim Lewis (Barbara), Kerrville
1975   Mrs. Robert D. Bergman (Anne), Weatherford
1977   Mrs. Jim Carhart (Vera), Houston
1979   Mrs. Henry C. Smyth, Jr. (Cathy), Dallas
1981   Mrs. Winfree L. Brown (Lou), Midland
1983   Mrs. Mark S. Campbell (Barbara), Dallas
1985   Mrs. Mark S. Campbell (Barbara), Dallas
1987   Mrs. Milton Fox (Ruth), Austin
1989   Mrs. Jay Patterson (Jan), Dallas
1991   Mrs. Al Kaufman (Beverly), Houston
1993   Mrs. Terry Saunders (Marcia), Lake Kiowa
1995   Mrs. James Thompson (Dianne), Boerne
1997   Mrs. Don Kennady (Jan), New Braunfels
1999   Mrs. Don Kennady (Jan), New Braunfels

SOURCE:
Texas Federation of Republican Women

APPENDIX 4

Ten Outstanding Republican Women, 1965–1999

1965

Mrs. W. J. Alexander
Mrs. John J. Andujar
Mrs. Dixie Crossman
Mrs. C. F. Hamilton
Mrs. Elmer G. Kreuber
Mrs. Jack Maxfield
Mrs. Malcolm Milburn
Mrs. Patricia Skinner
Mrs. Bill Steger
Mrs. Frank Wedding

1967

Mrs. John Culver
Mrs. Jack Eidson
Mrs. George Irving
Mrs. Gordon King
Mrs. Glen Leland
Mrs. J. P. Mason
Mrs. Violet Mottwiler
Mrs. Bradlee Postell
Mrs. H. J. Roper
Mrs. Loyd Winship

1969

Mrs. William Walker, Jr.
Mrs. Rudy Juedeman
Mrs. Lorraine Dyas
Mrs. Jack Pumphrey
Mrs. Alton Ray
Mrs. Noel Schroller
Mrs. William Dabney
Mrs. Ralph Bruse
Mrs. Robert McArthur
Mrs. George Pearson

1971

Mrs. Robert Black
Mrs. James Cochran
Mrs. Kendall French
Mrs. Baxter Grier
Mrs. Barney Johnson
Mrs. Pierce Langford
Mrs. Cornelius Olcott, Jr.
Mrs. Robert Paxton
Mrs. Adolf Stieler
Mrs. Earl Wischer

1973

Jo Kanowsky
Peggy Dunlap
Jane Burgland
Mary Kirchoff
Juandelle Lacy
Blanche Martin
Carolyn Messenger
Nancy Palm
Ellie Selig
Mildred Staley
Lou Stapleton

1975

Jewel Fleming
Jacque Allen
Lena Taylor
Jeanne Barnes
Patricia Duaine
Dorothy Crockett
Anna Mowery
Allie Jane Davis
Joan Cason
Nancy Elizabeth Judy
Special: Cleo Bohls

1977

Kit Sears
Iris Snell
Leibert Clinkinbeard
Mary Louise Johns
Joyce Pittman
Marguerite Binkley
Adele Luca
Carolyn Knight
Joy Rash
Dorothy Reed

1979

Elizabeth Paterson
Mary Lou Mergele
Myrtis Gibson
Ann Mason
Shirley Green
Dixie Clem
Ruth Potter
Marion Doubleday
Ada Gibbs
Carolyn Huchton

1981

Mary Jane Allen
Bette Hervey
Ann Covert
Jane Juett
Ruth Fox
Ruth Schiermeyer
Audrey Cannon
Barbara Foreman
Penny Butler
Anne Bergman

1983

Patti Clapp
June Deason
Peggy Engelhardt
Beverly Fisher
Kay Bailey Hutchison
Gerry Johnson
Jean Rheudasil
Helen Rutland
Laveta Sealy
Estelle Teague

1985

Martha Weisend
Ruth Tansey
Rickey Thompson
Beulah Childress
Pat Berry
Jan Patterson
Jane Berberich
Gwyn Shea
Fran Chiles
Natalie Sadler Kern

1987

Cindy Brockwell
Shirley Costello
Maxine Grothouse
Barbara Lockard
Florence Neumeyer
Jane Pieper
Marcia Saunders
Claudene Spellios
Nancy Stevens
Jane Yancey

1989

Nancy Boston
Rita Britow
Barbara Campbell
Alma Carter
Laverne Evans
Louise Foster
Ramona Kennedy
Yvonne Kohutek
Shirley McSpedden
Edith Schuler

1991

Harriet Armstrong
Vera Carhart
Jan Crow
Mary Denny
Florence Kling
Dolly Peralta
Margaret Rhea
Carolyn Robertson
Dottie Sanders
Theo Wickersham

1993

Kay Baird
Anna Claire Rice
Betty Strohacker
Jeanne Cotellessee
Rose Farmer
Gerry Hardway
Marjorie Nunn
Carol "Teddy" Peterson
Peggy Hamric
Phyllis Cole

1995

Lou Brown
Beverly Kaufman
Betsy Lake
Gayle West
Jeanne Musselman
Taffy Goldsmith
Sandra Logan
Neomi Godfrey
Patsy Standerfer
Ann Smith

1997

Dona Bruns
Mattie Friedlein
Sandra Halsey
Gladys Jeter
Mary Kochs
Jo Konen
Sonja L. Main
Bonnie Maynard
Peggy McDuff
Marvel K. Sayers

1999

Sue Bradley
Mary Belle Brown
Merri Easterly
Ann Harrington
Annette Hopkins
Barbara Jordan
Willie Lawley
Barbara Nowlin
Dianne Thompson
Kris Anne Vogelpohl

SOURCE:
Texas Federation of
Republican Women

Index

*The Index is for the main text only
and excludes the participants' hometowns.*